Emory Symposia in Cognition 3

Knowing and remembering in young children

Knowing and remembering in young children

Edited by

ROBYN FIVUSH
and
JUDITH A. HUDSON

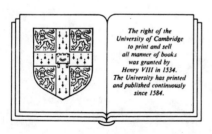

The right of the
University of Cambridge
to print and sell
all manner of books
was granted by
Henry VIII in 1534.
The University has printed
and published continuously
since 1584.

CAMBRIDGE UNIVERSITY PRESS

Cambridge
New York   Port Chester   Melbourne   Sydney

Published by the Press Syndicate of the University of Cambridge
The Pitt Building, Trumpington Street, Cambridge CB2 1RP
40 West 20th Street, New York, NY 10011, USA
10 Stamford Road, Oakleigh, Melbourne 3166, Australia

First published 1990

Printed in the United States of America

Library of Congress Cataloging-in-Publication Data

Knowing and remembering in young children / edited by Robyn Fivush and
Judith A. Hudson.

p.   cm. – (Emory symposia in cognition ; 3)

ISBN 0-521-37325-5

1. Memory in children – Congresses.   2. Cognition in children –
–Congresses.   I. Fivush, Robyn.   II. Hudson, Judith A.
III. Series.
BF723.C5K587   1990
155.42′3312 – dc20   90–34283
                                                                     CIP

British Library Cataloguing in Publication Data

Knowing and remembering in young children. – (Emory symposia
in cognition ; 3).

1. Children. Memory. Development
I. Fivush, Robyn   II. Hudson, Judith A.   III. Series
155.4131

ISBN 0-521-37325-5 hardback

Contents

Preface

This is the third volume in the *Emory Symposia in Cognition* series. The previous two books, *Concepts and Conceptual Development: Ecological and Intellectual Factors in Categorization* (edited by Ulric Neisser, 1987) and *Remembering Reconsidered: Ecological and Traditional Approaches to the Study of Memory* (edited by Ulric Neisser and Eugene Winograd, 1988), explored the intersection of traditional laboratory-based approaches and more naturalistic, ecological approaches to basic issues of human cognition. This volume represents a bit of a deviation from the previous volumes in at least two ways: First, although developmental issues were addressed in the previous volumes, this is the first of the series to focus specifically on development. Second, all of the research reported in this volume takes the "ecological" approach as its starting point, in that the research is based on the assumption that in order to understand how young children represent and remember experience, we must begin by examining activities, events, and tasks in which young children naturally and spontaneously engage.

The book comes out of a conference we held at Emory University in October 1987. The impetus for organizing such a conference stemmed from the exciting new research that was being conducted on very young children's memory abilities; in contrast to much of the research conducted in the seventies, research in the eighties emphasized young children's capabilities. This emphasis has challenged fundamental beliefs about early memory and representation, and changed our conceptions of the course of memory development. We wanted to bring many of these new findings and ideas together in order to provide a coherent view of knowing and remembering in young children. Thanks to our contributors, we think we have managed to do this.

Obviously, a conference and a book do not happen without the help of many people. First and foremost, we are indebted to Dick Neisser, not only because he is the director of the Emory Cognition Project, which provided the funds for the conference and for Judith Hudson to come to

Emory as a visiting scholar in the summer of 1987, but, more important, because he is always a supportive and intellectually stimulating colleague. Beth Shapiro was an invaluable help during the planning phases of the conference, and the Emory graduate students – in particular, Nina Hamond, Ira Hyman, Eric Bergman, and Marion Eppler – helped in ways too numerous to mention. Helen Wheeler at Cambridge provided excellent editorial assistance.

And, of course, we want to thank all of our contributors. All the work that went into the conference and this book is worth it because the ideas and research of our contributors are so exciting.

Robyn Fivush
Judith A. Hudson

Contributors

Christine Aman
Department of Psychology
University of Denver

Patricia J. Bauer
Institute of Child Development
University of Minnesota

Bette L. Bottoms
Department of Psychology
State University of New York,
  Buffalo

Stephen J. Ceci
Department of Human Development and Family Studies
Cornell University

Judy S. DeLoache
Division of Human Development and Family Ecology
University of Illinois at
  Urbana–Champaign

Michael Jeffrey Farrar
Department of Psychology
University of Florida

Robyn Fivush
Department of Psychology
Emory University

Gail S. Goodman
Department of Psychology
State University of New York,
  Buffalo

Nina R. Hamond
Department of Psychology
Emory University

Judith A. Hudson
Department of Psychology
Rutgers, The State University
  of New Jersey

Jean M. Mandler
Department of Cognitive
  Science
University of California, San
  Diego

Jayanthi Mistry
Kamehameha PreKindergarten Project

Ulric Neisser
Department of Psychology
Emory University

Katherine Nelson
Developmental Psychology
  Program
Graduate Center of the City
  University of New York

Robert J. Padgett
Department of Psychology
Butler University

Hilary Horn Ratner
Department of Psychology
Wayne State University

K. Ann Renninger
Program in Education
Swarthmore College

Barbara Rogoff
Department of Psychology
University of Utah

David F. Ross
Department of Human Devel-
    opment and Family Studies
Cornell University

Leslie Rudy
Department of Psychology
Ohio State University

Brenda S. Smith
Department of Psychology
Westmont College

Michael P. Toglia
Department of Psychology
State University of New York
    at Cortland

1

Introduction: What young children remember and why

JUDITH A. HUDSON AND ROBYN FIVUSH

This volume is based on papers presented at the Emory Cognition Project Conference, What Young Children Remember and Why, held in October 1987. The conference led to a reconsideration of what memory is and how it develops. The contributors examine memory in very different ways, but a common thread is that memory is no longer considered as a separate and distinct cognitive process that can be isolated from other cognitive processes; rather, remembering is viewed as a cognitive activity embedded in larger social and cognitive tasks. This view is the culmination of several changes in the field of cognitive development during the last decade.

First, recent studies of cognitive development have focused on the competencies of young children rather than on the limitations of preschool thought when compared to older school-aged children's in a variety of experimental tasks (e.g., Gelman, 1978). A focus on preschool competence began as a reaction to the portrayal of the young child by Piaget (1951) as egocentric, pre-operational, and pre-logical. This portrayal was refuted by research on preschoolers' classification (e.g., Markman, 1981), memory (e.g., Myers & Perlmutter, 1978), and perspective taking (e.g., Borke, 1975). Additionally, research on the impressive language-learning abilities of infants and toddlers (e.g., Brown, 1973; Halliday, 1975) and a proliferation of studies showing that infants are capable of complex cognitive processing (e.g., Reznick & Kagan, 1982) contributed to this new appreciation of the cognitive abilities of very young children.

Second, as part of the study of young children's competencies, researchers have used more ecologically valid assessments of cognitive ability. Decades of laboratory research have documented young children's failures in laboratory situations, but in the context of activities that are meaningful to them, preschoolers' true competence is revealed (Donaldson, 1978). Studies of children's event knowledge, story recall, search strategies, and play activities have uncovered impressive memory, discourse, and problem-solving strategies during the toddler and preschool

1

years (DeLoache, Cassidy, & Brown, 1985; Mandler, 1984; Nelson, 1986).

Finally, the shift in methods and contexts of assessment has been accompanied by a theoretical shift toward a more socially and contextually oriented approach to cognitive development as put forth by Soviet psychologists (Leont'ev, 1981; Vygotsky, 1962, 1978). These approaches emphasize the importance of meaningful goals in cognitive activity and the emergence of intellectual development within a social-cultural context. According to Vygotsky, a culture defines which cognitive activities are necessary and arranges opportunities for those activities to be acquired. The acquisition process is always socially mediated – both by the goals of the larger culture and through social interactions between individuals, specifically, between children and experienced adults. In this view, cognitive development is considered within a larger social-historical context and the appropriate unit of analysis is the interaction between children and adults.

Thus, research in the last decade has produced evidence that young children are actively involved in making sense of their physical and social world. Through many types of social interactions and real-world experiences, children develop discourse routines; schematic representations of stories, scenes, and events; spatial representations of locations and routes; and object categories based on functional as well as formal properties. Preschool children perform quite well in tasks that draw on these representations, but they typically fail in tasks in which their knowledge cannot help them understand the context or the procedures that are called for. In addition, they may possess knowledge relevant to a task, but may not always access or use that knowledge in an unfamiliar context. Thus, an important direction in cognitive developmental research has been to investigate the content, organization, and accessibility of children's emerging knowledge structures as well as the interaction between developing knowledge and developing cognitive abilities (Bjorklund, 1985; Chi, 1988; Nelson & Hudson, 1988).

In line with these theoretical reformulations, this volume takes a serious look at recent research on the development of memory and representation in young children. We take the position that in order to understand what children remember from a given experience (including such diverse experiences as a demonstration of where an object is located, presentation of a list of items to be put into a sack lunch, presentation of a list of names of toys, real-world events that have been experienced, and events that have been observed), we need to know what kind of knowledge structures children bring to that experience, how the experience is structured (temporally, causally, hierarchically, spatially, categorically, etc.), and whether children can make sense of the structure of the experience. Whether or not children can appreciate the structure of the experience depends on the status of their knowledge base as well as more general cognitive development.

We also need to consider the social and functional context of the experience and the context in which the experience is remembered. How children participate in an experience (as a participant, as an observer, as it is explained to them, etc.) can influence how the experience is represented. When remembering an experience, different contexts require different types of memory performances. For example, recalling an event for an experimenter who was not present at the original experience imposes different memory and discourse demands than recalling the same event in a conversation with someone who was also a participant. It is not our goal to specify which context is more "natural" or a better assessment situation – in fact, children may report more information to an experimenter because they know that the experimenter will require more background information. Rather, the point is that we need to take into consideration how children's understanding of the social context and their goals in the activity affect any kind of memory performance.

Chapters 2–5 examine the development of children's event representations, exploring the relationship between the structure of experienced events and the structure of children's representations of events. This line of research builds upon the literature on children's event representations in several ways. Nelson's (1986) research has shown that preschool children have temporally organized event schemas for events they are familiar with. Yet one important issue has been when and how event schemas are acquired. A second issue is whether young children understand the causal connections between actions in a causally organized event sequence, or whether they simply attend to temporal regularities. These two issues are addressed in Chapter 2, where Bauer and Mandler present research on how the temporal and causal structure of an event influences very young children's ability to organize and recall the event. Their data demonstrate that children as young as 16 months are sensitive to the causal connections among actions and use this information in organizing and recalling events.

A third issue in the study of children's event knowledge has been the relationship between general event knowledge and memory for specific episodes. Hudson (1986) proposed that children's generalized event representations influenced the content and accessibility of memories for specific events. In Chapter 3, Farrar and Goodman systematically explore the relationship between memory of a recurring event and memory of an unusual episode of that event. Their findings suggest there are developmental differences in the extent to which preschool and school-age children rely on event schemas as recall guides. Their discussion of the *schema-activation* and *schema-deployment* stages of script processing helps illuminate this finding and adds to our understanding of how event schemas influence memory for specific episodes.

Children's ability to appreciate the temporal and causal structure of events has by now received considerable attention. Yet events can also be structured hierarchically in terms of superordinate–subordinate links based on partonomy (as opposed to inclusion) relations (Barsalou & Sewell, 1985). Chapter 4 addresses the issue of whether young children's event representations are hierarchically organized after the first experience with an event. Ratner, Smith, and Padgett present a series of studies of children and adults' ability to appreciate the hierarchical organization of a real-world clay-making event. Their findings suggest that there are developmental differences in the ability to hierarchically organize event knowledge, at least in the initial stages of script acquisition.

DeLoache (Chapter 5) presents a different approach to the study of representational processes in young children. Her research focuses on children's ability to understand that one event can serve as a representation of another event. Research on children's search strategies has shown that toddlers can represent large-scale spatial layouts in order to locate hidden objects over long time-delays (DeLoache, 1985). Although children from 30 to 32 months can use their own internal spatial representations to locate objects, they are not able to use an external model of a spatial layout to accomplish the same task. They seem to have difficulty with *dual orientation,* that is, the ability to understand that a model is both a real, three-dimensional object and at the same time a representation of something else. This duel orientation, which emerges at the age of 36–39 months, is an important milestone in children's memory development because it signals children's ability to understand the correspondence between a memory representation and a real-world situation. They can now use their memory representations to help them understand new situations. As DeLoache points out, what good is a memory representation if it cannot be activated when needed?

Thus far, we have considered age-related differences in the organization of children's knowledge base and in general cognitive ability as mediating variables influencing what children represent and remember from experiences. Renninger's research (Chapter 6) adds yet another dimension – children's interests – that affects the specific content and organization of children's representations. Her research shows that individual differences in interests influence how children interact with objects in play, what they represent to themselves about various play objects, and how they perform in attention and memory tasks. These findings are further discussed in terms of the role of specific content in representation

and the implications of individual variation in representation for understanding structure and function in cognitive development.

The social context of remembering is the focus of the remaining chapters. The interaction between the rememberer and the audience as well
as the purpose or goal of remembering are shown to affect not just how
well children display competencies in remembering, but how the process
of remembering develops. In Chapter 7, Hudson investigates the role of
parent–child conversations in the development of 2-year-olds' ability to
remember and report past experiences. Here the emphasis is not just
demonstrating young children's memory competence in a naturalistic
context – although their ability to recall aspects of events up to 10 months
in the past is impressive – but to examine how the process of repeatedly
recalling events affects the emergence and development of early autobiographical memory. Developments during this early age period may have
implications for understanding the phenomenon of childhood amnesia,
that is, adults' difficulty in recalling events from early childhood.

Continuing the theme that memory skills develop within socially and
culturally defined memory activities, Rogoff & Mistry (Chapter 8) provide a comprehensive overview of a variety of ways in which memory
development is "channeled" by the social and cultural environment.
They show that children perform better in more meaningful memory
tasks that take advantage of real-world knowledge structures (i.e., knowledge of spatial layouts), and that children's memory performance actually declines when formal strategies such as rehearsal are misapplied to
tasks in which meaningful relationships serve as better memory organizers. Further, the development of verbal displays of memory (e.g., retell-
ing a story or narrating an autobiographic memory) depends on cultural
values and practices. In contrast to children from Western, middle-class
families, Mayan children are discouraged from speaking freely to adults:
Relating a story to an adult is a very unusual, highly stressful, and therefore difficult task for them. Finally, the need for adult guidance in remembering is shown to be related to the memory task at hand. In meaningful activities when the goal of remembering is evident to children, less
guidance is needed than in unfamiliar situations where the goal of remembering is understood only by the adult.

The social and functional context of early autobiographical memory is
considered further in Chapter 9, by Fivush and Hamond. In tracing children's autobiographical memory reports from age 2½ to age 4, they identify two processes that may help explain both developmental changes in
early autobiographical memory and the phenomenon of infantile amnesia. First, there appears to be a shift from focusing on the routine, or
typical, aspects of novel events to focusing on the more unusual, distinctive, and memorable aspects of events. Second, younger children have not

yet learned the conventionalized framework for recounting the past, and therefore depend more on the adult's questions to guide their recall than do older children.

The next two chapters extend research on the social and functional dimensions of remembering by moving beyond consideration of parent–child and experimenter–child relationships and exploring the social and functional context of children as witnesses. Goodman, Rudy, Bottoms, and Aman (Chapter 10) discuss the limitations of research that relies solely on children's recall of presented stimuli such as stories and films and that fails to consider the social and affective context of children's experience. Their research shows that we need to consider what is important from the child's perspective (such as a concern for personal safety or social acceptance) in evaluating children's eyewitness testimony.

Despite the preponderance of research showing young children's impressive memory abilities, we cannot lose sight of the fact that young children's memory (like older children's and adults') is sometimes inaccurate. In Chapter 11, Ceci, Toglia, and Ross discuss the accuracy and validity of children's eyewitness testimony by placing the issue in a larger, sociohistorical context. Using the Salem witch trials of the 17th century as a point of departure, the authors discuss how cultural conceptions of children have influenced the degree to which children's testimony is considered valid, and present research on factors that can foster distortions in young children's recollections.

Chapters 12–14 are commentaries. Nelson (Chapter 12) discusses the functions of early memories and how a functional approach offers explanations for the development of general event knowledge and the emergence of autobiographical memory during the years 1 to 3. Nelson also discusses how the results of several investigations reported in this volume contribute to understanding childhood amnesia. When children learn that memories can be shared with others, Nelson argues, remembering takes on a new social and personal significance. This development, which occurs sometime between the ages of 2 and 4, can account for discontinuities between toddlers' and preschool children's autobiographical memory as well as discontinuities in adults' recall of the toddler and preschool years.

Mandler (Chapter 13) raises a critical issue underlying much of the research reported in this volume, namely, the reliance on verbal measures of children's recall. As Mandler aptly points out, in discussing when children recall information, what kind of information they recall, and how much information they recall, we need to be cautious about equating verbal report and recall. For a variety of reasons, which Mandler elucidates, young children are most likely remembering more than they are telling us.

In the final commentary, Neisser (Chapter 14) exhorts psychologists interested in adult memory to pay attention to the developmental literature. It seems quite evident that in order to understand adult memory, we must understand the developmental process. Perhaps most important, Neisser argues, is that by considering memory development, the importance of viewing remembering as a social activity embedded in specific interactional contexts becomes clear.

The interface between knowing (representation) and remembering (process) as displayed in socially mediated memory activities is an exciting area of developmental research. The concerns are varied, the methods are eclectic, and the results are at times both convergent and divergent; but together, the chapters presented here attest to the value of adopting a functional perspective on the development of young children's memory.

REFERENCES

Barsalou, L., & Sewell, D. (1985). Contrasting the representation of scripts and categories. *Journal of Memory and Language, 24,* 646–665.

Bjorklund, D. F. (1985). The role of conceptual knowledge in the development of organization in children's memory. In C. J. Brainerd & M. Pressley (Eds.), *Basic processes in memory development: Progress in cognitive development research* (pp. 103–142). New York: Springer-Verlag.

Borke, H. (1975). Piaget's mountains revisited: Changes in the egocentric landscape. *Developmental Psychology, 11,* 240–243.

Brown, R. (1973). *A first language: The early stages.* Cambridge, MA: Harvard University Press.

Chi, M. T. H. (1988). Children's lack of access and knowledge reorganization: An example from the concept of animism. In F. E. Weinert & M. Perlmutter (Eds.), *Memory development: Universal changes and individual differences* (pp. 169–194). Hillsdale, NJ: Erlbaum.

DeLoache, J. S. (1985). Memory-based searching in very young children. In H. Wellman (Ed.), *The development of search ability* (pp. 151–183). Hillsdale, NJ: Erlbaum.

DeLoache, J., Cassidy, D. J., & Brown, A. L. (1985). Precursors of mnemonic strategies in very young children's memory. *Child Development, 56,* 125–137.

Donaldson, M. (1978). *Children's minds.* New York: Norton.

Gelman, R. (1978). Cognitive development. *Annual Review of Psychology, 29,* 297–332.

Halliday, M. A. K. (1975). *Learning how to mean: Explorations in the development of language.* London: Edward Arnold.

Hudson, J. A. (1986). Memories are made of this: General event knowledge and the development of autobiographic memory. In K. Nelson (Ed.), *Event Knowledge: Structure and function in development* (pp. 97–118). Hillsdale, NJ: Erlbaum.

Leont'ev, A. N. (1981). The problem of activity in psychology. In J. V. Wertsch (Ed.), *The concept of activity in Soviet psychology.* Armonk, NY: M. E. Sharp.

Mandler, J. M. (1984). *Stories, scripts, and scenes.* Hillsdale, NJ: Erlbaum.

Markman, E. M. (1981). Two different principles of conceptual organization. In M. E. Lamb & A. L. Brown (Eds.), *Advances in developmental psychology* (Vol. 1, pp. 199–236). Hillsdale, NJ: Erlbaum.

Myers, N. A., & Perlmutter, M. (1978). Memory in the years from two to five. In P. A. Ornstein (Ed.), *Memory development in children* (pp. 191–218). Hillsdale, NJ: Erlbaum.

Nelson, K. (1986) (Ed.), *Event knowledge: Structure and function in development.* Hillsdale, NJ: Erlbaum.

Nelson, K., & Hudson, J. A. (1988). Scripts and memory: Functional relationships in development. In F. E. Weinert & M. Perlmutter (Eds.), *Memory development: Universal changes and individual differences* (pp. 147–167). Hillsdale, NJ: Erlbaum.

Piaget, J. (1951). *Play, dreams and imitation in children* (C. Gattegno & F. M. Hodgson, Trans.). New York: Norton.

Reznick, J. S., & Kagan, J. (1982). Category detection in infancy. In L. P. Lipsitt & C. K. Rovee-Collier (Eds.), *Advances in infancy research* (Vol. 2, pp. 80–111). Norwood, NJ: Ablex.

Vygotsky, L. S. (1962). *Thought and language.* Cambridge, MA: MIT Press.

Vygotsky, L. S. (1978). *Mind in society.* Cambridge, MA: Harvard University Press.

2

Remembering what happened next: Very young children's recall of event sequences

PATRICIA J. BAUER AND JEAN M. MANDLER

Research on children's memory has amply demonstrated that when children are working in a familiar and meaningful context they exhibit memory skills far more advanced than they do when working in an unfamiliar context stripped of meaning. This lesson has provided the impetus for research on children's memories for familiar events and routines. By interviewing 3- to 8-year-old children about their participation in everyday events, researchers have shown that children as young as 3 years of age recall events in a fashion similar to that of older children and adults (Nelson & Gruendel, 1981, 1986).

The apparent similarities in the structure underlying the event representations of preschoolers and adults has led to the question of whether or not the event representations of even younger pre- and early-verbal children are similar as well. In this chapter we focus on three issues, all dealing directly with the question of whether or not the event representations of very young children share characteristics with those of older preschoolers. Briefly, the questions are these: First, do very young children include temporal order information in their representations of events? Second, do they use order information to organize their recall of newly experienced events? Third, do they organize their recall around causal relations?

Theoretical and empirical foundations

The most comprehensive studies of the recall of events by preschool-age children has been conducted by Katherine Nelson and her colleagues (Nelson, 1986). They have used the script model to describe children's early event-representations. The script model originally was devised to characterize adults' representations of routine events. As described by Schank and Abelson (1977) a script has three components: (a) it contains actions or elements appropriate to a particular spatial-temporal context; (b) it is organized around a goal; and (c) it is temporally ordered. Nelson and colleagues began their studies of children's recall of events by asking

9

whether it was consistent with the expectations of the adult script model. In effect, they examined whether or not young children's recall of events was similar to that of adults. Positive indications would lend support to the argument that children's underlying representations of events are structurally similar to those of older children and adults (Nelson & Gruendel, 1986).

In their initial studies, Nelson and Gruendel (1981) used a semi-structured interview format, sometimes supplemented by props to assist the subjects in their reporting. They interviewed children as young as 3 years about "what happens" in the course of everyday events and routines. The results of these and subsequent studies of children's responses to interviews about a variety of familiar as well as relatively novel events demonstrated that young children's recall of events is much like that of adults. The youngest children in their studies tended to mention fewer components of an event, relative to the older children, but they almost invariably mentioned the main or central act (e.g., "eating" in a meal-associated event). At all ages, the children almost invariably mentioned the components of the events in their usual or canonical order. In addition, the children demonstrated a good deal of consistency in their accounting of the events over 1- to 4-week intervals between interviews.

Assuming, therefore, that preschoolers' representations of events are structurally similar to those of adults, we have been led to ask whether or not the event representations of even younger pre- and early-verbal children are similar as well. Thus far, we have focused on three aspects of this issue. First, there is the question of whether or not very young children represent information about temporal order in their early representations. On conceptual grounds, Nelson (1986) and Mandler (1984) argue that in their earliest representations of events, children include information about the components of the event as well as information about the order in which they occur. However, the alternative view that early representations are unorganized is held by some researchers. Case and Khanna (1981), for example, have speculated that general changes in information-processing capacity occur around 24 to 28 months of age. Such changes allow children to coordinate multiple pieces of information, and thus make temporal ordering as an organizing principle available for the first time. Other researchers have noted correlations between the grammaticization process in language and developments in sequencing in symbolic play, again occurring between 24 and 28 months. They have argued that both changes are based on a general change in the capacity to order a series of components according to convention (e.g., Bates, O'Connell, & Shore, 1987; Shore, Bates, Bretherton, Beeghly, & O'Connell, in press). These conceptualizations would predict that the event representations of very young children might not be temporally ordered. Rather, early representations of events might be unorganized collections of individual components.

The second question is whether or not children encode information about temporal order in their very first representation of a new event. The alternative is that information about correct temporal order is abstracted over repeated experiences. This question has obvious implications for the accuracy of children's recall of an event they have experienced only once or a few times before. However, it also has implications for our most fundamental assumptions about the level of continuity between the psychological processes employed by very young children compared to adults. Again, on conceptual grounds, Nelson (1986) argued that event representations are *necessarily* temporally ordered. For adults, although it is not uncontroversial, it is argued that temporal information is encoded automatically (e.g., Hasher & Zacks, 1979; although see Zacks, Hasher, Alba, Sanft, & Rose, 1984, for qualifications). One of Hasher and Zacks's criteria for an "automatic" process is that it show little developmental change. Thus, if it is shown that even very young children organize events according to their temporal order, there will be evidence of continuity in the psychological processes used by children and adults. However, it is important to keep in mind that temporal order information might not be used until after one has had repeated experience with an event.

The third question is intimately related to the second; it concerns whether or not different types of temporal structure influence children's initial representations of an event. Two factors affect temporal structure. One is the temporal variance or invariance of the event. That is, is the event always performed in the same order? The second is the nature of the connections underlying the event. The elements of an event can be connected by causal relations, or they can be merely temporally connected. A causal relation exists when one item in a sequence *must* be performed before another in the same sequence. For example, you must open a door before you can go through it. In this example, as in the others we will discuss, the relation really would be more appropriately described as enabling, rather than as causal. That is, opening a door does not *cause* one to go through it, but it does make the next step possible. We will adopt the parlance of those working in this area and refer to these relations as "causal." Regardless of whether these relations are truly causal or merely enabling, they nevertheless *require* that the event always be performed in the same order. However, elements in a sequence need not be causally connected; they can be merely temporally connected. The order in which such elements occur is arbitrary, and therefore, they are at least *potentially* temporally variant.

On the basis of children's narratives about events, we know that they recall aspects of events with causal and temporal invariances more frequently and at a younger age than they do aspects of events lacking such structure (Hudson & Nelson, 1983; Slackman, Hudson, & Fivush, 1986). The question of interest here is whether or not very young children also organize their recall around causal relations. Further, do they do so after a single experience of an event, or only after repeated experience of it? We will reserve discussion of these latter two issues until after we have addressed the question of the presence or absence of temporal organization in pre- and early-verbal children's recall.

Recall of temporal order by pre- and early-verbal children

Investigation of the structure of event representations in preverbal children is obviously hampered by the response limitations of the young subjects – they are unlikely to engage in verbal recall. When working with children 2 years of age and younger, it is important that the verbal component of both the response medium and the task instructions be kept to a minimum. Therefore, the semistructured interview technique used in work with preschool-age children, even with the added support of props, is not useful because it requires verbal responses. Picture-ordering techniques, such as those used by Fivush and Mandler (1985) with 4- to 6-year-olds, also may not be of use with very young subjects because of the large verbal component involved in the instructions. One technique that has been used successfully is delayed imitation of actions. A specific event or action is modeled by the experimenter, and the subject is encouraged to imitate. Recently, Meltzoff (1988) employed this technique to study immediate and delayed recall (24-hour delay) of a single-act event by 9-month-old children. By combining a number of components or elements into an event sequence, delayed imitation can be used to study recall of events that are more analogous to those studied in older children. Further, by imposing longer temporal delays over which the event is to be remembered, we can gain information about long-term recall of event sequences by very young children.

Negative evidence

O'Connell and Gerard (1985) used delayed imitation to examine 20- to 36-month-old children's recall of three-element event sequences. The sequences depicted familiar events such as "having a snack," "going to bed," and "taking a bath." They presented the subjects with familiar event sequences in their canonical or usual order and also in reversed order. For example, a familiar event in canonical order would be modeled as: take off a teddy bear's clothes, put him in the bathtub, and 'wash' the bear. The reverse order of presentation of this event would be modeled as: 'wash' the bear, put him in the tub, take off his clothes. O'Connell and Gerard also presented subjects with a "scrambled" sequence of unrelated but meaningful actions. For example, they would model: cover the bear with a blanket, the bear pays money, wipe the bear's mouth. O'Connell and Gerard argued that if young children's representations of events are temporally organized, even their youngest subjects should demonstrate ordered recall of the familiar, canonically ordered event sequences.

Although the 20-month-old subjects reproduced some of the elements of the canonical and reverse-order sequences, they demonstrated little or no ability to reproduce the modeled order of the elements in any of the conditions. Further, the 20-month-old subjects produced fewer of the components and fewer different components in the scrambled sequences, relative to the canonical and reverse-order sequences. This led O'Connell and Gerard (1985) to conclude that their youngest subjects "appear to understand *that* some actions go together, but they demonstrated little understanding of *how* they go together" (p. 679; original emphasis). Twenty-four-month-old subjects were able to reproduce the modeled order of the sequences only when they were familiar and presented in their canonical order. The 28-month-olds produced both canonical and reverse-order sequences in their canonical order. That is, they, in effect, "corrected" or "repaired" the order of the reverse sequences. The 36-month-olds were better able to reproduce the model order of all of the sequence types.

O'Connell and Gerard (1985) concluded that children's early representations of events lack coherent organization or structure. On the basis of their data, it appeared that temporal ordering as an organizing principle was something imposed on a set of originally loosely related components or elements. It appeared that familiarity with an event was necessary before recall of it would be temporally ordered. In effect, their data suggested that until about 24 months of age, children's memories of events resembled a group of unorganized snapshots of individual components; the temporal organization necessary to combine the components into a coherent motion-picture was something imposed only later, with familiarity and/or development.

Evaluation of the negative evidence

The data from O'Connell and Gerard (1985) would appear to suggest that children's early representations of familiar events and *initial* representations of new events are not temporally ordered. However, for methodological and conceptual reasons, the data make it difficult to draw conclusions about children's abilities to use temporal information to order recall. Some objections to this work have been discussed in detail elsewhere (Bauer and Mandler, 1989; Bauer and Shore, 1987), and we will review them only briefly here. We also want to point out that some of the concerns we raise were discussed by O'Connell and Gerard (1985) themselves.

On the basis of O'Connell and Gerard's data it is difficult to evaluate children's abilities to engage in ordered imitation of familiar event sequences for three reasons. First, one-half of the sequences in their study involved using a teddy bear as a patient. That is, the child was to brush the bear's teeth or give it a drink. The other half of the sequences required that the subjects use the teddy bear as an active agent. That is, the bear itself was made to hold a toothbrush and brush its teeth, or made to hold a cup and drink from it. In addition to the motoric difficulty associated with such actions, this level of role complexity is usually not observed until about 24 months of age (see McCune-Nicolich, 1981, for a review). Even after this age, agent manipulation adds to the overall complexity of a task (Bretherton, 1984, p. 22). Second, the subjects experienced the same event sequences modeled in their canonical order as well as in reverse order within the same experimental session. We know from the adult literature that presentation of conflicting order information has a detrimental effect on recall of temporal order. Third, the subjects were required to imitate a total of 18 event sequences, two-thirds of which were "unusual." That is, they involved either violations of order expectations, as in the reverse-order sequences, or violations of expectations about "what goes together," as in the scrambled sequences. O'Connell and Gerard's (1985) unusually high attrition rate in their youngest age group, 65% of whom were dropped from the sample for lack of participation, speaks to the disturbing effect that such violations have on young subjects. It is likely that the high density of sequences involving violations of real-world knowledge had a detrimental effect on performance, across the board.

From O'Connell and Gerard's data it also is difficult to evaluate children's abilities to engage in ordered imitation of novel event sequences. We would like to be able to use children's responses to new sequences as an indication of their ability to use temporal order information to organize recall of novel events. However, the new sequences presented by O'Connell and Gerard (i.e., the reverse and scrambled sequences) actually were novel concatenations of components of familiar events. Thus, although the *sequences* were novel, the events depicted therein were not. In fact, if a child's representation of an event includes order information, presenting her with an unfamiliar ordering of that event would violate existing order expectations. As a result, the new sequences presented by O'Connell and Gerard were not a good test of response to novel events. Truly novel events are those for which one has no order expectations.

A genuine test of whether or not young children include order information in their representations of newly experienced events requires that they be presented with sequences of events that truly are novel and do not violate any existing real-world knowledge. Further, to evaluate whether or not very young children are likely to organize their event representations around causal and temporal invariances, it is necessary to contrast novel sequences of events lacking causal relations with novel sequences of events containing causal relations. Novel sequences are necessary in order to separate the effects of familiarity from the effects of the causal relations themselves.

Positive evidence

In the studies of temporal structure to be described we wanted to maximize subjects' opportunities to demonstrate temporally ordered recall. Therefore, we used delayed imitation to assess immediate and delayed recall of event sequences. Each subject was seen in the laboratory for two visits. In the first study, the visits were separated by 6 weeks; in the second study, they were separated by 2 weeks. At each session, each subject was tested on three different sequence types; familiar-event sequences presented in their canonical order; novel sequences characterized by causal or enabling relations among the elements (hereafter referred to as "novel-causal"); and novel sequences lacking causal or enabling relations among the elements (hereafter referred to as "novel-arbitrary"). In Study 1, each subject was tested on three sequences, one of each type. In Study 2, each subject was tested on six sequences, two of each type. Description of the sequences will follow.

For each sequence, the subjects first were allowed to manipulate the props to be used before modeling of sequence. This provided a baseline measure of the spontaneous occurrence of the targeted behaviors. We measured the number of target components that the subjects produced as well as the number of pairs of target components that they produced in the to-be-modeled order. The sequence of actions then was modeled, with narration, by the experimenter (E). After E had modeled the sequence, the props were returned to the subjects, and they were encouraged to imitate. Performance immediately after modeling provided our measure of immediate recall. All of the subjects returned to the laboratory either 2 or 6 weeks later and the procedure was repeated. At the second session, the children's performance *before* modeling constituted our measure of delayed recall.

It is important to note that the two studies we are describing were conducted in two different laboratories, at two different points in time. As a result, there are several minor methodological differences between them. As will become evident, these differences do not influence the conclusions that can be drawn. In that sense, then, the differences between the studies add to the strength of our conclusions.

First, we will focus on the data from the familiar event sequences. These sequences are most analogous to those tested by O'Connell and Gerard (1985) and Nelson and colleagues (e.g., Nelson and Gruendel, 1986). However, unlike in O'Connell and Gerard, our subjects were not required to use a teddy bear as an active agent, only as a patient in one of our sequences. Further, our subjects did not see the familiar events modeled in any other than the canonical order. In the first study, conducted by Bauer and Shore (1987), the familiar event sequence was giving teddy bear a bath. In the second study, conducted by Bauer and Mandler (1989), a "clean the table" sequence was used as well. The sequences were modeled as follows:

1. "Bath" – the subject was given a stuffed bear dressed in a T-shirt, a terry hand towel, and a dishpan. E modeled taking off teddy's shirt, putting him in the bathtub, 'washing' the bear, and 'drying' him.[1]
2. "Clean the table" – the subject was given a small spray bottle (empty, of course), a small wastebasket, and a paper towel. E modeled spraying the table at which they were seated, wiping it with the towel, and throwing the towel in the basket.

After the sequence had been modeled, the props were returned to the subjects and they were encouraged to imitate the sequence with instructions such as "Can you give the dirty bear a bath?" When the subjects returned at Session 2, they were simply given the props with no prior instruction.

In Study 1, thirty children, aged 17.5 to 23 months, with a mean age of 21 months, participated as subjects. In Study 2, twenty 16-month-olds and twenty 20-month-olds participated. There were an equal number of females and males in each study.

The measures of interest are the mean number of components produced by the subjects and the mean number of pairs of components produced in the target order. For example, if the subject produced all three components in the modeled order, she would receive a score of 3 for the "components" measure, and a score of 2 for the "pairs in modeled order" measure: pair 1–2, 2–3. If a subject omitted component number 2, she would receive credit for producing the pair 1–3.

Table 2.1 reflects the raw scores for the dependent measures. The analyses focused on significant differences between measures of baseline performance and measures of immediate recall, and measures of base-

Table 2.1. *Studies 1 and 2 – Familiar sequences: Mean number of components and number of components in target order*

	Study 1 21-month-olds (mean)	Study 2 16-month-olds (mean)	Study 2 20-month-olds (mean)
Components produced	(max.=4)	(max.=3)	(max.=3)
Baseline	1.0	.4	.3
Immediate recall	2.7	2.1	2.5
Delayed recall	2.4	1.3	1.9
Adherence to target order	(max.=3)	(max.=2)	(max.=2)
Baseline	.2	.1	.1
Immediate recall	1.1	.8	1.3
Delayed recall	.7	.3	.9

line performance and measures of delayed recall. Because recall is measured as performance above and beyond baseline, a low baseline score is preferable.

Analyses of variance and subsequent Tukey tests revealed that in both studies, all groups demonstrated evidence of both immediate and delayed recall for both the components of the familiar events and their order in the sequence.[2] Additionally, in Study 1, subjects showed no significant decrement in their level of recall of either the components or their temporal order even over the 6-week interval between sessions. In Study 2, the 20-month-old subjects also showed no significant decrement in their recall of the temporal order of the components over the 2-weeks-between-session interval, although they did show a significant decrement in their recall of the individual components over the same period. The 16-month-olds in Study 2 showed a decrement in their level of recall both of the components and of their temporal order. However, their level of performance before modeling at Session 2, although low, still was significantly greater than their baseline level of performance at Session 1. The results of these two separate studies provide clear evidence that at least by 16 months of age, subjects are encoding information about temporal order in their representations of familiar events. Further, at least by 20 months of age, the children can organize representations of familiar events sufficiently well to enable immediate as well as long-term recall.

Recall of the temporal order of novel events

On the basis of the data discussed thus far we can draw conclusions about whether or not children include order information in their representations of familiar events. However, the data do not enable us to conclude that children encode order information in their *initial* representations of events, since they are based on children's recall of events with which they are already familiar. Therefore, we still are left with two questions. First, do children encode order information in their initial representations? Or, alternatively, is information about correct temporal order later imposed on a set of originally unordered components? Second, do young children organize their recall around causal relations? Further, is this organization evident from children's initial experience of the event? Information about children's recall of novel event sequences is necessary in order to address these questions.

The data relevant to these questions are derived from subjects' performance on two different types of equally novel event sequences. The difference between the two sequence types is that structurally, one contains causal or enabling relations among the elements in the sequence whereas the other does not. Ordered recall of these novel events would indicate that children do encode order information in their initial representations of events. Any differences in level of recall for sequences of these two types would suggest that pre- and early-verbal children are differentially sensitive to the underlying structure of event sequences, even in the absence of information about temporal variance or invariance that would come from repeated experience of them.

The data to be presented were obtained in conjunction with the familiar-sequence data from Studies 1 and 2, already discussed. Thus, the subjects and the procedure were the same. In Study 1, the novel sequence characterized by causal relations (novel-causal) was making a "rattle." In Study 2, the rattle sequence was used as well as a "frog jump" sequence. The novel-causal sequences were modeled as follows:

1. "Rattle" – the subject was given a rubber ball and two graduated nesting or stacking cups. E modeled putting the ball into one of the cups, covering it with the other cup, and shaking the 'rattle' near her ear.
2. "Frog jump" – the subject was given a wooden board, a wedge-shaped block, and a toy frog. E modeled leaning the board against the block to form a teeter-totter, putting the frog on the board, and hitting the board, thereby causing the frog to 'jump.'

The important feature of the novel-causal sequences is that they contain relations that must be performed in the order in which they were modeled. For example, in the rattle task, if you put the cups together before you put the ball inside, the final product does not produce the "rattle" sound.

In contrast, the novel-arbitrary sequences to be described can be performed in any order with no implications for the final outcome. In Study 1, the novel sequence lacking causal or enabling relations was "bang the ring." For reasons to be discussed, two different novel-arbitrary se-

Table 2.2. *Study 1 – Novel-arbitrary and novel-causal sequences: Mean number of components and number of components in target order (21-month-olds)*

	Novel-arbitrary (mean)	Novel-causal (mean)
Components produced		
(max.=3)		
Baseline	1.0	.6
Immediate recall	1.0	2.2
Delayed recall	.8	1.5
Adherence to target order		
(max.=2)		
Baseline	.1	.1
Immediate recall	.2	1.2
Delayed recall	0	.5

quences were used in Study 2, namely, "train ride" and "make a picture." The novel-arbitrary sequences were modeled as follows:

1. "Bang the ring" – the subject was given a flat block, a dowel stick, and a stacking ring. E modeled banging the ring to the block, turning the ring, and stacking it on the stick.
2. "Train ride" – the subject was given two train cars that could be attached with Velcro, a 'driver' designed to fit inside either car, and a piece of train track. E modeled attaching the cars together, putting them on the track, and putting the driver in the car.
3. "Make a picture" – the subject was given a small chalkboard, a piece of chalk, a sticker, and an easel. E modeled attaching the sticker to the chalkboard, leaning the chalkboard against the easel, and scribbling on the chalkboard.

It should be apparent that for each of these last three sequences, the components of the event could be combined in any order, without resulting in a qualitatively different product or outcome.

We turn first to discussion of the data obtained from Study 1 for the novel-arbitrary sequence. The data from Study 1 are presented in Table 2.2. Analyses of variance and subsequent Tukey tests revealed that the subjects showed no immediate or delayed recall of either the components of the novel-arbitrary sequence or their temporal order.[3] On the basis of these data alone, one would conclude that children's *initial* representations of events are not temporally organized. However, subjects' difficulty with the novel-arbitrary task cannot be attributed entirely to its novelty, since a different pattern of performance was evident in the novel-causal condition. In the latter condition subjects showed clear evi-

Table 2.3. *Study 2 – Novel-arbitrary and novel-causal sequences:*
Mean number of components and number of components in target order

	Novel-arbitrary		Novel-causal	
	16-month (mean)	20-month (mean)	16-month (mean)	20-month (mean)
Components produced (max.=3)				
Baseline	.8	.9	.7	.8
Immediate recall	1.9	2.4	2.2	2.6
Delayed recall	1.4	2.1	1.6	1.9
Adherence to target order (max.=2)				
Baseline	.2	.1	.1	.2
Immediate recall	.7	.7	1.0	1.4
Delayed recall	.2	.6	.5	.8

dence of both immediate and delayed recall for both the elements of the sequence and their temporal order.

The low level of production of the components of the novel-arbitrary sequence was a source of concern because the two dependent variables are not independent of each other. The subjects in Study 1 were involved with the props provided, but they produced very few of the targeted behaviors. Instead, they might use the dowel stick as a bat and hit the ring. As a result, their lack of adherence to the target order could have been artificially low mainly because of lack of production of the target components, not because of the nature of the temporal connections among the components. Therefore, for Study 2, we modeled the train-ride and make-a-picture sequences, which we hoped would increase the likelihood of production of the target behaviors.

The data from Study 2 are presented in Table 2.3. Analyses of variance and subsequent Tukey tests showed clear evidence of immediate and delayed recall of the components of both the novel-causal and the novel-arbitrary sequences for both age groups. In fact, subjects recalled more of the components of the novel-causal task than of the familiar task discussed in the preceding section (see Table 2.1).

For the 16-month-olds, immediate recall of the temporal order of the events was evident for both novel sequence types, just as it was for the familiar sequences. However, delayed recall was not evident for either of the novel sequences. For the 20-month-olds, immediate and delayed recall of the temporal order of the events was evident for both the novel-causal and the novel-arbitrary sequences, just as it was for the familiar sequences. Overall, across recall conditions, adherence to the target order was best on the novel-causal sequences, followed by the familiar sequences, and finally by the novel-arbitrary sequences. This order was observed even though in terms of production of the individual components of the sequence (as discussed in the preceeding paragraph), a different relative order was observed.

Summary of Studies 1 and 2

Taken together, these separate studies demonstrate that as early as 16 months of age, children engage in ordered recall not only of familiar sequences of events but also of completely novel events. As young as 16 months of age, children's immediate ordered recall of novel events involving causal relations among the components of the sequence was equal to or higher than their ordered recall of the more familiar event sequences; the order of novel sequences lacking causal relations among the components was not recalled as consistently. The differential level of ordered recall of the two different novel sequence types raises the possibility that children are sensitive to causal temporal relations independent of information about temporal variance or invariance.

The two studies also provide evidence of long-term recall of familiar event sequences by children as young as 16 months, and long-term recall of novel-event sequences by 20-month-olds. Other investigators have provided evidence of long-term recall by children in this age range and even younger. However, the existing data are limited primarily to parental diary accounts of memories for specific people, places, and object locations from 7- to 11-month-old children (Ashmead & Perlmutter, 1980), and reports of recall of single object-specific actions by 9-month-olds (Meltzoff, 1988). The existing data on recall of event sequences by preverbal and early-verbal children primarily are derived from parental diary accounts of the memories of 21- to 27-month-olds (Nelson & Ross, 1980), and an extensive study of the crib speech of one 21-month-old girl (Nelson, 1984). These examples provide evidence of long-term recall by very young children of both familiar and novel events. However, to the best of our knowledge, the present studies are the first reports in the literature of long-term ordered recall for specific, experimentally controlled, multiple-element event sequences by children in this age range. We have seen that both familiarity with an event and the characteristics of its underlying structure influence children's recall. A further exploration of these influences is the subject to which we now turn.

Factors affecting recall of events

Elsewhere, Mandler (1986) has made the argument that the ability to recall an event that has happened in the past is influenced by the organization of its underlying representation. Two factors are implicated in this organization: familiarity, and the types of relations among the items of the sequence. In this context, by "familiarity" we mean simply the experience of the event on more than one occasion. This implies that information about temporal variance or invariance is available. Discussion of familiarity is resumed in a later section. The types of relations among the items of the sequence refer to the presence or absence of causal and enabling relations among the elements. We saw that in both Studies 1 and 2, subjects' immediate and delayed recall was superior for novel sequences characterized by causal relations, compared to novel sequences lacking such relations. This raised the possibility that children are sensitive to causal temporal relations in event sequences independent of information about temporal variance or invariance.

Causal and enabling relations

In the two studies we have been discussing, we presented subjects with two different types of equally novel events. Because both events were new, the subjects did not have access to information about the temporal variance or invariance that would be associated with each of the sequences over repeated experience of them. Nevertheless, the subjects were differentially sensitive to the structure of causally connected versus merely temporally connected events. We will argue on the basis of these data, and on the basis of data to be discussed, that our young subjects were already sensitive to the differences in the structure underlying the surface form of the causal versus the arbitrarily ordered event sequences.

In Study 3 (Bauer and Mandler, 1989), we presented a total of forty 18-, 24-, and 30-month-old subjects with two types of events sequences, each containing an irrelevant component.[4] The first sequence was the novel-causal "rattle" sequence with an irrelevant component added to it: A sticker was introduced in the second position of the sequence. Thus, E modeled putting the ball in one cup, putting a sticker on the other cup, putting the cups together, and shaking the 'rattle.' The second sequence was the arbitrarily ordered "train ride" sequence, also with a sticker introduced in the second position. The arbitrary sequence was modeled as putting the driver in the car, putting a sticker on its head (like a hat), attaching the cars, and putting them on the track.

The point of interest is what happened to the irrelevant component in each sequence. If the subjects had constructed a simple linear representa-

Table 2.4. *Study 3 – Novel events with irrelevant elements:*
Order of reproduction (N = 40)

	Causal		Arbitrary	
	%	(*N*)	%	(*N*)
Sequence ordering				
Exact reproduction	40	(16)	35	(14)
Displacement of irrelevant				
component	45	(18)	22	(9)
Other orderings	15	(6)	43	(17)

tion of both events, the irrelevant component would not necessarily be treated differently in the two different sequences. If, however, the subjects had constructed a representation of the causal sequence such that the causal relations already were playing an organizing role, we might expect to see correct ordering of the causal portion of the sequence and displacement of the irrelevant component. We examined the number of times that the sequence was reproduced exactly as modeled (exact reproduction); the number of times the irrelevant element was omitted or displaced but the order of the rest of the sequence was preserved (displacement of irrelevant component); and the number of times that any other than the irrelevant component was displaced or omitted (other orderings).

The results of Study 3 are presented in Table 2.4. In terms of exact reproduction of the four-element sequences, there were no differences between the causal and the arbitrary sequences. However, in terms of displacement of the irrelevant component and other ordering "errors," there *were* differences between the two sequence types. Twice as many subjects preserved all but the order of the irrelevant component in the causal sequence compared to the arbitrary sequence. Additionally, almost three times as many subjects made other ordering errors on the arbitrary sequence compared to the causal sequence. Thus, failure to reproduce the exact modeled order involved greater displacement of the irrelevant component in the causal sequence compared to the arbitrary sequence.

It is obvious from these data that the young subjects were sensitive to the different relations among the elements of the sequences, in spite of their surface similarities. This result provides evidence that the causal relations among elements in a sequence influence the event representations of children as young as 18 months of age. This influence is observed even in the absence of the information about temporal variance or invariance that would come with repeated experience of an event. We currently are conducting more extensive studies of the effects on recall of causal relations as compared to arbitrary temporal relations.

We certainly do not mean to imply by this interpretation that children's understanding of events is not influenced by repeated experience. Familiarity with a sequence of events has been shown to influence recall by our subjects as well as older preschool- and school-age subjects (e.g., Fivush & Mandler, 1985). But what does it mean to say that the repeated experience of an event or familiarity with an event strengthens the organization of the representation? What are the factors that influence the organization of an event with which you are familiar? This is the final question to which we now turn.

Familiarity

The underlying structure of familiar events as well as that of novel events is influenced by the presence or absence of causal relations among the elements. Some familiar events, like dressing your feet, are causally constrained; for a given foot, you must put on your sock before you can put on your shoe. Other familiar events are arbitrarily ordered. For example, in eating a meal, it is arbitrary whether you eat your soup or your salad first, or whether you eat your salad before or after your pasta. Most events with which we are familiar contain a mixture of causal and arbitrary relations. The now famous "birthday party" event is a classic example. Some of its elements are causally related (you must cut the cake before you can serve it), whereas many of the elements are arbitrarily ordered (whether you open presents before or after eating cake).

Regardless of the arbitrary or nonarbitrary nature of the temporal relations underlying an event, a familiar event is, by definition, one that has been experienced on more than one and perhaps on many occasions. Thus, for a familiar event, information about temporal variance or invariance is available. Many events with which we are familiar are temporally invariant. Either they are causally constrained or their invariance is determined by cultural convention. For example, in our culture, you eat your soup at the beginning of the meal; in Chinese culture, you eat it at the end. Thus, the order of soup eating in each culture is invariant and determined by convention. In the familiar events we have presented to children thus far we have made no attempt to isolate the causal and arbitrary relations inherent in them. However, the order in which the events usually occur has been temporally invariant.

We recently tested a sample of twelve 20-month-old children with some familiar temporally *variant* event sequences. In pilot work we used parental report to verify that the familiar-variant events depicted in the sequences are familiar to children of this age. The parents also indicated that the components of the sequences are highly typical of the events depicted. The events we used were "going for a walk" and "getting ready to go." For example, the getting-ready-to-go sequence was modeled as: put on teddy's shirt, brush his hair, pack his diaper bag (all performed with appropriate props). For the familiar temporally variant events, there are no causal temporal relations and there is no culturally agreed-upon order of occurrence. We compared the children's recall of the familiar-variant event sequences with recall of familiar temporally invariant sequences, of the type used in Studies 1 and 2 (e.g., giving a teddy bear a bath). In addition, we tested recall of novel sequences of arbitrarily ordered, and thus, *potentially* temporally variant events (e.g., making a picture).

Across the three different sequence types, the subjects produced an approximately equal number of *components* on all of the sequences (a mean of 2.5 out of 3 components were produced). Subjects' recall of the target *order* of the familiar-invariant events was superior to that on the familiar-variant events (mean sequencing scores of 1.7 and 1.1 out of 2, respectively). Recall of the target order of the familiar-variant events was not statistically different from that of the novel arbitrarily ordered events (a mean sequencing score of .9 out of 2) (Bauer, 1989, Experiment 1). These data suggest that the organizational advantage afforded by familiar events is derived from the invariance of their underlying temporal structure rather than from familiarity with their components.

Conclusions

In the data we have been discussing, we have highlighted subjects' recall of temporal information. We have done so because some investigators argue that children's earliest representations of events are unorganized. In their view, the ability to use temporal information as an organizing principle is dependent on familiarity with or repeated experience of an event. Alternatively, it is thought to be dependent on general changes in information-processing capacity that do not occur until about 24 to 28 months of age. In effect, it has been suggested that early memories of events resemble a group of unorganized snapshots of individual components; the temporal organization necessary to combine the components into a coherent motion-picture is something imposed only later with experience or development.

On the basis of our data, it appears that as young as 16 months of age, children can organize representations of events sufficiently well to enable immediate recall of both familiar and novel events, as well as some delayed recall of familiar events. By at least 20 months of age, the representations are able to support delayed recall not only of familiar events but of novel events as well. The temporal order of novel events characterized by causal relations among the components is consistently better remembered than the temporal order of equally novel events lacking this structure.

The organization of children's recall appears to be different for sequences of events characterized by different ordering relations. The difference is apparent in better recall of novel-causal compared to novel-arbitrary event sequences. The difference also is apparent in the children's handling of a component irrelevant to an event as a whole. When an irrelevant element is introduced into a sequence characterized by causal relations, it is often displaced to another position in the sequence or left out entirely. When an irrelevant element is introduced into an arbitrarily ordered sequence, it is treated no differently than any of the other components of the sequence. By this behavior our young subjects are demonstrating their sensitivity to the enabling connections inherent in causal sequences.

In addition to causal relations, familiarity with an event sequence influences subjects' recall. Familiar sequences with an agreed-upon temporal order are well remembered over 2- to 6-week intervals between sessions, even by young subjects. In contrast, particular instantiations of familiar events having variable temporal structures are not as well ordered by 20-month-olds. Thus, it appears that the organizational advantage afforded by familiarity with an event is derived primarily from the repeated experience of the event in an invariant temporal order, rather than from familiarity with the components themselves.

We opened this chapter by noting similarities in the structure underlying the event representations of preschool children and adults. The general question we have explored is whether or not the event representations of even younger pre- and early-verbal children are similar as well. It is obvious from our data that one of the most fundamental characteristics of the representation of events – namely, their temporally ordered nature – is present in children as young as 16 months of age. Recently, work using a modified version of the delayed-imitation technique has shown that even 14-month-olds encode the order in which familiar events occur (Mills, Mandler, Schreibman, & Oke, 1988). As one might expect, 14-month-olds do not evidence recall abilities as advanced as those of children in the age range we have tested. They are, however, more successful at imitating events modeled in their usual or canonical order than events modeled in backward or reverse order. Such data indicate that already established knowledge of the order in which events usually occur influences children's reproduction of a model's actions.

The data reported here, as well as those of Mills et al. (1988), suggest an essential continuity in the organizational tendencies of young children and adults. As noted in our opening remarks, adults apparently encode temporal order information virtually automatically (Hasher & Zacks, 1979). Work with 3½- to 5-month-old infants indicates that they are sensitive to temporal order information as well. They have been shown to use order information to anticipate the next event in a sequence (Haith, Hazan, & Goodman, 1988; Smith, 1984). Recalling an event sequence in the correct temporal order obviously involves capacities beyond merely anticipating the next step in a sequence. However, very young infants' demonstrated sensitivity to order information indicates continuity in the capacity to encode temporal order and also holds out the promise of continuity with the later ability to use temporal order to organize recall.

NOTES

1 In Study 1, all four components were included. In Study 2, only three components were modeled: take off teddy's shirt, put him in the tub, 'wash' the bear.
2 Details of the analyses are available for Study 1 in Bauer and Shore (1987); for Study 2, in Bauer and Mandler (1989, Experiment 1).
3 Subjects did show an increase in performance after modeling at Session II.
4 We thank Alan Leslie for suggesting this manipulation. Details of the analyses are available in Bauer and Mandler (1989, Experiment 2).

REFERENCES

Ashmead, D., & Perlmutter, M. (1980). Infant memory in everyday life. In M. Perlmutter (Ed.), *Children's memory* (New directions for child development, No. 10, pp. 1–16). San Francisco: Jossey-Bass.

Bates, E., O'Connell, B., & Shore, C. (1987). Language and communication in infancy. In J. Osofsky (Ed.), *Handbook of infant development* (2nd ed., pp. 149–203). New York: Wiley.

Bauer, P. (1989, April). Holding it all together: Effects of causal and temporal invariance on young children's event recall. *Abstracts of the Society for Research in Child Development, 6*.

Bauer, P., & Mandler, J. (1989). One thing follows another: Effects of temporal structure on 1- to 2-year olds' recall of events. *Developmental Psychology, 25*, 197–206.

Bauer, P., & Shore, C. (1987). Making a memorable event: Effects of familiarity and organization on young children's recall of action sequences. *Cognitive Development, 2*, 327–328.

Bretherton, I. (1984). Representing the social world in symbolic play: Reality and fantasy. In I. Bretherton (Ed.), *Symbolic play: The Development of social understanding* (pp. 3–41). Orlando, FL: Academic Press.

Case, R. & Khanna, F. (1981). The missing links: Stages in children's progress from sensorimotor to logical thought. In W. Fischer (Ed.), *New directions for child development* (pp. 21–32). San Francisco: Jossey-Bass.

Fivush, R., & Mandler, J. (1985). Developmental changes in the understanding of temporal sequence. *Child Development, 56,* 1437–1446.

Haith, M. M., Hazan, C., & Goodman, G. S. (1988). Expectation and anticipation of dynamic visual events by 3.5 month-old babies. *Child Development, 59,* 467–479.

Hasher, L., & Zacks, R. T. (1979). Automatic and effortful processes in memory. *Journal of Experimental Psychology: General, 108,* 356–388.

Hudson, J., & Nelson, K. (1983). Effects of script structure on children's story recall. *Developmental Psychology, 19*(4), 625–635.

Mandler, J. (1984). Representation and recall in infancy. In M. Moscovitch (Ed.), *Infant memory: Its relation to normal and pathological memory in humans and other animals* (pp. 75–101). New York: Plenum.

Mandler, J. (1986). The development of event memory. In F. Klix and H. Hagendorf (Eds.), *Human memory and cognitive capabilities – Mechanisms and performance* (pp. 459–467). New York: Elsevier North-Holland.

McCune-Nicolich, L. (1981). Toward symbolic functioning: Structure of early pretend games and potential parallels with language. *Child Development, 52,* 785–797.

Meltzoff, A. (1988). Infant imitation and memory: Nine-month-olds in immediate and deferred tests. *Child Development, 59,* 217–225.

Mills, D., Mandler, J. M., Schreibman, L., & Oke, J. (1988). *Order in the script: Temporal organization of event knowledge in one-year-olds.* Unpublished manuscript, University of California, San Diego.

Nelson, K. (1984). The transition from infant to child memory. In M. Moscovitch (Ed.), *Infant memory: Its relation to normal and pathological memory in humans and other animals* (pp. 103–130). New York: Plenum.

Nelson, K. (1986). Event knowledge and cognitive development. In K. Nelson (Ed.), *Event knowledge: Structure and function in development* (pp. 1–19). Hillsdale, NJ: Erlbaum.

Nelson, K., & Gruendel, J. (1981). Generalized event representations: Basic building blocks of cognitive development. In M. E. Lamb & A. L. Brown (Eds.), *Advances in developmental psychology* (Vol. 1, pp. 131–158). Hillsdale, NJ: Erlbaum.

Nelson, K., & Gruendel, J. (1986). Children's scripts. In. K. Nelson (Ed.), *Event knowledge: Structure and function in development* (pp. 21–46). Hillsdale, NJ: Erlbaum.

Nelson, K., & Ross, G. (1980). The generalities and specifics of long-term memory in infants and young children. In M. Perlmutter (Ed.), *children's memory* (New directions for child development, No. 10, pp. 87–101). San Francisco: Jossey-Bass.

O'Connell, B., & Gerard, A. (1985). Scripts and scraps: The development of sequential understanding. *Child Development, 56,* 671–681.

Schank, R. C., & Abelson, R. P. (1977). *Scripts, plans, goals and understanding.* Hillsdale, NJ: Erlbaum.

Shore, C., Bates, E. Bretherton, I., Beeghly, M., & O'Connell, B. (in press). Vocal and gestural symbols: Similarities and differences from 13 to 28 months. In V. Volterra and C. J. Erting (Eds.), *From gesture to language in hearing and deaf children.* New York: Springer-Verlag.

Slackman, E., Hudson, J., & Fivush, R. (1986). Actions, actors, links, and goals:

The structure of children's event representations. In K. Nelson (Ed.), *Event knowledge: Structure and function in development* (pp. 47–69). Hillsdale, NJ: Erlbaum.

Smith, P. H. (1984). Five-month-old infant recall and utilization of temporal organization. *Journal of Experimental Child Psychology, 38,* 400–414.

Zacks, R., Hasher, L., Alba, J., Sanft, H., & Rose, K. (1984). Is temporal order encoded automatically? *Memory and Cognition, 12*(4), 387–394.

3

Developmental differences in the relation between scripts and episodic memory: Do they exist?

MICHAEL JEFFREY FARRAR AND
GAIL S. GOODMAN

Studies of young children's memory for naturally occurring events reveal a much richer and more structured memory system than earlier laboratory studies suggest. Naturalistic studies have demonstrated, for instance, that preschool children are capable of recalling personally significant events over long periods of time (e.g., Hudson & Fivush, 1988); develop abstract memory schemas (e.g., scripts) rapidly (e.g., Fivish, 1984); are sensitive to the temporal and causal connections between actions within an event (e.g., French & Nelson, 1981); and rely on schemas to infer expected information and retain discrepant information (Hudson & Nelson, 1986; Myles-Worsley, Cromer, & Dodd, 1986; Slackman & Hudson, 1984; see Mandler, 1983, and Nelson, 1986, for reviews). Children thus evidence many similarities to adults in the nature and use of general event representations and autobiographical memory. Similarities such as these have prompted the proposal that across the preschool and adult years, developmental differences do not exist in the relation between general and autobiographical memory (Hudson, 1986; Hudson & Nelson, 1986). Given the extent of change in cognitive skills, knowledge, and experience that occurs across this age range, can this proposal be true? The intent of this chapter is to answer this question.

To do so, we begin by briefly reviewing the basic assumptions of schema-memory models, with particular attention to the relation between general knowledge and episodic memory. This review is followed by an outline of our theoretical perspective on how schemas and scripts function in the encoding and retention of event information. Interleaved within these two sections is a review of the relevant adult and developmental literatures. We then present the results of our research on the relation between children's script and autobiographical memory development. Our studies indicate that younger children are often more dependent on a script or general event representation when recalling specific autobiographical memories than older children, and that they often confuse different event instantiations. Our findings also show that increased event experience can facilitate autobiographical memory for

30

an event. The theoretical framework we develop explains why developmental differences in the relation between general and autobiographical memory exist in certain situations but not in others. It predicts that young children are at times more dependent on scripts than older children and adults when recalling autobiographical memories, but that this is not invariably so.

It is important from the start to define several key terms that will appear throughout this chapter. We will use the terms *episodic* and *autobiographical* memory interchangeably to refer to memory for specific instances of events, ones that deviate from typical encounters. The terms *schemas, general event representations,* and *generic representations* will refer to semantic memory for repeated events of a similar kind. The term *script* will refer to a type of schema whose domain concerns routine, real-life events.

Schemas and scripts

General assumptions

Schemas have a long history of usefulness in theories of cognition and memory. Bartlett (1932) proposed that schemas are organized unconscious mental structures comprising old information used to comprehend new information. Following Bartlett, more recent models of schema memory generally assume that when an event is experienced, schemas guide attention, retention, and retrieval of episodic experience (Mandler, 1983, 1984; Minsky, 1975; Taylor & Crocker, 1981; see Brewer & Nakamura, 1984, for a review). Schemas are said to support accurate memory for episodic information in a number of ways by, for example, promoting correct inferences for prototypical information (e.g., Schank & Abelson, 1977), providing a retrieval framework for recall (e.g., Anderson & Prichert, 1978; Goodman, 1980), and lessening the burden of remembering anew every occurrence of similar events. Schemas can also interfere with accuracy, however. This occurs, for example, when schemas incorrectly bias episodic memory toward the expected. Thus, schema-supported inferences may distort perception and memory for an event (Bartlett, 1932; Bransford & Franks, 1971; Bruner & Postman, 1949; Pompi & Lachman, 1967).

Schema-memory models are intimately linked with reconstructive approaches to memory. Reconstructive models emphasize that retrieval of episodic information represents a combination of general knowledge with virtual information. Neisser (1982), for instance, proposed that similar episodes of an event become confused among each other. When a person attempts to recall a specific event episode, details from similar episodes are often included, creating a type of memory referred to as "repisodic," indicating the reconstructive nature of episodic memory. Similarly, Linton (1982) argued that a general event representation reflecting similar event episodes is formed through repeated experiences. When a new event is first encountered, it is possible to discriminate among related events. But as similar events are repeatedly experienced, it becomes increasingly difficult to discriminate individual episodes. Consequently, the details of particular events are difficult to specify.

In most of these models, summarized or generic memories are thus the primary level of representation for events. The available empirical work generally supports the primacy of generic summarizations of autobiographical events (e.g., Abbott, Black, & Smith, 1985; Linton, 1975, 1982). For example, Reisser (Reisser, 1986a, 1986b; Reisser, Black, & Abelson, 1985) found that when adults retrieve a particular event from memory they appear to begin their retrieval process at a generic level to locate a specific episode. Barsalou (1985) also found that generic events are the preferred mode for recalling autobiographical memories.

One version of schema theory that has become both theoretically and empirically prominent, and that is of particular importance to us in the present chapter, is the *script*. Script theory was developed by Schank and Abelson (1977) as a guide for comprehension and prediction of event sequences by artificial intelligence programs. Nevertheless, a large body of research has shown the usefulness of this theory in explaining both adults' and children's cognition (e.g., Bower, Black, & Turner, 1979; Nelson, 1981, 1986). A script in Schank and Abelson's (1977) early work was defined as a generic or abstract knowledge structure that reflected people's understanding of temporal and causal sequences of events as they occur in very specific contexts, such as grocery shopping, going to the doctor's office, or attending a classroom lecture. According to this formulation, scripts contain slots for variables that define the actors, actions, and so forth, of the event. When a relevant, real-life event is experienced, these variables are instantiated by specific episodes of events. Thus the script, like the more general notion of a schema, guides the establishment of an episodic representation.

In Schank's (1982) revised model, he proposed that scripts do not exist in large precompiled units. Instead, when people try to understand an event, the most abstract knowledge structures available to them are used. These generic structures are often scripted abstractions of the various event *scenes* or components of the larger event experience, such as ordering a meal at a restaurant. Only those scenes needed to comprehend a particular event instantiation are utilized at that time.

How do schema-memory models explain retention of discrepant information? Many schema-memory models contend that schema-consistent events are absorbed by the schema whereas schema-discrepant information is retained distinctly. To the extent that episodic memories must be retained uniquely in order to be accessible, this question is of central concern in the present chapter. Bartlett (1932) addressed this question in his *schema-plus-correction* hypothesis. According to this hypothesis, a cognitive representation of an event consists of a schema along with specific corrections to it. The corrections are deviations to the schema and thus represent discrepant information. The deviations are distinctly captured in memory. In Schank and Abelson's original script formulation, script-inconsistent information is retained in a separate representation linked to the script (see also Graesser, Gordon, & Sawyer, 1979). In Schank's more recent model, an episodic memory occurs only when the more abstract general event memory fails to permit comprehension of a particular event. In that case, new discrepant information is retained as an episodic memory linked to the more abstract representation. This new information can serve as a source of predictions if the same set of deviations is encountered again in a similar context. Although Schank's new model provides for a more dynamic, alterable memory and for greater discrimination between similar episodes, it is in agreement with the original formulation in that deviations from generic knowledge are retained in representations linked to abstract knowledge structures.

In sum, adults appear to form generic memories quite easily. A number of theorists propose that schemas play an important role in the establishment of episodic memories. When retrieval of a specific episode is attempted, the generic schema provides a basis for reconstructing the event. One consequence of schematic processing often proposed is that a more distinctive representation is formed for information that deviates from schema expectations.

Developmental research

Children's scripts. Scripts and schemas play an important role in children's cognitive development as well. Katherine Nelson (e.g., Nelson, 1986; Nelson & Gruendel, 1981) has convincingly argued that general event representations are the basic building blocks of cognition from which more comprehensive and complex cognitive skills develop. Event representations are considered basic because they correspond most directly to the child's experience in the world. From these event-based representations, more abstract cognitive structures are constructed, such as semantic categories (Lucariello & Rifkin, 1986).

To investigate children's scripts, Nelson and her colleagues conducted a series of interviews with children concerning their event knowledge. The format of the script interview was to ask young children (typically 3-

to 5-year-olds) about "what happens" during events such as birthday parties, baking cookies, and the like. In contrast to initial expectations that children's reports would be disorganized and idiosyncratic, Nelson (1978) found that children gave ordered and conventionalized reports of what typically occurs during these events. As is now documented in several studies (Fivush, 1984; Fivush & Slackman, 1986; Myles-Worsley et al., 1986), children report the component acts of scripts corresponding to the order in which they occur in the real world. Younger children are also sensitive to the temporal order of events, although they report fewer acts (but see Price & Goodman, 1985).

A second characteristic of children's scripts is that they are abstract representations of events. Interestingly, scripts begin as fairly abstract, even after one experience, and become increasingly abstract or schematized with experience (Fivush & Slackman, 1986). Thus, children who are just forming a script might include typical instantiations of script variables, although these instantiations are not necessarily from any particular episode, whereas for more abstract scripts these details would be omitted. For example, in the early stages of a birthday script, a child might recall that "You play 'pin-the-tail-on-the-donkey' and eat chocolate cake." A more abstract script of this same event-type would eliminate these typical instantiations and include more general labels for these actions, such as "You play games and eat cake." In this example, "games" and "cake" are superordinate labels for the typical activities. Both cases, however, are examples of abstract scripts because they do not correspond to any specific event episode.

Episodic memory development. As with the adult research, the relation between schemas and autobiographical memory has been of interest in developmental work. Many developmentalists have posited the same link between script and autobiographical memories as the adult-oriented models. For instance, Hudson (1986) and Nelson and Gruendel (1981) argued that events that deviate substantially from scripts are more likely to be retained as distinct autobiographical memories. Nelson and Gruendel (1981) added an important developmental prediction, however. They suggested that general event memories may be a prerequisite for the development of autobiographical memories, particularly for younger children. They argued that children initially rely on scripts to guide their recall of events (see also Nelson, 1986). Once the script is established, unique aspects of particular episodes can be recalled. This characterization primarily applies to episodes within repeated events: Novel, one-time events can be remembered with considerable accuracy (Fivush, Hudson, & Nelson, 1984), probably because they suffer little interference from similar episodes.

As with the adult research, direct investigations of these relations in childhood are limited. Nonetheless, some interesting patterns concerning the link between script and autobiographical memory in children have been identified. Preschoolers evidence greater difficulty recalling specific episodes of events than recalling a script memory (e.g., Hudson, 1986). Fivush (1984) found that 5-year-olds had well-developed school scripts but had problems recalling specific instantiations of school activities. These studies indicate that, overall, children tend to recall scripts better than autobiographical events.

When studies have specifically addressed the question of developmental differences in the relation between scripts and autobiographical memory, inconsistent results have emerged. The story-memory literature indicates that with age, reliance on schemas wanes (e.g., Hudson & Fivush, 1983; Mandler, 1979). For example, in Hudson and Nelson's (1983) study of children's recall of scripted stories, preschoolers compared to first-graders recalled less information from stories that did not match their event representations (see also Mandler & Robinson, 1978, for a similar finding in the picture-memory literature). The preschoolers' recall was best for stories based on familiar as compared to unfamiliar events, and the preschoolers had the least difficulty sequencing more logically structured stories. Finally, they often incorrectly reported script-based information in their story recall. In these ways, young children are said to be more dependent on their scripts than older children.

Thus, one hypothesis regarding children's event memory is that younger children are more dependent on schematic knowledge structures and have trouble handling deviations from their schemas, limiting the establishment of autobiographical or episodic memories. As will be described, a similar set of predictions emerges from our own theoretical framework. However, in one of the few experimental investigations of the development of autobiographical memory for real-life events, Hudson (1990) failed to uncover developmental differences in schema dependence. In Hudson's study, nursery school and kindergarten children participated in either one or four creative movement workshops. In contrast to studies of story recall, she reported no developmental differences in the degree of reliance on script memory for the younger children. Hudson suggested that the younger children's extensive reliance on scripts is limited to story recall and not recall of real-life events. Similarly, Hudson and Nelson (1986) in a naturalistic study of children's event memories also failed to find developmental differences in children's use of schemas in guiding recall of specific episodes (see also Hudson, 1986). They concluded that there are no age differences in children's memory organizations. Instead, episodic memory is organized around general event representations with particular episodes marked by distinctive characteristics regardless of age.

In summary, studies of script and autobiographical memory have not found developmental differences in children's reliance on schema-based memory. The younger children do not appear to use schemas more than other children in recalling autobiographical memory. This is in contrast to research on story memory showing that younger children are more reliant on schemas than older children. It seems unlikely to us, however, that different memory procedures would be involved for different types of experiences or information. Instead, prior failure to find developmental differences may derive from a number of factors. One is the inclusion of a limited age-range. Hudson (1990), for example, compared the performance of 4- and 5-year-old children. Developmental differences may not be evident across this small age-span. Additionally, prior failure to find developmental differences may result from lack of information concerning the actual content of autobiographical events, so that the relation between script and autobiographical memory cannot be precisely evaluated (e.g., Hudson & Nelson, 1986). Finally, prior failures may have resulted from differences in the ease of organizing the events experienced in naturalistic studies compared with the text presented in story-memory studies. Children may often find it easier to organize naturally occurring events than to organize text-based material.

Schema confirmation and deployment

The *schema confirmation–deployment hypothesis* can potentially resolve discrepant findings concerning the presence or absence of developmental differences in the relation between scripts and autobiographical memory. That is, it describes the conditions under which children will and will not form distinct episodic memories for schema-discrepant events. This hypothesis was first posited to resolve a very similar discrepancy in the adult cognitive literature, specifically, whether or not schema-consistent or schema-inconsistent information is better retained in memory (Goodman, 1981; Goodman & Golding, 1983). In this theoretical framework, schemas function in both the encoding and retention of event information. Two stages in this process are proposed: schema confirmation and schema deployment (see Goodman & Golding, 1983). Specifically, it is hypothesized that when an event or situation is encountered, a person attempts to facilitate comprehension of that event by selecting an appropriate schema or by formulating a new one. Assuming that an appropriate schema is available, the person initially focuses cognitive resources on information that supports schema verification, that is, on schema-expected information. By focusing attention on schema-expected information, the person ensures that an appropriate schema has been activated. If, on the other hand, a schema for an event type does not exist, then the person cannot selectively attend to schema-expected information, because he or she has no basis for making this distinction. Instead, the person will attempt to formulate a new schema based on past experience, generalization from existing schema, and so forth (see Fischer & Farrar, 1987, for a related discussion). In constructing the schema, the person will attend to a broad range of event information. These processes are collectively referred to as *schema confirmation*.

Schema confirmation has different effects on memory performance depending on the level of schema development. If the schema exists, then information consistent with the schema will receive as much if not more processing than information that is inconsistent with it. Thus schema-consistent information is more likely to be recalled and recognized than schema-inconsistent information. If, however, the schema is just developing, then event information will be retained more or less equally, other factors being equal.

After the schema is confirmed, it structures the episodic representation of the event and serves as a framework for recognition and recall. A second information processing phase, termed *schema deployment,* can then begin. The schema-deployment phase has different consequences for memory than the schema-confirmation phase. During schema deployment, information consistent with the schema requires limited processing because it is expected via the schema (Friedman, 1979; Goodman, 1980). Attention is thus freed for the processing of inconsistent information, for the establishment of a distinct memory for that information, and for linking discrepant information to the schema. Schema deployment cannot take place until schema confirmation has occurred and may not occur at all for newly developing schemas.

There is ample evidence to support a distinction between a schema-confirmation and a schema-deployment phase of processing, but the evidence derives from different subareas, traditions, and paradigms in psychology. Within the cognitive tradition, evidence for the schema-deployment phase prevails. In typical studies of schema memory, participants are asked to view scenes or read stories that largely convey highly familiar themes and information. The use of easily recognized themes permits subjects to select and confirm appropriate schemas rapidly and thus to enter the schema-deployment phase very quickly. Loftus and Mackworth (1978), for example, presented adults with a picture of a farm scene that included an octopus as a schema-inconsistent item. The adults' first fixation was to the octopus. Loftus and Mackworth concluded that highly informative information, such as schema-inconsistent items, receives extra processing. Because the theme of a real-world scene can be abstracted in milliseconds, even before an eye movement can be made (Beiderman, 1982), Loftus and Mackworth's subjects may have activated and confirmed the appropriate schema almost instantaneously and entered the schema-deployment phase so quickly as to elude detection of schema confirmation.

Friedman (1979) also presented adults with pictures of familiar scenes, such as a kitchen, that contained schema-consistent and schema-inconsistent information. Subjects' longest fixations fell on schema-inconsistent information. On a later recognition test, adults recognized the schema-inconsistent information better than the schema-consistent information. Again, given that the pictured information could be quickly organized around preexisting schemas, the subjects may have quickly passed into the schema-deployment phase of processing.

In the story memory literature, Graesser et al.'s (1979) research also indicates that schema-inconsistent information is retained with greater "discriminative accuracy" than is schema-consistent information, although the strength of effect varies over time (see Graesser, 1981, for a review). The use of stories about familiar events, such as eating at a restaurant, would be expected to lead to the detection of schema-deployment but not schema-confirmation effects. In general, schema-deployment effects such as these underlie proposals, evidenced in most schema-memory models, that schema-inconsistent information is retained in a representation separate and distinct from the schema.

Evidence for a schema-confirmation phase of processing derives largely from problem-solving, social cognition, and developmental research. These fields share an interest in stimuli that are not readily categorized or interpreted by subjects, either because the stimuli are complex or are not easily organized (as in the problem-solving and much of the social cognition literature) or because the subjects are relatively less advanced cognitively (as in the developmental literature). In a well-known experiment, Johnson-Laird (1983) uncovered strong confirmation biases in a problem-solving task, especially when the stimuli were less familiar and therefore presumably less easily organized. White and Carlson (1983), in a study of social cognition, report findings quite in line with the proposed two stages of processing. They presented adults with background information about one of two target actors (e.g., that the actor was honest), in effect providing the subjects with a schema with which to interpret the actor's behavior. Subjects then viewed a videotape of the two actors engaged in separate but overlapping conversations. The conversations were structured so that the primed actor at first behaved in a schema-neutral manner and then in a schema-inconsistent manner. It was found that subjects first attended to the primed actor (schema confirmation), then to the unprimed actor, and finally back to the primed actor when he performed the inconsistent activity (schema deployment). This study is consistent with the proposition that subjects first attempt to confirm their schema and then attend to discrepancies.

The developmental literature also offers support for the schema confirmation-deployment hypothesis. This support derives, for example, from studies of infant attention and memory. In experiments that rely on standard habituation and preference techniques, infants are said to develop schemas of stimuli presented during familiarization trials (e.g., Kagan, 1970). These trials are followed by novel test stimuli that violate the schema. Hunter, Ross, and Ames (1982; see also Rose, Gottfried, Melloy-Carminar, & Bridger, 1982) found that infants, regardless of age, prefer familiar stimuli when the stimuli are complex and when the infant has not had sufficient time to encode (e.g., habituate to) them. On the other hand, when the infant has sufficient encoding time, a preference for novelty develops. According to the schema confirmation–deployment hypothesis, infants would be expected to first develop and confirm a schema and only then to show preferential attention and better memory for discrepant stimuli. The complexity of the stimuli in relation to the subject's age would influence whether schema-confirmation or schema-deployment effects are evidenced at the time of test. Complex stimuli would be more difficult for infants to encode and organize; younger infants will find more stimuli to be complex in relation to their knowledge and abilities than will older infants, with the result that younger infants will remain in the confirmation phase longer than older infants. Once the younger infants encode the stimuli and confirm their schema, they then enter the deployment phase and preference for novelty is evidenced. As described in the paragraphs that follow, a similar pattern would be expected to hold for the relation between schemas and episodic memory in childhood.

Existing research thus suggests that schema-confirmation and schema-deployment effects operate across developmental levels. That is, whenever a person encounters a situation, she or he attempts to activate relevant schema. If the schema for the event exists and is confirmed, the person is in a position to attend selectively to discrepant information. If a script does not exist or is still being formed, the person will have more difficulty establishing a separate memory for a particular episode because that event instantiation is being utilized in the formation of the schema.

There are several developmental implications of our theoretical framework for the study of children's memory development. Because of processing limitations and less developed knowledge bases, it may take longer for younger than older children to develop and confirm a schema and consequently establish distinct episodic memories for a particular repeated event. Because they take longer to develop and confirm an appropriate schema, they remain in the schema-confirmation phase longer than older children. Thus, younger children may appear in many situations to be more dependent on schemas in recalling events than older children, at least until the younger children have established and confirmed the appropriate schema. In contrast, older children may more readily form an autobiographical memory because they can establish and confirm a schema more quickly.

A second developmental implication derives from the likelihood of qualitative differences in individuals' ability to organize information schematically. In certain developmental periods, an individual may be restricted in the types of schematic organizations possible. In infancy, perceptual organizations may predominate. In childhood, a plethora of readily accessible symbolic organizations emerges. Later, more abstract, formal-operational organizations become increasingly common. Unevenness, that is, *decalage*, in the type of organization a single child can control is expected (Fischer, 1980), but regardless of the dominant nature of the organization (perceptual, symbolic, or formal operational) or the degree of decalage across domains, the schemas guiding encoding and retrieval within a specific domain should conform to the predictions of the schema confirmation–deployment hypothesis.

Thus, at issue is whether younger children are more script-dependent than older children in recalling an episodic memory of an event. Prior studies of story memory support this general pattern, whereas studies of episodic memory for real-world events do not. The schema confirmation–deployment hypothesis argues that under the appropriate circumstances, such effects should be found for episodic memories of real-life events as well.

Methodological issues

To address these conceptual issues, adequate investigative methods and procedures are needed. The procedure typically used for studying children's script and autobiographical memory development is naturalistic. In this approach children are interviewed about real-world events they have experienced. These studies take advantage of the natural richness of children's real-world experiences, a richness often missing from traditional laboratory studies of memory. The study of memory development has profited enormously by leaving the laboratory and studying children's memory in the real world. It has brought to the forefront a number of phenomena regarding children's memory that might have otherwise remained aloof or ignored. At the same time, this research raises both conceptual and methodological questions concerning the study of script and autobiographical memory that may be difficult to answer without returning to a more controlled laboratory environment. Ecological richness often comes at a price – namely, the ability to control those factors affecting memory. Consequently the ability to understand memory development may be affected (see Hudson, 1990, for a related discussion). In the paragraphs that follow, specific methodological issues raised by naturalistic research are discussed.

One issue concerns the best way to assess and distinguish script and autobiographical memories. Typically, children's use of different linguistic forms is relied on to discriminate these two types of memories (Nelson, 1981, 1986). For instance, children include different information in their recall of a script memory than in their recall of an autobiographical memory. Specifically, script reports tend to comprise actions, elaborations of actions, and conditionals (i.e, "if . . . then" statements), whereas autobiographical reports tend to comprise optional and particular information unique to a specific instantiation of an event. Children also often use the general *you* when referring to the activities of an event, as opposed to the more specific *I*. The use of *I* might be expected if the child is recalling a specific episode in which he or she participated. For instance, if recalling a specific episode about what happened in McDonald's, a child might recall "I ate a Happy Meal and got a toy truck," whereas if recalling a script, a child might report that "You get your food and sit down." Finally, children use the tenseless or present-tense verb form when recalling a script memory, rather than the past-tense verb form, which would again be expected if children were recalling a specific episode. As children's script representations become more abstract, the proportion of their recall containing only script-related propositions and script-related noun and verb forms should increase. These are clever and innovative techniques that provide an initial way to distinguish between script and episodic event memories. However, as noted by Fivush and Hamond (this volume) one of the memory skills that children acquire is how to talk about past events. Furthermore, researchers use different linguistic forms in their questions, such as different verb tenses, to elicit script and autobiographical memories. Thus, the possibility exists that the differences in how children talk about script and autobiographical memories are at least partially attributable to some combination of these factors. Therefore, it is important also to use alternative methods for assessing script and autobiographical memories.

The use of previously occurring real-world events to investigate memory also has several drawbacks. As Neisser (1982) pointed out, it is often difficult to verify the accuracy of someone's recall. When such verification is available, it can be of benefit in understanding memory, as in

Neisser's case study of John Dean's memory for Watergate-related conversations. Another difficulty with using previously occurring events, particularly with developmental studies, is that age and experience are generally confounded (see Slackman, Hudson, & Fivush, 1986, for a related discussion). That is, older children typically have more experience in an event than younger children, making it difficult to determine whether differences are due to age or to experience. Finally, when naturalistic studies of scripts and autobiographical memory utilize previously established knowledge structures, it is difficult to study the initial formation of schemas and the resulting effects on memory.

Another important limitation of the use of naturally occurring events is the absence of control over the similarity and differences between various instantiations of the events. Recall that script theory (e.g., Schank, 1982) argues that only events that differ substantially from a generalized event are retained in memory. If all instantiations of an event are similar, which is likely in the case of events such as eating at McDonald's and baking cookies, there is not much need to retain a specific experience in memory. Furthermore, if all the visits are the same, it is more difficult to distinguish between script and autobiographical memories, since the content would be highly similar. Children could simply be recalling a specific episode instead of a more generic memory. The failure to remember specific episodes with increased experience could be because there was nothing unique about these experiences.

A final limitation concerns the interview techniques used to access script and autobiographical memory. Children may remember a great deal about the events, but a single interview procedure may not be adequate for assessing their memories. Without precise knowledge of what occurred during an event, as is common in many naturalistic studies (but see Fivush et al., 1984; Hudson, 1990; Myles-Worsley et al., 1986), memory assessment techniques are generally limited to free recall. However, when a record exists of what happened, more effective recall techniques, such as "contextual" recall (i.e., recall of the events where they occurred), can be used to elicit event memory (Price & Goodman, 1985).

To summarize, research on the development of scripts and autobiographical memory for real-world events has made important contributions to our understanding of memory development. This research has illustrated that when children's memory abilities are studied using real-world events they show more competence than typically demonstrated in laboratory tasks. This research has also raised many intriguing questions concerning script development and its relation to autobiographical memory. With the groundwork laid through naturalistic studies, we believe it is advantageous at this time to return to the laboratory, but to do so in

Table 3.1. *Experimental design of Study 1 and Study 2*

Day Group	Visits				
	Visit 1	Visit 2	Visit 3	Visit 4	Visit 5
Study 1					
Day 1	e	s	s	s	i
Day 4	s	s	s	e	i
Study 2					
Day 1	e	i			
Day 1	s	i			
Day 2	s	e	i		
Day 4	s	s	s	e	i

Note: s = script visit; e = episodic visit; i = interview.

such a way as to combine as much as possible the richness of children's real-world experiences with experimental control.

In our experimental approach, we tried to create ecologically valid, novel events for children to experience in a laboratory setting. We believe that if this can be done in a controlled and systematic fashion and still capture the complexity of children's real-world experiences, a more comprehensive understanding of the relation between children's script and autobiographical memory development is possible. Moreover, to the extent that these studies replicate the findings of more naturalistic research, greater confidence can be placed in both approaches to the study of children's memory.

Experimental Investigations

Overview

The research reported below examined the relation between script and autobiographical memory development in 4- and 7-year-old children. The focus of this research was children's ability to recall a specific event visit (i.e., an *episodic event*) that deviated from a repeated visit (i.e., *script visit*) depending on the level of event experience. We approached this issue using two different experimental designs. As illustrated in Table 3.1, the first study gave children the same amount of total event experience, but varied when they were exposed to the episodic visit relative to the script visit. The second study varied the total amount of event experience, with the episodic visit always occurring last. This design equated the delay between visit and interview.

Study 1

Method

Subjects and procedures. Thirty-two children visited our laboratory five times over a 2-week period. During the first four visits each child played with an adult who guided the child through a sequence of four events. These events were linked by a common theme of playing "animal games." Each game consisted of the child and adult using two unique toy animals to perform a unique action. A typical event might involve the child and adult playing with a rabbit and frog puppet and having them jump over a fence. The other events involved different animals and different actions. Figure 3.1 provides a description of the entire event structure.

During the visits, the adult guide also wore an animal costume, designed to serve two functions. The primary function was to act as a powerful retrieval cue for the child. Earlier work by Hudson and Nelson (1986) suggests that temporal cues, such as *yesterday* are not effective retrieval cues. Similarly, Barsalou, Lancaster, Spindler, George, and Farrar (in preparation) also found that temporal cues were not effective cues for adults recalling specific autobiographical memories. Thus, in our studies when children were asked about their visits we were able to ask specific questions such as "What happens when you play with the cat?" as opposed to a general temporally based question, such as "What happens when you played animal games the first time you came?" A secondary function of the costume was to make the visits enjoyable for the children.

During each visit, the child entered the "animal room" and was greeted by the adult guide dressed in an animal costume. After a brief warm-up period, the adult explained that they were going to play some animal games. The child was encouraged to put on a simplified version of the adult's costume. The adult then announced the name of the first event table and took the child to its location, where they completed that table's prescribed activity. This procedure was followed at each of the four event-tables.

Visit types. Three of the four visits were identical in every aspect. We will refer to these identical, repeated visits as the *script visits*. During either the first or last visit, deviations or changes of the script visit were introduced. This visit will be referred to as the *episodic visit*. Of course, for the children who experienced the episodic visit during the first session, there was no discrepancy or deviation from their perspective. All four visits took place within a 7-day period.

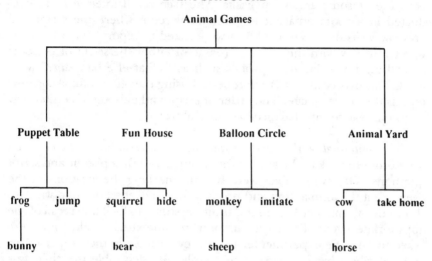

Figure 3.1. Hierarchical structure of the experiment event.

Deviation changes. Three types of deviation changes to the four event-tables were made during the episodic visit. First, one of the script event tables was eliminated and replaced with a totally new event table (i.e., the *Animal Workshop* involving the building of two new toy animal figures). Second, a change was made in the instantiations of the animals, actions, and props of a script event table while maintaining the theme and location of that event table (e.g., at the *Puppet Table* this involved two new puppets crawling under a bridge). Three, a change occurred in the sequence of the two remaining event tables (e.g., reversing the sequence of the *Fun House* and the *Balloon Circles*). Each child received all three types of deviation changes and the deviation changes were counterbalanced across the different event tables. In addition, the same adult wore a new animal costume. The costumes used for the two visit types were counterbalanced across script and episodic visits.

Interview

One week following the fourth visit, children were interviewed under both free recall and contextual recall conditions. This interview was videotaped and was conducted by an adult unfamiliar to the children. Previous research has indicated that if children believe that an adult knows what occurred in an event, they will provide less information (Fivush, Gray, Hamond, & Fromhoff, 1986).

Free recall. In the free recall condition, children were asked about both the episodic and script visits. The free recall interview was conducted in a room adjacent to the animal room where the script and episodic visits occurred. Children were asked to report "What happens when you play with the – – – ?" (name of either the script or episodic animal guide). Additional probes such as "What else happens?" were used. This procedure was then repeated using the other animal costume type as the retrieval cue. The order of script and episodic visit interview questions was counterbalanced across children.

Contextual recall. For the contextual recall condition, the children were brought back to the animal room, and asked the episodic and script questions. The event tables were present marking the locations of the events, but the animal toys and props were removed. The child was also shown the animal mask from the adult's costume to facilitate recall of the appropriate event. For each question in contextual recall, they were asked to take the experimenter to each event table in the proper order and describe what happens at that table. At each table the child was asked, "What happens when you play at this table with the – – – ?" (name of either the script or episodic adult–animal guide). Additional probes were used at each table, such as "What else happens?" "What animals do you play with?" and "What do you do with the animals?" After completing this procedure with either the script or episodic question, the procedure was repeated for the other event visit type. The order of event-type questions was counterbalanced across children. However, for each child, the order that the script and episodic questions were asked in the free recall condition was maintained in the contextual recall condition.

There were a number of procedural differences between the free recall and contextual recall conditions. We were not concerned with isolating the particular property of these conditions that was responsible for any differences in memory performance. Rather, we were simply interested in identifying the degree to which children's memory performance could be improved by creating a context designed to increase children's recall.

Results

Script and episodic memory

Overall event memory. In the first group of analyses, we examined how well children recalled both the script and episodic visits overall. This included memory for both the script visit information and the deviation

Table 3.2. *Mean proportion of event information recalled in Study 1*

	Script visit			Episodic visit		
	4 years	7 years	Overall	4 years	7 years	Overall
Event tables	.55	.83	.69	.39	.70	.54
Animals	.34	.62	.48	.25	.45	.35
Actions	.36	.70	.53	.21	.55	.38
Props	.33	.61	.47	.17	.32	.25

changes. All analyses involved a 2 (Age) × 2 (Deviation day: Day 1 vs. Day 4) × 2 (Visit type: script vs. episodic) × 2 (Recall: free vs. contextual) repeated measures ANOVA. Age and deviation day were between-subject factors and visit type and recall were within-subject factors.

The dependent measures for this first analysis were proportion of: event tables recalled (5 possible), animals recalled (10 possible), props recalled (5 possible), and actions recalled (5 possible). Proportion was calculated as the ratio of the number of correct events recalled to the number of possible events recalled plus the number of incorrect events.[1]

Table 3.2 shows mean proportion correct recall for these measures as a function of visit type. Children's recall of the script visit was significantly better than recall of the episodic visit across all measures of event visit memory. Considering recall of the event tables, for instance, the children recalled 69% of them from the script visit compared to 54% of them from the episodic visit, $F(1, 28) = 13.76$, $p < .05$. This finding is in line with prior script memory research for naturalistic events in which children have more difficulty recalling episodic memories. Not surprisingly, the 7-year-olds recalled more than the 4-year-olds for all measures of event visit recall, for instance, proportion of event tables recalled, $F(1, 28) = 31.17$, $p < .05$. Children's recall of the event tables was also generally higher than the specific instantiations of those event tables (e.g., the animals, actions, and props).

Episodic memory. The previous analyses looked only at children's recall of the two types of visits overall. They did not address the question of children's ability to recall the episodic material per se (i.e., the deviation changes) as a function of level of script development when the episodic visit occurred. The next analyses directly examined the relation between memory for the script and episodic visits.

We first considered total recall of the deviation changes and its three components. Four proportional measures of memory for the deviation changes were computed: (1) recall of the new instantiations of an old

Table 3.3 *Mean proportion of deviation changes recalled in Study 1*

	Script visit			Episodic visit		
	Day 1	Day 4	Overall	Day 1	Day 4	Overall
Total deviation changes						
4-year-olds	.12	.22	.16	.09	.18	.14
7-year-olds	.13	.04	.09	.45	.36	.40
New event instantiations						
4-year-olds	.04	.29	.16	.06	.15	.11
7-year-olds	.12	.06	.09	.29	.23	.26
New event table						
4-year-olds	.19	.17	.18	.12	.15	.14
7-year-olds	.06	.00	.03	.56	.50	.53
Order change						
4-year-olds	.12	.12	.12	.06	.25	.32
7-year-olds	.19	.06	.13	.44	.25	.35

event table (i.e., script visit table); (2) recall of instantiations of a new event table; (3) recall of the change in event order; and (4) recall of total deviation changes (i.e., the summed average of the proportions constituting measures 1–3). Proportions were calculated as number of correct items recalled divided by number of possible correct items. Table 3.3 provides the means for the proportion of deviation changes recalled. It is important to note that children could and often did report the deviation changes as occurring in both the script visit and in the episodic visit. Of course, it is only correct to report them as part of the episodic visit. Not surprisingly, the 4-year-olds recalled less of the deviation changes than the 7-year-olds, but as the next section describes, this was affected by visit type.

Script-based recall of the episodic visit. Of particular interest was whether younger children were more schema or script bound than the older children. Several methods were available to assess this. The traditional method measures *script intrusions* in episodic recall. This involved examining children's inclusion of the script instantiations, rather than the deviation changes, in their recall of the episodic visit.

A second method of measuring dependence on scripts is through assessing *episodic intrusions* in script recall. According to the schema-confirmation hypothesis, if children are establishing a general script or event memory to guide their recall, then any particular component of an

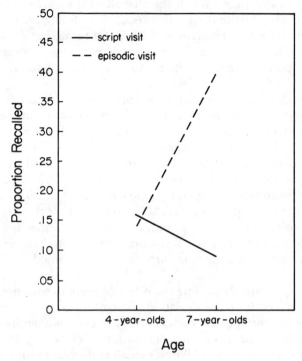

Figure 3.2. Total deviation changes recalled by age and visit type in Study 1.

event instantiation should become part of the script rather than maintained as a separate episodic memory, and should appear as an episodic intrusion.

Regardless of which intrusion measure was used, the results indicated that the younger children were more dependent on the script when recalling the episodic visit than were the older children. Consider episodic intrusions first. There was a significant age × visit interaction for the total deviation changes recalled, F (1, 28) = 17.99, $p < .05$. Using data from Table 3.3 but collapsing over deviation day, Figure 3.2 graphically represents this relation. Specifically, the 4-year-olds often reported that the event deviations occurred during the script visit and relied on their general event memory in reporting what happened with both types of visits. That is, when the 4-year-olds were asked about both the script and episodic visits, they reported that the deviation changes occurred in both the script and episodic visits. They reported about 14% of the total deviation changes in their episodic recall and 16% in their script recall. In contrast, the 7-year-olds were more likely to have formed separate, distinct memories for the two different types of visits. They correctly included the deviation changes in their recall of the episodic visit and excluded the changes from their script recall. Specifically, they reported only 9% of the deviation changes in their script recall, but 40% of the deviations in their episodic recall. This general pattern was obtained for the total deviation changes and its components, except for the order changes.

This same pattern was found for the script intrusions. Again, there was a significant age × visit interaction for most measures of deviation changes recalled, including total deviation changes, $F(1, 28) = 12.76$, $p < .05$. *The 4-year-olds did not distinguish the script and episodic visits, but* falsely included the script instantiations in their episodic recall at the same level of incorporation, 39%, as in their script visit recall, 36%. The 7-year-olds, however, were more likely to exclude correctly the script-based instantiations from their episodic recall, 33%, and to include them correctly in their script visit recall, 61%. Importantly, even when controlling for the fact that the 7-year-olds often recalled more information than the 4-year-olds, this developmental pattern of intrusions is maintained.

Event experience. Regarding the effect of event experience, the 4- and 7-year-olds' recall of the deviation changes was also differentially affected by the day the episodic visit occurred. There was a significant age × day interaction for the new event instantiations, $F(1, 28) = 4.36$, $p < .05$ (see Figure 3.3). The younger children's recall of the new event instantiations was significantly higher when the episodic visit took place on Day 4 than on Day 1, whereas the 7-year-olds' recall was not affected by event experience. These means represent the averaged recall from both the script and episodic because the three-way interaction was nonsignificant.

Recall condition. Finally, there were strong effects of recall condition for most of the measures of script and episodic memory. Contextual recall was higher than free recall for both age groups. For example, there was a significant main effect of recall condition for proportion of script animals recalled, $F(1, 28) = 208.92$, $p < .001$. Children recalled only 17% of the script animals in free recall, but 77% of the script animals in contextual recall. There were no systematic age interactions involving the recall condition factor.

Summary

The results of Study 1 suggest developmental differences in how children organized their event memories, in accordance with the predictions of the schema confirmation-deployment hypothesis. Specifically, the younger children had difficulty forming episodic memories, as indicated by the

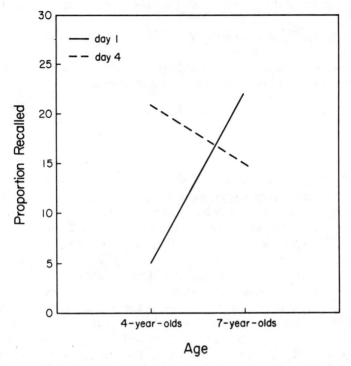

Figure 3.3. New event instantiations recalled by age and deviation day in Study 1.

pattern of both script and episodic intrusions. These results indicate that the younger children were able to confirm the schema but could not yet deploy it. The 4-year-olds may have utilized a script or general event summary when recalling either type of visit as indicated by the intrusions. In contrast, the 7-year-olds maintained separate memories for the event visits, suggesting they were able to both confirm and deploy the schema, marking the deviation changes as atypical instantiations of the general event memory (see Schank, 1982). These results support earlier research showing that young children are more reliant on schemas in structuring their recall of particular schema-based story instantiations (Hudson & Nelson, 1983). However, this pattern has not typically been found for episodic memory (Hudson, 1987; Hudson & Nelson, 1986).

Study 1 also found that all children had poorer recall of the episodic visit than of the script visit. This may be because the script memory is the primary form of event representations or simply because the children had more experience in the script visit than in the episodic visit.

Finally, Study 1 found that 4-year-olds' memory for some of the deviation changes of the episodic visit increased with event experience. For the 7-year-olds, recall of the deviation changes of the episodic visit was generally unaffected by experience. This suggests that event experience facilitates the establishment of episodic memory for repeated events. We return to these issues and also discuss the relevance of these results for models of memory development after considering Study 2.

Study 2

Method

Overview. The results of the first experiment were informative and suggested that an experimental approach can be used to study the development of children's episodic memory. However, several modifications of our procedure were needed to clarify the findings. First, the recall of the episodic visit from the first visit could have been influenced by additional script experience. That is, the children who had the episodic visit in the first session then had three additional script visits. This made it impossible to assess memory for the episodic visit as a novel, nonscript-based event. In essence, we lacked a baseline measure for the recall of this visit. We also lacked a baseline measure of recall of the script visit. Second, the delay between event experience and the interviews was different for the deviation day groups. The children who had the episodic visit first had a longer delay to their interview than the children who had the episodic visit last.

Consequently, the total number of event experiences children had were varied in Study 2. Specifically, children had one, two, or four event visits in which the episodic visit always occurred last. The single exception was the Day 1 script-visit group who experienced a script visit only. This design eliminated differences in delay between the episodic visit and interview, and provided baselines for recall of the visits.

Experimental procedure. The event visit and structure were the same as in Study 1. Each child was randomly assigned to the event experience condition (i.e., one, two, or four visits). It is important to note that the data from the children who had the four visits in Study 1 were utilized in the second study. Thus, only two new groups of children went through the procedure, the one- and two-visit children. As in the first study, all event visits occurred within a 7-day period and generally within a day or two of each other.

The script visit(s) was defined as the visit(s) before the episodic visit. The episodic visit was the last event visit and utilized the same deviation changes as Study 1.

Table 3.4. *Mean proportion of event information recalled in Study 2*

	Script visit			Episodic visit		
	Day 1[a]	Day 2	Day 4	Day 1[a]	Day 2	Day 4
Event tables						
4-year-olds	.58	.40	.53	.54	.49	.36
7-year-olds	.80	.71	.88	.78	.81	.68
Animals						
4-year-olds	.24	.17	.30	.32	.26	.11
7-year-olds	.53	.34	.60	.49	.42	.37
Actions						
4-year-olds	.45	.30	.35	.45	.33	.21
7-year-olds	.69	.57	.70	.73	.61	.55
Props						
4-year-olds	.30	.23	.29	.23	.27	.18
7-year-olds	.66	.48	.59	.64	.52	.42

[a]Script and deviation recall based on different groups.

One week following the last visit, each child returned for the interview. The same interview procedure used in Study 1 was employed here, with the exception that children who had only one visit were interviewed only about that one experience.

Results

Script and episodic memory

Script memory. The first group of analyses examined children's recall of the script visit as a function of experience. Only the one-visit children who experienced the events associated with the script visit were included here, providing baseline information for this visit type. A 2 (Age) × 3 (Deviation day: Day 1 vs. Day 2 vs. Day 4) × 2 (Recall: free vs. contextual) repeated measures ANOVA was employed. Age and day were between-subject factors and recall was a within-subject factor. Since the one-visit children only had the script visit, memory for the script and episodic visits was not compared in this analysis.

The left half of Table 3.4 provides mean proportions for the event information recalled from the script visit. There was a significant main effect of deviation day for the majority of the script visit measures (e.g., proportion of event tables recalled, $F (1, 42) = 4.62$, $p < .05$). Both 4-

and 7-year-olds who had either one or four visits recalled the script visit significantly better than the children with two visits. One interpretation of this U-shaped effect is that the one-visit children had no interference from the other visits and the four-visit children had ample opportunity to learn the script. In contrast, the two-visit children's poorer memory for the script visit may have resulted from confusion between the two visits.

Episodic memory. We next considered children's memory for the episodic visit as a function of event experience with a 2 (Age) × 3 (Deviation day) × 2 (Recall: free vs. contextual) repeated measures ANOVA. This analysis included the one-visit group who experienced the deviation changes, although for these children the events were not deviations from a previous visit since they had none. As was true for the one-time script visit, this condition provided a baseline for the children's recall of the events associated with the episodic visit. (Interestingly, these visits were of equal memorability.) As before, it was not possible in the present analysis to compare the recall of the script and episodic visits directly. This comparison is made in the next section from those children who had repeated visits.

As with overall script memory, there was a main effect of deviation day for most measures; for example, event tables recalled, $F (2, 42) = 3.94$, $p < .05$. However, in contrast to the U-shaped effect of deviation day described above, increased event experience produced a significant decline for overall episodic memory as shown in the right half of Table 3.4. Similarly, when memory for only the deviation changes of the episodic visit was examined there was also a decline in recall for the children with repeated visits as shown in the right half of Table 3.5. For the new event instantiations, for instance, there was a main effect of day, $F (2, 42) = 8.26$, $p < .05$. The decline shown in Table 3.5 resulted primarily from a drop in performance between the Day 1 condition compared to the Day 2 and Day 4 conditions.

Relations between script and episodic memory. The next analyses addressed the primary question of whether younger children show more script dependency than the older children. To do this, we examined recall of the deviation changes for only those children who had repeated visits through a 2 (Age) × 2 (Deviation day: Day 2 vs. Day 4) × 2 (Visit type: script vs. episodic) × 2 (Recall: free vs. contextual) repeated measures ANOVA. This permitted a direct comparison between children's recall of the script and episodic visits, and clarified some of the findings from the previous analyses.

These analyses again showed developmental differences in the rela-

Table 3.5. *Mean proportion of deviation changes recalled in Study 2*

	Script visit			Episodic visit		
	Day 1	Day 2	Day 4	Day 1	Day 2	Day 4
Total deviation						
4-year-olds	–	.12	.19	.37	.14	.18
7-year-olds	–	.15	.04	.49	.33	.36
New event instantiations						
4-year-olds	–	.08	.29	.40	.08	.15
7-year-olds	–	.17	.06	.48	.19	:23
New event table						
4-year-olds	–	.27	.17	.33	.23	.15
7-year-olds	–	.21	.00	.56	.50	.60
Order change						
4-year-olds	–	.00	.12	.37	.12	.25
7-year-olds	–	.06	.06	.44	.31	.25

tion between children's script and episodic memory. There was a significant age × visit type interaction for both the episodic and script intrusions, for example, proportion of total deviation changes recalled, F (1, 28) = 11.18, $p < .05$. As in Study 1, the 7-year-olds were able, in large part, to keep separate their memories for the script and episodic visits. That is, there were few script or episodic intrusions into their episodic or script recall, respectively. The 4-year-olds, however, did not show this same pattern. Similar to Study 1, the 4-year-olds did not have distinct memories of the two types of visits. Figure 3.4 illustrates this effect with the total deviation changes measure. It should be noted, however, that the similarity with Study 1 is partially but not completely attributable to the fact that the Day 4 group is the same in both studies.

Event experience. Further support for this developmental pattern is seen when the effect of event experience is examined for recall of the two types of visits. As Figure 3.5 shows, there was a significant age × day × visit interaction for recall of the new event instantiations. The 4-year-olds with four visits were more likely to include this deviation change in their recall of the script visit than in their recall of the episodic visit. Apparently, the 4-year-olds had distinguished the two-visit types, but in the wrong direction, which suggests they were using a general event or script memory to recall the visits. The 7-year-olds also showed greater separation of the script and episodic visits with increased experience,

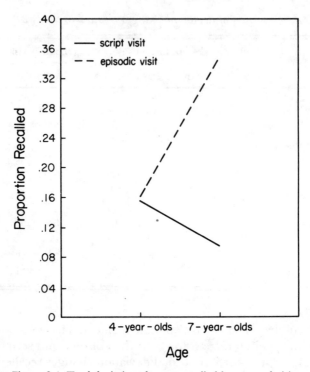

Figure 3.4. Total deviation changes recalled by age and visit type in Study 2.

although in the correct direction. That is, they correctly included the new event instantiations in their recall of the episodic visit and excluded them from their script visit recall. Interestingly, both the 4- and 7-year-olds with only two visits failed to distinguish between the two visits for the new event instantiations, indicating that they did not have enough experience to establish a separate episodic memory.

General Discussion

Implications for models of memory development

Do developmental differences exist? The results of Studies 1 and 2 indicate developmental differences in the ability of 4- and 7-year-olds to recall specific details of events that deviate from a script or schema. The younger children behaved according to the predictions of the schema confirmation–deployment hypothesis. They were much more likely than 7-year-olds to include the deviation changes in their script visit recall rather than in their episodic recall, indicating that their

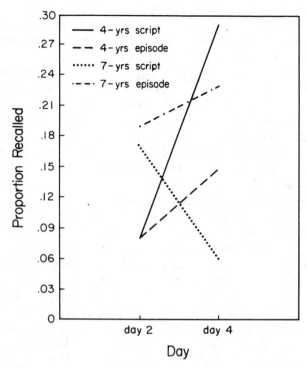

Figure 3.5. New event instantiations recalled by age, deviation day, and visit type in Study 2.

script memory was still being formed. Thus, they were not able to enter into the schema-deployment phase to establish an episodic memory. The 7-year-olds also behaved in accordance with the schema confirmation–deployment hypothesis. The older children were able to keep separate their memory for the two types of event visits, indicating that the 7-year-olds were able to learn the schema quickly, confirm it, and then deploy the schema to organize their memory for the episodic visit. Interestingly, those 7-year-olds with only two visits had difficulty establishing a separate memory for at least some details of the episodic memory. These children were probably still in the schema-confirmation stage. It was only those 7-year-olds with four visits who were able to enter the schema-deployment stage.

Together, the results of Study 1 and Study 2 indicate that younger children, under certain circumstances, are more schema-dependent than older children for an episodic or autobiographical memory of a repeated event. The 4-year-olds had difficulty establishing a separate episodic memory but, rather, relied on their general event memory, which absorbed information from both the script and episodic visits, in recalling the event. This pattern matches findings from studies of story recall in which younger children also rely on schemas in recalling episodic memories (see Mandler, 1979). Our results contradict those from investigations of children's script and episodic memory for naturally occurring events (e.g., Hudson, 1987; Hudson & Nelson, 1986). We feel that these failures to find developmental differences are primarily attributable either to small age differences in the groups studied or an inability to assess the accuracy of children's recall. Thus, we believe that our results in combination with studies of story recall do indicate that young children are often more schema-dependent than older children for many memory tasks.

We do not want to suggest, however, that this schema dependency always occurs or that this pattern of results is specific to the particular age groups studied. Rather, according to the schema confirmation–deployment hypothesis, the schema dependency displayed by the 4-year-olds should occur with any age group when they experience an event that is difficult to organize schematically. This means that for more complicated events, the 7-year-olds would be expected to show greater schema-based recall and more difficulty deploying the schema. Similarly, with simpler events the 4-year-olds would be expected to show less schema dependency and an increased ability to deploy the schema. The general point is that any age group will function at different levels of schema dependency depending on the complexity of the event being encountered.

The structure of script and episodic memory. The results of these studies also support current conceptualizations of script and episodic memory (e.g., Hudson & Nelson, 1986; Schank, 1982). Although our findings do not allow us to decide among various specific proposals, they do support claims regarding the primacy of script representations for event memory. Similar to the findings of other studies, our results reveal that young children's script memory is generally better than episodic memory and is used in organizing episodic memory. For instance, increased event experience generally improved overall script memory, suggesting an increasing schematization of the event memory. In contrast, increased experience tended to decrease overall episodic memory compared to a one-time novel event. At the same time, however, once a repeated event was encountered, event experience facilitated memory for those specific details (i.e., the new event instantiations) representing deviations from the script, as most memory models would argue (e.g., Schank, 1982).

Caveats and concerns

We want to be cautious in characterizing the structure and form of the "script" memory we studied. That is, it is unclear whether we can properly say that children's memory for the script visits indicates a script structure. Our working assumption was that a generic representation of the script visits was formed (a fair assumption, given theoretical discussions of the formation of scripts) and that the script-visit interview question tapped it. It is possible, however, that what we tapped corresponded more to an autobiographical memory and not to a script memory per se. This could have been the case for the 7-year-olds, who demonstrated an ability to distinguish between the two visits. That is, the 7-year-olds may have been recalling two different episodic memories. The 4-year-olds did not recall separate visits, however. Regardless of how the script visits are conceptualized, the interpretation of the results would remain, namely, that the younger children merged the different visits and were in that sense more schema-bound than the older children.

A second concern relates to the animal costume cues used to mark the different types of visits. Perhaps the reason the 4-year-olds often failed to distinguish between the two visits was not because they were more reliant on the script, but because they simply were not aware that the different animal costumes signaled or cued the different event types. Although this is a reasonable interpretation, the evidence does not support it. First, the younger children were clearly aware of the change of costume and would often comment about it. Second, and more importantly, the data suggest that they do use these cues to distinguish the visits. For instance, as Figure 3.5 revealed, the 4-year-olds did not always report the exact same information for the two types of visits. For example, on Day 4, the 4-year-olds used the different animal costume cues to access different information about the script and deviation visits. This result stands in contrast to their Day 2 performance, when they failed to differentiate the script and deviation information. If children had not used the costumes to distinguish the events, their recall should have been almost identical because they would not have been able to use the cues to recall different event memories. Finally, the findings are predictable and consistent with previous research (e.g., Mandler, 1979, 1983).

A third concern is whether the event we created has any sort of ecological validity. There is nothing to indicate that this event is greatly different from certain other events children experience, particularly when viewed from their perspective. Our event is similar to the type of experiences a child might have at an amusement park, circus, or carnival, or to the games he or she might play with friends. From the child's point of view, the event they experienced in our laboratory may be just another of the many strange, mysterious, and fun events that parents often take them to, for whatever reasons. Moreover, from the researcher's point of view, the event had the advantage of being unfamiliar so that script formation could be studied. To the extent that ecological validity is equated with the study of natural events in the real world, it is more difficult to study the effects of initial script formation on memory. Thus, we believe that this and similar experimental events can be properly used to study children's event memory, especially when studies primarily concern theoretical issues. It would be beneficial, of course, for researchers to attempt to replicate our findings in more naturalistic studies, but they would need to keep a variety of factors, such as the ease of organizing the event, in mind.

A final concern is why increased event experience improved recall of event changes for only the new instantiations of an old script event table, but not the other deviation changes. It is unclear whether this effect was due to the particular class of event deviations or the way this deviation was realized in this particular study. Recall of the new instantiations might be considered a fairly difficult task in that it required memory of new details introduced into a familiar event. It may be that since these instantiations were deeply embedded within the hierarchy of the event, the additional experience was needed to mark their salience. In contrast, the new event table (i.e., the Animal Workshop) may have been more salient since it represented an entirely new event node and may not have required the same extensive event experience.

Conclusions

Our findings show that young children are more dependent *in some situations* than older children on scripts in organizing their autobiographical memories. Consistent with the predictions of the schema confirmation-deployment hypothesis, when young children are faced with a complex event that is difficult to organize, they are less likely than older children to remember deviations from a repeated event. Instead, the younger children remain in a schema-confirmation phase in which they attempt to establish and confirm an organizing framework to understand and encode the event. Presumably, if the younger children had been given more experience with the repeated event, they would have evidenced schema-deployment effects, assuming they could then organize the information schematically. Or, if a simple event had been chosen, one for which the younger children already possessed a schema, the younger children would have evidenced distinct memories for script and deviations visits.

NOTES

The research reported in this chapter was supported by a University of Denver Biomedical Research Grant awarded to Michael Jeffrey Farrar and Gail S. Goodman, by a NIMH Postdoctoral Grant awarded to Michael Jeffrey Farrar through the Department of Psychology at the University of Denver, and by a Department of Health and Human Services grant awarded to Gail S. Goodman. Special thanks go to Daniel MacIntosh and to Christine Aman for serving as research assistants. We also thank Bonnie Buddin and Mary Jo Jones for their assistance. Dr. Marshall M. Haith provided valuable comments on this project during its inception.

1 The amount of incorrect information recalled was included as part of the denominator in order to provide a more sensitive assessment of overall recall accuracy of the event. We were not interested in simply assessing recall of a particular event instantiation (e.g., tables, animals, etc.), but rather we were concerned with memory for the event episode(s) as distinct from other episodes. It is important to note, however, that if incorrect information is not used in the denominator, the pattern of results does not change substantially, except that the effect of day is not as strong.

REFERENCES

Abbott, V., Black, J., & Smith, E. (1985). The representation of scripts in memory. *Journal of Memory and Language, 24,* 179–199.

Anderson, R. C., & Prichert, J. W. (1978). Recall of previously unrecallable information following a shift in perspective. *Journal of Verbal Learning and Verbal Behavior, 17,* 1–12.

Barsalou, L. W. (1985). Free recall of natural events. *Proceedings of the Second Annual Workshop on Conceptual Information Processing.* New Haven, CT.

Barsalou, L., Lancaster, J., Spindler, J., George, B., & Farrar, M. J. (in preparation). The organization of autobiographical memories.

Bartlett, F. C. (1932). *Remembering: A study in experimental and social psychology.* Cambridge: Cambridge University Press.

Beiderman, I. (1982). Perceiving real-world scenes, *Science, 177,* 77–79.

Bower, G. H., Black, J. B., & Turner, T. J. (1979). Scripts in memory for text. *Cognitive Psychology, 11,* 177–220.

Bransford, J. D., & Franks, J. J. (1971). The abstraction of linguistic ideas. *Cognitive Psychology, 2,* 331–350.

Brewer, W. F., & Nakamura, G. V. (1984). The nature and function of schemas. In R. S. Wyer & T. K. Srull (Eds.), *Handbook of social cognition.* Hillsdale, NJ: Erlbaum.

Bruner, J., & Postman, L. (1949). Perception, cognition and behavior. *Journal of Personality, 18,* 14–31.

Fischer, K. W. (1980). A theory of cognitive development: The control and construction of hierarchies of skills. *Psychological Review, 87,* 477–531.

Fischer, K. W., & Farrar, M. J. (1987). Generalizations about generalizations: How a theory of skill development explains both generality and specificity. *International Journal of Psychology, 22,* 643–678.

Fivush, R. (1984). Learning about school: The development of kindergartners' school scripts. *Child Development, 55,* 1697–1709.

Fivush, R., Gray, J., Hamond, N., & Fromhoff, F. (1986). *Two studies of early autobiographical memory* (Tech. Rep. No. 11). Emory University Cognition Project, Atlanta.

Fivush, R., Hudson, J., & Nelson, K. (1984). Children's long-term memory for a novel event: An exploratory study. *Merrill-Palmer Quarterly, 30,* 303–316.

Fivush, R., & Slackman, E. (1986). The acquisition and development of scripts. In K. Nelson (Ed.), *Event knowledge: Structure and function in development* (pp. 71–96). Hillsdale, NJ: Erlbaum.

French, L., & Nelson, K. (1981). Temporal knowledge expressed in preschoolers' descriptions of familiar activities. *Papers and Reports on Child Language Development, 20,* 61–69.

Friedman, A. (1979). Framing pictures: The role of knowledge in automatized encoding and memory for gist. *Journal of Experimental Psychology: General, 108,* 316–335.

Goodman, G. S. (1980). Picture memory: How the action schema affects retention. *Cognitive Psychology, 12,* 473–495.

Goodman, G. S. (1981). *Schema-confirmation and schema-deployment.* Unpublished manuscript.

Goodman, G. S., & Golding, J. (1983, April). *Effects of real-world knowledge on memory.* In K. Nelson (Chair), *Memory and representation of the real world.* Symposium presented at the Society for Research in Child Development, Detroit.

Graesser, A. C. (1981). *Prose comprehension beyond the word.* New York: Springer-Verlag.

Graesser, A. C., Gordon, S. E., & Sawyer, J. D. (1979). Recognition memory for typical and atypical actions in scripted activities: Tests of a script pointer + tag hypothesis. *Journal of Verbal Learning and Verbal Behavior, 18,* 319–332.

Hudson, J. (1986). Memories are made of this: General event knowledge and development of autobiographic memory. In K. Nelson (Ed.), *Event knowledge: Structure and function in development* (pp. 97–118). Hillsdale, NJ: Erlbaum.

Hudson, J. (1990). Constructive processes in children's event memories. *Developmental Psychology, 26,* 180–187.

Hudson, J., & Fivush, R. (1983). Categorical and schematic organization and the development of retrieval strategies. *Journal of Experimental Child Psychology, 36,* 32–42.

Hudson, J., & Fivush, R. (1988, March). *As time goes by: Sixth graders remember a kindergarten experience.* Paper presented at the meeting of Conference on Human Development, Charleston, SC.

Hudson, J., & Nelson, K. (1983). Effects of script structure on children's story recall. *Developmental Psychology, 19,* 625–635.

Hudson, J., & Nelson, K. (1986). Repeated encounters of a similar kind: Effects of familiarity on children's autobiographical memory. *Cognitive Development, 1,* 253–271.

Hunter, M. A., Ross, H. S., & Ames, E. W. (1982). Preferences for familiar or novel toys: Effects of familiarization time in one-year-olds. *Developmental Psychology, 18,* 519–529.

Johnson-Laird, P. N. (1983). *Mental models.* Cambridge, MA: Harvard University Press.

Kagan, J. (1970). Attention and psychological change in the young child. *Science, 170,* 826–832.

Linton, M. (1975). Memory for real-world events. In D. A. Norman & D. E.

Rumelhart (Eds.), *Explorations in cognition* (pp. 376–404). San Francisco: W. H. Freeman.

Linton, M. (1982). Transformations of memory in everyday life. In U. Neisser (Ed.), *Memory observed* (pp. 77–91). San Francisco: W. H. Freeman.

Loftus, G. E., & Mackworth, N. H. (1978). Cognitive determinants of fixation location during picture viewing. *Journal of Experimental Psychology: Human Perception and Performance, 4,* 565–572.

Lucariello, J., & Rifkin, A. (1986). Event representations as the basis for categorical knowledge. In K. Nelson (Ed.), *Event knowledge: Structure and function in development* (pp. 189–203). Hillsdale, NJ: Erlbaum.

Mandler, J. M. (1979). Categorical and schematic organization in memory. In C. R. Puff (Ed.), *Memory organization and structure* (pp. 259–299). New York: Academic Press.

Mandler, J. M. (1983). Representation. In J. H. Flavell & E. M. Markham (Eds.), *Cognitive Development.* In P. Mussen (Ed.), *Handbook of child psychology* (4th ed., vol. 3, 420–494). New York: Wiley.

Mandler, J. M. (1984). *Stories, scripts and scenes: Aspects of schema theory.* Hillsdale, NJ: Erlbaum.

Mandler, J. M., & Robinson, C. A. (1978). Developmental changes in picture memory. *Journal of Experimental Child Psychology, 26,* 122–136.

Minsky, M. (1975). A framework for representing knowledge. In P. Winston (Ed.), *The psychology of computer vision* (pp. 211–280). New York: McGraw-Hill.

Myles-Worsley, M., Cromer, C., & Dodd, D. (1986). Children's preschool script reconstruction: Reliance on general knowledge as memory fades. *Developmental Psychology, 22,* 22–30.

Neisser, U. (Ed.) (1982). *Memory observed: Remembering in natural contexts.* San Francisco: W. H. Freeman.

Nelson, K. (1978). How young children represent knowledge of their world in and out of language. In R. S. Seigler (Ed.), *Children's thinking: What develops?* (pp. 255–273). Hillsdale, NJ: Erlbaum.

Nelson, K. (1981). Social cognition in a script framework. In J. H. Flavell & L. Ross (Eds.), *Social cognitive development: Frontier and possible futures* (pp. 97–118). New York: Cambridge University Press.

Nelson, K. (Ed.) (1986). *Event knowledge: Structure and function in development.* Hillsdale, NJ: Erlbaum.

Nelson, K., & Gruendel, J. (1981). Generalized event representations: Basic building blocks of cognitive development. In M. E. Lamb & A. L. Brown (Eds.), *Advances in developmental psychology* (Vol. 1, pp. 131–158). Hillsdale, NJ.: Erlbaum.

Pompi, K. F., & Lachman, R. (1967). Surrogate processes in the short-term retention or connected discourse. *Journal of Experimental Psychology, 75,* 143–150.

Price, D., & Goodman, G. S. (April, 1985). *Children's comprehension of recurring events.* Paper presented at the meeting of the Society for Research in Child Development, Toronto.

Reisser, B. J. (1986a). Knowledge-directed retrieval of autobiographical memories. In J. L. Kolodner & C. K. Reisback (Eds.), *Experience and reasoning.* Hillsdale, NJ: Erlbaum.

Reisser, B. J. (1986b). The encoding and retrieval of memories of real-world experiences. In J. Galambos, R. Abelson & J. Black (Eds.), *Knowledge structures.* Hillsdale: NJ: Erlbaum.

Reisser, B. J., Black, J. B., & Abelson, R. P. (1985). Knowledge structures in the organization and retrieval of autobiographical memories. *Cognitive Psychology, 17*, 89–137.

Rose, S. A., Gottfried, A. W., Melloy-Carminar, P., & Bridger, W. H. (1982). Familiarity and novelty preferences in infant recognition memory: Implications for information-processing. *Developmental Psychology, 18*, 704–713.

Schank, R. C. (1982). *Dynamic memory: A theory of reminding and learning in computers and people.* New York: Cambridge University Press.

Schank, R. C., & Abelson, R. P. (1977). *Scripts, plans, goals, and understanding.* Hillsdale, NJ: Erlbaum.

Slackman, E., & Hudson, J. (1984, October). *Filling the gaps: Inferential processes in children's comprehension of oral discourse.* Paper presented at the meeting of the Ninth Annual Boston University Conference on Language Development, Boston.

Slackman, E., Hudson, J., & Fivush, R. (1986). Actions, actors, links, and goals: The structure of children's event representations. In K. Nelson (Ed.), *Event knowledge: Structure and function in development* (pp. 47–69). Hillsdale, NJ: Erlbaum.

Taylor, S. E., & Crocker, J. (1981). Schematic bases of social information processing. In E. T. Higgins, C. P. Herman, & M. P. Zanna (Eds.), *Social cognition: The Ontario symposium* (Vol. 1). Hillsdale, NJ: Erlbaum.

White, J. D., & Carlson, D. F. (1983). Consequences of schemata for attention, impressions and recall of complex social interactions. *Journal of Personality and Social Psychology, 45*, 538–549.

4
Children's organization of events and event memories

HILARY HORN RATNER, BRENDA S. SMITH, AND
ROBERT J. PADGETT

For all of us the world comes to be known through our own and others'
actions, but for young children this is especially true. Compared to older
children or adults, preschoolers must rely more on their experiences in
the world and their memory of these experiences to learn. They simply
do not have the means available to acquire as much information from
books or oral instruction. Thus, most of the remembering that young
children do in order to construct knowledge of their world involves
memory for events – information that is action based, goal motivated,
and contextually embedded.

The importance of event memory is indicated by its central place in
the study of children's cognitive development (e.g., Mandler, 1984a;
Nelson, 1986a). Nelson and Gruendel (1981) suggest that generalized
event representations form the basic building blocks of early learning
and memory. Such representations reflect the knowledge gained from
multiple experiences involving the same event and are less specific than
any of the individual episodes. These generalized event representations,
or scripts, have been found to underlie the development of organization
in memory (e.g., Lucariello & Nelson, 1985), word meaning (e.g., Barrett, 1986), categorization skills (e.g., Nelson, 1982), and play (e.g.,
Seidman, Nelson, & Gruendel, 1986).

We know a great deal about the contents and structure of children's
scripts. For instance, even though the number of actions that can be
reported increases with age, preschoolers and older children alike focus
on central acts that are highly related to the goal of the episodes (e.g.,
Nelson & Gruendel, 1981). Furthermore, children at all ages sequence
actions very accurately, and as children grow older their action sequences
become more complex (McCartney & Nelson, 1981). They also become
better able to incorporate more optional and variable-order actions and
refer more to conditional constraints embedded within the sequence
(e.g., Slackman, Hudson, & Fivush, 1986). The amount of information
reported and the accuracy of the sequence also depends on the nature of
the actions composing the event. Scripts constructed from causally con-

65

nected actions contain more information and are sequenced more accurately than temporally related sequences (e.g., Myles-Worsley, Cromer, & Dodd, 1986; Nelson & Gruendel, 1986).

These findings and others have led to a now common formulation of the contents and organization of scripts. Event actions are seen as hierarchically nested within more general, superordinate categories that form scenes (e.g., Mandler, 1984a, Schank & Abelson, 1977). In contrast to taxonomic categories, these superordinate–subordinate links are based on partonomy rather than inclusion relations (e.g., Barsalou & Sewell, 1985). Typically, the representation is depicted as a tree structure, consisting of a main goal, several subgoals, actions, and outcomes. As one moves down through the structure, the level of detail and concreteness increases, so that information at the lower levels of the hierarchy is specific, detailed, and often less critical to understanding an instance. Information becomes more general and sometimes more important as one moves up through the hierarchy (Kintsch & van Dijk, 1978; Omanson, 1982; Thorndyke, 1977). Certain actions are more central than others based on their relationship to the superordinate goals of the event (e.g., Trabasso & Sperry, 1985). In addition to hierarchical organization and graded structure (i.e., centrality), scripts are also organized by temporal sequence (e.g., Barsalou & Sewell, 1985) and by temporal properties (e.g., Galambos & Rips, 1982; Nottenburg & Shoben, 1980). Actions are linked together in a linear chain that specifies their order of occurrence and are described by properties that indicate their relative temporal position within the sequence (i.e., early, late, etc.). (See also Farrar & Goodman, this volume.)

Many of these characteristics apply to representations of novel episodes, events that have occurred only once. Children very accurately report the actions within an episode in temporal sequence (e.g., Fivush, Hudson, & Nelson, 1984) and report the main goal and most central acts of the event (e.g., Myers & Bluhm, 1985; Ratner, Smith, & Dion, 1986; Smith, Ratner, & Hobart, 1987). This suggests that generalized representations take the form of the episodes that constitute them and can be created from one event experience (e.g., Nelson & Gruendel, 1986). We do not know, however, whether hierarchical organization, one of the principal characteristics of scripts, is present after one experience and whether it changes with repeated exposure to the event. In fact, we know very little about how the representation of single, novel episodes are related to or transformed into a generalized representation containing information about several instances.

In this chapter we examine whether the organization scheme, which seems to be present when an event has been repeatedly experienced, emerges after the first experience. If it does not, we can ask which parts of the structure, if any, are present and whether their presence or absence is related to the age of the person participating in the event or how often the event is repeated. We review the results of our earlier studies and present our findings from more recent projects.

Our answer to "what young children remember and why" depends, then, on the internal organization of children's event memories. More precisely, we assume that children remember in accordance with their organizing schemes and that the content and form of their memories reflect these schemes. By specifying what those schemes might be and how they change, we can make predictions about the types of information most memorable to children and how this is affected by age or experience.

To preview our findings, our research suggests that young children do exhibit parts of a hierarchical structure in their recall even after one event experience. Nevertheless, when an event is experienced repeatedly, more of the hierarchical structure emerges – just as would be expected if organization in scripts arises from event frequency and familiarity (e.g., Mandler, 1986). Adults and older children, however, appear more sensitive than preschoolers to this sort of organization and construct it more quickly. Before well-integrated scenes or categories emerge within the hierarchy, understanding of the causal connections among the actions appears to guide encoding and recall and may serve as organizers of the categories.

Memory and organization of a novel event

The paradigm

In order to assess event memory and organization, children and adults in our studies participate in a standardized clay-making event and then are asked to recall it. In some studies we also ask participants to organize the elements of the event into categories. From their verbal responses we can make inferences about how the event is represented and can examine whether organization within the event influences how it is reported. Like others (e.g., Nelson, 1986b), we rely on verbal reports and assume a correspondence between the report and the event's internal representation. Verbal reports do underestimate the amount of information in memory (e.g., Smith, Ratner, & Hobart, 1987) but nonetheless reveal important information about at least one layer of event representation.

Our event has four important characteristics. First, because the event is standardized, the conditions present during the experiencing of it are controlled. Individual variations in the event do not occur, which permits us more easily to draw conclusions about how the event is remembered.

Second, our event contains actions that children can and are willing to carry out so that the standardized procedures can be maintained. Children can easily perform the clay-making task because they are familiar with baking, a related event. Even though most of the children have helped bake something, very few have made clay. Therefore, familiar elements are present but are combined in a novel fashion. This distinction is critical if we are to examine memory for novel events and memory changes with additional experience. A second advantage of the novelty of the task is that children are interested and motivated to participate.

Third, the clay-making event can be varied. Actions and objects can be added, subtracted, or rearranged; actions can be performed by the child, the experimenter, or both. The event can even be filmed, talked about, or shown in pictures. This flexibility provides information about how the nature of the event influences its memory.

Finally, the event can be organized hierarchically. The actions that compose the event are organized into superordinate categories, which in turn define the overall goal. By examining recall and other measures we can explore whether this hierarchical structure is used to organize memory of the event. In our studies the number of actions making up the event has been no less than 24 and no more than 40. These actions have been organized into four or five superordinate categories. The four superordinate categories that are always present are: getting ready to make clay, adding the dry ingredients, adding the liquid ingredients, and mixing everything together. In some studies we add a fifth category, cleaning up.

To ensure that the superordinate categories and actions making them up are uniformly perceived and agreed on, we chose one version of the event to verify. All five superordinate categories were included and each category contained six actions. The actions and categories appear in Table 4.1. Twenty-five college students identified the actions that made up the event and 25 additional students identified its hierarchical structure. To familiarize themselves with the event, both groups watched a videotape of the second author performing the clay-making actions we had previously defined. Those identifying the actions then watched the tape again. This time the event was divided into ten segments that were 20 to 30 seconds in length and that contained an average of three actions. (Eight segments contained three actions, one contained two actions, and one contained four actions.) After each segment was shown, the students wrote down the actions they saw. To verify their descriptions they saw the event two more times. During the first of these reviews the event was presented in segments. During the second, it was shown continuously. All but two of the actions were identified by at least 88% of the subjects.

The group who verified the hierarchical structure of the event was

Table 4.1 *Clay-making actions and superordinate categories*

Get ready	*Mix everything together*
1. Put apron on	19. Stir ingredients with spoon
2. Get bowl, spoon, and food coloring	20. Sprinkle flour on table
3. Get flour & scoop	21. Gather pieces of clay together
4. Get oil and cinnamon	22. Put clay on table
5. Get water, measuring cups, and spoon	23. Knead clay
6. Get salt	24. Roll clay into a ball
Add the dry ingredients	*Clean up*
7. Measure flour	25. Put clay back in bowl
8. Put flour in bowl	26. Put spoons and cups in basket
9. Measure salt	27. Wipe crumbs off table
10. Put salt in bowl	28. Throw crumbs in wastebasket
11. Measure cinnamon	29. Brush off hands
12. Pour cinnamon in bowl	30. Take apron off
Add the liquid ingredients	
13. Measure water	
14. Pour water in bowl	
15. Measure oil	
16. Pour oil in bowl	
17. Measure color	
18. Pour color in bowl	

told that events could be divided into natural units or scenes (following Mandler & Murphy, 1983). They were given a list of the 30 actions. The names of these actions were listed one per line, were not capitalized, and were not punctuated. After the initial viewing, the students watched the tape a second time. We instructed them to think about what the natural units were in this event. The third time they viewed the tape they divided the event into segments by drawing a line between the last action in one unit and the first in the next unit. While viewing the tape for the fourth and final time, they reviewed their choices and labeled each of the units. We counted the number of subjects who ended each unit with the action, plus or minus one, that we had identified as the final action in the unit. According to this criterion, three of the five units were identified by 22 or more of the subjects. The other two units were grouped together by 20 of the subjects and labeled as *put everything in.* Five more divided this unit into two, *put in the dry ingredients* and *put in the liquid ingredients,* as we had. Although we defined the category more precisely than the subjects, they agreed that this set of actions belonged together. These results demonstrated that the actions and categories we had defined were valid and could be reliably identified.

Cuing study

Rationale. In the first study, we manipulated the recall context to examine whether hierarchical organization was present in preschoolers' and college students' recall of a novel event (Smith et al., 1987). Before children and adults reported the event we presented cues from various levels of the hierarchical tree. We expected performance to vary as a function of cue type if memory of the event were organized hierarchically or if children and adults searched their memory hierarchically. Using this technique we discovered that parts of the organizing structure do seem to be present after one experience, even for young children.

Procedure. In this study the event contained 4 superordinate categories and 35 actions. Kindergartners and adults recalled the clay-making event under four cuing conditions immediately after the event and 2 weeks later. They were cued only during immediate recall.

In the first condition, which served as a baseline, children and adults received no cues at all. We simply asked them to tell us what they had done. At delayed recall, all children and adults received this no-cue condition.

A second group was given the main goal of the event as a cue. We asked them how they had made the clay. In our earlier studies (e.g., Ratner, Smith, & Dion, 1986; Smith et al., 1987, Experiment 1), 60% to 80% of our subjects reported the main goal of the event, indicating very clearly that it was represented. If subjects search down the hierarchical tree while reporting the event, then presenting the main goal might lead to increased production of the superordinates related to it (i.e., get ready, add the dry ingredients, etc.).

A third group was given one of the superordinate labels as a cue. We asked subjects in this group if they had used dry things. We expected that if links existed between the superordinate and the actions subsumed by it, then recall would be enhanced for that category and perhaps for other categories as well. By using only one of the superordinate labels we could also determine where subjects began their recall. Would they report an action within the dry-ingredients category, or would they report another superordinate? The first pattern would suggest links between the superordinate label and the actions organized by it. The second pattern would indicate that links occur across categories between the superordinate labels.

Finally, a fourth group was given a subordinate cue, the last action in the dry-ingredients category. We asked subjects if they had used cinnamon. If strong links do not exist among superordinates or between a superordinate and the actions organized by it, links may exist among the

Table 4.2. *Mean proportions of superordinate and subordinate actions reported in the cuing study*

	Time of interview	Cuing condition			
Age		None	Goal	Subordinate	Superordinate
Superordinate recall					
5-year-olds	Immediate	.286	.358	.242	.540
	Delayed	.200	.214	.186	.272
Adults	Immediate	.428	.314	.314	.358
	Delayed	.328	.114	.172	.200
Subordinate recall					
5-year-olds	Immediate	.143	.167	.169	.155
	Delayed	.102	.124	.100	.086
Adults	Immediate	.300	.237	.190	.241
	Delayed	.318	.294	.255	.288

Source: Ratner, Smith, & Hobart (1987), p. 19. Reprinted by permission of Academic Press.

actions themselves. If so, subjects would report the next action in the sequence. By choosing the last action in a category as a cue, we could determine whether the first action recalled was categorically or temporally related to the cue. If the cue and first action recalled were members of the same superordinate category (i.e., both dry ingredients), we could conclude that subjects were using the categories to direct their recall. If the first action recalled was from the category next in the sequence, we could conclude that subjects were reporting the actions in the order of occurrence, a temporal strategy.

If a hierarchical tree organizes memory of the clay-making event and cues influence the use of the organization, then more actions should be reported in the superordinate cue condition than the others. Performance was expected to be next best in the goal-cue condition and poorest in the no-cue and subordinate-cue conditions. If adults are more active organizers than children, cues should not influence their recall.

Results. In Table 4.2, subordinate recall appears for the four conditions at the two age-levels. Although adults reported more information than children, recall was equivalent among the cuing conditions. Even when we examined the number of actions reported for the category that was directly cued, there were still no differences among conditions. This suggests that strong links may not be present between the superordinate category labels and the actions summarized by them, at least when the event is experienced only once.

Table 4.3. *Number of subjects who began their recall in a given category*

		Condition			
Age	Category	No cue	Goal cue	Subordinate cue	Superordinate cue
Immediate					
Children	Dry	7[a]	10	7	3
	Liquid	4	4	6	11
	Other	2	0	1	0
Adults	Dry	6	7	7	9
	Liquid	0	1	4	0
	Other	8	6	3	5
Delayed					
Children	Dry	10[a]	10	7[a]	4
	Liquid	3	3	5	10
	Other	0	1	1	0
Adults	Dry	1	2	3	6
	Liquid	0	0	3	0
	Other	13	12	8	8

[a]One subject reported no information

Source: Smith, Ratner, & Hobart (1987), p. 19. Reprinted by permission of Academic Press.

There was some evidence that the superordinate labels were linked together. First, children reported more superordinate labels in the superordinate and goal-cue conditions than in the other conditions. Adults, in contrast, reported more superordinates in the no-cue condition than in the other three. For children, then, the presence of one superordinate label led to the production of others, whereas for adults more superordinates were reported when they directed their own recall.

More persuasive evidence that there are links among the superordinates was provided by the starting point in recall. Those who received a superordinate cue could (1) begin reporting within the cued category, the dry ingredients; (2) within the next category, the liquid ingredients; or (3) ignore the cue and report the first action of the event. The number of subjects who began their recall in each of three categories of the event was tallied. These three categories were adding the dry ingredients, adding the liquid ingredients, and "other," which included getting ready and mixing everything together. "Other" responses almost always involved the get-ready actions. The results appear in Table 4.3 for each age group and for immediate and delayed recall.

Most of the children in the no-cue, goal-cue, and subordinate-cue conditions began recalling the event when the dry ingredients were measured and put into the bowl. Very few started with get-ready actions. For these kindergartners, the event appeared to begin when the ingredients were placed into the bowl. This point is reinforced by the results from delayed recall. Two weeks later, in the absence of cues, even more children began recalling the event by naming actions involving the dry ingredients. This is not surprising because adults rate these actions as more central to the event than getting ready (Padgett & Ratner, 1987; Smith et al., 1987), but it indicates that children separate preparatory actions from the event.

In contrast, almost all of the children in the superordinate-cue condition started reporting the actions involving measuring and pouring the liquid ingredients. Of the 11 children in this category, 7 started by reporting the superordinate itself (i.e., we put the wet stuff in). This pattern was maintained even during delayed recall. Two weeks later without the superordinate cue, these same children started reporting the event in the liquid-ingredients category. Thus, categories that were used initially to direct recall were maintained either in a structured representation or as part of the retrieval process. This was our strongest indicator that at least some of the categories were meaningful to the children and that the rudiments of a hierarchical structure had formed, at least among the superordinates themselves. But notice, too, that temporal links were present because children began reporting from the category next in the sequence. Consistent with this interpretation, more of the subordinate-cue children, in comparison to those in the no-cue and goal-cue conditions, reported actions from the liquid ingredients category.

Adults also showed evidence of an emerging hierarchical structure, but the specific indicators were different. During the immediate interview, about half the adults began by recalling the dry-ingredients actions and about half began in the "other" category. During delayed recall most started in the "other" category. All of the adults assigned to this category began their recall with get-ready actions. In contrast to the children, then, the adults were more likely to define the preparatory actions as the beginning of the event. This pattern occurred fairly consistently across the four conditions, although there was some tendency for more adults to begin in the dry-ingredients category if they had received the superordinate cue. This pattern was also maintained over time. This suggests that when adults were given the cue, they were better able than children to direct their attention to actions within the category. Furthermore, their delayed recall was influenced by cuing in the same way as the children's; how the event was initially recalled influenced how it was reported 2 weeks later. This suggests that the act of recall changes the representation of the event or creates a separate representation of its report.

Summary. After one experience, representations of relatively novel and complex events are hierarchically organized to some extent, but this structure is incomplete and not well integrated. Links seem to be present among the superordinate category labels, but connections between them and the subordinate actions do not seem as strong. At the same time, category distinctions were made within the event. Children, for instance, separated the get-ready actions from the rest of the event, which suggests that some sets of actions did cohere to form units. The superordinate labels may have been represented primarily as verbal statements because they were socially provided through language. Initially the labels may not act as true organizers of subordinate actions or as symbols for the categories. Children may not verbally identify or activate these categories, and consequently, may create two levels or types of organization that have little connection between them. This discrepancy may reflect the presence of two memory "systems." One, a socially accessible system, may be primarily mediated by language, and the other may principally involve percepts – actions, feelings, locations, or objects that may or may not be decoded into language (Pillemer & White, in press). The first may come to organize the second, but additional experience may be necessary to coordinate the two levels.

Young children appear to construct action categories most easily when actions are presented and recalled in verbal form. Huttenlocher & Lui (1979) found that children as young as age 3 recalled verbally presented lists of related actions better than unrelated lists. Others (e.g., Foellinger & Trabasso, 1977; Foley & Johnson 1985; Johnson, Perlmutter, & Trabasso, 1979), however, have found that actions are not always organized into categories even by 6-year-olds. When 6-year-olds recalled sets of related actions they had performed or watched someone else perform, they organized them according to actor not action class. When person was removed as a basis for organization, the younger children did rely on action class just as older children and adults did. For young children, performing an action may activate elements of meaning that initially interfere with recognizing similarities across actions in form or function. Later we will show that objects may have played this role in the clay-making event. We are currently investigating whether verbal and motoric presentation of actions leads to use of different organizing schemes.

Although memory of the event did not seem to be organized into a well-integrated hierarchical structure, our paradigm may not have been sensitive enough to detect the extent to which the event was organized. Even after one experience, organization may have been greater than we observed. To assess this possibility, we examined organization in a different way.

Sorting study

Rationale. To uncover the organization of object categories, children and adults are often asked to sort pictures of objects or objects themselves into groups (e.g., Inhelder & Piaget, 1964; Rosch, Mervis, Gray, Johnson, & Boyes-Braem, 1976). The groupings are assumed to reflect the underlying organization of these objects in memory. Although young children have been found to use more thematic (e.g., Liberty & Ornstein, 1973), complementary (e.g., Denney & Ziobrowski, 1972), or functional (e.g., Bruner, Olver, & Greenfield, 1966; Lange & Jackson, 1974) groupings than older children, they can organize items taxonomically, especially if objects are central members of the category (e.g, Whitney & Kunen, 1983) or if performance demands are minimized (Markman, Cox, & Machida, 1981). To assess more directly whether actions within the event are organized into categories, 15 kindergartners and 15 college students were asked to sort pictures of the actions into groups and explain their groupings after they made the clay.

Next, we asked the participants to recall the event. When they had reported everything they thought they could, all the superordinate category labels were presented as cues. In the previous study we did not find that the dry-ingredients cue facilitated recall, but some of the other category cues might be more effective. When several different categories are represented in object word lists and their labels are presented during recall, performance is facilitated (e.g., Moely, 1977), even for children as young as 3 years of age (e.g., Myers & Perlmutter, 1978). Analogously, we assumed that if event categories are represented and can be accessed verbally, then more actions should be reported when cues are given.

Procedure. For this version of the event, 24 actions were organized into four categories: get ready, add the dry ingredients, add the liquid ingredients, and mix the clay together. There were six actions in each of the four superordinate categories. Color photographs were taken of the second author performing each of the clay-making actions. A photograph illustrating the action to be performed was presented and verbally labeled during its execution to make clear which action was depicted.

The experimenter first explained that the photographs showed each step in making the clay and then labeled the first superordinate (i.e., "To make the clay, we have to get ready"). Then the first action of the event (i.e., "We have to put on the T-shirt") was labeled, and the corresponding photo was presented. When the action had been accomplished, children and adults were shown the next photograph, and the depicted action was labeled. This continued throughout the event. Thus, the main goal, every superordinate, and all of the subordinate actions were labeled by the experimenter before they were performed or accomplished by the subject.

After the clay was made, the utensils and ingredients were covered, and the experimenter shuffled the 24 photos of the event actions and randomly arranged them before the subject, labeling the action in each photo. In order to verify that the main goal had been encoded, the experimenter asked what they had been trying to do when performing all the actions shown in the pictures. Next, the subject was told that some of the steps "go together somehow" and that he or she should put the actions that "go together" in the same group. When the groups were formed, subjects were asked to explain them.

Then the pictures were removed and the child or adult recalled the event, pretending that the experimenter knew nothing about making the clay. After subjects had reported all that they could, each superordinate cue was presented in a random order. To determine if the superordinate categories could be identified, we sorted the photos into the four groups and asked subjects to explain why the pictures went together in these groups.

Sorting results. Of the 13 children and 15 adults who were asked what they were trying to do when they performed the actions, 12 of the children and all of the adults responded with the main goal, making clay. We know, then, that the main goal of the event was readily understood and is easily accessible.

Children sorted the picture into more groups ($M = 6.6$) than the adults ($M = 4.7$), who more accurately identified the actual number of superordinate categories in the event. Children's division of the actions into a larger number of groups is similar to their sorts of object categories (e.g., Saltz, Soller, & Sigel, 1972; Worden, 1975).

More importantly, children organized their groups along different dimensions than the adults did. We classified the sorting explanations into five categories and calculated the proportion of groups that were of each type. The five categories are as follows: (1) *superordinate,* in which the subject referred to one of the four categories in the event; (2) *action,* in which only an event action was given as the basis for sorting; (3) *object,* in which only a common ingredient or utensil was mentioned; (4) *action–object,* in which both a common action and object were described; and (5) *other,* in which complexes and unjustified groupings were combined. Complexes were explained by listing the individual actions or action–object pairings. The proportions of groups that were of each type, along with examples, are reported in Table 4.4.

Table 4.4. *Proportion of sorting responses as a function of age and type*

	Explanation type				
	Superordinate	Action	Action–object	Object	Complexes or unjustified
Examples:	Adding dry things	Pouring things	Pouring water	All these have flour	Pour & mix I don't know
Children	.29	.11	.09	.38	.13
Adults	.53	.33	.10	.00	.03

Adults were most likely to justify their groups using a superordinate label, but they also used actions. In contrast, children referred to an object most often to explain their groupings. Some children did, however, rely on superordinate and action explanations. Still others were confused about why they had sorted the pictures as they did and were unable to explain their groups. This difficulty resulted in higher proportions of descriptions of the individual actions selected (i.e., complexes) and unjustified explanations than for adults. College students produced more superordinate and action explanations than children, whereas children produced more object and unjustified explanations than college students ($p < .05$). The superordinate, action, and action–object groups accounted for as much as 97% of adults' responses, whereas these three categories accounted for only 48% of children's explanations.

This pattern was repeated when we presented the superordinate groups for identification. When the pictures were sorted into the four superordinate categories, 86% of the adults' responses involved superordinate explanations, but only 27% of the children's responses reflected superordinate reasoning. Those children who did provide more superordinate explanations in the sorting task were very likely to be the same children who identified more of the superordinates when we sorted them, ($r = .92, p < .001$).

Children were most likely to sort and identify categories that contained actions most causally central to the event (Padgett & Ratner, 1987). Two-thirds of their own superordinate sorts involved either adding the dry or liquid ingredients. Only one-fourth involved the get-ready actions, and less than one-tenth involved mixing the clay together. This suggests that causal connections between the actions underlie the organization of these categories.

Mixing the clay together was not salient in the children's sorts either. Yet, when we asked children to identify the superordinates *we* sorted,

35% of their correct identifications involved the mixing actions. Apparently, they encode these actions (which are defined by adults as the most critical in the event) but do not spontaneously organize them together. Not surprisingly, 47% of the children's correct identifications were either dry- or liquid-ingredient actions and only 18% involved getting ready.

Children did identify some of the superordinate categories and could spontaneously produce superordinate and action groupings. In accordance with the results of our first study, some parts of the hierarchical structure were in place after one event experience. Children's recall reflected this organization even more clearly.

Recall results. The number of actions reported before cuing was compared to the total number of unique actions reported both before and after cuing. If actions in the event are organized by category and can be verbally accessed, their labels should serve as effective cues and improve recall. Children did report more information after cuing, but only in response to two of the cues, *get ready* (2.0 vs. 4.2) and *add the liquid ingredients* (1.9 vs. 2.5) ($ps < .05$). Just as in our first study, *add the dry ingredients* (2.6 vs. 3.2) did not serve as an effective cue. Providing the label, *mix together,* also did not improve recall significantly (3.2 vs. 3.7). Thus, our earlier conclusion that few links existed between superordinates and subordinates was conservative because of the cue we chose to use. The fact that two of the cues were effective in the present study confirms that superordinate category labels did organize some of the subordinate actions and that they aided access of event information. Nevertheless, it is also clear that both levels were not entirely integrated. (Adult performance could not be examined. Their recall was at ceiling during both free [$M = 21.5$] and cued recall [$M = 22.5$]).

Summary. The results of the sorting task suggest that preschoolers were less likely than college students to use the hierarchically structured information in the event. Children seem to have focused on the objects as the basis of their memory organization, whereas adults used superordinate and action categories to organize the episode. Children's greater difficulty creating these categories is not particularly surprising. Tasks that require abstraction of even object categories can be difficult for young children (see Mandler, 1983). Furthermore, the elements to be organized in these tasks are actions. In comparison to objects, action concepts (i.e., verbs) are organized less cohesively (Graesser, Hopkinson, & Schmid, 1987; Huttenlocher & Lui, 1979) and are organized along dimensions of similarity later in development (e.g., Brown & Berko, 1960). This suggests that hierarchical organization of actions would be more difficult than even objects, and indeed, children did not organize these actions as abstractly as adults. This difference occurred in spite of the fact that the actions in the event were related to the superordinate goals in a part–whole fashion. Collections, which are organized on the basis of part–whole relations, are easier for children to organize than classes (Markman, 1981). Therefore, children might have performed similarly to adults in the present task. Perhaps the relational characteristics of the classified entity (i.e., actions vs. objects) exerts as much, if not more, influence on performance than the form of the relationship that binds the group together.

As in our first study, children did find some of the most central categories in the event meaningful. When they received the category labels as cues, their recall improved. These findings mirror children's organization and use of object categories in recall. If asked to produce categories, children often use a different and less abstract scheme of organization than adults (e.g., Flavell, 1985). Yet their recall is improved when they are cued with taxonomic category labels that organize and describe the items in the to-be-remembered list (e.g., Myers & Perlmutter, 1978). Children apparently generate hierarchically organized representations of both object and action categories but are not able to benefit fully from the structures they create.

Children are not the only ones who do not make full use of their organizational skills. The college students did not rely exclusively on hierarchically organized categories to structure the event either. They created more superordinate categories than the children, but many of their categories were based on actions or action–object relations. The extent to which hierarchical organization is used, then, may depend less on the developmental level of the individual and more on the factors relevant to the event and the context in which it is experienced. As is becoming increasingly clear, knowledge structures share more similarities than differences across different ages (e.g., Chi & Ceci, 1987).

One factor that may influence recall and organization of an event is the perceptibility of its causal chain (Trabasso & van den Broek, 1985). The clay-making event has many steps whose interrelationships are complex and varied. Young children do not comprehend its causal structure as well as older children and adults, even though kindergartners do recall more of the actions that are most causally related to the goal of the event (e.g., Smith et al., 1987). A separate sample of kindergartners and second-graders was presented with clay that was either too dry or too liquid to appropriately be called "clay." We asked them to tell us what had gone wrong. Even second-graders were much better able than kindergartners to identify the problem and to explain which steps in the event were critical in producing the outcome. Thus, if adults and children in the sorting and recall studies had understood the event equally well, organization of the event probably would have been more similar. It is not that individuals organize events differently because they are young or old; they organize events differently because they understand them or not (e.g., Chi, 1978). This is not to say that our results are inconsequential. Children do not understand many of the events in which they participate. Many of their activities are organized by adults and are motivated by goals and plans that are not their own (Nelson & Gruendel, 1986).

Memory and organization of familiar events

Matching study

Rationale. If event processing depends on factors other than age, adults and children should organize events similarly in some situations and differently in others. To explore these similarities and differences and to replicate our earlier findings, we decided to examine organization in a matching task. If our results were generalizable to a new task, we could be more confident that we described characteristics representative of more general processing rather than behaviors restricted to the clay-making event.

Procedure. In this study we presented college students and kindergartners with 21 sets of three actions each. Their task was to choose which two actions in the set went together best. On each trial, two items matched along one dimension, two matched along another dimension, and two were unrelated. Three different problem types were presented: (1) superordinate–subordinate; (2) superordinate–object; and (3) subordinate–object. They are described in the paragraphs that follow, and examples are presented in Table 4.5.

In superordinate matches the two actions went together because they were parts of a larger event; that is, together they accomplished a higher goal. For example, *dust the table* and *wash the floor* were superordinate matches because if performed together, they would accomplish the goal of housecleaning.

In subordinate matches the actions were identical but were performed on different objects. For example, one of the subordinate matches was *wash the floor* and *wash the apple*. Although we have called these matching action pairs subordinate to be consistent with our previous studies, it is important to note that these are basic-level categories. These actions share the same name but are different instantiations of that name; that is, they are performed on different objects.

In object matches the actions differed but the objects were the same. Grouping *roll the bat* and *swing the bat* would be an example of an object

Table 4.5. *Examples of problem and match types*

Problem types	Match types			
	Superordinate	Subordinate	Object	Unrelated
Superordinate–subordinate	Dust the table Wash the floor	Wash the floor Wash the apple	X[a] X	Dust the table Wash the apple
Superordinate–object	Swing the bat Throw the ball	X X	Swing the bat Roll the bat	Roll the bat Throw the ball
Subordinate–object	X X	Wave the flag Wave the scarf	Wave the scarf Tie the scarf	Wave the flag Tie the scarf

[a]An X indicates that a match of that type is not possible for the given problem.

match. The items for object matches were chosen so that the two actions were not likely to accomplish a common goal.

If the subject chose two actions that shared no common goal, action, or object, an unrelated match was made.

Actions such as *dust the table, wash the floor,* and *wash the apple* were presented together in superordinate–subordinate problems. If the subject chose *dust the table* and *wash the floor,* he or she made a superordinate match. If *wash the floor* and *wash the apple* were chosen, a subordinate match was made. If *dust the table* and *wash the apple* were chosen, an unrelated match was made. This problem type and the various matches that could be made are illustrated on the first line of Table 4.5.

Superordinate–object problems involved actions such as, *roll the bat, swing the bat,* and *throw the ball.* If *swing the bat* and *throw the ball* were chosen, a superordinate match was made. If *roll the bat* and *swing the bat* were chosen, an object match was made. If *roll the bat* and *throw the ball* were chosen, an unrelated match was made. This problem type is presented on the second line of Table 4.5.

The last problem type was subordinate–object, in which two items matched because the actions were the same and two items matched because the object was the same. For example, the following three actions could make up a subordinate–object problem: *wave the flag, wave the scarf,* and *tie the scarf.* A subordinate match would involve *wave the flag* and *wave the scarf,* whereas an object match would involve *wave the scarf* and *tie the scarf.* This problem type is shown on the third line of Table 4.5.

Seven problems of each of the three types were presented to three groups of twelve college students and one group of ten 4-year-olds. Two of the three adult groups were given the problems in written form. In one of these groups, we asked subjects to choose the two items that went

Table 4.6. *Number of subjects who preferred particular match types (total N in parentheses)*

Match Type	Age and condition			
	Adults Written Standard (12)	Adults Written Causal (12)	Adults Picture Causal (12)	Preschoolers Picture Causal (10)
Superordinate–subordinate	6	12	11	5
	6	0	1	4[a]
Superordinate–object	7	11	6	4
	5	1	6	6
Subordinate–object	11	4	1	3[a]
	1	6	11	6

[a]One subject did not consistently choose one type over another.

together best (standard instructions). In the other, we asked subjects to choose the two that went together best to make something else happen (causal, or superordinate, instructions). The third adult group and the one group of children were also given causal instructions, but for these two groups the items were depicted in photographs. We were concerned that children would have difficulty solving the problems if the items were not depicted, and we wanted to see if mode of presentation would affect the choices. When items were depicted, the background was always the same because the three actions and context cues were eliminated.

Results. The first question we wished to answer was whether children and adults responded consistently in the task. We looked to see if subjects chose the related matches more often than would occur by chance. In Table 4.6, the number of people in each of the four groups who chose each type of match more often than by chance is reported for the three problem types. All the adults in each of the three conditions showed a clear preference for one of the two types of related items available in each problem. Two children responded randomly; one when solving the superordinate–subordinate problems, and the other, when solving the subordinate–object problems. Nevertheless, the majority of children preferred one of the two types of related matches. Thus, for every problem type in every condition, a significant number of adults and children consistently preferred related over unrelated matches.

The next question was whether a significant number of people within each group for each problem type chose one type of match over another. Specifically, did adults prefer superordinate matches in the

Table 4.7. *Mean number of matches made by type, age, and condition*

| Match type | Age and condition | | | |
	Adults written standard	Adults written causal	Adults picture causal	Preschoolers picture causal
Superordinate–subordinate	3.5[a] *	5.8	5.6 *	4.1
	3.4 *	1.0	1.3 *	2.6
Superordinate–object	4.1	4.7 *	3.5	2.6
	2.8	2.0 *	3.5	3.8
Subordinate–object	4.9 *	3.1 **	2.0	2.8
	1.8 *	3.3 *	4.9	3.8

[a]Differences between adjacent pairs of means are indicated by the asterisks between them and are significant at the indicated levels: * $p < .05$, ** $p < .10$.

superordinate–subordinate and superordinate–object problems? Did adults prefer subordinate matches in the subordinate–object problems? Did children prefer object matches in the two object problems and subordinate actions in the superordinate–subordinate problems? These are the patterns we would expect if the results from the clay-making studies generalize to this task. We did find support for this pattern but the results, especially for the subordinate–object problems, were more complex because consistent patterns within age group also depended on instructions and mode of presentation.

Superordinate–subordinate problems are considered first. We will start by examining the performance of the three groups who were instructed the same: the children and the two adult groups who received causal (super-ordinate) instructions. Their data appear in the second, third, and fourth columns of Table 4.6. As expected, the adults preferred superordinate matches, whereas the children did not prefer either type. In Table 4.7, the mean number of matches made of each type is given. Children chose more subordinate and fewer superordinate matches than the adults. Both sets of results, then, are consistent with and confirm our earlier findings that adults are more likely to create superordinate categories and children are more likely to create subordinate, or basic-level, categories.

The choices of the adult group who received standard instructions are an exception to this pattern. Adults in this group were asked to choose the items that went together best and no mention of accomplishing a higher goal was made. In contrast to the other adult groups, these sub-jects did not choose either type of match more frequently than the other (see Table 4.6). As a consequence, they chose fewer superordinate and more subordinate matches than the other two adult groups (see Table 4.7). Apparently, causal reasoning needs to be evoked before adults select superordinate matches. Superordinate groupings may have been created more often in the clay-making task because the actions in the event had just been performed. The goal, which binds the actions together into a causal sequence, is a tangible accomplishment and may structure the event into part–whole relations. We suggested earlier that acting may focus children's attention away from the action and toward its arguments (i.e., actors, objects, locations, instruments); but for adults, acting may increase attention to the causal sequence. The difference may depend on whether the actions can be organized causally and whether the causal structure is understood. Whatever the reason, even adults do not always process events in a superordinate fashion. This is consistent with our suggestion that hierarchical processing is more a matter of understanding and context than developmental level.

Superordinate–object problems are considered next. The similarity between adults and children is even more apparent here. Only when the items are presented in written form and causal instructions are given, do a significant number of adults prefer superordinate matches. Again, for adults to choose superordinate pairs consistently, causal reasoning must be evoked.

Subordinate–object problems, the final problem type, led to complex patterns of performance. Performance differences among conditions are less clear because there are no superordinate matches available even though instructions for three of the conditions request superordinate (i.e., causal) thinking. In the standard condition where causal reasoning is not requested adults clearly prefer subordinate matches (matches in which the action is the same but the objects differ). With causal instructions, however, adults are more likely to choose object matches, and do so as frequently as the children.

Why is this the case? It may be easier to construct an event category or event sequence from two different actions performed on the same object than from two identical (and parallel) actions performed on different and unrelated objects. Adults and children choose object matches as often in this problem, but perhaps they have different reasons for doing so. Adults may be able to generate categories that are abstract enough to contain the two unrelated objects, but because of the difficulty of this process, children may choose objects because of their similarity and nothing more.

In order to test this hypothesis, we examined the reasons people gave for the matches they made. Each reason was classified as one of three types: superordinate, subordinate, or object. Superordinate reasons made reference to two actions accomplishing some other goal. Subordi-

Table 4.8. *Percentage of total explanations provided of particular types*

Match type	Explanation type	Adults written standard	Adults written causal	Adults picture causal	Children picture causal
		Age and condition			
Superordinate	Superordinate	69.5	80.8	67.3	27.9
	Subordinate	28.5	19.2	31.5	43.2
	Object	2.0	0.0	1.5	28.9
Subordinate	Superordinate	22.0	38.2	44.2	10.0
	Subordinate	78.0	54.2	55.8	88.0
	Object	0.0	7.5	0.0	2.0
Object	Superordinate	0.0	30.3	0.0	2.0
	Subordinate	69.0	64.7	86.9	17.0
	Object	31.0	4.9	13.1	81.0

nate reasons named a common action or described the two actions as occurring in sequence. Object reasons referred to a common object, object property, or object location. In Table 4.8, the percentage of each of the possible reasons is given for each match type. We collapsed across the three problem types to simplify the table.

Our predictions were partially confirmed. For object matches children overwhelmingly gave object reasons. When superordinate reasons were supplied, adults were more likely to give them; but subordinate reasons were adults' more frequent response. Usually a sequence between the two dissimilar actions was constructed.

The children's greater reliance on objects and their properties is also apparent when considering the reasons given for the superordinate matches. Although we had selected the pairs because the two actions accomplished a higher goal, the children found an object-related reason to link them together almost a third of the time. Adults' reasons were much more likely to match our own for including the items in the task. In fact, the percentage of superordinate reasons given by adults (72.5) and children (27.9) for the superordinate matches closely matched the justification responses given by adults (86.0) and children (27.0) in the sorting study.

Finally, for subordinate matches, both children and adults were most likely to give subordinate reasons.

Summary. The results of this matching study show that children are more likely than adults to base their categories of actions on the objects these actions share. Adults, in contrast, more often rely on superordinate and subordinate categories to organize the same actions. When actions can be organized along multiple dimensions, older children and adults are most likely to focus on the action itself and not on the actor or objects involved (Foley & Johnson, 1985). Their categories reflect similarities in the action's form or function. This sequence is reminiscent of the development of action concepts themselves. Huttenlocher, Smiley, and Charney (1983) showed that verbs referring to actions with which objects are highly associated (e.g., sweep, drink, wash) are among those learned first. Only later are verbs that encode complex goals acquired. Indeed, Huttenlocher & Lui (1979) argue that actions are conceptually dependent upon objects for meaning. When organizing actions in an event younger children may focus on these more elementary units. Thus, the organization of actions within events may reflect the same processes that are responsible for the acquisition of individual action concepts. In essence, the formation of superordinate action categories may involve the same procedures that generate basic-level categories.

Therefore, the findings from our clay-making studies do seem to reflect differences between adults and children that are more broadly representative of event processing. These differences in organization have implications not only for organization within episodes but also for organization between episodes. When an event is experienced more than once, a representation is formed that is more general than any of the separate episodes it comprises (e.g., Nelson & Gruendel, 1981), but a basic question concerns the relationship among representations of separate episodes of the same event. Which cues are used to determine similarity? Common goals? Common actions? Common objects? Common locations? These findings suggest that children may rely more on common objects and their properties, including location, than adults. Adults may focus more on common goals and actions. Mandler (1984b) suggests a similar sequence during infancy and childhood: "[T]he initial basis for forming units in an event schema may be more primitive than a goal-based analysis, perhaps involving instead analysis in terms of objects, their locations, and changes in their locations over time" (p. 89).

As we have mentioned before, the performance differences between adults and children are probably best considered as an interaction between the demands of the task and the prior experience of the participants involved; it is a mistake to focus principally on age per se. For instance, Mandler, in the quote above, was describing the cues that *infants* might use in forming event representations. She suggested that goal-based analyses of events are achieved at least by the preschool years. Yet we have seen that this does not always occur for preschoolers or even adults. We are suggesting, then, that as one understands more of the causal connections in an episode, he or she is more likely to rely on goals and actions to guide processing of the episode and those related to it in subsequent encounters. Among other factors, the likelihood of understanding these connections appears to be based on the length and complexity of the event, how much attention is focused on its goal, and prior experience (Mandler, 1986).

Sorting study

Rationale. With greater experience children should come to understand the hierarchical structure of an event more clearly, and this understanding should be reflected in event recall and organization. Means and Voss (1985) found exactly this result. They selected children and adults who had seen the movies *Star Wars* and *The Empire Strikes Back* many times (four or more) or only a few (three or fewer). These experts and novices from second grade through college were asked to identify basic actions, subgoals, and high-level goals of the stories' protagonists. Experts correctly identified more subgoals and high-level goals than novices at each grade level, indicating that more of the movies' hierarchical structure was understood and remembered by those with more experience. Experts and novices performed differently, however, at different ages, especially with respect to high-level goals. The differences between experts and novices widened as age increased. As individuals grow older they apparently benefit more from experience.

These results are consistent with a study in which we varied experience with the clay-making event. Children who made clay several times came to organize the event differently than those who made clay only once. Furthermore, older and younger children learned differently from their experience.

Procedure. Kindergartners and fourth-graders participated in the clay-making event once or four times. For the first group, then, it was novel; for the second, it was familiar. The procedures used were virtually identical to those of our earlier studies. The event was made up of 30 actions, organized into five superordinate categories of 6 actions each: get ready, add the dry ingredients, add the liquid ingredients, mix the clay together, and clean up. Seven to 9 days after children made clay for the last time, they recalled the event and then received the superordinate category labels as cues. Next, they sorted pictures of the clay-making events into groups and explained the reasons for their groups. To complete the task, we sorted the pictures into the five superordinate groups and asked the children to explain the basis for our organization.

Table 4.9 *Mean number of superordinate labels and subordinate actions reported*

Grade	Experience	Superordinate		Subordinate	
		Free	Total	Free	Total
Kindergarten	Novel	.6	.6	4.6	11.4
	Familiar	1.8	2.2	5.4	12.4
Fourth	Novel	2.0	2.3	8.5	16.3
	Familiar	2.4	2.4	13.8	22.2

Recall results. Our results are only preliminary, so our conclusions must be regarded as tentative. We coded protocols from five subjects in each age and experience group. In Table 4.9 the number of superordinate and subordinate actions reported before (free recall) and after cuing (total recall) appear. For all groups, cuing with the superordinate labels led to greater recall of the subordinate actions. Again, we have evidence that these subdivisions of the event had meaning for the participants and facilitated recall. Cuing did not increase superordinate recall, however. We did not find that reporting actions within one category cued recall of the superordinate, so cross-category cuing only seems to occur from superordinate to superordinate and not from subordinate to superordinate.

Children also recalled more of the subordinate actions when the event was familiar. Both before and after cuing, more of the subordinate actions were produced after participating in the event four times. In contrast, only the kindergartners reported more of the superordinates after greater experience with the event. This is consistent with our earlier findings that only portions of a hierarchical structure are actively used or reproduced by children after only one experience. But it is clear that this structure can become more elaborated with additional experience – at least when the hierarchical structure is verbally described during the event.

Sorting results. We examined the number of categories created, the percentage of these groups for which the children gave superordinate or object explanations, and the percentage of superordinate categories that were recognized during the identification task. We suggested earlier that superordinate labels may come truly to organize the actions they summarize and that two separate levels of organization become integrated with experience. If so, then children should produce and identify more superordinate categories as the event becomes familiar. Fourth-graders' performance in this task was consistent with our prediction. The familiar-event group created fewer categories than the novel-event group (6.6 vs. 9.8) and produced almost twice as many superordinate categories in their sorts (65.4% vs. 37.0%). The percentage of superordinates correctly identified when we sorted the pictures into the five categories also increased (55% vs. 68%). In addition, the percentage of object groups dropped dramatically (34% vs. 1.6%). When objects were identified, they were always mentioned in combination with actions. The younger children's performance did not differ much with additional experience.

Summary. Although these findings are tentative, they support our contention that changes in event organization are related to the frequency of experiencing the event and are not solely dependent on the age of the participant. At the same time, older children apprehend the hierarchical structure of the event more easily than kindergartners and profit more from additional experience. In addition, their category sorts are more consistent with their recall. The younger children could make use of the superordinate labels as cues and reported more of them after experiencing the event more often, but they were not very likely to identify the superordinates or to create groups based on them. These findings support and extend our earlier conclusions that after one experience some of the superordinate structure is represented and used to facilitate recall regardless of age.

General summary and conclusions

From the first encounter with a new experience, children are active organizers of an event and its memory. Actions are collected together to form categories within the sequence and these parts are connected to higher goals that define the episode. Children can provide descriptions of an event that summarize its components and do not focus solely on isolated bits of information that may be salient to them.

Although the process of creating a script is evident at very young ages, changes in this process occur as children grow older. Younger children do not generate an integrated hierarchy as easily as older children or adults. Some of the categories and links between them may be represented only through language, and only some of the more causally central categories may be created at all. Not all of these categories appear to be linked to one another. This indicates that the causal connections among actions guide initial encoding and help define the categories that are constructed.

Younger children focus less on actions and goals in an event when they understand the sequence less completely or when their attention is directed to other action components. In both the sorting and the matching tasks, younger children relied more on objects and their properties, including location, to organize the event actions. More concrete aspects of the event seem to guide their construction of it, just as objects are more likely to aid comprehension of action concepts earlier in development.

With greater experience, however, children focus more on actions and their goals and rely less on objects as organizing cues. We found that as the event was experienced more often more of the category structure emerged. In previous research we have also found that additional experience leads to more frequent recall of the most causally central actions (Smith et al., 1987). Apprehending more and more of the event's causal structure may be related to developing a hierarchically organized representation of an event. Certainly in the matching task, even adults were more likely to think about actions as parts of an event when their attention was directed to the causal relation between actions and the goals they accomplish. Thus, the extent to which hierarchical organization is used seems to depend on factors relevant to the event and its context, such as attention to the event's goal, the complexity of the sequence, and perhaps which aspects of the event are labeled or who participates.

Greater experience with an event also influences how it is remembered, and how it is remembered may influence the nature of the event's representation. More actions and more of the categories within the hierarchical structure were reported as the event became familiar. Furthermore, these categories were maintained in an event's representation over time and were used to direct recall on subsequent occasions. In our first study we found that when children received a category cue during recall they incorporated the label into their subsequent reports and used it to organize recall. The act of recalling information again and again and using these categories to direct recall may contribute substantially to the presence of categories, or scenes, in scripts. Organization may reflect not only direct experience but reflections on it. Categories that are used initially to structure memory of a novel event or its report may become incorporated into a generalized representation of multiple experiences or may be used to generate a description of what happens during the occurrence of a prototypical instance.

NOTE

The first author was supported by grant #MCJ-260554-01-0 from the Division of Maternal and Child Health, Bureau of Health Care Delivery and Assistance while writing this report. We would like to thank the children and parents of the

Child Development Laboratory School, Wayne State University, and its director, Elizabeth Marriott. Thanks are also due Rick Sweet and David Daniel for their help in data collection. Portions of this research were presented to the Society for Research on Child Development, April 1987, Baltimore, MD.

REFERENCES

Barrett, M. (1986). Early semantic representations and early word usage. In S. Kuczaj & M. Barrett (Eds.), *The development of word meaning* (pp. 39–67). New York: Springer-Verlag.

Barsalou, L., & Sewell, D. (1985). Contrasting the representation of scripts and categories. *Journal of Memory and Language, 24*, 646–665.

Brown, R., & Berko, J. (1960). Word association and the acquisition of grammar. *Child Development, 31*, 1–14.

Bruner, J., Olver, R., & Greenfield, P. (1966). *Studies in cognitive growth.* New York: Wiley.

Chi, M. T. H. (1978). Knowledge structures and memory development. In R. S. Siegler (Ed.), *Children's thinking: What develops?* (pp. 73–96). Hillsdale, NJ: Erlbaum.

Chi, M. T. H., & Ceci, S. (1987). Content knowledge: Its role, representation, and restructuring in memory development. In H. W. Reese (Ed.), *Advances in child development and behavior* (Vol. 10, pp. 91–142). Orlando, FL: Academic Press.

Denney, N., & Ziobrowski, M. (1972). Developmental changes in clustering criteria. *Journal of Experimental Child Psychology, 13*, 275–282.

Fivush, R., Hudson, J., & Nelson, K. (1984). Children's long-term memory of a novel event: An exploratory study. *Merrill-Palmer Quarterly, 30*, 303–316.

Flavell, J. (1985). *Cognitive development.* Englewood Cliffs, NJ: Prentice-Hall.

Foellinger, D., & Trabasso, T. (1977). Seeing, hearing and doing: A developmental study of memory for actions. *Child Development, 48*, 1482–1489.

Foley, M. A., & Johnson, M. (1985). Confusions between memories for performed and imagined actions: A developmental comparison. *Child Development, 56*, 1145–1155.

Galambos, J., & Rips, L. (1982). Memory for routines. *Journal of Verbal Learning and Verbal Behavior, 21*, 260–281.

Graesser, A., Hopkinson, P., & Schmid, C. (1987). Differences in interconcept organization between nouns and verbs. *Journal of Memory and Language, 26*, 242–253.

Huttenlocher, J., & Lui, F. (1979). The semantic organization of some simple nouns and verbs. *Journal of Verbal Learning and Verbal Behavior, 18*, 141–162.

Huttenlocher, J., Smiley, P., & Charney, R. (1983). Emergence of action categories in the child: Evidence from verb meaning. *Psychological Review, 90*, 72–101.

Inhelder, B., & Piaget, J. (1964). *The early growth of logic in the child.* New York: Norton.

Johnson, L., Perlmutter, M., & Trabasso, T. (1979). The leg bone is connected to the knee bone: Children's representation of body parts in memory, drawing, and language. *Child Development, 50*, 1192–1202.

Kintsch, W., & van Dijk, T. (1978). Toward a model of text comprehension and production. *Psychological Review, 85*, 363–394.

Lange, G., & Jackson, P. (1974). Personal organization in children's free recall. *Child Development, 45,* 1060–1067.

Liberty, C., & Ornstein, P. (1973). Age differences in organization and recall. *Journal of Experimental Child Psychology, 15,* 169–186.

Lucariello, J., & Nelson, K. (1985). Slot-filler categories as organizers for young children. *Developmental Psychology, 21,* 272–282.

Mandler, J. (1983). Representation. In J. H. Flavell & E. M. Markman (Eds.), *Handbook of child psychology: Vol. 3, Cognitive Development* (4th ed., pp. 420–494). New York: Wiley.

Mandler, J. (1984a). *Stories, scripts, and scenes: Aspects of schema theory.* Hillsdale, NJ: Erlbaum.

Mandler, J. (1984b). Representation and recall in infancy. In M. Moscovitch (Ed.), *Infant memory* (pp. 75–100). New York: Plenum.

Mandler, J. (1986). The development of event memory. In F. Klix & H. Hagendorf (Eds.), *Human memory and cognitive capabilities: Mechanisms and performance* (pp. 459–467). New York: Elsevier North-Holland.

Mandler, J., & Murphy, C. (1983). Subjective judgments of script structure. *Journal of Experimental Psychology: Learning, Memory, and Cognition, 9,* 534–543.

Markman, E. M. (1981). Two different principles of conceptual organization. In M. Lamb & A. Brown (Eds.), *Advances in developmental psychology* (Vol. 1, pp. 199–236). Hillsdale, NJ: Erlbaum.

Markman, E., Cox, B., & Machida, S. (1981). The standard object-sorting task as a measure of conceptual organization. *Developmental Psychology, 17,* 115–117.

Means, M., & Voss, J. (1985). Star wars: A developmental study of expert and novice knowledge structures. *Journal of Memory and Language, 24,* 746–757.

McCartney, K., & Nelson, K. (1981). Children's use of scripts in story recall. *Discourse Processes, 4,* 59–70.

Moely, B. (1977). Organizational factors in the development of memory. In R. Kail & J. Hagen (Eds.), *Perspectives on the development of memory and cognition* (pp. 203–236). Hillsdale, NJ: Erlbaum.

Myers, N., & Bluhm, C. (1985, April). *Preschool children's memory for a classroom event.* Paper presented at the meeting of the Society for Research in Child Development, Toronto, Ontario.

Myers, N., & Perlmutter, M. (1978). Memory in the years from two to five (pp. 191–218). In P. A. Ornstein (Ed.), *Memory development in children.* Hillsdale, NJ: Erlbaum.

Myles-Worsley, M., Cromer, C., & Dodd, D. (1986). Children's preschool script reconstruction: Reliance on general knowledge as memory fades. *Developmental Psychology, 22,* 22–30.

Nelson, K. (1982). The syntagmatics and paradigmatics of conceptual representation. In S. Kuczaj (Ed.), *Language development: Language, thought and culture* (pp. 335–364). Hillsdale, NJ: Erlbaum.

Nelson, K. (1986a). *Event knowledge: Structure and function in development.* Hillsdale, NJ: Erlbaum.

Nelson, K. (1986b). Event knowledge and cognitive development. In K. Nelson (Ed.), *Event knowledge: Structure and function in development* (pp. 1–19). Hillsdale, NJ: Erlbaum.

Nelson, K., & Gruendel, J. (1981). Generalized event representations: Basic building blocks of cognitive development. In M. E. Lamb & A. L. Brown (Eds.), *Advances in developmental psychology* (Vol. 1, pp. 131–158). Hillsdale, NJ: Erlbaum.

Nelson, K., & Gruendel, J. (1986). Children's scripts. In K. Nelson (Ed.), *Event knowledge: Structure and function in development* (pp. 21–46). Hillsdale, NJ: Erlbaum.

Nottenburg, G., & Shoben, E. (1980). Scripts as linear orders. *Journal of Experimental Social Psychology, 16*, 329–347.

Omanson, R. (1982). The relation between centrality and story category variation. *Journal of Verbal Learning and Verbal Behavior, 21*, 326–337.

Padgett, R., & Ratner, H. (1987). Older and younger adults' memory for structured and unstructured events. *Experimental Aging Research, 13*, 133–139.

Pillemer, D., & White, S. (in press). Childhood events recalled by children and adults. In H. W. Reese (Ed.), *Advances in child development and behavior* (Vol. 22). New York: Academic Press.

Ratner, H., Smith, B., & Dion, S. (1986). Development of memory for events. *Journal of Experimental Child Psychology, 41*, 411–428.

Rosch, E., Mervis, C., Gray, W., Johnson, D., & Boyes-Braem, P. (1976). Basic objects in natural categories. *Cognitive Psychology, 8*, 382–439.

Saltz, E., Soller, E., & Sigel, I. (1972). The development of natural language concepts. *Child Development, 43*, 1191–1202.

Schank, R., & Abelson, R. (1977). *Scripts, plans, goals, and understanding.* Hillsdale, NJ: Erlbaum.

Seidman, S., Nelson, K., & Gruendel, J. (1986). Make believe scripts: The transformation of ERs in fantasy. In K. Nelson (Ed.), *Event knowledge: Structure and function in development* (pp. 161–187). Hillsdale, NJ: Erlbaum.

Slackman, E., Hudson, J., & Fivush, R. (1986). Actions, actors, links, and goals: The structure of children's event representations. In K. Nelson (Ed.), *Event knowledge: Structure and function in development* (pp. 47–69). Hillsdale, NJ: Erlbaum.

Smith, B., Ratner, H., & Hobart, C. (1987). The role of cuing and organization in children's memory for events. *Journal of Experimental Child Psychology, 44*, 1–24.

Thorndyke, P. (1977). Cognitive structures in comprehension and memory of narrative discourse. *Cognitive Psychology, 9*, 77–110.

Trabasso, T., & Sperry, L. (1985). Causal relatedness and importance of story events. *Journal of Memory and Language, 24*, 595–611.

Trabasso, T., & van den Broek, P. (1985). Causal thinking and the representation of narrative events. *Journal of Memory and Language, 24*, 612–630.

Whitney, P., & Kunen, S. (1983). Development of hierarchical conceptual relationships in children's semantic memory. *Journal of Experimental Child Psychology, 35*, 278–293.

Worden, P. (1975). Effects of sorting on subsequent recall of unrelated items: A developmental study. *Child Development, 46*, 687–695.

5

Young children's understanding of models

JUDY S. DeLOACHE

Memory obviously plays a central role in cognitive development, and developmental researchers have always been concerned with what experiences and information children remember and why they remember those things. Of equal importance, however, is the transfer of what is remembered about one situation to other situations. Without the ability to generalize or transfer, everything a child learned and remembered would remain specific to the particular context in which it was first acquired. There could be no general skills or knowledge.

Understanding when and how transfer occurs is a basic problem in the study of memory and memory development (Brown & Campione, 1984). It is especially important to determine what conditions influence children's perception of the relation between two situations, objects, or events: The realization that one thing or event is in some way like another is a prerequisite to transferring what is known about one to the other (Gentner, 1983; Gick & Holyoak, 1980, 1983; Holyoak, Junn, & Billman, 1984). This chapter concerns a marked discontinuity, not in young children's ability to remember some information about an event but in their propensity to transfer or apply their memory of that information to a different, but related, situation.

Consider a 2½-year-old who watches carefully as an adult hides an appealing toy dog behind the couch in a room. The child and adult leave the room for some period of time. When they return, the adult asks the child, "Where's Snoopy? Can you find Snoopy?" Most 2½-year-old children, on most such occasions, immediately find the hidden toy.

This scenario exemplifies the well-established fact that very young children are very competent at remembering the location of hidden objects. When asked to retrieve an object hidden in a distinctive location in a differentiated space, they succeed in doing so 80% or more of the time (DeLoache, 1985). Young children are clearly capable of attending to a hiding event, encoding the information about the location of the object, and retrieving that information from memory. An important part of the retrieval process is their recognition of the appropriate context for

94

retrieval; upon reentering the room, they know to use their memory for the location of the hidden object to guide their search.

Consider a second 2½-year-old child who watches as an adult places an appealing toy dog behind the couch in a room. The child is then asked to find not the toy that he just saw being hidden in the room, but a miniature toy dog hidden in the corresponding place in a scale model of the room. Most 2½-year-old children, on most such occasions, fail to find the hidden toy.

The difference in performance in these two situations is surprisingly large. In both cases, the children remember the location of the toy they saw being hidden: If the child in the second example returns to the room and is asked to find the toy he originally watched being hidden, he can do so. Thus, the 2½-year-old's failure to find the miniature toy in the model is not a simple memory problem. The real difficulty seems to be that the child does not recognize the model as a context in which it is appropriate to retrieve and apply his memory for the hiding event he observed in the room.

The 2½-year-old's failure in this situation is especially surprising in view of the fact that children only a few months older are extremely successful in it. Most 3-year-olds who see the toy being hidden in the room know just where to find the miniature toy in the model.

The above example represents a situation in which the young child's problem is not in forming a memory of some experience but in knowing when to use that memory, in recognizing its relevance to a context different from that in which it was originally acquired. It does an individual little good to have a memory representation if that representation is not activated at the appropriate time. This example (involving the understanding of a scale model) concerns the general problem of the detection of correspondence, a problem that lies at the heart of the classic areas of transfer and analogical reasoning. Both transfer and analogical reasoning depend on recognition of the correspondence between two entities, x and y. Something about one's perception of y provides access to one's knowledge representation of x. That knowledge can then be used to help achieve a better understanding of y. If y fails to activate x, one's existing skills and knowledge are not brought to bear to comprehend or solve y. Transfer and reasoning by analogy require flexible access, the activation of a representation by a variety of objects or contexts similar, but not identical, to those involved in its acquisition.

It is becoming increasingly clear that accessibility and the flexible application of knowledge can be surprisingly problematic for individuals of any age (e.g., Gentner, 1989; Gick & Holyoak, 1980, 1983). These processes have long been considered especially unreliable early in development (Mandler, 1983, 1988), and children's knowledge often seems restricted to the specific context in which it was acquired (Gelman & Baillargeon, 1983). The puzzle of predicting when young children will succeed or fail in applying what they know of one situation to a different one continues to attract the attention of developmental researchers. The research summarized in this chapter concerns a sharp age-related disparity in accessibility, a dramatic developmental shift in young children's detection of a particular type of correspondence relation.

In this chapter, I (1) describe the basic phenomenon – an extremely large difference between the performance of 2½- and 3-year-olds in a task that requires using a scale model; (2) summarize a series of experiments investigating the effect of several variables, including perceptual similarity and explicit instructions, on young children's understanding of the correspondence between a model and the larger space it represents; (3) present another series of studies designed to elucidate why young children find a scale model so difficult to understand; and (4) propose a model for understanding young children's understanding of scale models.

An abrupt developmental shift in understanding the correspondence between a scale model and the large space it represents

The original question motivating this research concerned cognitive flexibility in young children, specifically, their ability to take their memory for something experienced in one context and apply it in a new and different context. A task involving memory for the location of a hidden object was used because previous research had established that very young children have excellent memory for the location of an object hidden in a natural or well-differentiated space (DeLoache, 1985; DeLoache & Brown, 1979, 1983, 1984; DeLoache, Cassidy, & Brown, 1985).

The basic experimental format was that a 2½- or 3-year-old child watched as a small toy was hidden in a scale model of a room. Then the child was asked to find not the small toy, but a larger toy hidden in the analogous location in the room itself. In order to find the larger toy, the child had to (1) recognize the correspondence between the scale model and the larger room and (2) map the location of the hidden toy in the model onto the corresponding location in the room.[1]

The original study will be described in some detail, because all the subsequent research used the same basic method. Each experimental session began with an extensive *orientation* phase during which the experimenter explicitly instructed the child regarding the correspondence between the room and the model. First, she introduced the two toys that would be hidden as "Big Snoopy" (a stuffed dog 15 cm high) and "Little

Snoopy" (a plastic dog 2 cm high). She then oriented the child to the room and to the model, explaining that "This is Big Snoopy's big room, and this is Little Snoopy's little room. Look – their rooms are just alike; they both have all the same things in their rooms." The model (71.1 cm × 64.8 cm × 33.0 cm) was in an adjacent room, in the same spatial orientation as the room (4.80 m × 3.98 m × 2.54 m). It contained miniature versions of all the items of furniture in the room (e.g., couch, chair, dresser, pillows, etc.), arranged in the same relative spatial positions. Next, the experimenter demonstrated the correspondence between the individual pieces of furniture in the two spaces. She carried all the items of furniture from the model into the room and placed each one on its counterpart: "Look – this is Big Snoopy's big couch, and this is Little Snoopy's little couch. They're just the same."

Immediately following the orientation phase, the child received four *experimental trials*, each with three parts: (1) *Hiding Event*. The child watched as the experimenter hid one of the toys in one of the spaces. For half the subjects the hiding event was in the model, for half it was in the room. This variable has never affected the results in any study. (For ease of communication, I shall refer to the case in which the child observed the miniature toy being hidden in the model.) A different hiding place was used for each trial. The experimenter always called the child's attention to the act of hiding ("Look, I'm hiding Little Snoopy here"), but she never referred to the hiding place by name. (2) *Retrieval 1 – Analogous Object*. Without retrieving the toy he or she had seen being hidden, the child was led into the adjoining room and asked to find the analogous toy. Before every retrieval, the child was reminded of the correspondence between the two hiding events ("Remember, Big Snoopy is hiding in the same place as Little Snoopy"). (3) *Retrieval 2 – Original Object*. Next, the child was taken back to the first room and asked to retrieve the original toy that he or she had observed being hidden at the beginning of the trial. Retrieval 2 served as a memory check and was crucial for interpreting the children's behavior on Retrieval 1. If the child could find the original toy on Retrieval 2, poor Retrieval 1 performance could not be due to simple forgetting or lack of motivation.

The subjects for the initial study were 32 children, 16 in a younger group (30–32 months, $M = 31$ months) and 16 in an older group (36–39 months, $M = 38$ months). The sample for this and all subsequent studies was predominately middle class and white.

The results were dramatic. Figure 5.1 shows the proportion of errorless retrievals for the two age groups. (An errorless retrieval is defined as the child searching *first* at the correct location.) The interaction shown in Figure 5.1 is highly significant. The Retrieval 2 data indicate that both age groups knew where the original object was hidden. This

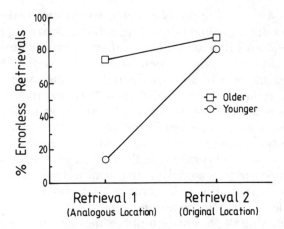

Figure 5.1. Percentage errorless retrievals achieved by the two age groups. (Reprinted from DeLoache, 1987, by permission. Copyright 1987 by the AAAS.)

high level of performance was very comparable to that reported in previous research on young children's memory for location (DeLoache & Brown, 1979, 1983, 1984; DeLoache et al., 1985).

Based on their knowledge of the location of the toy they saw being hidden, the older children also knew where to look for the analogous toy (Retrieval 1). In other words, they used their memory for the location of one hidden object to draw an inference about where a different object must be. This inference came so easily that their success in finding the toy they had not seen being hidden equaled their success in retrieving the toy they had observed being hidden. Unlike the older children, the younger ones drew no inference from their knowledge of where the original object was hidden. Their knowledge of where the miniature dog was concealed in the model was restricted to that situation; they failed to transfer from one space to the other.

One aspect of the model task that makes the younger children's failure even more surprising is that the children very clearly understand the basic memory situation. Brown (1989; Brown & Kane, 1988; Brown, Kane, & Echols, 1986) has argued that transfer can be expected, even for very young children, so long as the underlying structure of the information to be transferred is well understood. She and her colleagues have reported several studies in which analogical transfer is a function of the level of the children's knowledge. The better or the more deeply children understand what they have learned, the more likely they are to transfer to a new, related instance. In the model task, however, the 2½-year-old children have a complete understanding of the original hiding event; nevertheless, they fail to transfer.

One important feature of the younger children's Retrieval 1 behavior in this and all subsequent studies is that they do search for the analogous toy (although they do not make highly systematic errors). They understand (1) that this is a finding game, (2) that there is an analogous toy hidden in the second space, and (3) that they are supposed to search for and find it. However, the 2½-year-olds seem not to realize that they have any basis for knowing where the toy is. To the younger children, then, Retrieval 1 is a guessing game; to the older children, it is a memory or reasoning game.

Further indication that the younger children in the model task regard their experience with the model as being separate from their experience with the room comes from the report that one of our 2½-year-old subjects gave to her mother when asked what she had done in our laboratory. The little girl said that first she had played a game with Little Snoopy and that then "it was Big Snoopy's turn." She seemed to feel she had played one game with Little Snoopy and a different game with Big Snoopy.

The most striking aspect of the results of this study is that so large a difference in performance occurred with such a relatively small difference in age. There was little evidence of intermediate levels of performance, in either the group or individual data; all the younger children did extremely poorly, almost all the older children did very well.

The apparent all-or-none nature of the performance in this task was examined further in a study (DeLoache, 1989b, Experiment 1) that focused on children intermediate in age between the two age groups in the original study. The overall Retrieval 1 performance of a group of 16 children between 33 and 35 months of age was 38% – a figure intermediate between the very high and very low performance of the old and young groups in the first experiment. However, this intermediate level of performance did not reflect a gradual overall improvement between 2½ and 3 years of age. Rather, it reflected the fact that some of the children in the intermediate age group performed extremely poorly and some, extremely well. A close look at aspects of the children's behavior other than their retrieval performance revealed that children who gave independent evidence that they realized that the room and model were related to each other were highly successful at retrieving the analogous toy (75%). Children of the same age who gave no clear sign of awareness of the correspondence were unsuccessful (15%); their knowledge of where the original toy had been hidden remained specific to that toy in that space.

In both the original (DeLoache, 1987) and the intermediate-age study (DeLoache, 1989b), extreme differences in performance were observed. In the former, the large difference in Retrieval 1 performance was between the two age groups; in the latter, the comparably large difference was between the performance of children of a single age who either did or did not give independent evidence of understanding the correspondence between the two spaces. The two studies, taken together, make two main points: (1) Understanding the relation between a scale model and the larger space it represents is quite difficult for young children. They can perform competently within either space, but the correspondence between the two is surprisingly elusive. (2) Sensitivity to this correspondence seems to develop rather abruptly. In these samples, the transition appeared to occur between 34 and 36 months of age.

Understanding the correspondence between the model and room thus appears to be the crucial first step to being able to transfer one's memory for an event from one to the other. According to this line of reasoning, 2½-year-old children – the age group that performed so poorly in the original model study – should show similar difficulty with any task that requires them to understand and use the correspondence between two spaces. In other words, if successful performance in a task demands that the child realize the correspondence between a scale model and a larger space, then 2½-year-olds should fail, regardless of what the task is.

To test this prediction, an experiment was designed in which 2½-year-old children observed the experimenter perform an action in one space and then were asked to imitate that action in the second space. To make the data as comparable as possible to the studies just described, everything was as much like the model task as possible, except for what the child was asked to do. The same extensive orientation as in the standard model task was given to the children. Following it, the experimenter demonstrated one *placement* of the toy. She put either Little or Big Snoopy on its table and then placed the second toy in the corresponding location in its space. As she did so, she informed the child that "Little and Big Snoopy like to do the same things." After this demonstration, the experimental trials began. On each trial, the experimenter placed the toy somewhere in either the room or the model, depending on the condition to which the child had been assigned. She said, "Look, Big [Little] Snoopy is sitting here. Can you put Little [Big] Snoopy in the same place in his room?" The experimenter never named the objects of furniture on which the toys were placed. The same locations (i.e., items of furniture) that served as hiding places in the model task were used for the placements, with a different one used on each trial. The only difference was that the toy was simply *placed on* the piece of furniture rather than hidden behind or under it. A liberal scoring criterion was adopted: If the child put the toy anywhere on the appropriate item of furniture, it was counted as a correct response. (For example, if the experimenter placed the first toy on the left end of the couch, the child's response was scored as correct if his or her toy was anywhere on the couch.)

This imitation task is ideal for the purposes of this study: (1) It requires understanding something about the correspondence between the two spaces for successful performance. (2) It may be simpler than the model task because the child only has to remember where he or she saw the experimenter place the original toy and then duplicate that placement. No retrievals of hidden objects are required. (3) Its close similarity in other respects to the model task facilitates comparison across studies.

The results were exactly as predicted: The older children were highly successful in the imitation task, while the younger ones were very rarely successful. The absolute levels of performance were very similar to those reported in the original model study for the same two age groups – 16% and 15% for the younger groups and 75% and 77% for the older subjects. Thus, young children's performance is almost identical in two different tasks, both of which require understanding the relation between a scale model and a larger space. Furthermore, exactly the same level of performance was achieved by another group of eight subjects between 29 and 32 months of age. These children were asked to imitate the experimenter's *hiding* of the toy rather than the placement of it. They hid the toy correctly 16% of the time.

The results of the imitation study support the argument that the underlying factor responsible for young children's performance in the model task is whether they realize there is any correspondence between the two spaces in the first place. Children who are aware of the correspondence are able to transfer the stipulated action across the spaces, whether it is placing, hiding, or finding a toy, whereas children who are unaware of the correspondence have no basis for knowing what to do.

These results raise several questions. What is responsible for the large age difference in performance previously observed with the model task? In other words, what variables support the excellent performance of the older children, and conversely, what impedes the younger children's understanding of the situation? Are 2½-year-olds *incapable* of recognizing the correspondence between a model and room, or might there be some way to induce them to succeed? What is responsible for the development of competence in this task, and why is development so abrupt? Answers to some of these questions will be found in the research summarized in the following sections.

Variables that influence young children's understanding of scale models

Verbal instructions

Is the 2½-year-olds' poor performance due to inadequate verbal skills? One possible source of the large discrepancy in performance between the 2½- and 3-year-old children is the information presented to them in the course of the experiment. As stated earlier, the standard model task involves a full explanation: The correspondence between the two spaces, the objects within them, and the hiding events are all explicitly, even painstakingly, described and demonstrated by the experimenter. Perhaps the greater verbal abilities of the older children enable them to understand this description of the correspondence, but the younger children are hampered by inadequate verbal skills.

There are several reasons to doubt this explanation. For one thing, the younger children appear to understand everything about the experimental procedure, *except* the correspondence between the room and model. They know that on Retrieval 2 they should search for the toy where they remember seeing it being hidden, and they do so. They know that on Retrieval 1 they should search for the hidden toy, and they do so. In fact, they are usually quite happy to search on Retrieval 1 and show no evidence of surprise at either finding or not finding the toy at any given place they search. Thus, the *only* thing the 2½-year-olds fail to understand is that they have any basis for knowing where to search on Retrieval 1. This singular failure does not seem compatible with an explanation based on age differences in comprehension of the instructions.

Furthermore, we have independently verified that children of this age understand the meaning of the term "the same." When asked to pick which of two objects is "the same" as a standard object, 2½-year-old children are able to choose appropriately. They are able to do so whether the standard and target are identical or only similar in appearance. Hence, it seems unlikely that the 2½-year-olds in the model task fail because of not understanding the experimenter's comments that "Big and Little Snoopy have the *same* things in their rooms" or that "Big Snoopy and Little Snoopy like to do the *same* things in their rooms."

Further evidence against the importance of differences in verbal abilities comes from a study in which 2½-year-olds were provided with verbal labels for the hiding places. The reasoning for this experiment was that differences between the two age groups in verbal ability might be important in terms of verbal mediation. In the previous studies using the model task, the hiding places were never explicitly referred to as the experimenter hid the toy. She always said, "I'm hiding Snoopy *here*," never naming the item of furniture used as the hiding place. Perhaps the older children spontaneously labeled the hiding place for themselves, and that helped to mediate their transfer from one space to another. Perhaps the younger children failed to provide such labels for themselves. If differences in verbal labeling were important, one would expect that labeling the hiding places for the younger children might improve their performance. It is well established that labeling items that are to be remembered improves young children's performance in a variety of situations (e.g., Cantor, 1965; Ornstein & Naus, 1978; Reese, 1966; Stevenson, 1972).

For this study, the experimenter said as she was hiding the toy on each trial, "I'm hiding Little Snoopy here behind the dresser [under the pillow, etc.]." The results indicated unequivocally that providing 2½-year-old children with verbal labels did not improve their performance in the model task: The Retrieval 1 and Retrieval 2 scores of 16% and 88% are essentially the same as those achieved by the same age group in the original model study (DeLoache, 1987). Thus, differences in verbal ability–verbal mediation appear not to play any substantial role in the large age difference observed in previous model studies.

It should also be noted that the results of this study fit with the argument advanced above that the 2½-year-old subjects fail to recognize the correspondence between the room and model. If a child does not realize that the room and model are related in the first place, labeling the individual hiding places on the experimental trials should be irrelevant. It should not help to hear the word *couch* as one watches Little Snoopy being hidden in the model unless one realizes that the small couch is related to or represents the larger couch in the room. From this perspective, the absence of an effect for labeling is not surprising.

Does the 3-year-old's success depend on explicit instruction? A very different sort of question arises with respect to the role of the explicit instructions provided in the model task in supporting the excellent level of performance achieved by the 3-year-old subjects. In our research, the subjects have always been given extensive, explicit information about the correspondence between the two spaces. Does the success of the 3-year-olds depend on having the correspondence pointed out to them?

On the one hand, their high level of success suggests that they might recognize the correspondence between room and model on their own. Indeed, children occasionally anticipate the experimenter's explanation of the correspondence. Some children make comments such as "they're the same," or "they match," before the experimenter has mentioned the correspondence.

On the other hand, we know that people of all ages are much more likely to perceive an analogy between entities or situations and to transfer information from one context to another if the relation between the two is pointed out to them. Examples abound in the analogical reasoning literature. Adults often fail to notice spontaneously that two problems are analogous and that they have a common solution. A simple hint that two problems are alike is often enough to induce the realization that the solution already learned to one problem is also applicable to the second (Gick & Holyoak, 1983).

The same responsivity to hints is seen in analogical reasoning studies with young children (e.g., Brown & Kane, 1988; Holyoak et al. 1984). In a series of studies by Crisafi and Brown (1986), 2- to 4-year-old children who were told that all the problems were analogous – "all my games are candy games and you play them all the same way" – showed significantly better transfer than children not given such hints.

To see whether 3-year-old children in the model task must have the correspondence between the model and the room explicitly pointed out to them by the experimenter, a group of 3-year-olds was given a modified task in which the experimenter gave less explicit instructions than in the previous model studies. The only changes were that the experimenter omitted saying to the child that the two rooms were just alike and had the same things in them, and she also omitted the direct comparison of the furniture from the two spaces. She named the objects in each space, but did not bring the items of model furniture into the room to demonstrate their correspondence with their larger counterparts. All other information given was the same as in the preceding studies.

The omission of the explicit instruction had a pronounced negative effect on the 3-year-old's Retrieval 1 performance: They found the hidden toy on only 25% of their Retrieval 1 attempts, a figure significantly below the 75% to 80% achieved by the same age group with full instructions about the correspondence. These results leave little doubt that *most* 3-year-old children are unlikely to notice the correspondence between a scale model and a larger space unless they are told of its existence. (One subject in this study and a few of the children in other studies have appeared to appreciate the correspondence before it was explained to them, but most have not.)

Perceptual similarity between model and room

A second variable that comes immediately to mind as a candidate for influencing young children's awareness of the relation between a model and the space it represents is the degree of perceptual similarity between the two. It seems reasonable to suppose that the more the model looks like the room, the more likely a child is to recognize the correspondence between the two.

In the domain of analogical reasoning, the surface similarity of two analogues has been shown to exercise a strong effect, especially for children (Brown & Kane, 1986; Gentner, 1988; Gentner & Toupin, 1986; Holyoak et al., 1984). Perception of the underlying structural similarity of two analogues is enhanced by a high degree of physical similarity between the elements within the analogues. Gentner and Toupin (1986) reported that children who first heard a story with a chipmunk, robin, and horse as characters found it easier to transfer the story plot to a second character set comprising a squirrel, robin, and zebra than to an elephant, shark, and cricket. Similarly, Brown and Kane (1988) found that young children's success at solving story problems was facilitated when the solution to a series of superficially different problems involved using the identical object in the same way. Gentner (1988, 1989) argues that the primary effect of perceptual similarity is on the process of gaining access to or becoming aware of the existence of an analogy.

In considering the role of similarity, one must distinguish between similarity of objects and similarity of relations among objects. Gentner (1988) has argued that one reason surface similarity has such a pronounced effect on analogical reasoning in young children is that they tend to focus on objects more than on relations among objects. Smith (1989) has also stressed the primacy of objects over relations in young children's reasoning. With development, as well as with the growth of knowledge in any particular domain, children become increasingly capable of reasoning about relations, a phenomenon Gentner (1988) refers to as the "relational shift." Several experiments have been directed toward assessing the role of object and relational similarity in the model task.

Similarity of objects. In the first study in this series, the physical similarity of the objects within the room and model was manipulated, along with the similarity of the surrounding space. An artificial room was constructed of a plastic-pipe frame supporting opaque white fabric walls. Although smaller (2.57 m × 1.85 m × 1.88 m) than a normal room, it was large enough for an adult and child to move around in.

The design of the study called for four conditions: the combination of high and low similarity of objects (furniture) within the spaces – place – and high and low similarity of the external surround (the walls) – space. Accordingly, two models were constructed. One was made of the same pipe and fabric as the room itself (high space similarity), and the other was a cardboard box painted white (low space similarity). Each model was furnished either with pieces of furniture that looked as much as possible like those in the room (high place similarity) or that were perceptually different (low place similarity). For example, in the high place condition, the large and small chairs were both covered in the same blue print fabric, the dressers were both covered with the same contact paper, etc. In the low place condition, the model chair had a solid brown fabric cover, the surface of the dresser was different, and so on. The 64 subjects for this study were from the same two age groups as in the original experiment (older $M = 38$ months, younger $M = 31$ months).

The results are shown in Figure 5.2. The main finding was that, as expected, surface similarity did have a pronounced effect on the chil-

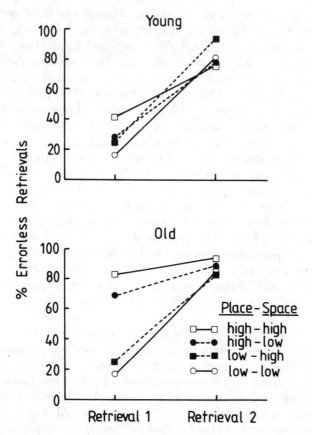

Figure 5.2. Percentage errorless retrievals as a function of age and similarity between the individual hiding places and the surrounding spaces of the model and room. (Reprinted from DeLoache, 1989a, by permission.)

dren's Retrieval 1 performance. However, it is apparent that similarity of the objects themselves – the hiding places – was much more important than similarity of the overall surround.

Our manipulation of the similarity of the overall surround of the two spaces had only a small effect. This result is not surprising, given the preeminence of objects in young children's reasoning (Gentner, 1988; Smith, 1989). However, a more extreme manipulation might have a more pronounced effect. Suppose, for example, that the walls had been not only of a different material but also of a different color, or that the overall shape of the model spaces had been radically altered (perhaps a circle instead of a rectangle).

Our object similarity manipulation had an especially large effect on the older subjects. Although increasing this type of similarity slightly elevated the Retrieval 1 performance of the younger children, decreasing it had a pronounced negative effect on the older children's performance. As long as the individual hiding places within the model and room looked very much alike except for size (high place similarity), the 3-year-olds were quite successful; they clearly recognized the correspondence between the two, and they transferred what they knew from one to the other. However, when the objects within the spaces differed in appearance, even though they were exemplars of the same categories of furniture, the older children failed to transfer. Thus, even though 3-year-old children are capable of establishing the conceptual equivalence of room and model, this equivalence is still very much based on perceptual similarity.

Similarity of spatial relations. The experiment just described clearly established the importance of physical similarity of the objects within the room and model. However, it said nothing about a different type of similarity relation between the two – similarity of the spatial relations among the objects within the spaces. In the standard model task, the items of furniture are always in the same spatial positions relative to each other and to the surround; in both the room and model, the chair is in the corner to the right of the couch and to the left of the dresser. Is the success of the 3-year-old subjects in this task based solely on their perception of the similarity of the individual objects in room and model, or do the congruent spatial relations among those objects also contribute? If these children are essentially unaware of the relations among objects, then it should not matter whether the spatial relations among the furniture within the two spaces are congruent or not.

Two experiments were designed to get at different aspects of this issue. In the first, we asked about the importance of relative spatial position in young children's performance in the model task. We know that 3-year-old children are very successful in this task: They recognize the model–room correspondence and, having seen the miniature toy being hidden somewhere in the model, they know where to find the larger toy in the room. What assumption do they make about what specifies the location of the analogous toy? There are at least two plausible possibilities: (1) The larger toy is hidden behind the corresponding piece of furniture in the room; (2) the larger toy is hidden in the same relative position in the room. In the standard model task, these two possibilities are congruent; that is, the analogous toy is always hidden behind the corresponding item of furniture in the corresponding position. What if these two possibilities were separated? Which assumption would guide 3-year-olds' behavior?

To address these questions, we gave a group of 3-year-olds one day's experience in the standard model task and then brought them back a second day. On that occasion, the furniture in the model had been rearranged; on Day 2, the spatial relations among the objects in the model were different from the spatial relations among the objects in the room. For this study, we used the artificial room and the high place–high space Similarity model. In addition to the standard contents of these spaces, we added a picture on the wall and a potted plant. These objects were not rearranged on Day 2; they remained in the same spatial positions to serve as stable landmarks to help the children identify relative spatial position within the spaces.

For half the children, the object group, the toy was hidden with the same object (piece of furniture) in the model and in the room. Thus, if the toy was hidden behind the miniature dresser on the west wall of the model, it was behind the large dresser, but on the north wall of the room. For the other half of the subjects, the spatial position group, the object was hidden in the same relative spatial position in the two spaces, but with different objects. Thus, if Little Snoopy had been placed behind the chair in the southwest corner of the model, it was hidden in the southwest corner of the room, behind the couch. The only other change was that instead of instructing and reminding the children that Big Snoopy was hidden in the "same place" as Little Snoopy, the experimenter told the children she was hiding Big Snoopy in the "same way" as Little Snoopy. The question was to what extent the lack of congruent spatial relations between room and model would affect the children's performance. Because of the possibility that a child might start out Day 2 with the wrong hypothesis about where the toy should be found, we gave more trials than usual (six instead of four) to allow for learning effects. In other words, a child in the spatial position group might assume that the toy would be with the same object but discover that that was not the correct rule. We expected to see evidence of such learning by some children in both groups.

Figure 5.3 shows the Retrieval 1 results for this study. The Day 1 performance was exactly as expected: Retrieval 1 scores were very high and equal for the two groups (which had been treated exactly alike at this point). However, Day 2 provided some surprises. The children in the object group showed absolutely no decrement in Retrieval 1 responding. With the two toys hidden behind the analogous items of furniture, the children readily found them. (Although not shown here, Retrieval 1 was equal to Retrieval 2). This result indicated that these 3-year-old children firmly expected that the toys would be hidden with the same items of furniture in the room and model, even though those items were in different positions within the spaces. Thus, it appears that the rule that the 3-year-olds abstracted from their first day's experience with the standard model task, with the spatial relations among objects congruent across the two spaces, was something like: "Little Snoopy is hidden behind the same piece of fur-

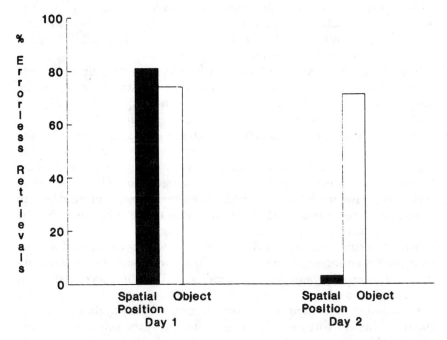

Figure 5.3. Percentage errorless retrievals on Retrieval 1 with congruent spatial relations (Day 1) or noncongruent spatial relations (Day 2). For the object group, the toy was hidden behind the corresponding object; for the spatial position group, the toy was hidden in the corresponding spatial position within the room.

niture in his little room that Big Snoopy is hidden behind in his big room. If Big Snoopy was hidden behind the big chair, look for Little Snoopy behind the little chair." The strength of the children's belief in this rule is reflected in the fact that there was no change over trials; the children held and acted on this belief right from the start and hence did very well.

The data for the spatial position group offer a marked contrast. As is apparent in Figure 5.3, their Retrieval 1 performance was almost totally disrupted on Day 2. Their extremely low performance indicates that they, like the children in the object group, firmly expected the toy to be hidden with the analogous object rather than in the analogous spatial position. Indeed, the most common "error" was to search for the analogous toy with the corresponding piece of furniture.

As was true for the object condition, there was again no trials effect. However, in the object condition, the children had started out with the correct idea and hence had nothing to learn. In the spatial position condition, they started out with the wrong idea and had everything to learn. They failed to do so. The children in the spatial position condition *never* figured out the relevance of spatial position, and they failed to abandon the object rule when they discovered that it did not lead to a successful retrieval. Indeed, several of the children chastised the experimenter for hiding the toy in the "wrong" place.

The results of this study tell us that when 3-year-old children perform successfully in the standard model task, they apparently do so on the basis of object-to-object correspondences. They equate the miniature and full-size objects within the two spaces and encode the location of the hidden toy in terms of those objects. Having successfully retrieved the analogous toy from behind the corresponding item of furniture in the corresponding spatial position, they assume that it is the piece of furniture that determines the location of the analogous toy. Thus, given mastery of the basic model task, individual objects are much more salient to young children in reasoning from one space to the other than are the relations among those objects.

What this study fails to establish, however, is whether relational similarity is equally unimportant in the child's *initial* awareness of the correspondence between the room and the model of it. Thus, in a second study of the role of similarity of relations among objects, we simply asked whether there was a difference in 3-year-old children's initial understanding of the room–model correspondence as a function of the congruence of the spatial relations among the two spaces. Does the 3-year-olds' appreciation of the correspondence between the room and its model depend on having all the analogous objects in corresponding spatial positions within the two spaces?

In one condition, congruent spatial relations, the items of furniture were arranged exactly alike in the two spaces (i.e., the standard procedure). In the second condition, discrepant spatial relations, the same objects were arranged differently. Thus, the chair that was in the northwest corner of the room was in the southeast corner of the model. Eight 3-year-old subjects ($M = 38$ months) participated in each condition. The two toys were always hidden behind the corresponding objects and hence in different spatial positions. (Since the preceding study had indicated such extreme inattention to spatial position, it did not seem necessary to include a spatial position condition in this study.) The artificial room and the high similarity model (high place–high space) from the preceding object similarity study were used.

The results left little doubt as to the importance of congruent spatial relations. As Figure 5.4 shows, there was a large difference in Retrieval 1 performance as a function of congruence of the spatial relations among the objects within the two spaces. When the similar-looking objects were in different relative positions, our 3-year-olds failed to appreciate the correspondence between the model and room.

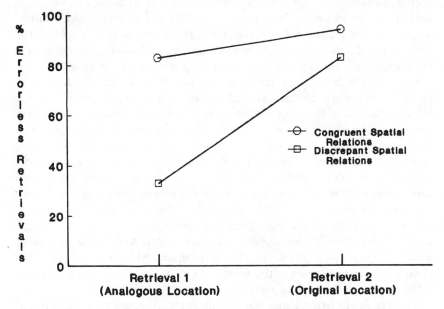

Figure 5.4. Percentage errorless retrievals with congruent verses discrepant spatial relations among objects. Toy was always hidden with corresponding object.

These three studies on the role of object and relational similarity make it very clear that young children's awareness of the correspondence between a scale model and the larger space it represents depends crucially on a high degree of perceptual support. The 3-year-olds' initial appreciation of the room–model correspondence is based on both object and relational similarity: The objects within the two spaces must look very much alike, except for size, *and* they must occupy the same relative positions within the spaces. It appears that the overall perceptual gestalt of the model must evoke the child's representation of the room for him or her to grasp the relation between the two. Once the conceptual equivalence between them has been established, object correspondence seems to be much more salient than spatial position or relational correspondence.

Similarity of scale. Another physical property of a room and model that might affect young children's perception of the correspondence between them is scale or, more precisely, the degree of difference in size between the two spaces. Acredolo (1977; Acredolo, Pick, & Olsen, 1975), among others, has cautioned that large- and small-scale spaces might have different effects on various aspects of spatial cognition. A large-scale space is a surrounding space, and only a portion of it can be seen at any one time. In contrast, one does not enter a small-scale space, and the entire space can be surveyed all at once. If 2½-year-old children were asked to perceive the correspondence between two spaces of the same general scale, they might be more successful than they are at appreciating the relation between a surrounding and a surveyable space.

Accordingly, an experiment was conducted in which children were given the standard model task with the exception that, instead of being asked to transfer from a small-scale model to a large-scale room, they were asked to transfer from a small model to a slightly larger model. The small model (the same one used in the previous study of perceptual similarity) measured 62.9 cm × 48.3 cm × 38.1 cm; the large model measured 91.5 cm × 68.5 cm × 57.0 cm. In both cases, a child could (and they sometimes did) kneel down inside the model to search for the toy, but the walls were sufficiently low that they did not provide a surrounding space and the child could always see over them. The models and the items of furniture within them were constructed to be as perceptually similar as we could make them. A screen separated the two spaces so the child could not see both at the same time. The standard procedure was followed to test a group of ten subjects ($M = 30.8$ months).

The results indicated that decreasing the difference in scale between the two spaces substantially enhanced the likelihood that young children would realize they were related and would transfer what they knew from one to the other. Figure 5.5 shows the results for the two-model study in comparison to the results for the same age group in the high space–high place similarity condition of the perceptual similarity study summarized earlier. As the figure shows, the degree of discrepancy between the two spaces made a difference. Retrieval 1 performance was much better when the two spaces differed minimally in size, that is, when they were both the same type of space. Indeed, the Retrieval 1 performance of the children in the similar scale condition was fully equivalent to that of the older children in the standard model task. Apparently it is much easier to recognize the correspondence relation between two spaces that one can survey than it is to realize that a surveyable space corresponds to a surrounding space. Thus, overall size is a dimension of perceptual similarity that influences young children's performance in the model task.[2]

To summarize the findings with respect to perceptual similarity: (1) It is clear that young children's apprehension of the conceptual equivalence of two spaces is very much affected by how alike they look. The surface appearance of the objects within the spaces must be highly similar, and they must be in the same relative positions, or even 3-year-olds will fail to detect the relation between them. (2) Further increasing the perceptual similarity of the spaces by reducing the difference in scale between them dramatically enhances the performance of even younger

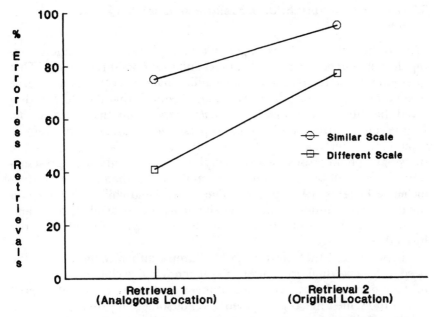

Figure 5.5. Percentage errorless retrievals as a function of the extent of size difference between two spaces.

children; 2½-year-olds successfully transfer what they learn from one model to a second slightly larger model.

The research summarized so far qualifies the dramatic age difference in performance reported by DeLoache (1987). The extremely good performance of 3-year-old children in the model task is highly replicable, but it depends on the children being explicitly instructed about the model–room correspondence and there being a high degree of perceptual similarity between them. Thus, the model task is actually more challenging for 3-year-olds than it might at first appear to be.

The abysmal performance of the 2½-year-old children in the model task is also highly replicable, even in the face of a variety of efforts to improve their performance, including labeling, increasing surface similarity, and other manipulations not described here. At the same time, however, we have found that 2½-year-olds can be highly successful when the model and the larger space differ minimally in size. Thus, the model task can be made more accessible to 2½-year-olds than it originally appeared to be.

These studies clearly establish the crucial role of perceptual similarity in young children's ability to grasp conceptually the correspondence between two separate entities. We turn now to a very different, but equally crucial, determinant of the early understanding of models.

The source of young children's failure to understand scale models

What is the source of the younger children's difficulty with understanding the relation between a scale model and the room it represents? That question was the focus of a series of studies that concentrated on the role of a model as a symbol. The model task requires that the child understand that the model *represents* or *stands for* the room, that it is a symbol for the room. "Symbolization is the representing of an object or event by something other than itself" (Potter, 1979, p. 41). Scale models – like drawings, photographs, maps, sculptures – are symbolic representations. "A symbol brings to mind something other than itself" (Huttenlocher & Higgins, 1978, p. 109). The 2½-year-old children's failure in the model task cannot be due to a general absence of symbolic functioning, but it might have to do with some aspect of symbolization required by models.

I hypothesized that the younger children's difficulty stems from the need to have a "dual orientation" to the model. The child must respond to the model both as a real, three-dimensional object (or set of objects) and at the same time as a representation of something else. Perhaps the younger children have difficulty representing the model in two different ways at the same time; they may see the model only as a real thing and not as a symbol of something other than itself.

The test of the above hypothesis was to compare performance in the standard model task with performance in a similar task that used a different, purely representational medium – pictures – to give the child information about the location of the object hidden in the room. Although a photograph or other two-dimensional representation is, of course, a real object and hence has a certain "double reality" (Sigel, 1978), its primary function is as a representation of something else. It should not require a dual orientation in the way a model does and should, therefore, be easier to interpret.

It should be noted that the prediction of better performance with pictures than with real objects is counterintuitive on several grounds. We generally think of two-dimensional stimuli as impoverished relative to three-dimensional stimuli, which are considered to be richer, more salient, more informative. A large body of developmental and cross-cultural research has shown better learning and memory with real objects than with pictures (e.g., Daehler, Lonardo, & Bukatko, 1979; DeLoache, 1986; Deregowski & Serpell, cited in Cole & Scribner, 1974; Hartley, 1976).

To test the dual orientation hypothesis, 2½-year-old children served as subjects in a series of picture studies. In the first (DeLoache, 1987, Ex-

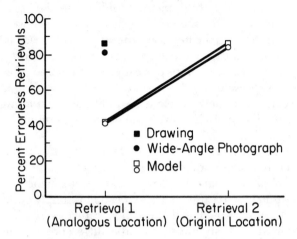

Figure 5.6. Percentage errorless retrievals for pictures versus model.

periment 2), information about the location of the toy in the room was conveyed via a set of four color photographs, each of which depicted one or more of the hiding places (pieces of furniture) in the room. In another study, children were presented with a wide-angle color photograph showing all the relevant portion of the room. A third group of children had a simple line drawing of the room with some of the furnishings lightly colored in. The pictures were always sitting on a table in the room adjacent to the room they depicted. For each of the four trials, the experimenter pointed directly at the appropriate place in the picture and said, "Snoopy's hiding back [under] here." Then the child was asked to find the toy in the room. A different hiding place was used for each trial. In each of these studies, all children received both the picture and standard model tasks, each on a different day, with task order counterbalanced across subjects.

Figure 5.6 shows the results for the wide-angle photograph and the line drawing. The results for the multiple-photographs study (DeLoache, 1987) were the same. As can be seen in the figure, the hypothesis was supported: The 2½-year-old children's performance with the pictures was substantially and significantly above their performance on Retrieval 1 of the model condition. The same child who was unable to find the toy after watching it being hidden in the model was able to find it after seeing a picture of its hiding place. Young children are thus much more successful at acquiring and applying information from a two-dimensional representation than they are from a three-dimensional representation of the same information. The latter's status as a real thing distracts them from its representational role.

One potential criticism of these picture studies and the conclusions drawn from them concerns the method by which the children were given the information. In the model conditions, the subjects observed a hiding event. In the picture conditions, the experimenter simply pointed to the correct place on the picture. Perhaps it is easier for a child to represent a point than it is to represent a hiding event. If so, it is possible that the difference between the model and picture conditions has nothing to do with the specific media involved or with the necessity of multiple representations of the model.

The results of a control study rule out this possible artifact. If performance in the picture task is good because the correct location is denoted through pointing rather than a hiding event, performance with the model should be much better if the correct location is simply pointed out to the child. Note, however, that if the child's difficulty resides in the dual nature of models, it should make little difference whether one points to the relevant location or hides a miniature toy in it. In either case, the younger children should fail. Accordingly, a group of 2½-year-olds watched as the experimenter pointed to the hiding place in the model, saying, "This is where Big Snoopy is hiding in *his* room" (the same thing said in the picture tasks). These children were unable to find the toy – their Retrieval 1 performance was exactly the same as that of a comparable group tested in the standard model task. Thus, the dramatic difference in the performance of 2½-year-old children in the model and picture tasks is not attributable to differences in how the relevant information is conveyed. The results therefore support the claim that the difference is attributable to the different representational demands of the two media.

An additional very important result emerged from the line drawing and wide-angle photo studies – a transfer effect. Figure 5.7 shows the level of performance in the model and picture conditions as a function of order of task. The transfer effect is most clear-cut for the line drawing study, shown in the right panel of the figure. As expected, the children who experienced the model on Day 1 were almost totally unsuccessful. Also as expected, the same children were highly successful in the drawing task. The interesting data came from the other group of children, those who participated in the picture task on the first day and the model task on Day 2. As the figure shows, these children achieved the expected high level of success with the drawing. They also achieved an unexpectedly high level of success in the model task. Having first experienced the situation in which they used information presented to them in a picture to find the hidden toy, they were able to exploit the same information presented via the model. Their performance was equivalent to the level typically achieved by 3-year-olds. A similarly significant, though less ex-

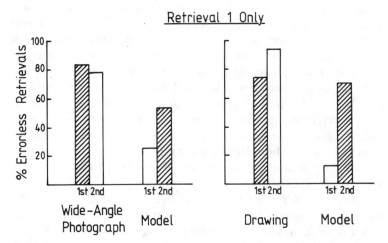

Figure 5.7. Percentage errorless retrievals in the picture and model tasks as a function of order of task. All model data are for Retrieval 1.

treme, transfer effect was also found for the wide-angle photo study (left panel of Figure 5.7).

It should be noted that transfer was not universal. Half the children in these two groups (8 of the total of 16 subjects) transferred; that is, they achieved high scores (75% errorless retrievals or better) with the model after experiencing a picture task first. The other half still did not understand the room–model correspondence. In addition, there was no evidence of transfer in the initial picture study reported in DeLoache (1987). Thus, the experience of applying information from a two-dimensional stimulus to the room provokes some, but by no means all, 2½-year-olds to become aware of the correspondence between the three-dimensional model and the room.

The transfer effect has important implications for interpreting the younger children's performance in the model studies. The 2½-year-old's usual failure in the standard model task cannot be attributed to an absolute *inability* to recognize the correspondence between a model and the larger space it represents. Under certain circumstances, some of them *can* do so.

Why does participating in a picture task enable some 2½-year-olds to succeed with the model? Perhaps the experience of using one symbolic medium to find the hidden toy alerts the children to the symbolic possibilities of a different medium. These children presumably understand something about the symbolic status of drawings and realize that the drawing represents or stands for the room. This realization is relatively easy because (1) they are familiar with the general representational role of pictures, and (2) a two-dimensional representation does not require a dual orientation, nor does it invite a response to it as a real object. Although a drawing or photograph is undeniably a real, tangible object, its only familiar function is a representation, and its features as a real object are relatively nonsalient and uninteresting.

An important question raised by the transfer effect is whether or not it is highly specific. In the studies just described, the pictures and the model both represented the *same* larger space. In other words, on Day 1 the children had experience with a picture of a room and used it to know where to find an object hidden in that room; on Day 2, they encountered a model of that same room and were able to use it to guide their searching in the room. It may be that 2½-year-old children would show the transfer effect only under these very restrictive conditions. In other words, the children may simply be learning to transfer to that particular room.

A different, and much more interesting, possibility also exists. Perhaps the transfer effect reflects some genuine advance in symbolic functioning. Perhaps their experience with the picture task sensitizes 2½-year-olds to the general idea or possibility of representational relations among objects. If so, transfer should occur, even if the picture and model represent different rooms.

An experiment was conducted to test for generalized transfer. On Day 1, a group of thirteen 2½-year-olds was given a picture task in which a line drawing of room A was used to indicate where a toy was hidden in the room. On Day 2, each child received a model task in which the model was of room B. Thus, the drawing and model had different referents.

The results supported the notion of generalized transfer. For those subjects who scored 75% or better on the picture task, Retrieval 1 in the model task was 56%, slightly lower than the previous transfer effect, but still higher than would otherwise be expected of this age group. Of the 13 subjects, 6 succeeded in the model task (their Retrieval 1 score was 75% or more). Without the previous experience, we would expect no more than one or two children to have done well in the model task. The results of this study indicate that experience with a different symbolic medium facilitates success in the model task at least in part because it alerts children to the general concept of symbolic representation.

This transfer effect is in some sense an example of learning to learn. According to Brown and Kane (1988), preschool children are able to develop a mind-set to look for analogies. Having experienced one pair of problems in which the second could be solved by analogy to the first, children quite readily use analogy to solve the second of a subsequent pair of problems. In the model transfer study, the first day's experience with the picture test may have similarly lead the children to expect to apply what they learned in one context to the other.

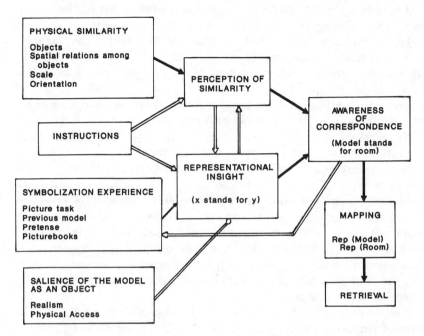

Figure 5.8. A Model for understanding young children's understanding of models.

Four conclusions can be drawn from the picture studies: (1) 2½-year-old children are able to find an object when its location is conveyed to them via a picture, even though they are unable to apply the same information from a model. (2) These children apparently understand the representational relation between the picture and the room; hence, they apply information gained from the former to the latter. (3) Prior experience with a symbolic medium that they at least partially understand enables 2½-year-old children to succeed in the model task. (4) Such experience apparently induces them to recognize the symbolic nature of the model.

A Model for understanding young children's understanding of models

The results of the studies reviewed in the preceding section (and some others not included here) contributed to the development of a Model (Figure 5.8) of the variables involved in understanding and using a scale model. This Model, as any model is meant to do, (1) helps to organize the body of data collected to date, making evident ways in which the specified variables should interact; (2) generates predictions for future research; and (3) suggests a probable source of development.

The pivotal role in this Model is taken by *Awareness of the Correspondence* between the room and model. This precedence is dictated by the all-or-none extremes of performance in both the group and individual data that have appeared in nearly all the previous studies. The vast majority of children aged 3 years and above whom we have tested have succeeded (i.e., scored 75% or better) in the standard model task; nearly all 2½-year-olds have failed (scored 25% or less). Most intermediate-age subjects have scored either very high or very low.

Furthermore, the overall pattern across studies is an unusual combination of extreme stability and extreme lability. With respect to stability, the results of the original study (DeLoache, 1987), with its very large age difference between 2½- and 3-year-olds, have been replicated numerous times using the same and different stimuli (i.e., different rooms and models). Levels of performance have proved to be impervious to many manipulations that could reasonably be expected to have some impact. The superiority of pictures over the model has consistently appeared in several different studies.

With respect to lability, it is possible to cause extreme changes in the level of performance of both age groups. The older children, who in numerous studies appeared to be fully competent, were reduced to chance performance by decreasing the surface similarity of the objects within the spaces and by omitting explicit instructions about the correspondence. The younger children, who in numerous studies appeared totally hopeless (I used the phrase *apparently ineducable* in an earlier paper – DeLoache, 1989a), reached a high level of success with the standard model following related experience with pictorial stimuli. This same age group also performed extremely well with two spaces that differed in size by a relatively small amount.

These extremes of performance suggest that the crucial factor is whether or not a child *recognizes the correspondence* between the model and the room. If the child does not understand that the model stands for the room, then there is no basis for transfer, no basis, other than chance and persistence, for finding the hidden object. According to the Model, then, variables demonstrated or hypothesized to affect young children's performance in the model task do so by either promoting or impeding the child's *Awareness of the Correspondence*.

Two intervening variables are hypothesized to influence the child's awareness (or lack of it). The first of these, *Perception of Similarity* between room and model, is influenced primarily by the level of *physical similarity* between them. Noticing that the model looks like the room – more precisely, that certain objects in the model look like certain objects in the room – increases the probability that the child will become aware of the correspondence, or symbolic relation, between the two spaces. As was demonstrated in the perceptual similarity study, a high level of surface similarity is necessary to support the 3-year-olds' grasp of the conceptual equivalence of the room and model. If a high level of surface similarity is present and the perceptual similarity of the two spaces is increased even more by decreasing the size discrepancy between them, 2½-year-olds now see the relation between the two and successfully transfer from one to the other.

The second mediating variable is the activation of a *Representational Insight* – a readiness to realize that one object or event may stand for a different one. Three variables are hypothesized to influence the likelihood that the child will be sensitive to the symbolic potential of a model. One of these is previous *symbolic experience*. In the research conducted to date, an immediate experience with a related task using a different symbolic medium – pictures – enabled some 2½-year-olds to succeed in the model task. The effect was shown to generalize, suggesting that the children were alerted to the possibility of representational relationships. The importance of a second variable, explicit *instructions* about the correspondence between the two spaces, has also been shown. Most 3-year-olds succeed only if they are fully instructed by the experimenter. Being told that the room and model are alike may lead the child to look for a symbolic relationship. The third variable hypothesized to affect sensitivity to symbolic relations in general is the *salience of the model* as an object. This variable has a negative influence; the more salient the "objectness" of the model is, the less likely children are to become aware of its symbolic potential. Responding to the model as an object blocks responding to it as a symbol. The picture-versus-model studies support this hypothesis.

The last feature of the Model is *mapping*. Given awareness of the correspondence between the model and room, the child's mental representation of the model must be mapped onto the representation of the room. In the standard model task, this step appears to be trivially easy. However, one could presumably design tasks in which mapping would be more difficult.

The Model generates several predictions about how its different components should interact. For example, the Model stipulates that previous symbolization experience should influence the likelihood that the child is sensitive to the symbolic potential of a scale model. We know that 36-month-olds fail to appreciate the correspondence between a room and a model when there is not a high degree of surface similarity between them. The Model leads us to predict that if this age group of children experienced and succeeded with the high similarity model used in the perceptual similarity study summarized above, such experience should sensitize them to the general possibility of symbolic relations among objects. Hence, if they are subsequently given the low similarity model, they should be more likely to interpret it correctly than they would do without the previous model experience.

In terms of interactions among variables, the Model suggests that decreased physical similarity might be compensated for by even more explicit instructions to the children (for example, discussing the fact that although the two corresponding items of furniture do not look at all alike, they are nevertheless the same kind of thing). Increased symbolic experience, which comes naturally with increasing age, should decrease the need for high physical similarity and explicit instructions. Hence, one would expect that children older than those tested to date could succeed in the standard model task without explicit instructions and with low levels of surface similarity between room and model.

The Model also predicts that reducing the salience of the model as a real object ought to make it easier for 2½-year-olds to recognize its symbolic potential. Perhaps precluding physical access to the model would improve the performance of the younger age group. If 2½-year-olds watch through a window as the miniature toy is hidden in the model and are not allowed to interact directly with it, they might be more likely to appreciate the information thus given to them.

One of the most important aspects of the Model depicted in Figure 5.8 is that it specifies a probable source of development – symbolic experience. The more experience a child has had with various forms of symbolization, the more likely it is that he or she will be sensitive to the symbolic potential of a new medium. Specific experiences that may be very relevant are picturebooks and symbolic play. Beginning sometime in the second year of life, most young children in this culture have a great deal of exposure to picturebooks, and they become increasingly knowledgeable about the symbolic functions of books and pictures (DeLoache & DeMendoza, 1987; Ninio & Bruner, 1978). Symbolic play also occupies a substantial portion of the young child's day (McCune-Nicholich, 1981). Object substitution (e.g., using a block of wood as a car) involves a type of dual orientation – the child may know the identity and nature of the substitute object but still treat it as a symbol or substitute for something else. Pretend play, picturebook experience, and other materials and activities (possibly including television) that involve some form of "dual reality" – responding to one thing in two different ways – should all increase young children's understanding of and sensitivity to symbolic representation in general.

One reason that young children are capable of simple forms of pretense and understand something about picturebooks before the age at which they show any competence with models has to do with the "referential specificity" of a model. A model represents or refers to a particular other reality, and the child has to apply the information gained from the model in a highly specific way. In contrast, young children's picturebooks rarely if ever represent something in the child's immediate environment or direct experience. From their books, children learn about zoo animals in general, but not about any particular real animal; they learn about lions and tigers, dragons and unicorns. Similarly, in symbolic play, the substitute or replica objects with which young children play involve generic representation: the Fisher-Price farm set includes prototypical horses and cows, not Old Dobbin and Elsie; their toy MacDonald's represents a general concept of hamburger stands, not any particular MacDonald's. The 2½-year-old who comes into our lab may be asked, for the first time in his or her life, to interpret and apply a symbolic relation that requires a relatively complex mapping onto a specific referent.

Conclusion

The research summarized here has concerned the flexible use of memory by very young children. The situation studied is one in which memory is not enough – it is necessary, but by no means sufficient. In the model task, performance is often very bad even though memory is very good.

This highlights the importance of considering not just the development of memory processes per se, but also the child's emerging ability to have flexible access to his or her own memory system. Remembering a statistical formula does you no good unless you can recognize problems to which it applies. Knowing that the note in the second space up in the treble clef is A is useless unless you are also aware of the correspondence between the notes on the page of sheet music and the keys on the piano. Between 2 and 3 years of age, children show a substantial increase in flexible access, resulting from their increasing readiness to appreciate the correspondence, the symbolic relation, between disparate entities.

The most important questions for future research in this domain are to try to specify more precisely what processes subserve the awareness of the correspondence between a model and what it represents and to understand why there is such volatility in young children's understanding of this relation.

NOTES

This research and the preparation of this chapter were partially supported by Grants HD-05951 and HD-25271 from the National Institute for Child Health and Human Development and by HATCH Grant 60-309 from the University of

Illinois Agriculture Experiment Station. I am deeply indebted to Kathy Anderson for her extremely capable assistance at all stages of this research.

1 Please note that a scale model differs in several important ways from a simple replica-type toy. For one thing, a scale model represents a particular other reality, and there are specific correspondences between objects within the model and the larger space it represents. Children's toys typically lack such specificity. A replica car has many of the most important features of cars in general (e.g., basic shape, wheels), but the cars played with by very young children usually do not represent any particular car. In addition, using a scale model involves matching one's representation of the model with one's representation of the larger space. Such precise representational mapping is not necessary in simply playing with replica toys. A child can engage in pretend play with a toy car without necessarily mapping his or her representation of the miniature car onto any specific, familiar car or, indeed, onto any real car at all. Many investigators of early pretense have argued that in part children's early pretend play involves play routines (e.g., making a "vroom-vroom" sound while pushing the car along the floor) that the child has learned from adults and older siblings (Bates, Benigni, Bretherton, Camaioni, & Volterra, 1979; DeLoache & Plaetzer, 1985; Sachs, 1980). It is not clear that more than minimal mapping is carried out in the mind of the child between these play routines and the events they seem to represent to an adult observer. In other words, young children are taught how to play with toys, and they can engage in these routines without necessarily thinking about the real-life counterparts of those toys as they do so. In contrast, a model can be used *as a model* only by thinking about its relation to the larger space it represents.

2 There is a clear limit to the advantage gained by decreasing the size disparity between the model and the space it represents. Retrieval 1 performance is much worse with two *identical* spaces than it is with two spaces that are of similar scale but that are still discriminately different in size. See DeLoache (1989a) for a summary of this research and for an explanation of why identical spaces present unique difficulties in this context.

REFERENCES

Acredolo, L. P. (1977). Developmental changes in the ability to coordinate perspectives of a large-scale space. *Developmental Psychology, 13,* 1–8.

Acredolo, L. P., Pick, L. L., & Olsen, M. G. (1975). Environmental differentiation and familiarity as determinants of children's memory for spatial location. *Developmental Psychology, 11,* 495–501.

Bates, E., Benigni, L., Bretherton, I., Camaioni, L., & Volterra, V. (1979). *The emergence of symbols: Cognition and communication in infancy.* New York: Academic Press.

Brown, A. L. (1989). Analogical learning and transfer: What develops? In S. Vosniadou & A. Ortony (Eds.), *Similarity and analogical reasoning* (pp. 369–412). London: Cambridge University Press.

Brown, A. L., & Campione, J. C. (1984). Three faces of transfer: Implications for early competence, individual differences, and instruction. In M. Lamb, A. Brown, & B. Rogoff (Eds.), *Advances in developmental psychology* (Vol. 3, pp. 143–192). Hillsdale, NJ: Erlbaum.

Brown, A. L., & Kane, M. J. (1988). Preschool children can learn to transfer. *Cognitive Psychology, 20,* 493–523.

Brown, A. L., Kane, M. J., & Echols, C. H. (1986). Young children's mental models determine analogical transfer across problems with a common goal structure. *Cognitive Development, 1,* 103–122.

Cantor, J. H. (1965). Transfer of stimulus pertaining to motor paired-associated and discrimination learning tasks. In L. P. Lipsitt & C. C. Spiker (Eds.), *Advances in child development and behavior* (Vol. 2, pp. 19–58). New York: Academic Press.

Cole, M., & Scribner, S. (1974). *Culture and thought.* New York: Wiley.

Crisafi, M. A., & Brown, A. L. (1986). Analogical transfer in very young children: Combining two separately learned solutions to reach a goal. *Child Development, 57,* 953–968.

Daehler, M. W., Lonardo, R., & Bukatko, D. (1979). Matching and equivalence judgments in very young children. *Child Development, 50,* 170–179.

DeLoache, J. S. (1985). Memory-based searching in very young children. In H. Wellman (Ed.), *The development of search ability* (pp. 151–183). Hillsdale, NJ: Erlbaum.

DeLoache, J. S. (1986). Memory in very young children: Exploitation of cues to the location of a hidden object. *Cognitive Development, 1,* 123–137.

DeLoache, J. S. (1987). Rapid change in the symbolic functioning of very young children. *Science, 238,* 1556–1557.

DeLoache, J. S. (1989a). The development of representation in young children. In H. Reese (Ed.), *Advances in child development and behavior* (Vol. 22, pp. 2–39). New York: Academic Press.

DeLoache, J. S. (1989b). Young children's understanding of the correspondence between scale model and a larger space. *Cognitive Development, 4,* 121–139.

DeLoache, J. S., & Brown, A. L. (1979). Looking for Big Bird: Studies of memory in very young children. *Quarterly Newsletter of the Laboratory of Comparative Human Cognition, 1,* 53–57.

DeLoache, J. S., & Brown, A. L. (1983). Very young children's memory for the location of objects in a large scale environment. *Child Development, 54,* 888–897.

DeLoache, J. S., & Brown, A. L. (1984). Where do I go next? Intelligent searching by very young children. *Developmental Psychology, 20,* 37–44.

DeLoache, J. S., Cassidy, D. J., & Brown, A. L. (1985). Precursors of mnemonic strategies in very young children. *Child Development, 56,* 125–137.

DeLoache, J. S., & DeMendoza, O. A. P. (1987). Joint picturebook reading of mothers and one-year-old children. *British Journal of Developmental Psychology, 5,* 111–123.

DeLoache, J. S., & Plaetzer, B. (1985, April). Tea for two: Joint symbolic play by mothers and young children. In J. S. DeLoache and B. Rogoff, *Collaborative cognition.* Symposium presented at the meeting of the Society for Research in Child Development, Toronto.

Gelman, R., & Baillargeon, R. (1983). A review of some Piagetian concepts. In J. H. Flavell and E. M. Markman (Eds.), *Handbook of child psychology: Vol. 3, Cognitive development* (pp. 167–230). New York: Wiley.

Gentner, D. (1983). Structure-mapping: A theoretical framework for analogy. *Cognitive Science, 7,* 155–170.

Gentner, D. (1988). Metaphor as structure mapping: The relational shift. *Child Development, 59,* 47–59.

Gentner, D. (1989). Mechanisms of analogical learning. In S. Vosniadou & A. Ortony (Eds.), *Similarity and analogical reasoning* (pp. 199–241). London: Cambridge University Press.

Gentner, D., & Toupin, C. (1986). Systematicity and surface similarity in the development of analogy. *Cognitive Science, 10*, 277–300.

Gick, M. L., & Holyoak, K. J. (1980). Analogical problem solving. *Cognitive Psychology, 12*, 306–355.

Gick, M. L., & Holyoak, K. J. (1983). Schema induction and analogical transfer. *Cognitive Psychology, 15*, 1–38.

Hartley, D. G. (1976). The effects of perceptual salience on reflective-impulsive performance differences. *Developmental Psychology, 12*, 218–225.

Holyoak, K. J., Junn, E. N., & Billman, D. O. (1984). Development of analogical problem-solving skill. *Child Development, 55*, 2042–2055.

Huttenlocher, J., & Higgins, E. T. (1978). Issues in the study of symbolic development. In W. A. Collins (Ed.), *Minnesota Symposia on Child Psychology* (Vol. 11, pp. 98–140). Hillsdale, NJ: Erlbaum.

Mandler, J. (1983). Representation. In J. H. Flavell & E. M. Markman (Eds.), *Handbook of child psychology: Vol. 3. Cognitive development* (pp. 420–494). New York: Wiley.

Mandler, J. (1988). How to build a baby. *Cognitive Development, 3*, 113–136.

McCune-Nicholich, L. (1981). Toward symbolic functioning: Structure of early pretend games and potential parallels with language. *Child Development, 52*, 785–797.

Ninio, A., & Bruner, J. (1978). The achievement and antecedents of labeling. *Journal of Child Language, 5*, 1–15.

Ornstein, P. A., & Naus, M. J. (1978). Rehearsal processes in children's memory. In P. A. Ornstein (Ed.), *Memory development in children*. Hillsdale, NJ: Erlbaum.

Potter, M. C. (1979). Mundane symbolism: The relations among objects, names, and ideas. In N. R. Smith & M. B. Franklin (Eds.), *Symbolic functioning in childhood* (pp. 41–65). Hillsdale, NJ: Erlbaum.

Reese, H. W. (1966). Verbal effects in the intermediate-size transposition problem. *Journal of Experimental Child Psychology, 3*, 123–130.

Sachs, J. (1980). The role of adult–child play in language development. In K. H. Rubin (Ed.), *Children's play*. San Francisco: Jossey-Bass.

Sigel, I. (1978). The development of pictorial comprehension. In B. S. Randhawa & W. S. Coffman, *Visual learning, thinking, and communication* (pp. 93–111). New York: Academic Press.

Smith, L. B. (1989). From global similarities to kinds of similarities: The construction of dimensions in development. In S. Vosniadou & A. Ortony (Eds.), *Similarity and analogical reasoning* (pp. 146–178). London: Cambridge University Press.

Stevenson, H. W. (1972). *Children's learning*. New York: Appleton-Century-Crofts.

6

Children's play interests, representation, and activity

K. ANN RENNINGER

If you were to watch two 3-year-old children playing with trains, the first child could well be linking the cars of the train together, at the same time keeping an eye on the small colored blocks across the way, to which she then drives the train and proceeds to load its cars. The second child might also be linking the cars' couplers, but instead pulls the engine forcefully causing the cars to fly off the ground before they start to unhinge at the couplers and crash. In both instances, the children are employing a particular set of actions with essentially the same play object.[1] They both know that trains can be hooked together, and their actions suggest that they probably know a fair amount about trains – the engine is used to pull cars, the cars link together to form a line, the wheels enable the train to move forward, the cars can be used for carrying loads. There are still more things these two children could (and, in fact, may) do with the trains. (They could organize the cars by type, they could build a railroad track for the train using big blocks, they could issue tickets for a ride, etc.) Some of these actions may not appear for weeks, some of them may never appear – at least in train play.

It is the thesis of this chapter that the way in which children play with play objects reflects what they represent to themselves as potential actions for play with these objects and may serve to gate information available to them in their subsequent play activity. In particular, the chapter focuses on aspects of young children's identified interests, or stored knowledge and value, for the play objects in their nursery school class. Findings from two studies conducted on the same sample of children will be used as the basis for this discussion of the role of individually identified interests and noninterests in children's representation of possibilities for action and their subsequent engagement with play objects.

In the first study, a combined naturalistic-experimental methodology was employed to evaluate the effect of interest on attention and memory of 3-year-old children. In the second study, the naturalistic component of the first study was examined in more depth. In this study the play actions of each child in free play were evaluated as a function of the value (interest, noninterest) of the play object, the affordances of that play object generally, and the gender of the child. Discussion of both studies focuses on the interest–representation–activity relation, the role of specific content in representation, and the implications of individual variation in interests for understanding children's development.

Interest, a subject variable

Interest is here conceptualized as involving elements of both knowledge and value. Knowledge refers to information about classes of objects and events in a given domain that the child has stored from past experience with instances of those objects and events. Value also refers to information that the child has stored from previous experience with objects and events in a given domain; however, rather than information about the objects and events themselves, it is information about the relationship between the objects and events and the self (Mead, 1934). Value thus refers to that which underlies the feelings children bring to continued involvement with the objects and events in a given domain (Vygotsky, 1967).

Operationally, a child identified as having an interest in trains will play with trains more frequently than with other objects, might fashion a train out of blocks, and while pushing a boat, may announce that it is "on the railroad track." In the nursery school, children's interests are thought to be reflected in the degree to which children maintain attention over time to objects. As Norman (1976) has pointed out, differential attention of this sort bears a reciprocal relationship to memory. Sustained attention affects the ease and likelihood with which objects will be encoded in memory; knowledge and value as long-term memory structures direct and sustain attention.

Historically, experimental psychological research on memory and attention has had two traditions. One, heavily influenced by if not originating with Ebbinghaus (1885/1914), has generally focused on stimulus variables. A second, dating from the very earliest experimental research on attention (Bessel, 1823) and strongly reinforced by Bartlett's (1932) studies of remembering has focused on subject variables.

The "Ebbinghaus" tradition was founded on the notion that psychological research should parallel the work of the natural sciences by developing techniques that guaranteed maximum experimental objectivity. As Ebbinghaus described the basis for his work:

We must try in experimental fashion to keep as constant as possible those circumstances whose influence on retention and reproduction is known or suspected, and then ascertain whether that is sufficient. The material must be so chosen that decided differences of interest are, at least to appearances, excluded. (p. 12)

Ebbinghaus, in other words, realized that interest might exert an important influence on memory process. Rather than choose to study this influence, he chose to rule it out by employing nonsense stimuli that would presumably be equally interesting or uninteresting for all subjects and presented the stimuli under highly controlled conditions. Rather than subject variables, the stimuli themselves and stimulus variables such as order, frequency, and type of presentation became the focus of his research – a legacy that continues to influence many current investigators.

The "Bartlett" tradition, on the other hand, concentrated on the subject and on the subject as an individual. Thus, Bartlett felt that the study of meaningful material was essential to an understanding of the nature of memory as it functions in everyday life. As he suggested,

because process and course of recall are inevitably bound up with the kind of material that has to be learned, I have discarded nonsense syllable material. . . . The dissolving power of modern research seems to have split Memory into a number of variously related functions. . . . Remembering is not a completely independent function, entirely distinct from perceiving, imaging, or even from constructive thinking, but it has intimate relations with them all. (pp. 11–12)

As a result, Bartlett chose to focus his investigations on "the conditions of response that have to be considered as resident within the organism," that is, in the subject.

With the transition to cognitive psychology (e.g., Berlyne, 1960; Broadbent, 1958; Bruner, Goodenow, & Austin, 1956; Hebb, 1949; Hunt, 1965; Miller, Galanter, & Pribram, 1960; Triesman, 1960) the two traditions of research on attention and memory became better integrated in a subject–stimulus interactionism. For example, Moray's (1959) use of the subject's name in shadowing experiments illustrated, at least in a limited way, that individual differences exist in information processing. Gray and Wedderburn's (1960) introduction of meaningful material in dichotic listening tasks demonstrated that meaning had to be taken into account in any analysis of processing mechanisms. Findings of this sort, together with the reemergence of a concern with cognitive development (Flavell, 1963; Piaget, 1954), eventually led to cognitive information-processing models of memory and attention in which performance was understood in terms of both conceptually driven (top-down) processes organized in relation to the subject's knowledge system and data-driven (bottom up) processes organized in relation to stimulus variables (Lindsay & Norman, 1976; Neisser, 1966; Norman, Rumelhart, & the LNR Research Group, 1975).

This focus on the interaction between stimulus and subject variables led to a shift from linear, single-task research models to multidimensional, multitask methods. Such methods permit both analysis of individual differences in the subject and for the study of relationships between these individual differences and performance across tasks. As Mostofsky (1970) noted, attention in particular requires multidimensional analysis for it involves the attentional process, the attentive subject, and the attention-getting stimulus. Similarly, Jenkins's (1979) tetrahedral research model goes even further by addressing the additional need to focus on subject variables in relation to orienting tasks (directions, instructions, etc.), criterial tasks (recall, recognition, etc.), and materials (psychological organization, psychological sequence, etc.) across similar problem-solving contexts. This need has also been touched on in discussion by Bransford (1979); Brown (1982); Hasher and Zacks (1979); Hunt (1978); Kahneman (1973); and Wellman and Somerville (1980).

Interest is only one of several subject variables to which Jenkins (1979) refers in his tetrahedral model. He also categorizes abilities, knowledge, and purposes as subject variables, and observes that investigators of subject variables have typically studied "a single paradigm of acquisition, a fixed body of material, a single dependent measure" (p. 432). The present conceptualization of interest is not intended to describe interest as a paradigm, as a fixed body of material, or as a single dependent measure. Instead, interest is conceptualized as reflecting the stored knowledge and value of an individual's prior engagements, and the representation requisite to this activity. Among adults, interests are thus assumed to take the form of a particular pattern of questioning or challenge setting which may but does not necessarily have to be described by a specific domain. With young children, on the other hand, it appears that the challenge setting and possibilities for action in which they engage are more readily identified with particular play objects. Thus, although train is the object with which interest is identified, it is not the object train that is "interest," rather, train is the content of the activity. Interest is the individual's cognitive and affective engagement with intended objects of interest. It is thought to vary among individuals and to serve as an organizer of individual activity. As such, interest involves perception of possibilities for action, representation of these possibilities to the self, and the setting, resolving, and resetting of challenges with that object.

Interest, as individually varying psychological state

In this section, literature specific to the study of interest is reviewed briefly, to provide an understanding of the possibilities afforded by study of interest as a subject variable and as one approach to describing variation between individuals in development. The study of interest has a long, if uneven, history in psychology. The importance of interest for study of attention and subsequent recall was noted at least as early as 1840 by Goethe (1914) in his classic analysis of color perception, and continued to be discussed among psychologists throughout the 19th and early 20th centuries. It virtually disappeared from the literature in the 1930s when "consciousness" and "attention" began to be eschewed as constructs relevant to psychological explanation and has only recently resurfaced as a "hot topic" for cognitive psychologists (Hidi & Baird, 1988). This renewed interest in interest appears to stem from at least four sources: increased attention to subject variables as potential influences on the way in which an orienting response is interpreted (Bransford, 1979; Brown, 1982; Jenkins, 1979); attention to individual differences across a variety of domains (Dillon 1985; Dillon & Schmeck 1983); detailing of task affordances (Gibson, 1979) and domain-specific knowledge (Chi, 1978); and a concurrent concern with identifying and understanding affect, emotion, and value in development (Mandler, 1975).

Generally speaking, conceptualizations of interest can be organized in terms of their orientation with respect to two characteristics: (a) focus on interests as a function of individual differences or on interest as a universal characteristic of human beings; and (b) conceptualization of interests as a trait or interest as a psychological state. Contemporary discussions have tended to focus on interest either as a trait stressing individual differences, or as a psychological state ignoring individual differences. Probably the most influential approach has been the individual difference–trait approach of psychometrics (Strong & Feder, 1961).

The psychometric approach, which uses quantitative indices to evaluate individual interest traits, evolved in the 1920s with the vocational-guidance movement. Within the context of this movement, employee–employment fit became the focus of study (see Fryer, 1931). Psychological research was oriented toward identifying personal traits through matching people to jobs that better suited their particular interests.

Another more recent approach to study of interest, exemplified by Izard (1977, 1979), has focused on observable behaviors characteristic of interest as a psychological state. This "interest expression" is identified through coding facial movement and is conceived of as a basic positive emotion presumed to provide motivation for facilitating cognitive and motor processes. In general, this approach has focused on the universal qualities of interest as a psychological state.

By contrast, early conceptualizations of interest focused on interest as a psychological state, which varied as a function of individual differences in experience. These conceptualizations first described interest solely in terms of experience and gradually became more elaborate, describing interest in terms of individual knowledge and value, both of which were thought to be rooted in experience. Theorists involved in this development included: Baldwin (1897, 1906, 1911); Dewey (1913, 1916); James (1890); Thorndike (1935), Piaget (1940), and Vygotsky (1967).

James (1890) discussed interest in terms of the organization of experience:

Millions of items of the outward order are present to my senses which never properly enter into my experience. Why? Because they have no *interest* for me. *My experience is what I agree to attend to.* Only those items which I *notice* shape my mind – without selective interest, experience is utter chaos. Interest alone gives accent and emphasis, light, and shade, background and foreground – intelligible perspective, in a word. (vol. 1, p. 402)

James's notions of perceptual learning foreshadowed the Gibsonian (Gibson, 1966, 1979) argument that practice schools attention to distinctive features. James's view, however, was even broader than Gibson's in that he felt not only practice, but interest, also improved a subject's ability to discriminate. Thus, interest was described by James as "a sharpener of discrimination alongside of practice" (vol. 1, p. 515). The effect that James associated with interest was that of molding the individual's experience.

Baldwin (1911) took a different approach in his discussion of interest. He described it in terms of the activities in which an individual engaged. Interest was described as a function of both knowledge of and involvement with an activity. Thus, for Baldwin, both cognitive structures that the child brought to activity in the world and the competence the child experiences in action and its accompanying affect characterized interest.

In his discussion of interests, Dewey (1916) elaborated on this relationship between interest and competence in action by suggesting that interest was in the material. He labeled the worth of materials in continuously engaging activity as their interest value. Dewey advised teachers to link new material with the child's purposes, to "discover objects and modes of action, which are connected with present powers. The function of this material in engaging activity and carrying it on consistently and continuously is its interest" (p. 149).[2]

Thus, Dewey felt children could only act on tasks that were within their "present power," which included both ability level and interests. The teacher who tried to create "an interest" in something which was not "of interest" to the child would probably be unsuccessful.

Thorndike (1935) expanded on these discussions. A student of James, he spoke of interest as the past experience of a person that acts as a tendency to "cause attention, practice, satisfaction or success, and so increased ability" (p. 45). For him both the motivational value as well as the competence involved in sustained attention were important components of interest.

This affective aspect of interest was also stressed by Vygotsky (1967) in his critique of play theories. He described interest as a need of the child in activity and argued for more attention to subject variables generally and interest as a reflection of the child's commitment in action more specifically:

... the trouble with a number of theories of play lies in their tendency to intellectualize the problem. .... I think that the mistake of a large number of accepted theories is their disregard for the child's needs – taken in the broadest sense from inclinations to interest, as needs of an intellectual nature – or, more briefly, the disregard of everything that can come under the category of incentives and motives for action. (pp. 538–539)

Finally, Piaget (1940) brought the cognitive and motivational components of interest together while also linking interest to the acts of mental assimilation which construct experience.

Interest is the proper orientation for every act of mental assimilation. .... [It] commences with the beginnings of psychological life and plays an essential role in the development of sensorimotor intelligence. But with the development of intuitive thought interests multiply and differentiate and give rise to a progressive dissociation between the energizing mechanisms that imply interest and the values interest engenders. (p. 340)[3]

Taken together, the early theorists suggest that interest organizes experience as a function of both knowledge and value. Embedded in these discussions are suggestions that: (a) interest schools attention; (b) interest organizes experience; (c) interest is reflected in the task (play object, idea, text, etc.); (d) experience gates information stored in memory; and (e) different types of experience gate what gets stored in memory. Underlying these discussions is an assumption that individuals vary in their experience and interest.

In contrast, most recent discussions of interest have tended to elaborate interests as universal psychological states. These discussions have primarily had two focuses: (a) interest as affect or emotion (e.g., Izard, 1977, 1979), and (b) the "interestingness" of the text (or, more generally, tasks) with which the subject engages. In his work on interest, Izard has been primarily concerned with the affective content of interest. Findings from his laboratory suggest that 2- to 8-month-old infants differentiate between stimuli as a function of interest, suggesting that interest is a significant predictor of visual fixation (Langsdorf, Izard, Rayias, & Hembree, 1983).

Research on interestingness, on the other hand, is focused on ways in which text can be modified to enhance interest. Findings from these studies indicate that individuals will attend to (Garner, Gillingham, & White, 1989), and recall both narrative and expository text (Hidi & Baird, 1986; 1988) as well as sentences (Anderson 1982; Anderson, Mason, & Shirey, 1984) that create a positive valence for the reader. The aspects of context that have been manipulated to contribute to interestingness include: characterization, plot, theme, and setting (Anderson, Shirey, Wilson, & Fielding, 1986). In addition to manipulation of context, structural features of texts such as insertions, elaborations, and seductive details have been employed to increase the interestingness of text (Hidi & Baird, 1988; Garner et al., 1989).

Substantial effects of interest on both subject fixation and comprehension provide powerful arguments for continuing to research subject interest and the interestingness of text. Such research provides specific information about subjects and texts, respectively, and, as such, contributes to ways in which environments and texts can be organized. However, this research does not address the interdependence of the individual child's response and features of the text or task. For purposes of application in particular, consideration of subject and task interdependence is important because it is this interaction that specifies the way in which information is processed by the individual. Such data are potentially useful in remediating children's "faulty rules" (Ginsburg, 1977), mapping the range of individual variance in a variety of aspects of learning, and addressing individual variation in children's development. Focus on particular subject–task interaction (system, or activity) that incorporates the individual subject's understanding of task as a function of experience (Rogoff & Mistry, 1985) not only facilitates evaluation of contextual effects of both subjects and tasks as independent influences on learning, but provides a lens for understanding the respective contributions of each to the other as well.

One approach to the study of subject–task interaction involves controlling for individual differences between children with respect to the variables under study. In the present studies, differences between children with respect to the content of their interests was expected based on findings from psychometric studies of interest indicating that interests vary across individuals. On the other hand, that each individual could be identified as having an interest further suggested that the discussion of universal characteristics of interestingness as an influence on comprehension could be thought of as an alternate and complementary level of analysis. Thus, it was expected that although the impact of interest on cognitive functions might be universal, the specifics of what the individual child brings to his or her understanding of task affordances (Gibson, 1966) might well vary as a function of personal experience. Such an argument appears to have general support in discussion of cognitive mapping (Neisser, 1976) and the child as craftsperson (Feldman, 1980); although these discussions do not focus specifically on differences between individuals in the way in which information from the environment is picked up and how it might impact on subsequent activity.

The present discussion of interest focuses on interest as an individually varying, but universal, psychological state. It draws on previous conceptions of interest to address three relatively applied aspects of child–task engagement. Specifically: (a) Do individual interests affect the way in which children engage and learn from tasks with which they do have experience? (b) Do children represent tasks (their demands and potentials) that are of interest to them differently than they do tasks that are not of interest to them? (c) What is the effect of identified interests on a child's subsequent task engagement or activity?

Such questions focus on the individual learner as co-constructing his or her understanding, or theory (Carey, 1985) about the world, in conjunction with the objects and others that make up that world. Because of the individual nature of this construction, it seems reasonable that although the underlying structures are probably universal, the particular content of engagement may provide a specific function for the individual in terms of determining the kinds of questions with which he or she has practice, the challenges he or she sets for him- or herself – in short, the way he or she understands what it is that a task represents as possibilities for action. Specifically, if the kinds of things to which an individual attends and the comprehension one has in attending are influenced by what Piaget (1940) referred to as secondary interests (e.g., attractions, novel learning), it seems reasonable to assume based on the work of early theorists and the applied success of the psychometric approaches in ascertaining particular differences in the content of individual interests, that individual differences in interest may well have implications for understanding how individuals engage (and learn from) tasks.

Discussions of experts and novices in particular content areas (e.g., Chi, 1978; Chi, Glaser, & Rees, 1982; Chiesi, Spilich, & Voss, 1979; Spilich, Vesonder, Chiesi, & Voss, 1979) have demonstrated the importance of domain-specific knowledge with respect to memory performance. These findings suggest that based on knowledge of a domain, it can be expected that experts and novices will differ in performance. Recent findings from Ericsson and Crutcher (in press) suggest, however, that experts and novices in a domain generally do not differ in aptitude or general reasoning. Rather than contradict each other, these findings suggest that what may differ between the performance of experts and novices in domains may not simply be knowledge. Instead, the difference may be explained by both the stored knowledge and value, or interest, that the subject has for a particular domain. In other words, equating expertise with prior knowledge alone may be too simplistic an explanation for differences in expert and novice performance.

Findings from case studies of persons learning computers and music suggest that individuals who develop an interest in computers are more inclined to reengage with computer tasks, and to persevere longer in their task engagement than are those who do not report a developing interest (Prenzel, 1988). In other words, the task is represented to the self in such a way that an individual has predominantly positive emotions toward this task (whether computers or music, or some other domain), and if asked to compare this engagement with others in which the individual was involved, this task is ranked high in the individual hierarchy of values (Schiefele, 1987). In this conceptualization, interest is a specific "person–object relation" that includes an emotional as well as an affective component. The central feature of interest is its intrinsic character. Knowledge is understood to develop in coordination with the positive valence one holds for a particular object (task, etc.). With respect to subsequent action, interest is conceptualized as "a scheme within a structure of valences, linking a multitude of individual valences of actions, action outcomes, and consequences of action" (Schiefele, 1987). The questions that form the basis of this approach to the study of interest are questions of origins: how interest develops, and the characterization of progress in learning that leads to classification as an expert or novice relative to others working on the same task. Three aspects of the Educational Theory of Interest distinguish it from studies of experts and novices. First, this discussion of interest also includes a discussion of value. Second, this discussion identifies individuals as varying by domain with respect to the way in which knowledge emerges, rather than focusing on learning of the task domain per se. Third, this discussion suggests that individuals are reflectively aware of their interest(s).

In contrast, although the present discussion of interest focuses on interest as involving both stored knowledge and value, and on the individual as co-constructing his or her understanding of tasks, it does not address the way in which interests emerge, nor does it presume that individuals are always reflectively aware of interest as a psychological state. For the purpose of experimentation, the subject's engagement with a task is considered to be reflected in individually identified objects of interest and noninterest. As such, this approach to the study of interest focuses on the role of interest (stored knowledge and value) and noninterest (knowledge and low value) in learning and subsequent task engagements. It assumes that the individual's present task engagements reflect the way in which he or she has represented possibilities for action to himself or herself, the kinds of questions posed, and the challenges to which he or she responds.

There is some precedent for discussing interdependence of subject and task with respect to the way in which information is processed. Eckblad (1981), in particular, focuses on the importance of individual contributions to task engagement in her discussion of scheme theory, the relation between the schemes of a particular person and a set of stimuli. Eckblad reports that in all but one case, interesting stimuli were optimally arousing, being placed between *complex* and *pleasant* on a stimulus dimension. These findings build on those that established optimal levels of discrepancy in task presentation (e.g., Hunt, 1965) – that there are particular points in attending to tasks when attention is heightened because of the difference that exists between the task as previously experienced and the task as presented (or represented). If interest as psychological state can be characterized as reflecting the kinds of optimally discrepant possibilities for action, questions and challenges that individuals set for themselves in continued engagement with an identified object of interest, it seems reasonable to expect that studies where subjects received tasks that were personally interesting and noninteresting might significantly contribute to our existing understanding of child–task engagement, particularly individual differences in the processing of contents that children do learn. In addition, such findings would provide insights for facilitating children's learning in domains (or aspects of domains), for which they do not have an identified interest.

To begin to map the role of interest in what might best be described as experimental learning (ongoing play with familiar play objects), the studies described here were designed to evaluate (a) subject–task engagement with respect to the effect of the individual's identified interests across tasks assessing three dimensions of processing: attention, recognition, and recall memory; and (b) the role of both individual interests and task affordances in representation of and activity with naturally occurring tasks.

The studies reported here were designed to evaluate interest conceptualized as both the stored knowledge and value an individual brings to subsequent engagement with a task. They focus on tasks with which the individual is already knowledgeable, and they do not presume that the individual is aware that interest is influencing performance. In fact, identification of interest is based on naturally occurring task involvements of each individual studied, and is determined relative to that individual's involvement with every task in which he or she is involved.

Three-year-old children were selected as the focus of the studies because: (a) they are not able to feign interest and are not experimenter-wise; (b) they can follow directions necessary to follow up experimental tasks; (c) they accommodate easily to videotaping (so that identification of interest could be based on observed behaviors rather than self-report); (d) competence was not acquired so quickly with any play object that it was not possible to study their actions in free play; and (e) the nursery setting afforded the possibility of studying children's actions in a contained environment.

Both studies being discussed were conducted using the same sample of 3-year-old children. The children were videotaped during free play at nursery school over the second term of their nursery school year. As such, each of the 16 children (8 males, 8 females) was as familiar with each of the 16 available play objects and each of his or her peers as could be expected. The videotapes were coded once to identify individual interests and noninterests for each child. These identified interests were then employed to construct stimulus sets in the first study and to evaluate the role of interest and noninterest in the children's actions in the second study.

Naturalistic identification of children's interests (and noninterests)

Procedures

Following procedures outlined in Renninger and Wozniak (1985), six videotapes, each 40 minutes in length, were made of each child in free play at nursery school. For purposes of data reduction, each 40-minute tape was divided into 2.5-minute segments and the child's activity during each segment was continuously coded in terms of the object, content, and interpersonal nature of play. Thus, interest for a play object was determined by the quality and quantity of sustained attention maintained by the child for 2.5 minutes or more across the videotaped play sessions.

For experimental purposes, children were identified as having an interest in a particular class of objects if, over the sessions of free play, they: (a) returned to that object repeatedly; (b) spent more time playing with that object than with other play objects; (c) would at times play with that object in solitary play; *and* (d) would at times play in other than manipulative play with that object.

Alternatively, play objects of the children were identified as noninterest if the child did have knowledge of the object but lacked value for that object relative to the value demonstrated for objects of interest. Thus, using the same procedure for data reduction as that used to identify children's interests, children were identified as having a noninterest in a particular class of play objects if, over the videotaped play sessions, they: (a) did spend time with these objects; (b) could use something other than manipulative play with the noninterest object; *and* (c) did not spend as much time with these play objects as they did with their identified objects of interest; and (d) did not play with the object in solitary play. (In instances where more than one play object could have been identified as

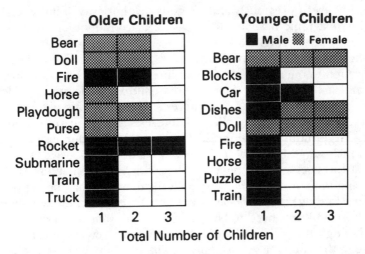

Figure 6.1 Children's interests by age and sex. (Reprinted from Renninger and Wozniak, 1985, by permission.)

a noninterest, a noninterest item was randomly selected from a pool of potential noninterests by an adult unfamiliar with the experiment.)

Only those objects continuously available to all children were considered potential objects of interest and noninterest. Therefore, interest is here discussed as being reflected in the experimental play behaviors of children with the play objects available to them in the nursery school setting.

Results and discussion

Two interests were identified for each child. Both of these were much stronger for that child than were other potential play interests present in the nursery environment. Findings regarding the content of children's interests are presented in Figure 6.1. These findings indicate that: (a) children's interests tend to be strong and relatively well focused; (b) between children interests vary widely; (c) by ages 2.9 to 4.2 years, the specific contents of the identified interests of boys and girls have almost totally diverged, boys' interests being in general more heterogeneous than those of girls; and (d) within this age range, older children as a group have somewhat different interests than younger children.

Although children do tend to maintain attention to certain classes of play objects in the environment longer and more frequently than they do with other objects, one child's interests are not, as a rule, the interests of other children. In fact, interests appear to vary widely. This dual characterization of interest as a psychological state on the one hand, and an individual difference variable on the other, supports the early views of interest viewed previously and suggests that intensity of individual interest for text topic may in fact be a useful consideration in subsequent studies of interestingness.

The variation in children's interests is even more striking when viewed in relation to the range and type of interests chosen as a function of the age and sex of the child. Among older children, males and females each had the same number (5) of interests. However, this pattern was not characteristic of younger children's interests. The group of younger boys had a larger number of interests (7) than did the group of younger girls (3), which suggests that older girls may be more responsive to new interests at this age and that boys may be solidifying their interest and thus focusing their attention more specifically than they had been previously. (These findings are cross-sectional and based on a limited sample of children, and thus need to be considered with some reservation.)

Although the girls in the older group had a few more interests than those in the younger group, only two of all of the girls' interests, horse and play-dough, are not sex-stereotyped. These interests were held only by older girls. A contrasting tendency is present with respect to age and type of boys' interests, however. The boys in the younger group were somewhat less stereotypical in their choice of interests (blocks, dishes, horse, and puzzle) than the boys in the older group, who all chose sex-stereotyped interests. Others such as Van Alstyne (1932) have noted similar patterns of sex-stereotyped interests among this age group.

In contrast to the differences in direction of interest among children, the relative strength of interest between children seems to be quite consistent. A little boy with an interest in trains may in general be expected to be neither markedly more nor markedly less strongly interested in his trains than a little girl with an interest in bears will be interested in her bears. From a constructivist perspective, interest could be said to reflect the child's differential experience with the environment, particularly experience involving action on objects. As the child engages in play, the possibilities of action that the particular play objects afford presumably become more clear. Differences between the affordances of different objects and events, then, may provide the basis for a greater differentiation of attention (Gibson, 1966, 1979; Gibson and Rader, 1979) and thus greater differentiation of interest. Individual differences in the direction of interest, then, reflect individual differences in the children's stored knowledge and value.

As both Piaget (1940) and Vygotsky (1967) have suggested, interest also reflects the child's values. Presumably, as the child engages in action with various play objects and develops feelings of competence (White, 1959) with those objects, and as the child encounters objects in social contexts that enhance their value (Lewin, 1935; Mead, 1934), the child comes to feel positively toward them. It appears that regardless of the particular direction (specific content) in which their interests take them, young children will probably be highly motivated to engage objects of interest in any situation in which they find them. This notion – that interest would impel children to engage actively with particular play objects – was a major premise of the two studies that follow.

Interest, attention, and memory

This study of the effect of interest on attentional shift, recognition, and recall memory is detailed by Renninger and Wozniak (1985). It was specifically designed as a multidimensional, multitask analysis in which the effect of interest would be assessed across three processing situations. The study was designed to assess the performance of young children across a set of related tasks that would permit evaluation of both levels of processing, as well as within and between child differences on tasks as a function of interest.

Based on the work of the early theorists, and in particular the work of Arnold (1910) and Bartlett (1932), it was expected that interest would affect attention and recall. Arnold argued that the relation between attention and interest was reciprocal. He maintained that sustained attention led to the development of interest, and interest, in turn would increase the likelihood of sustained attention. For the purposes of studying interest as a variable reflecting experience, however, it seemed reasonable to expect that attentional shifts might in fact reflect attention to objects of interest. Such a possibility was implied by Turvey (1973) in his discussion of the way in which individuals constantly monitor information being received in the peripheral visual field. Specifically, if individuals use that part of experience which is not focal to determine subsequent shifts in attentional focus, it might be expected that when the presence of an object of interest was indicated, attention would involuntarily shift in the direction of that object.

Bartlett (1932) makes a similar point in discussing primacy–recency effects in serial recall, stating that:

> when material is arranged in serial order, items at the beginning and at the end occupy a favorable position so far as clearness in recall goes. It is of course no psychological explanation merely to refer to position as an objective factor, and to put the superiority down vaguely to greater expenditure of "attention." There is no actual evidence, and there seems to be no way of obtaining any evidence, that in such cases a greater amount of "attention," whatever this may be, is expended. . . . In fact, position function is probably of diminishing importance the further we get from the nonsense syllable type of memory work.
>
> The primary determinant of relative clearness in this series was the functioning of preformed interests. (p. 56)

According to Bartlett, recall performance improves as a function of the meaningfulness of the stimuli to the subject. He also notes diminished effects of order as tasks reflected such meaning. Thus, the hypothesis that an identified object of interest placed in the middle serial position, that position least likely to be recalled (Murdock, 1962), might in fact be recalled by young children was suggested by his findings. The recall portion of this study also follows up on his suggestion that one might think about the range of stimuli on a continuum the endpoints of which might be labeled "nonsense" and "preformed interest." The preformed interest of his study was a general group interest in World War II.

The present research extends Bartlett's research on interest by specifying individually meaningful stimuli – interests as individually assessed based both on stored knowledge and on value. The hypothesis for this aspect of this study, then, is based on the notion that interest is a specifically directed psychological state whose direction varies among individuals on the basis of their particular knowledge and value systems.

On the other hand, findings from study of young children's recognition memory suggest that because recognition memory is so well developed by 3 years of age, children typically reach a ceiling in recognition tasks. Thus, although interest might theoretically be expected to affect the way in which items presented for recognition were processed, it was also anticipated that such effects might be difficult to isolate experimentally. As such, it was anticipated that even if no effect of interest on recognition memory could be determined, this task would provide an instructive contrast to the children's performance on the attention and recall tasks.

Procedures

Based on the naturalistic identification of interests, objects identified as interests were embedded in experimental tasks that assessed attentional shift, recognition, and recall. Objects of a given child's interest were employed as that child's target stimuli in each task. For that same child, the objects of every other child's interest were employed as comparison stimuli. Thus, relative preference across children for objects of interest was not, in general, preference for the same objects and cannot therefore be attributed to variations in stimulus salience. In both the recognition and recall tasks, additional "filler" objects were also employed to provide context.

Because two objects of interest were identified for each child there were two sets of stimuli for each group of children studied. In addition, because there were two age groups involved in the study and these each had somewhat different interests, interest differed by age. Objects for the older group of children were: Set (1) horse, play-dough, purse, rocket, train, and water-toys; and Set (2) bear, blocks, doll, fire hat, truck, and submarine. Objects for the younger group were: Set (1) bear, book, dishes, fire hat, horse, and train; and, Set (2) blocks, car, doll, paint-brushes, play-dough, and puzzle.

Two female adults, familiar to the children, collected all of the data. The attention task was administered first, followed by the recognition and recall tasks. The tasks were designed to evaluate whether the pickup as well as the retrieval of information presented to young children would vary as a function of individual differences in interest. Thus, the attentional shift task consisted of a series of "interest wheels" in which the experimenter presented pictures of identified objects of interest and noninterest to the children's visual peripheral field. Shifts in eye gaze to these objects were then recorded and analyzed for the presence of interest effects.

The recognition task consisted of a "birthday game" in which drawings of interest and noninterest objects were shown to the children and then presented in a novel context for free-choice recognition. In this task, level of recognition and the order in which items were recognized were recorded and evaluated. Finally, a modified version of Perlmutter and Myers's (1977) recall task was used to present nine play objects from the nursery school to the children for recall. The identified object of interest was placed in the middle position (Position 5) of a series of identified noninterest objects, and the children were asked to recall what they saw. Overall level and order of recall were recorded and analyzed for the presence of interest effects.

Results and discussion

Overall findings from this study suggest that: (a) Children's individual interests exert a marked influence on shifts in focal attention to objects in their peripheral visual field; (b) children's individual interests influence both the likelihood that an item will be correctly recognized when en-countered again and the likelihood that an incorrect filler item will be falsely identified as previously encountered, at least within the particular task employed in this study; and (c) children's individual interests power-fully influence level of recall. So marked is this effect that recall of an interest object placed in that position (middle) generally least likely to be recalled is (for older subjects) equal to or (for younger subjects) even greater than recall of objects in that position (final) generally most likely to be recalled.

More specifically, results of the task assessing attentional shift sug-gested that children are substantially more likely to shift fixation, and to shift fixation first to an interest object than to comparison objects that are of interest to other children. Moreover, no differences were found in performance between trials indicating that the children's performance was remarkably even.

The potential implications of these findings are far-reaching. Processing of information from the peripheral visual field has been discussed as an important determinant of where the eye looks next (Turvey, 1973). There is, however, little research on the depth with which events in the periphery are processed as the eye is guided in its search for information necessary to adaptive action. The results of this portion of the study provide a foundation for arguing that shifts in attention are influenced not only by the perceptual characteristics of the peripheral objects or events, but by the value they have for the subject. This would seem to indicate that the children are processing peripheral stimulus information at a sufficient depth to be carrying out a process of evaluation, even if it is one of which they are not reflectively aware. Such a suggestion implies that although interest may influence the way in which knowledge develops, it is a psychological state of which the subject may not be aware. Finally, since no differences were found between the first and last trials of the interest wheel, it appears that the influence of interest on the direction of attentional shift is remarkably consistent phenomena. Interest, then, is not only a strong determinant of shifts in attention but also remains so over multiple encounters with the same situation.

Results of the recognition task mirror those of the attentional shift task. These findings suggest that children are more likely to recognize a given interest item and to choose a given interest item first than they are to recognize items of noninterest or to choose them first. Furthermore, when children make false positive recognitions, they are much more likely to involve items judged as related to their interests than would be expected by chance, or excitedly to mislabel objects as involving their identified object of interest. Thus, for example, a child identified as having an interest in trains, exclaimed, "What a long train," when presented with a filler item depicting a fishing rod.

Presumably, when children are shown an interest item embedded in a context of other items, they are more likely to attend to it and, possibly, to attend to it more closely. On recognition trials, in which the same item is embedded in a different context, the close attention children have paid to the item during the original presentation may facilitate the likelihood that it will be recognized, that is, that the children will experience a sense of familiarity with it on the second encounter.

It should be noted, however, that given the nature of the recognition task, another alternative is at least conceivable. The task is constructed so that the children are asked to help another child choose those items from among a larger set that were the toys the other child had received for his or her birthday. If the children projected their own desires onto the task, the high rate of interest items selected might as much reflect personal desire for those items as it does recognition of the items as belonging to the original set. The tendency for false positive recognitions to be associated with interest items could also reflect such an effect. On the other hand, levels of recognition are generally high for this age group (Brown & Campione, 1972; Brown & Scott, 1971; Corsini, Jacobus, & Leonard, 1969; Perlmutter & Myers, 1974) and should limit this type of effect. In addition, the results of the recall task suggest that young children are capable of recalling the presence of an interest object from a set of comparison objects. Thus, it stands to reason that if recall is possible – particularly because this age group has been characterized as limited in recall (Perlmutter & Lange, 1978) – recognition as a perceptual judgment of familiarity is certainly possible. Taken together, the findings for the recognition task suggest that, like attentional shift, recognition is powerfully influenced by interest.

Results of the recall task demonstrated differences in recall with respect to serial position (interest and recency) and, to a much lesser extent, age. First, older children tended to have higher overall levels of recall than did younger children, although this effect did not quite reach statistical significance. Second, younger children manifested a considerably weaker recency effect than did the older children. Third, and perhaps most importantly, the interest effect manifested by the level of recall for objects in Position 5 was strong for all children. For younger subjects, Position 5 had the highest level of recall, greater even than the level of recall for Position 9, the recency position. For older subjects, the level of recall for Position 5 was roughly equivalent to that for Position 9, but recall for these two positions was superior to all other positions.

Because this study represents a variation on that of Perlmutter and Myers (1979), it is instructive to contrast these findings with those which they reported. The first finding of higher overall recall for older subjects is consistent with that of Perlmutter and Myers. The fact that this finding did not reach statistical significance in this study, whereas it did in the Perlmutter and Myers research, probably reflects the fact that Perlmutter and Myers studied two more widely separated age groups (2.9 to 3.1 and 3.8 to 4.8 years of age) than were involved in this investigation (2.9 to 3.5 and 3.6 to 4.2 years of age).

The second finding, that the recency effect for younger children was weaker than that for older children, does not parallel that of Perlmutter and Myers, who found no differences between age groups as a function of serial position. It seems possible that this difference may be explained by the relative strength of the interest effect for the younger group – younger children manifested the highest level of recall for interest objects, objects at Position 5. Under the assumption that younger children have an overall recall limitation of 1 to 3 objects (as is also indicated by these data), high levels of recall for Position 5 brought about by systematically introducing an interest object into that position may have directly reduced the capacity available for recall of objects in the recency position.

This line of reasoning is supported by the presence of an age difference in intrusions noted by the observer during the testing. Half of the older children mentioned that their identified object of interest was *not* in the box, while younger children typically included an interest object in their recall just as though the object had actually been present during the given trial – even when that particular interest object was not part of that stimulus set. Possibly, younger children, thinking globally in terms of "toys" when asked was in the box, simply mentioned a favorite toy – namely their interest object. It is consistent with this that no objects other than objects identified previously as interest objects were observed to occur as intrusions.

The third finding, which recall of Position 5 was high and, for younger children, even higher than that for Position 9, is in marked contrast to that of Perlmutter and Myers's finding that low levels of recall occurred for all except the recency position.

Clearly, children's interest in the object of interest greatly influenced the likelihood that it would be recalled. Perlmutter and Myers have suggested that improvement in recall for serial positions other than the last requires the development of rehearsal strategy and increased general knowledge brought about by children's expanding experience with the world. It seems reasonable that both of these factors do, in fact, contribute to improved recall as children develop. However, the results of the present study suggest that the development of rehearsal strategies may not be necessary for recalling an object in the middle serial position when the object in that position is an identified object of interest.

In this particular task, the presence of interest effects suggests that, by age 3, enough knowledge has been acquired with respect to a class of play objects that the potential actions and challenges particular to that class of play objects have begun to characterize individual children's evolving knowledge structures and serve to differentiate the specific content of their knowledge base from that of other children. Thus, interest might be said to inform the differentiation of perception and, in turn, the quality of recall.

Furthermore, differential performance by the children with respect to identified objects of interest suggests that the experimental use of toys as stimulus objects for young children in recall needs to be reevaluated. Typicality of "toy" for a particular age group is not the same as interest in a given toy. Although a similar point has been made with respect to adult categorization (Malt & Smith, 1982), "toys" have generally been considered very appropriate and relatively similar stimuli for the study of young children.

Findings from this study of the effect of interest on attention and memory indicate that interest exerts a marked influence on attentional shift, recognition, and recall memory among young children. In fact, interest is so influential in the performance of children on these tasks that they shifted eye gaze to their identified items of interest first, and described these objects first on both the recognition and recall tasks. Clearly, if interest is such a powerful influence on performance, then it might be expected that study of these children's actions in free play would begin to provide insights about the way in which interest gates the kinds of possibilities for action these children represent to themselves and on which they subsequently act.

Interest, representation, and action

In the previous study, interest was employed as a dependent variable and its effect on attentional shift, recognition, and recall memory of young children was evaluated. Findings indicate not only that interest affects attentional shift, recognition, and recall memory, but that its effect is so overwhelming that no particular distinctions emerged between these three dimensions of children's processing. Thus, given observations of children's actions in free play that suggested there are substantial differences in their activity, it was anticipated that by specifying contrasts between interest and noninterest with respect to value, and by focusing on the structure of children's actions, it might be possible to evaluate further the role of interest (and noninterest) in children's task engagement.

To avoid conflation of knowledge and interest effects, noninterest was conceptualized as involving knowledge and low value. To avoid a confound between aptitude for performance with particular objects and identified objects of interest and noninterest, identified objects of interest and noninterest were individually identified for each child relative to that child's play with all available play objects, and were then studied relative to the mean proportion of their behaviors with these identified objects of interest and noninterest. Finally, to facilitate evaluation of child–task engagement as a function of interest and not simply the probability that some play objects actually afforded more possibilities for action than did others, a modal task affordance for each play object with respect to each of the variables studied was calculated based on all of the children's play actions. This rating was then employed as an independent variable in analyses. Thus, based on the assumption that children's actions in free play reflect their understanding of possibilities for action with those play objects (or at least the way in which they are able to carry out their understanding of these possibilities), the present study was designed to address the way in which different types of experience gate the content that children represent to themselves through evaluating children's play actions with those objects as a function of interest, task affordance, and gender.

In discussing current work on event presentation, Nelson (1986) notes that one of the assumptions underlying this research has been that "differences in initial perceptual representations imply differences in derived structures as well as in cognitive performance" (p. 17). She continues to suggest that because "schemas in part guide perception, perceptual representation of the same event may differ for children to the extent that their schemas for that event differ" (p. 17). In other words, Nelson suggests that there are individual understandings of events that deviate from the event representations the individual eventually will develop. Given that interest appears to affect attention and memory of young children powerfully, and that the specific contents of children's interests vary as they do, it seemed reasonable to suggest that in addition to the similarities that characterize the development of young children's understanding of "events," there may be some fairly systematic differences in this development as well. In order to investigate the possibility that children's interests might differentially influence their representation of tasks (and subsequently their activity), this study was designed to evaluate children's play across objects available in their nursery school classroom.

Procedures

The videotaped free play of each of the 16 children (8M, 8F) who were subjects of the previous study was independently reanalyzed to identify each child's actions with each of 16 play objects continuously available to the children. Following this, children's actions with those objects identified previously as interests and noninterests were evaluated as a function of value (interest and noninterest), task affordance, and gender.

Identification of children's actions with objects involved continuous coding of all tapes of each child in free play. Coding consisted of: (a) identifying the object of play, (b) the type of play, as well as (c) the particular action (within type of play) as these occurred. All data including duration of each data point were recorded by computer.

Although the specific actions with which children engage with discrete play objects may vary, observation of children's behaviors indicate that it is possible to describe the type(s) of play in which the child is engaged and types of play to which a child might shift in play across their play with each of the available play objects. To facilitate comparison of children's play across play objects (trains, dolls, etc.), a taxonomy of play types was developed, based on observations conducted using another sample of children playing in the same classroom with the same play objects as those employed in this study. The taxonomy identifies the structural features of children's actions with play objects. The types of play described by this taxonomy include: investigative, functional, operational, transformational, and facilitative play (Renninger, 1984). Each of these types of play is thought to reflect the child's exploration of challenge-setting, and as such different dimensions of child–task engagement.[4]

In *investigative play*, children's actions are described as reflecting exploration of the physical attributes of an object. Thus, for example, in investigative train play a child might drop the train, push it sideways, or play with the coupler. The kinds of challenges with which the child is thought to be engaging in investigative play, then, involve exploration of new options for play with the object, features with which the child has not previously been engaged. In *functional play*, children are described as continuing to explore the properties of a class of objects, but this exploration reflects convention. Thus, in functional train play a child might hook cars together, push the train (engine first), or load and unload the train. In functional play children demonstrate a culturally consistent understanding of what is and is not a train. The kinds of challenges with which children are thought to be engaging include mimicking and making connections between their play and the functional uses of these objects in the larger world in which they live.

In *operational play*, children's actions are sometimes described as exploration, but this exploration is generally described as reflecting preoccupation with relations such as: counting, dividing, ordering, and so on. Superficially, children's play may appear to be either investigative or functional; however, continuous monitoring of the play often reveals repetition of sequencing, counting, dividing, adding, subtracting, balancing, or attention to regularities of motion. For example, in operational train play the child might: connect and disconnect cars repeatedly, get down to eye level with the train, and pull it forward and backward while focusing on the wheels; or order the cars by size, color, and the like. Thus, the kinds of challenges with which the child is thought to be engaging include exploring and developing an understanding of systematic or programmatic action.

In *transformational play*, children's actions are described as reflecting the use of one object to represent another object. In transformational train play, a child might make tickets out of paper, use a line of chairs to denote a train, or step out of a large rocking boat and announce, "We're at the train station, Bill." Train is the object of play even though there are no trains or model trains being used. The challenges the child is thought to be engaging in transformational play involve maintaining the flow of an image in play. This requires substituting something else as the "object" when it is not available.

Finally, in *facilitative play*, the object is generally described as supporting children's actions in other play areas. In facilitative train play, the train might be carried to the easels and placed on a nearby window ledge. A child might paint, and when finished pick up the train and move with it to another play area. The challenges for the child in facilitative play are thought to include the ability to divide attention between objects, and separating from an object that provides security (Gay & Hyson, 1976).

Identification of particular actions within each type of play refers to what the child was doing. Thus, one child's investigative play with trains might involve holding the engine upside down and spinning one wheel and then another wheel, whereas another child's investigative play with trains might include pushing a train with one car sideways, stopping the pushing motion, pushing again, and then reorganizing the way the train was connected so that the wheels would allow the train to be pushed more smoothly.

All shifts in action were also coded, so that it was possible to evaluate the sequence of the child's actions both between and within play objects. Thus, for example, "pushing the train" and "stopping the pushing motion" would count as two actions. An action sequence might include: "pushing the train," "stopping the train," "pushing the train," "reorganizing the connections," and would be considered a repeated action sequence if it were employed by the child more than once.

This coding of children's play actions contrasts with that for identification of interests and noninterests in which the only play evaluated was that with objects that lasted for 2.5 minutes or longer. It further contrasts with the identification of objects of interest and noninterest in that it focuses on the process of the child's engagement with each play object. In this way it is possible to compare, for example, the individual child's investigative play with one play object with his or her investigative play with another play object.

Results and discussion

Children's actions in free play with each play object were evaluated with respect to each of the following variables: frequency and duration of play; number of types of play; shifts between types of play; number of shifts in action within each type of play; number of shifts between actions within level for each type of play; and repetition of action sequences. For the purposes of analysis, these data were employed in two ways. First, modal scores of all children's play with each play object were determined. On the basis of these scores each object was rated high or low on affordances for each of the variables under study. Then, based on the individually identified objects of interest and noninterest reported earlier, a score for object affordances specific to the identified object of

interest and the identified object of noninterest for that child was entered into analyses as an independent variable. Following this, and independent of the identification of each child's interest and noninterest,
scores for each variable were calculated for each child's play with his or
her identified objects of interest and noninterest.

Results from 2 (value: interest or noninterest) × 2 (object affordances: high or low) × 2 (gender: male or female) repeated measures
analyses of variance reveal that: (a) children are no more likely to play
with objects identified as interests than noninterests, although they are
more likely to play for longer periods of time with objects identified as
interests than those identified as noninterests; (b) children are more
likely to use more types of play with objects identified as interests than
they are with objects identified as noninterests. Additionally, children
are more likely to use more varying types of play with those objects
affording more varying types of play (e.g. play-dough) than they are on
those objects which were rated low on the possibility of employing a lot
of different actions in play (e.g. trains); (c) children are more likely to
shift between types of play with objects identified as interests than with
those identified as noninterests; (d) children are more likely to employ
more actions in play with objects of interest than with objects identified
as noninterests; (e) children are more likely to employ more shifts in
actions with objects identified as interests than with objects identified as
noninterests; (f) children are more likely to repeat particular sequences
of action with their identified object of interest than with objects of
noninterest; (g) children who shared the same identified object of interest did not necessarily share the same action sequences in play with their
identified object of interest; (h) children in play with objects identified
as noninterests are more likely either not to repeat prior action within
play types or only to repeat prior actions with no incorporation of
change in their action sequences.

In general, then, findings from this study suggest a powerful and
consistent effect of interest on children's play actions. That children
were not engaged in play with their identified objects of interest any
more frequently than they were with their identified objects of noninterest further corroborates that noninterest reflects a variation of the
quality of children's engagement with play objects and is not simply
reflecting a lack of knowledge for that play object. On the other hand, it
is interesting that although the children are playing no more frequently
with objects of interest, they are in fact playing with identified objects of
interest for longer periods of time than with identified objects of noninterest. This suggests that the children may see more possibilities for
action with their identified objects of interest and that they are better
able to recall prior actions with these objects and in engagement are in

fact setting challenges for themselves that vary from those they set for themselves with their identified objects of noninterest.

Clearly, main effects that indicate interest is a determinant of the number of types of play, shifts between types of play, number of shifts in action within each type of play, number of shifts between actions within level for each type of play, and repetition of action sequences all suggest that the children are in fact engaging differently with their identified objects of interest than with their identified objects of noninterest. If we can assume that the children's actions reflect what they re-present to themselves as possibilities for actions, then it seems reasonable to argue that the content of representation not only varies between individuals but does so in a consistent and reliable way across several types of children's play actions – at least with respect to individually identified objects of interest. In fact, differences in the quality of children's repeated actions with objects identified as interests and noninterests, as well as the finding that suggests that children who shared the same interests did not necessarily share the same repeated sequences of action, further suggests that individual interests may guide and regulate the individual's subsequent representation and activity.

In order to study further the role of value, affordance, and gender in children's actions, analyses specific to each identified play type were conducted as well. Findings from study of children's actions in *investigative play* (focus on an object's physical attributes) reveal: (a) females are most likely to re-engage in investigative actions and to shift actions with their identified objects of interest – these objects of interest also are most likely to be objects which afford the most possibilities for actions and shifts of action in investigative play; (b) all children spend the most time in facilitative play with identified objects of interest that are also objects affording possibilities for the longest actions. In addition, females are most likely to play the longest with objects which are identified as objects of interest – and females are most likely to play the longest with objects that afford possibilities for actions that last the longest; and (c) all children have more different types of investigative actions with objects identified as interests than those identified as noninterests. In addition, females are more likely to play with objects that afford the most possibilities for investigative play.

Given that the kinds of challenges with which children engage in investigative play include exploration of new options for play with the object, physical characteristics of the object with which the child has previously been engaged, the present findings can be interpreted as suggesting that in investigative play all children are employing more different types of actions or more different types of challenges and questions, and they persevere with these challenges longer when playing with objects identified as interests than when playing with objects identified as noninterests. However, these findings further suggest that females may be more disposed both to play with objects that afford novel challenges and to set novel challenges for themselves in free play than are males.

In contrast, findings from study of children's actions in *functional play* (focus on conventional use of the object) suggest: (a) all children have the most repeated engagements, lasting the longest periods of time, and the most shifts in action in functional play with their identified objects of interest; (b) males are most likely to have the most different types of actions in functional play with their identified objects of interest, which also are most likely to be objects that afford the most possibilities for action in functional play.

Given that the kinds of challenges with which children engage in functional play include exploration of relations between their play and the functions of their play objects in the larger world, the present findings can be interpreted as suggesting that in functional play children are more likely to have picked up on the cues provided by their environment about typical uses of their identified objects of interest than of their identified objects of noninterest. In addition, male children are more likely to incorporate actions that mimic those of the larger world in their play with identified objects of interest, and their identified objects of interest afford more possibility of conventional play than do those of female children. Taken together with findings from study of children's investigative play, it appears that, at least in the sample studied, female children are more likely to engage in and to play with objects that provide novel challenges, whereas male children are more likely to engage in and to play with objects that provide more opportunities for mimicking the larger world.

Findings from study of children's actions in *operational play* (focus on such relations as counting, sequencing, etc.) suggest further that: (a) all children re-engage with objects and shift actions most frequently to objects identified as interests during operational play. In addition, those objects most frequently engaged in operational play are most likely to be objects that afford the most possibilities for action and the most possibilities for shifts in action in operational play; (b) all children engaged in the longest periods of play in operational play with their identified objects of interest; (c) females are most likely to have the most different types of actions in operational play with their identified objects of interest, which also are most likely to be objects that afford the most possibilities for different actions in operational play.

Given that the kinds of challenges with which children engage in operational play include exploring and developing an understanding of systematic and programmatic action, findings from the present study can be interpreted as suggesting that in operational play children are most likely to re-engage objects identified as interests, and to do so for longer periods. In addition, female children are more likely to employ more different kinds of relations in their operational play than are male children and are more likely to play with objects that provide more possibilities for exploring these relations. Not only are these females more inclined to engage in novel challenge setting, as suggested by their investigative play, but they are also likely to explore the possible relations in play with their identified object of interest, and they seek out objects that enable them to have more possibilities for such engagement.

Findings from study of children's action in *transformational play* (focus on representation of the object) suggest: (a) females are most likely to have the most repeated engagements in transformational play with their identified objects of interest, which also are most likely to be objects that afford the most repeated engagement in transformational play; (b) all children have the longest engagement in transformational play with their identified objects of interest, all children have the longest engagements in transformational play with objects that afford the most possibilities for long engagements; (c) males are most likely to shift actions within level in transformational play with identified objects of interest, which also are most likely to afford the most likelihood of shifts in action within transformational play; (d) all children use the most different types of actions in transformational play with their identified object of interest, which are also the most likely to be objects that afford the most different types of action in transformational play.

Given that the kinds of challenges with which children engage in transformational play require maintaining the flow of an image in play through substituting another object for the "object" when it is not available, findings from the present study can be interpreted as suggesting that children are most likely to image or transform objects to represent their identified objects of interest. In particular, females are most likely to have the most repeated engagements in transformational play and to play with objects that facilitate the most possibilities of repeated engagements. Males, on the other hand, are most likely to shift actions in their transformational play with objects identified as interests, and these objects afford the most possibilities for shifting of actions in transformational play. That the females in this sample are able to have the most repeated engagements in transformational play and to select objects for play that permit more repeated engagements suggests that the females in this sample may generally be more focused on repeated opportunities to image than are the males, although the males, when in transformational play, are more likely actually to engage in more different kinds of actions. These findings complement those indicating that male children also engaged in more different kinds of functional play than did the female children. It appears that because the males engage in a greater range of actions in functional play and seek out objects that facilitate a greater range of actions in functional play, in transformational play their shifting actions reflect this repertoire of functional actions in the possibilities they have for play with objects in transformation. The females, on the other hand, with their tendency to explore novel challenges (investigative play) and types of relations (operational play) may repeatedly engage in transformational play as another challenge but do not bring an established repetoire of particular actions to their transformational play behavior.

Findings from study of children's actions in *facilitative play* (focus on the object as supporting play with another object) reveal: (a) all children engage in facilitative play most frequently with identified objects of interest; (b) children do not differ in the time they allot to facilitative play with identified objects of interest and noninterest; (c) all children are most likely to shift between actions in facilitative play with identified objects of interest, which are also most likely to be objects that afford the most possibilities for shifting of action in facilitative play.

Given that the kinds of challenges with which children engage in facilitative play include the ability to divide attention between objects and to separate from an object that provides security, findings from the present study suggest that children in facilitative play with their identified objects of interest are most likely to engage objects of interest and to employ a range of actions in their play with these objects in facilitative play, even though they do not engage in facilitative play with identified objects of interest for longer periods of time than they engage identified objects of noninterest. It appears that although the children have more capacity to engage in facilitative play with objects of interest and do so more frequently than with objects of noninterest, they do not actually engage in facilitative play for longer periods of time with their identified objects of interest because their value for these objects may actually distract them from the other objects with which they have been occupied.

In summary, findings from this study of children's actions in free play indicate that children's interests influence their representation of possibilities for action, and presumably their subsequent activity because this activity in all likelihood will also reflect their interests. Leont'ev (1981) observed that activity serves "to orient the subject in a world of objects . . . activity is . . . a system with its own structure, its own internal transformations, and its own development" (p. 46). In the present study, children's actions with respect to their own identified objects of interest and noninterest indicate that interests serve to increase the likelihood of particular engagement and the kinds of challenge setting such engagement makes possible. These findings further suggest that differences in the specific content of interest may in fact be influencing the aspect or affordances of play objects to which the child attends, with which the child engages, and what the child does in play with that object in subsequent activity. Thus, at least for children at 3 years of age, the activity of particular engagement may have a unique structure that reflects individual interests.

In his discussion of the development of representational competence, Sigel (1986) notes that children need first to conserve the meaning of the object to be represented, and following this they develop the capacities to make a plan (anticipate), to use hindsight (hindsight), and to go beyond present action (transcendence). Findings from the present study indicate that children as young as 3 years of age are developing abilities to repeat challenges for themselves, through the types of play in which they engage. Specifically, they are exploring manipulable aspects of the object's physical properties (investigative play); connections between their play and actions of their milieu (functional play); possibilities for systematic action (operational play); substituting one object for another (transformational play); and dividing attention (facilitative play). That these children distinguish between interest and noninterest objects in their engagement in each type of play suggests that these children are making choices (anticipating); drawing on experience (hindsight); and considering alternative possibilities for action (transcendence) in their play – at least with identified objects of interest – regardless of whether these actions are reflective or not. Their ability to represent to themselves information that subsequently influences activity requires a general ability to think about an object in two different ways at the same time. This ability appears to emerge first in play with identified objects of interest.

Furthermore, it appears that children are equally flexible with respect to their actions in play with objects identified as interests and equally inflexible with respect to their actions in play with objects identified as noninterests. Such findings provide a complement to those of Nelson and Gruendel (1986), who found in their study of 4- to 8-year-olds that older children were more likely to evidence both increased structural complexity in scripts and flexibility in describing strategies. The present study suggests that at least with respect to individual interests and noninterests, the actions of children differ between domains as a function of value and in some instances as a function of what the possibilities for action with that play object may be. Whatever the specific content of representation, it varies in a consistent way such that there is increased structural complexity in their play with objects identified as interests. What is less clear is the extent to which such actions have been internalized as procedural responses to particular objects and as such reflect unconscious reactions rather than emerging planfulness in children's activity.

Findings that suggest that children in play with identified objects of interest repeat patterns of action and incorporate new actions into these patterns indicate that children probably are not simply reacting to objects identified as interests but are evidencing an emerging planfulness. That children continue to re-engage their identified objects of interest, to repeat particular patterns of action that also incorporate systematic variations in these actions, and that these actions vary even when children share the same identified objects of interest, further suggests not only that the children are responding to the challenges the play object affords, but that they are setting challenges for themselves with these play objects that build on prior activity.

On the other hand, findings that indicate differences between children with respect to their actions in play as a function of gender, suggest that the specific form of their activity is probably a response to the others in their class, as well as the larger system of social relations of which they are also a part. What is of particular importance to the present discussion is the role of interest in the development of children's understanding. That systematic differences emerge between children with respect to the content of their interests, and then again with respect to the structure of their play with their interests when analyzed by play type, indicates that the influence of gender might be best understood as embedded in, rather than causally connected to, the content of individual interests. At very least, such differences suggest that there may be several kinds of "interests" that might be usefully studied.

Conclusions

There are probably more similarities than there are differences in the way in which individuals process information. However, differences that do exist between children in the way they understand the tasks with which they are presented and how they then proceed to accomplish these tasks are major stumbling blocks for both the child and those with whom they work. The literature is replete with findings suggesting the importance of meaningfulness, typicality, centrality, familiarity, and the like for the way in which individuals perform. These studies all attest to the importance of the tasks with which subjects are presented, although most such studies have grouped subjects together in order to describe individual contributions to subject–task engagement. In the present studies, by controlling for differences between children with respect to the content of their individually identified interest, and by employing mean proportions to evaluate differences between children in their actions with both interest and noninterest objects, it was possible to begin to evaluate the role of interest in the development of children as individuals. Findings from these studies indicate that individually identified interests and noninterests do affect the way in which children engage and perform on tasks requiring attention and memory, the way in which children represent the demands and potentials for tasks that are of interest to them, and what the child stores in the way of information for subsequent activity.

Furthermore, it appears that in experimental play (ongoing play with familiar objects) children have the most access to and more likelihood of storing information pertaining to objects identified as interests. The patterns of these children's activity between domains suggests an individual organization of activity that is guided and regulated by interest. To the extent that action outcomes, such as focus, type, and shifting of play actions, can be construed as evidence of an emerging planfulness, young children's specific organization also might be conceptualized as schematic. Whether such a scheme would take on a "structure of valences" as Schiefele (1987) suggests, is a question that the present studies only begin to address.

Krapp and Fink (1986) have reported that the pattern of children's actions with their interests, conceptualized as preferred person–object relationships, is maintained during the transition from the family into kindergarten, although which actions will be observed across time is not predictable. Rather, they find a high probability of determining reliable post hoc connections between present and past patterns of actions on a case-by-case basis. Such findings, together with those of the present studies suggesting that interests might be considered to reflect the kinds of questions and challenges the individual represents to himself or herself in engagement with an object (task, etc.), suggest that interest might be most appropriately conceptualized as embedded in the way in which the individual engages subsequent activity. This would explain why simple correspondences between patterns of action across environments are not easily made, and why two children in play with the same object are not necessarily involved in the same actions even when observed for long periods, over the course of an entire term at nursery school.

In discussing scene schema, Mandler (1979, 1983) notes that they are integrated into the knowledge structure and inform what it is that comes to be expected. In particular, what is known about the schema and what is anticipated "provide a great deal of economy in our processing of the surround [meaning] that much of what we think we have actually seen, we have only inferred" (1983, p. 454). This echoes James's (1890) discussion of interest and suggests an extension that includes information that is presumed or inferred, information that informs (whether accurately or not) subsequent activity.

In the attentional shift task reported in the first study, children were more likely to shift their gaze toward an object identified as an interest when it was projected in their peripheral visual field. Findings from this study were discussed as reflecting the perceptual characteristics of the peripheral objects as well as the value of these objects for the child. Together with findings from study of children's actions in play, it appears that the children in the present studies have internalized a process of evaluating the objects available to them in nursery school and this influences their subsequent engagements, whether these are explicit tasks of recognition and recall, or more implicit tasks involving subsequent action in free play.

Findings from the present studies further suggest that in addition to access of information that interests provide children, information stored about identified objects of interest and its concomitant influence on the process of children's representation for subsequent activity should be acknowledged as well. Although train play, for example, involves many actions shared across children, it also varies between children. In fact, the kinds of actions in which a child engages in train play are not necessarily the same actions as those of the next child, even if the train is an identified object of interest for both children.

Findings from the studies presented appear to suggest that the kinds of play objects for which children have an interest influence the kinds of possibilities for subsequent action, or challenges that the children set for themselves in response to these possibilities. They also suggest that children seek out play objects that match the kinds of challenges with which they feel comfortable. An important question for the present discussion is whether the challenges being posed by two children in play with trains are qualitatively different, and what the implications of such differences might be for thinking about the role of specific content in representation and the implications of individual variation in interests for understanding children's development.

Based on the present findings, it might be expected that two children in train play would engage qualitatively different kinds of challenges if train play were an identified object of interest for one child but not for the other child. Whether the child for whom train play was not an identified interest might be expected to be exploring similar challenges in play with his or her identified object of interest is another question. Findings from the second study presented suggest this is probably the case. On the other hand, given findings that suggest that particular play objects afford more possibilities for some actions than others, it may be that the specific class of objects of interest to children do influence the kinds of challenges with which they engage. It should be pointed out, however, that children in the present study are engaging on a regular basis with their identified interests and noninterests, along with a variety of other play objects. Thus, if they are limited in the challenges with which they engage, this is not because of a lack of alternate sources of possibilities and challenges in the environment and can be attributed to self-imposed constraints.

At present, interest as an individually varying, psychological state can be said to account for and may well contribute to differences between young children in both representation and subsequent activity. It appears there is an individual quality to representation involving both the kinds of possibilities that are more characteristic of an object and the process of representing and re-presenting information about a class of objects. Whether children's interests influence only the content of information that is processed, or whether interest might be more appropriately considered to have schemelike properties that influence the representational process, clearly needs further research. From either of these perspectives, interest appears to be an important reflection of, and source of, individual differences in task engagement.

However, some basic questions about the role of interest in the development of children need to be addressed. Interest appears to serve a particular function for young children by focusing, developing skills, schooling attention to particular features of tasks, and on the basis of these facilitating the setting of challenges for the child that are optimally discrepant. However, interest does not appear to have such a pervasive effect on information processing among older children. Findings from studies of fifth- and sixth-grade students' task engagement in reading and mathematics tasks (where the context of passage and word problem interest and noninterest was manipulated), for example, suggest that interest serves to influence comprehension of the task but not the skills requisite to such tasks (Renninger, 1988). Furthermore, it seems reasonable that once a student is more metacognitively able, and can acknowledge the influence of interest on activity, it may be possible for him or her to develop strategies to overcome the influence of interest (and noninterest).

Clearly, longitudinal evaluation of individual children's actions in free play should further knowledge about the importance of particular content and specific configurations of possibilities (Piaget, 1987) or challenges that characterize children's task engagement and the extent to which they could be said to vary as a function of interest. It would also permit evaluation of shifts in interest over time and determination of whether they are most appropriately identified with objects or perhaps more appropriately identified with possibilities afforded by particular engagements. On the other hand, case studies and protocol analyses of individuals on tasks allowing manipulation of interest and noninterest would offer additional insights about access to, and storage of, information that characterizes individual performance across tasks.

The present findings provide strong support for the influence of identified objects of interest on the way in which young children subsequently re-engage them. The implications of such representations for children's development longitudinally is a topic for further research. At this time, it appears that both researchers and practitioners can benefit from recognizing the power of young children's interests with respect to task engagement, appreciating that the task with which individual children may understand themselves to have been presented may not have been the task that was intended. As such, programs involving either research on or practice with young children would do well to account for and accommodate to the role of individual interests in children's representation and subsequent activity.

NOTES

The research reported in this chapter has been supported through grants from the National Academy of Education Spencer Fellowship Program, the Eugene M. Lang Faculty Fellowship Fund, the Swarthmore College Faculty Research Fund, and a Joel Dean Fellowship for student research assistance. Portions of this chapter have been presented as parts of papers at the meetings of the Jean Piaget Society (1983) and the Society for Research in Child Development (1987). The first study was reported in Renninger and Wozniak (1985). I would like to thank Usha Balamore, Marijka Gossens, Herbert Kerns, Barbara L. Klock, Tessa Prattos, Debra Van Aken, and Lucien T. Winegar for their research assistance on the studies presented.

1 Play object or simply object is used throughout this manuscript to refer to the class of objects or events with which children might engage in a nursery school class. Thus, object could refer to a doll, dramatic play, play-dough, or trains, among other objects.
2 Reprinted with permission of Macmillan Publishing Company from *Democracy and Education* by John Dewey. Copyright 1916 by Macmillan Publishing Company, renewed 1944 by John Dewey.
3 From *Six Psychological Studies*, by Jean Piaget, translated by Anita Tenzer. Copyright © 1967 by Random House, Inc. Reprinted by permission of the publisher.
4 This list is not, however, considered to be an exhaustive list of possible play types.

REFERENCES

Anderson, R. C. (1982). Allocation of attention during reading. In A. Flammer & W. Kintsch (Eds.), *Discourse processing* (pp. 292–335). Amsterdam: North-Holland.
Anderson, R. C., Mason, J., & Shirey, L. (1984). The reading group: An experimental investigation of a labyrinth. *Reading Research Quarterly, 20*, 6–37.
Anderson, R. C., Shirey, L., Wilson, P. T., & Fielding, L. G. (1986). Interestingness of children's reading material. In R. E. Snow & M. J. Farr (Eds.), *Aptitude learning and instruction: Vol. 3. Cognitive and affective process analyses* (pp. 287–299). Hillsdale, NJ: Erlbaum.

Arnold, F. (1910). *Attention and interest: A study in psychology and education.* New York: Macmillan.

Baldwin, J. M. (1897). *Social and ethical interpretations in mental development: A study in social psychology.* London: Cambridge University Press.

Baldwin, J. M. (1906). *Thought and things: A study of the development and meaning of thought (Vol. 1).* New York: Macmillan.

Baldwin, J. M. (1911). *Thought and things: A study of the development and meaning of thought* (Vol. 3). New York: Macmillan.

Bartlett, F. C. (1932). *Remembering: A study in experimental and social psychology.* New York: Cambridge University Press.

Berlyne, D. E. (1960). *Conflict, arousal, and curiosity.* New York: McGraw-Hill.

Bessel, F. W. (1823). *Astronomische Beobachtungen auf der Koniglichen Universitat: Sternwarte in Konigsberg, 8,* iii–viii.

Bransford, J. D. (1979). *Human cognition: Learning, understanding, and remembering.* Belmont, CA: Wadsworth.

Broadbent, D. E. (1958). *Perception and communication.* London: Pergamon.

Brown, A. L. (1982). Learning and development: The problems of compatibility, access and induction. *Human Development, 25,* 89–115.

Brown, A. L., & Campione J. C. (1972). Recognition memory for perceptually similar pictures in preschool children. *Journal of Experimental Psychology, 95,* 55–62.

Brown, A. L., & Scott, M. A. (1971). Recognition memory for pictures in preschool children. *Journal of Experimental Child Psychology, 11,* 401–412.

Bruner, J. S., Goodenow, J. J., & Austin, G. A. (1956). *A study of thinking.* New York: Wiley.

Carey, S. (1985). *Conceptual change in childhood.* Cambridge, MA: MIT Press.

Chi, M. T. H. (1978). Knowledge structure and memory development. In R. Siegler (Ed.), *Children's thinking: What develops?* Hillsdale, NJ: Erlbaum.

Chi, M. T. H., Glaser, R., & Rees, E. (1982). Expertise in problem solving. In R. J. Sternberg (Ed.), *Advances in the psychology of human intelligence* (Vol. 1). Hillsdale, NJ: Erlbaum.

Chiesi, H. L., Spilich, G. J., & Voss, J. F. (1979). Acquisition of domain-related information in relation to high and low domain knowledge. *Journal of Verbal Learning and Verbal Behavior, 18,* 257–274.

Corsini, D. A., Jacobus, K. A., & Leonard, S. D. (1969). Recognition memory of preschool children for pictures and words. *Psychonomic Science, 16,* 192–193.

Dewey, J. (1913). *Interest and effort in education.* New York: Houghton Mifflin.

Dewey, J. (1916). *Democracy and education: An introduction to the philosophy of education.* New York: Macmillan.

Dillon, R. F. (1985). *Individual differences in cognition* (Vol. 2). New York: Academic Press.

Dillon, R. F., & Schmeck, R. R. (1983). *Individual differences in cognition* (Vol. 1). New York: Academic Press.

Ebbinghaus, H. (1914). *Memory: A contribution to experimental psychology* (H. A. Ruger & C. E. Bussenius, Trans.). New York: Columbia University Press. Originally published in 1885.

Eckblad, G. (1981). *Scheme theory: A conceptual framework for cognitive-motivational processes.* New York: Academic Press.

Ericsson, K. A., & Crutcher, R. J. (in press). The nature of exceptional performance. In P. B. Baltes, D. L. Featherman, & R. M. Lerner (Eds.), *Life-span development and behavior* (Vol. 10). Hillsdale, NJ: Erlbaum.

Feldman, D. H. (1980). *Beyond universals in cognitive development.* Norwood, NJ: Ablex.

Flavell, J. H. (1963). *The developmental psychology of Jean Piaget.* Princeton, NJ: Van Nostrand.

Fryer, D. (1931). *The measurement of interests in relation to human adjustment.* New York: Holt.

Garner, R., Gillingham, M. F., & White, C. S. (1989). Effects of "seductive details" on macroprocessing and microprocessing in adults and children. *Cognition and Instruction, 6,* 41–57.

Gay, E., & Hyson, M. (1976). Blankets, bears, bunnies: Studies of children's contacts with treasured objects. In T. Shapiro (Ed.), *Psychoanalysis and contemporary science* (Vol. 5). New York: International Universities Press.

Gibson, E. & Rader, N. (1979). Attention: The perceiver as performer. In G. A. Hale and M. Lewis (Eds.), *Attention and cognitive development* (pp. 1–21). New York: Plenum.

Gibson, J. J. (1966). *The senses considered as perceptual systems.* Boston: Houghton Mifflin.

Gibson, J. J. (1979). *The ecological approach to visual perception.* Boston: Houghton Mifflin.

Ginsburg, H. (1977). *Children's arithmetic: How they learn it and how you teach it.* Austin, TX: Litton Educational Publishing.

Goethe, J. W. (1840/1914). *Theory of colours* (C. L. Eastlake, Trans.). London: John Murray.

Gray, J. A., & Wedderburn, A. A. I. (1960). Grouping strategies with simultaneous stimuli. *Quarterly Journal of Experimental Psychology, 12,* 180–184.

Hasher, L., & Zacks, R. T. (1979). Automatic and effortful processes in memory. *Journal of Experimental Psychology, General, 108,* 356–388.

Hebb, D. O. (1949). *The organization of behavior.* New York: Wiley.

Hidi, S., & Baird, W. (1986). Interestingness – a neglected variable in discourse processing. *Cognitive Science, 10,* 179–194.

Hidi, S., & Baird, W. (1988). Strategies for increasing text-based interest and students' recall of expository texts. *Reading Research Quarterly, 23,* 465–483.

Hunt, E. (1978). Mechanics of verbal ability. *Psychological Review, 85,* 109–130.

Hunt, J. McV. (1965). Intrinsic motivation and its role in development. In D. Levine (Ed.), *Nebraska Symposium on Motivation* (pp. 189–282). Lincoln: University of Nebraska Press.

Izard, C. E. (1977). *Human emotions.* New York: Plenum.

Izard, C. E. (1979). Emotions as motivations: An evolutionary developmental perspective. *Nebraska Symposium on Motivation, 1978* (pp. 163–200). Lincoln: University of Nebraska Press.

James. W. (1890). *The principles of psychology.* London: Macmillan.

Jenkins, J. J. (1979). Four parts to remember: A tetrahedral model of memory. In L. S. Cermak and F. I. M. Craik (Eds.), *Levels of processing in human memory* (pp. 429–446). Hillsdale, NJ: Erlbaum.

Kahneman, D. (1973). *Attention and effort.* Englewood Cliffs, NJ: Prentice-Hall.

Krapp, A., & Fink, B. (October, 1986). *The transition from family to kindergarten and its impact on person–object relationships.* Paper presented at the meeting of the International Association for the Study of People and Their Physical Surroundings, Haifa, Israel.

Langsdorf, P., Izard, C. E., Rayias, M., & Hembree, E. A. (1983). Interest expression, visual fixation, and heart rate changes in 2- to 8-month-old infants. *Developmental Psychology, 19,* 375–386.

Leont'ev, A. N. (1981). The problem of activity in psychology. In J. V. Wertsch (Ed.), *The concept of activity in soviet psychology*. Armonk, NY: M. E. Sharpe.

Lewin, K. (1935). *A dynamic theory of personality* (D. K. Adams and K. E. Zener, Trans.). New York: McGraw-Hill.

Lindsay, P. H., & Norman, D. A. (1976). *Human information processing: An introduction to psychology*. New York: Academic Press.

Malt, B. C., & Smith, E. E. (1982). The role of familiarity in determining typicality. *Memory and Cognition, 10,* 69–75.

Mandler, G. (1975). *Mind and emotion*. New York: Wiley.

Mandler, J. M. (1979). Categorical and schematic organization in memory. In C. R. Puff (Ed.), *Memory organization and structure*. New York: Academic Press.

Mandler, J. M. (1983). Representation. In Paul H. Mussen (Ed.), *Handbook of child psychology* (Vol. 3, pp. 420–494). New York: Wiley.

Mead, G. H. (1934). *Mind, self, and society from the standpoint of a social behaviorist*. Chicago: University of Chicago Press.

Miller, G. A., Galanter, E., & Pribram, K. H. (1960). *Plans and the structure of behavior*. New York: Holt.

Moray, N. (1959). Attention in dichotic listening: Affective cues and the influence of instructions. *Quarterly Journal of Experimental Psychology, 11,* 56–60.

Mostofsky, D. I. (1970). The semantics of attention. In D. I. Mostofsky (Ed.), *Attention: Contemporary theory and analysis* (pp. 9–24). New York: Appleton-Century-Crofts.

Murdock, B. B., Jr. (1962). The serial position effect in free recall. *Journal of Experimental Psychology, 64,* 482–488.

Neisser, U. (1966). *Cognitive psychology*. New York: Appleton-Century-Crofts.

Neisser, U. (1976). *Cognition and reality: Principles and implications of cognitive psychology*. San Francisco: W. H. Freeman.

Nelson, K. (1986). Event knowledge and cognitive development. In K. Nelson (Ed.), *Event knowledge: Structure and function in development*. Hillsdale, NJ: Erlbaum.

Nelson, K., & Gruendel, J. (1986). Children's scripts. In K. Nelson (Ed.), *Event knowledge: Structure and function in development*. Hillsdale, NJ: Erlbaum.

Norman, D. A. (1976). *Memory and attention: An introduction to human information processing*. New York: Wiley.

Norman, D. A., Rumelhart, D. E., & the LNR Research Group. (1975). *Explorations in cognition*. San Francisco: W. H. Freeman.

Perlmutter, M. & Lange, G. (1978). A developmental analysis of recall–recognition distinctions. In P. A. Ornstein (Ed.), *Memory development in children* (pp. 243–258). Hillsdale, NJ: Erlbaum.

Perlmutter, M., & Myers, N. A. (1979). Development of recall in 2- to 4-year-old children. *Developmental Psychology, 15,* 73–83.

Perlmutter, M., & Myers, N. A. (1974). Recognition memory development in 2- to 4-year-old children. *Developmental Psychology, 10,* 447–450.

Piaget, J. (1940). The mental development of the child. In D. Elkind (Ed.), *Six psychological studies*. New York: Random House.

Piaget, J. (1954). *The construction of reality in the child*. (M. Cook, Trans.). New York: Basic.

Piaget, J. (1987). *Possibility and necessity: Vol. 1. The role of possibility in cognitive development*. Minneapolis: University of Minnesota Press.

Prenzel, M. (April, 1988). Task persistence and interest. In U. Schiefele (Chair), *Content and interest as motivational factors in learning*. Symposium conducted at the annual meeting of the American Educational Research Association, New Orleans.

Renninger, K. A. (1984). Object–child relations: Implications for both learning and teaching. *Children's Environments Quarterly, 1*(2), 3–6.

Renninger, K. A. (1988, April). Effects of interest and noninterest on student performance with tasks of mathematical word problems and reading comprehension. In A. Krapp (Chair), *Differences in student performance across subject areas as a function of interest.* Symposium conducted at the annual meeting of the American Educational Research Association, New Orleans.

Renninger, K. A., & Wozniak, R. H. (1985). Effect of interest on attentional shift, recognition, and recall in young children. *Developmental Psychology, 21*, 624–632.

Rogoff, B., & Mistry, J. (1985). Memory development in cultural context. In M. Pressley & C. Brainerd (Eds.), *Cognitive learning and memory in children* (pp. 117–142). New York: Springer-Verlag.

Schiefele, U. (1987). The importance of motivational factors for the acquisition and representation of knowledge. In P. R. J. Simons & G. Beukhof (Eds.), *The regulation of learning* (pp. 47–69). Den Haag: S. V. O. Selecta.

Schiefele, U., & Krapp, A. (1988, April). The impact of interest on qualitative and structural indicators of knowledge. In U. Schiefele (Chair), *Content and interest as motivational factors in learning.* Symposium conducted at the annual meeting of the American Educational Research Association, New Orleans.

Sigel, I. E. (1986). Early social experience and the development of representational competence. In W. Fowler (Ed.), *Early experience and the development of competence* (New Directions for Child Development, No. 32). San Francisco: Jossey-Bass.

Spilich, G. J., Vesonder, G. T., Chiesi, H. L., & Voss, J. F. (1979). Text processing of domain-related information for individuals with high and low domain knowledge. *Journal of Verbal Learning and Verbal Behavior, 18*, 275–290.

Strong, D. J., & Feder, D. D. (1961). Measurement of the self-concept: A critique of the literature. *Journal of Counseling Psychology, 8*, 170–178.

Thorndike, E. L. (1935). *Adult interests.* New York: Macmillan.

Triesman, A. M. (1960). Contextual cues in selective listening. *Quarterly Journal of Experimental Psychology, 12*, 242–248.

Turvey, M. T. (1973). On peripheral and central processes in vision: Inferences from an information-processing analysis of masking with patterned stimuli. *Psychological Review, 80*, 1–52.

Van Alstyne, D. (1932). *Play behavior and choice of play materials of preschool children.* Chicago: University of Chicago Press.

Vygotsky, L. S. (1967). Play and its role in the mental development of the child. *Soviet Psychology, 3*, 62–76.

Wellman, H. M., & Somerville, S. C. (1980). Quasi-naturalistic tasks in the study of cognition: The memory-related skills of toddlers. In M. Perlmutter (Ed.), *Children's memory* (New Directions for Child Development, No. 10, pp. 33–48). San Francisco: Jossey-Bass.

White, R. (1959). Motivation reconsidered: The concept of competence. *Psychological Review, 66*, 297–333.

The emergence of autobiographical memory in mother–child conversation

JUDITH A. HUDSON

The following are excerpts from a conversation between an experimenter and a 3-year-old in which the child is asked to recall a visit to the circus:

Exp.: What about the circus?
Child: I went to the circus before.
Exp.: Can you tell me about that?
Child: Yeah, there were clowns there and nothing scared me.
Exp.: You saw clowns. What else?
Child: Elephants and horses.
Exp.: Well, what's the first thing that happened when you went to the circus?
Child: I saw tigers and they were there.
Exp.: Who did you go with?
Child: Gabby.
Exp.: You went with Gabby?
Child: It was fun there.
Exp.: And what happened when it was over?
Child: We went home, home to a birthday party. It was someone's party.

There are several noteworthy aspects of this conversation. First, the experimenter was not known to the child until introduced by the nursery school teacher just moments before the interview commenced. Second, there is no reason provided for why the experimenter wants to know about the events: The child is simply asked to report what happened. Third, the experimenter provides no specific cues or prompts to assist the child. When these factors are taken into consideration, the child's ability to provide a coherent account of past events and his ability to give this account to an unfamiliar adult for no apparent reason shows that he has mastered some fundamental skills in reporting past events. Like the child participants in the conversations reported by Fivush and Hamond (this volume), he is able to provide information about the significant aspects of the event from his perspective.

By the preschool years, many children have acquired a basic ability to

166

narrate an event, that is, they have mastered a very basic narrative structure for reporting personal narratives (Hudson & Hagreen, 1987; Hudson & Nelson, 1986; Hudson & Shapiro, in press). Although children's narratives become more elaborated and more complex over the preschool years, the basic form is acquired early on. This accomplishment is particularly impressive considering that kindergarten children have difficulty producing other types of narratives such as make-believe stories conforming to a basic episodic structure (Stein, 1988). In fact, when asked to tell a make-believe story, 4- and 5-year-olds tend to report personally experienced events instead of developing a fictional plot (Gruendel, 1980; Hudson & Shapiro, in press).

Another important finding demonstrated in the above example is that 3-year-olds do not seem to suffer from the phenomenon of *childhood amnesia* found in adults. When adults attempt to recall events from childhood, they rarely recall events occurring before the age of 3 and can remember very few events from the years 3 and 4 (Pillemer & White, in press; White & Pillemer, 1979). Although adults have trouble remembering when they were 2 and 3 years old, 3-year-olds do not display the same kinds of difficulties. Recent studies (e.g., Hudson, 1986; Hudson & Nelson, 1986; Fivush & Hamond, this volume) have shown that preschool children's memory for real-world events is quite extensive. Thus, by the preschool years children have mastered some important skills for remembering and reporting autobiographical memories.

When and how do these skills emerge? That is the question that motivated the research reported in this chapter. Clearly, we needed to study autobiographical memory in children younger than 3. The age range approximately from 24 to 36 months seems to be an important period to study. By 24 months, many children produce multiword utterances and by 30 months are able to sustain a topic in coversation. These accomplishments enable them to participate in conversations about past events with their parents. By 36 months, many children can produce event narratives on their own. How do children's memory and narrative skills develop during this age period? The focus of this chapter is how children learn to participate in conversations about the past with their parents and how these conversations provide the context in which children learn how to retrieve autobiographical memories.

Memory and discourse development in the years 2 to 3

In studying the relationship between discourse and memory it is important to keep in mind some issues that can become confounded. During the years 2 to 3, children's language skills develop quite rapidly, allowing them to communicate much more effectively. In particular, the use of temporally displaced talk, that is, talk about past and future events, emerges during this period. In conversations with their toddlers, parents begin to break away from talking exclusively about the "here and now" and discuss plans for the future as well as memories of the past. It has been proposed that temporally displaced talk referring to specific past events emerges in "conversational routines" established by mothers with their toddlers (Eisenberg, 1985; Sachs, 1983). Moreover, these interactions are more likely to occur in familiar, routinized situations (Lucariello & Nelson, 1987).

Two-year-olds are also experiencing a variety of different kinds of events that may influence their general knowledge about events and their memory for specific episodes. For example, young children soon learn the evening routine of dinner, bathtime, and bedtime. Once they have formed generalized event representations for these events, children can use this knowledge to anticipate event sequences. A friend of mine reported that her 2-year-old daughter became quite distressed one time when she was given a bath before dinner because the child thought she was not going to be fed that evening. Parents of toddlers report many such instances of their children anticipating familiar events. More impressive evidence comes from the work of Bauer and Mandler (this volume) and O'Connell and Gerard (1985) showing that by 14 months, children show evidence of temporally organized event representations. Having acquired generalized event representations, children can use these schemas to guide their recall of events. Reliance on event schemas typically results in more exhaustive memory for specific episodes. For example, preschool children who experienced four episodes of a novel event (a creative movement workshop) recalled more about specific episodes than children who had only experienced a single episode (Hudson, 1990).

Reliance on general event representations as memory guides for specific episodes can also distort recall. The children in Hudson's (1990) study who experienced the four workshops tended to confuse details from each of the workshops (see also Farrar & Goodman, this volume). There is also evidence that highly routine episodes of familiar events are extremely difficult to recall because they have become fused into the generalized event representation and are no longer available to recall as distinct episodes (Hudson & Nelson, 1986).

In contrast, both novel events and distinctive episodes of familiar events, that is, when something unusual or unexpected occurs, may be retained as specific event memories (Hudson, 1988). The 2-year-old who was upset at having bath before dinner may remember that evening because it was so different from all others. But had the evening routine always gone that way, the occurrences of that evening would quickly be forgotten.

During the preschool years, children's increasing experience with similar events helps them to appreciate what is routine and what is distinctive about particular episodes. The ability to appreciate events as novel or distinctive may contribute to developmental changes in the content of early autobiographical memories as children's memory becomes more focused on atypical experiences (Fivush & Hamond, this volume; Nelson & Ross, 1980). Thus, generalized event representations can help the young child remember specific episodes by providing a meaningful framework for comprehending an event as well as the background against which particular episodes are perceived as distinctive and therefore memorable.

Although children's event knowledge and discourse skills are expanding from 24 to 36 months, the passage of time can have a negative effect on recall. That is, memories can be expected to fade over longer retention intervals. Even adults have difficulty recalling events from long ago and need more specific cues to remember remote events. If a 2-year-old can remember an event occurring 3 days ago better than an event occurring 3 months ago, the difference is likely to be due to the difference in retention interval between the two events. But what if the event that occurred 3 months ago is remembered better 3 months later than 3 days after the occurrence? Can we find improvement in recall of events over time due to improved language skills or the development of general event knowledge?

Effects of verbal rehearsal

One factor that may contribute to improvement in recall at any age and particularly in recalling these very early and very fragile memories is verbal rehearsal. Recent experiments have shown that memories that are repeatedly recalled are later remembered in more detail than memories that are seldom discussed. In Hudson's (1990) study of preschool children's recall of either repeated or single episodes, all children, regardless of amount of experience with the event, recalled more about the workshops in delayed recall at 4 weeks if they had also been asked to recall the workshop on the same day. Hamond (1988) asked 3- to 6-year-olds to recall a very salient and novel event – a trip to Disney World – and found that children who had frequently talked about the event with their families recounted more information. Of course, talking about an event is different from a rehearsal strategy used as a deliberate mnemonic device to improve later recall. But they are similar in that both involve reviewing information and both produce a similar effect, that is, enhanced recall.

There is evidence that repeated verbal recall improves later recall, but there is no consensus on how this happens. The critical issue seems to be whether verbal recall strengthens the original memory or replaces it. This question is important to consider because autobiographical memories are frequently elicited in conversations with others. For very young children, the conversational partner is most likely a parent who guides the child's participation. Is it the process of recall – the child's internal retrieval processes – that strengthens recall, or is it the interaction – that is, the information provided by the adult and incorporated by the child – that contributes to later recall? Three models of how repeated recall of an event affects autobiographical memory have emerged from a number of different literatures. The models will be presented as if they are mutually exclusive. However, it is possible that all or none may be applicable.

Information-processing perspective. From an information-processing perspective, bringing an event memory to consciousness and reflecting on an experience may activate nodes and paths in a semantic network and strengthen them in memory. Those nodes and paths then become more accessible to activation at a later time. Frequently recalled events are more accessible to recall because there are more and stronger paths available to access information. In addition, nodes of information that are activated by thinking of the event are strengthened. In this model, it is not necessary that a particular unit or node is reported verbally for the unit to be activated: It just needs to be activated. For example, if a child remembers a trip to the zoo and says, "We saw lions," more information may actually be activated – seeing tigers and elephants, and that Mommy and Daddy were there as well. Paths to those units may also be strengthened when the child says "We saw lions."

Support for this model comes from the work of Rovee-Collier (Rovee-Collier & Hayne, 1987) showing that reactivation of infant memory immunizes against forgetting. In this research, infants learn to kick to produce movement in a mobile suspended over their crib. A ribbon tied to the infant's ankle is connected to the mobile to produce the movement. To test for their memory of the learning, a mobile is reintroduced, but the ribbon is not attached, and memory is measured as the amount of kicking that babies produce. At 3 months, infants "remember" how to move the mobile for about 8 days, but by 2 weeks they have forgotten. That is, they simply look at the mobile but do not kick. If after 13 days the memory was reactivated by showing the infant the moving mobile (the movement was produced by an experiment and was unrelated to infants' movements), the infants "remembered" the mobile in a test session on the 14th day (Rovee-Collier, Sullivan, Enright, Lucas, & Fagan, 1980).

Extending this paradigm, research has shown that 3-month-olds can remember up to 4 weeks later with reactivation and that similar, but not identical, stimuli can also serve as reminders (Rovee-Collier & Hayne, 1987). The implication from this line of research is that experiences that are reactivated persist in memory, whereas those that are not reactivated are forgotten. Moreover, there seems to be a critical period in which infant memories can be reactivated; after that time, the experience is treated as a novel event and does not reactivate the earlier memory.

Fivush and Hamond (in press) have also found evidence that reinstatement of an event can improve 2-year-olds' memory. In this study, 24- and 28-month-olds participated in a novel laboratory play event. Half of the children came back after 3 months and were asked to reenact the event. The other half were asked to reenact the event at both 2 weeks and 3 months. Children in the repeated recall condition showed evidence of remembering more information than children in the single experience condition, suggesting that reexperiencing an event may help prevent long-term forgetting.

It is also possible that simply talking about an event can reactivate a memory. Thus, talking about events with toddlers may prevent early memories from being forgotten during the early years. However, new information can also be incorporated into memory each time the memory is reactivated, so that over successive retrievals, memories may change.

Rote-learning model. According to this model, as an event is recalled over and over again, what is said about the event becomes incorporated into the memory for the event. Eventually, memory for the actual experience is replaced by rote recall of what happened as described in past discussions. For example, in recalling a trip to the zoo a parent may say, "Do you remember when we went to the zoo? Remember the big lion? What did he do? Did he roar? Yeah, he roared. And what did you do? Did you cry? Yeah, you were so scared of that lion." After participating in this kind of conversation a number of times, when the child is asked, "Do you remember when we went to the zoo?" she responds, "Big lion scared me. I cry." Years later this incident may still be remembered, but anything else that happened, even other fairly distinctive events, are lost to recall.

The same effects could be found even if the child was not explicitly coached. For example, on the day after the trip to the zoo, when asked what happened, the child might willingly volunteer information. When asked to tell Grandma what happened the following week, she reports the same information. Three months later, when viewing a picture book of zoo animals, the child repeats once again her "memory" of what happened when she went to the zoo. But by now she seems to be reciting a story about the event that does not deviate over retellings. Eventually, she may be able to recite the story verbatim but may no longer remember the actual event.

The rote-learning model has been used to account for the few memories of early childhood that persist into adulthood: They are remembered because they have become part of the family folklore. In addition, it can explain some distortions and inaccuracies in autobiographical memory. For example, Piaget (1962) reported a vivid childhood memory he had of his nurse saving him from being kidnapped. Much later, he discovered that this event had never happened, but was a false story told by the nurse to account for injuries he received due to her negligence in watching him. Apparently the episode had been talked about so often that he remembered it as an actual experience.

Thus, in the rote-learning model, children learn to memorize a story about the event through repeated conversations; they do not necessarily strengthen their original memory of the event. In fact, the original memory is no longer activated at all but is replaced by memory of a narrative about the event. This type of replacement is different than merely incorporating new information. The implication is that another "layer" has been added – the verbal narrative, which is reactivated over successive retrievals.

Interactive-learning model. In the interactive-learning model, remembering is considered more than just activating units of information, but it also involves giving a coherent narrative of what happened. When children are engaged in remembering events, especially very young children who depend on an adult to elicit and guide their recall, they are also learning how to narrate the event. As they are asked questions like "Who was there?" "Where did we go?" "What did we do?" "Then what happened?" they are learning to organize a memory narrative, to give the who, what, where, when, and why information in sequence.

In this model, it is the verbal exchange between the participants that is essential for development. Because children are being tutored in how to remember, how the adult structures the conversations and the child's participation in the process of remembering are crucial for the development. This model is based on Vygotsky's (1978) theory that all higher mental functions develop in the context of social interaction. Remembering can be viewed as an activity that is at first jointly carried out by parent and child, then later performed by the child alone.

As discussed above, early talk about the past is largely elicited by parents in routinized conversations. The parent introduces the topic of the conversation and frames the child's contributions. Over time, children become less dependent on this type of adult scaffolding and are able on their own to provide more information about the past. In addition, children may internalize the process of retrieving information from memory through participation in parent-guided memory conversations (Eisenberg, 1985; Lucariello & Nelson, 1987). By providing probes and prompts for children in the form of questions, parents model the memory-search process. Children can then use this structure to ask themselves questions about events when they are engaged in later memory conversations. In support of this interpretation, Ratner (1984) found that mother's memory-demand questions were correlated with children's performance on memory tasks at ages 3 and 4. Ratner argues that children internalize the use of questioning and retrieval cues first provided by parents in order to search their own memories.

The difference between the interactive-learning model and the rote-learning model is that in the interactive-learning model, children are internalizing the skills for remembering and narrating events; they are not memorizing particular stories about particular events. This model also predicts that the acquisition of strategies for retrieving autobiographical memories and the development of a narrative structure for reporting memories can generalize to recall of events that have not been repeatedly remembered. Increased experience with recalling events in general can result in better recall of many events because children have acquired the cognitive skills for directing their own memory search, not just strengthened particular paths.

An important difference between the interactive-learning model and both the information-processing and the rote-learning models is that the interactive-learning model is primarily applicable to memory development in children. Presumably, most older children and adults already know how to narrate an event (although the form and function of a memory narrative may vary by culture). Repeated recall of particular events may only enhance recall of those particular events. But for very young children, learning how to remember may be more important than rehearsing specific content.

Of course, it is possible that more than one model can account for the relationship between talking about the past and the development of memory. In repeated memory conversations, children may be internalizing memory and discourse skills for remembering and reporting events; at the same time, they may be strengthening paths and nodes in long-term memory, and they may also be memorizing routinized formats for talking about some particular events.

Finally, we also have to consider the possibility that there is no relationship between talking about events and later recall. With age, children's language ability improves, which may not affect their memory per se but simply their ability to talk about what they remember. Thus, over repeated recall conversations we may see improvement in children's recall, but this has nothing to do with improvements in memory. It merely reflects the fact that they are acquiring better language skills to report what they have been remembering all along. In this case, it could be argued that younger children remember just as much as older children, but simply lack the verbal skills to communicate their memories.

Summary

In studying autobiographical memory in very young children, we need to account for how social, cognitive, and linguistic factors influence memory development. As children's communication skills, autobiographical memory, and general event knowledge expand during the years 2 to 3, children are able to communicate autobiographical memories to the adults in their lives. A critical issue is the degree to which parent–child conversations about past events contribute to children's autobiographical memory development. Three models of how repeated recall conversations affect children's autobiographical memory were proposed. In the *information-processing model,* repeated conversations serve to reactivate memories. Reactivation prevents memories from being forgotten, strengthens retrieval paths, and may serve to reorganize memories such that multiple cues can be used for retrieval. In the *rote-learning model,* repeated conversations provide children with a narrative about the event which replaces the original memory. Over successive recall conversations, children recall the narrative, not the original event. In the *interactive-learning model,* memory conversations with parents provide the context in which children acquire discourse skills for talking about the past and retrieval strategies for searching their memory.

Rachel's memory: A case study

This study attempted to tease apart the effects of age, retention interval, and repeated recall on the development of autobiographical memory through a longitudinal case study of one mother–child dyad. Conversations about past events between a mother (the author) and her daughter, Rachel, were tape-recorded from the time Rachel was 21 months old until she was 28 months old. Rachel was the only child in the family, and her language ability could be considered advanced for her age. However, the particular ages she remembered certain things are not important for this investigation. What is more interesting are the changes over time in the memory conversations.

Method

Most conversations were initiated by the mother for the purpose of taping. Data collection was discontinued at 28 months because at this time Rachel frequently initiated conversations about past events on her own that were not recorded, and she began to lose interest in mother-initiated conversations. Conversations generally occurred at mealtimes, lasted from 3 to 30 minutes, and covered 1 to 6 events. From the total corpus, 86 events were selected for analysis representing only conversations about specific, one-time events. For example, visits to the library were not included because this event occurred relatively frequently and it was not possible to distinguish one episode from another.

What is unique about these data is that each event could be dated and retention intervals computed. The retention interval for the events ranged from 0 to 126 days. In addition, during the first 4 months of the study, the events were not discussed at any time other than the recorded conversations. Thus, what Rachel remembered in the conversations from 21 to 25 months was exhaustive of her verbal reporting of the events. It was therefore possible to assess the effects of repeated recall in the very early stages of remembering and to examine the content of what was reported over repeated conversations.

Coding

Each conversation was first coded in terms of structural characteristics. As is typical of mother–child conversations during this age period, Rachel's contributions consisted primarily of responses to various questions. Three kinds of questions were asked: *General questions* such as "Can you tell me about when we went to the beach?" and "What else did we do?" served to introduce the event topic and encourage discussion, but did not specify the kind of information that was expected in response. *Information requests* were who, what, where, when, and why questions that queried particular aspects of the event, as in "Who came with us?" "What did you wear at the beach?" Here the type of information desired is specified in the questions. *Yes–No* questions simply asked for an affirmative response to the provided information, for example, "Did Grandma Pat come to the beach with us?" "Did you wear a bathing suit?" Four additional maternal contributions were coded: *offers* of information in which new information is provided without asking a question, *repetitions* of previously mentioned information, and *verifications* ("That's right. You did have a red bathing suit").

Rachel's contributions were coded into six categories. An *offer* of information occurred when she provided information without a specific request, either spontaneously or in response to a general question. An *information response* occurred when she provided the specific information requested ("What color was your bathing suit?" "Red"). A *yes–no response* was simply a yes or no usually, but not always, given in response to a yes–no question. *Repetitions* of previously mentioned information were also coded. In addition, some responses were coded as *unintelligible* and *no response* to questions were also coded.

Results

The proportions of each participant's contributions consisting of these coding categories were computed for each event discussed. Then the proportions were correlated separately with Rachel's age in weeks, retention interval in days, and the number of conversations that had taken place about that particular event. For each correlation, the other two factors were partialed out. That is, correlations between changes in the proportion of each type of contribution over time were computed with the retention interval of the events and the number of times they had been discussed partialed out. Next, these proportions were correlated with retention interval, partialing out age of the child and number of recalls. Finally, partial correlations were computed for the proportions and frequency of recall (for those events where this could be determined) with age of the child, and retention interval partialed out.

Changes in the structure of the conversations with age. Partial correlations for proportions of each type of contribution with age of the child are shown in Table 7.1. Maternal contributions consisted largely of yes–no questions, requests for information, and repetitions of previously mentioned information; most of these were repetitions of what the child had just said. Rachel gave primarily yes or no responses and offered information more often than she answered requests for information. In addition, 24 percent of the questions asked were not responded to by the child. (These were not included in the overall proportions of the child's contributions because they indicate a lack of contribution.)

The partial correlations show how the conversations changed over time. First, note that the total number of contributions increased for both participants. Looking at maternal contributions, we see that the proportions of general and yes–no questions decreased with time, whereas the proportions of offers and verifications increased. At the same time, Rachel produced proportionally fewer yes–no responses and fewer no responses. What this seems to indicate is an increasing ability on Rachel's part to participate in the conversations in general, and an increasing ability to provide information, both spontaneously and in re-

Table 7.1. *Structure of mother–child conversations, Study 1*

	Mean frequencies	Mean proportions	Partial correlations, proportions with age of child
Mother's contributions			
General questions	1.66	.05	−.38**
Information requests	6.34	.18	.20
Yes–no questions	13.24	.39	−.42**
Offers	1.58	.04	.38**
Repetitions	7.84	.21	.12
Clarifications	1.68	.04	.01
Verifications	3.50	.10	.52***
Total	36.20		(.44)***
Child's contributions			
Offers	8.44	.28	.30*
Information responses	3.08	.12	.28*
Yes–no responses	12.42	.43	−.25*
Repetitions	3.51	.11	−.15
No response	5.16	.24	−.41**
Total	28.87		(.50)***

*$p < .05$
**$p < .01$
***$p < .001$

sponse to specific requests. Her mother's role also shifted. Over time, proportionally fewer yes–no questions were asked and there were more offers of information in statement form. This seems to indicate that Rachel was treated as a more equal participant. It is likely that in memory conversations among peers there would be many offers and few yes–no questions. The decrease in general questions may reflect the fact that the topic of the conversation is increasingly provided by Rachel obviating the need for a general opening question on the part of her mother.

There were only three significant partial correlations between the structural measures and retention interval and frequency of recall. Over longer retention intervals, both participants produced fewer total contributions (correlations of −.35 and −.27). In other words, the conversations became shorter. Over repeated recalls, there were more verifications (.30).

Changes in Rachel's responses to questions. Of course, the overall proportions of different kinds of contributions made by Rachel do not reflect how she responded to particular kinds of questions. Table 7.2

Table 7.2. *Child's responses to mother's questions, Study 1*

	Mean frequencies	Mean proportions	Partial correlations, proportions with age of child
General questions			
No response	25	.47	−.24
Offer	29	.53	.24
Information requests			
No response	26	.32	−.38*
Information	45	.56	.34*
Offer	8	.10	.12
Yes–no questions			
No response	13	.15	−.52**
Yes–no response	53	.62	−.10
Offer	18	.21	.57**

*p < .05
**p < .01

shows the frequencies and proportions of different kinds of responses made by Rachel to various types of questions. This table also shows the correlations between the proportions of each type of response and age of the child with retention interval and frequency of recall partialed out.

With age, Rachel responded more to general questions and produced more offers, although these correlations did not reach significance. A request for information could be answered with the particular information queried, or could elicit an offer of information other than what was requested, or was not responded to at all. With age, there was a significant increase in the proportion of requests for information that produced information responses, and a significant decrease in the proportion of no responses.

Most interesting are the changes in Rachel's response to yes–no questions. These only required a yes or no response, but over time, she responded with more offers of information, whereas the proportion of no responses decreased. This indicates that Rachel changed her interpretation of the questions over time. She began to interpret yes–no questions as prompts to contribute more memory information. Although maternal questions shifted over time, Rachel also changed her responses to those questions. The only significant correlation between Rachel's responses and either retention interval or frequency of recall was that over longer retention intervals, she produced proportionally fewer offers in response to yes–no questions.

To illustrate these changes in the structure of the conversations, examples of conversations at 21, 24, and 27 months are shown in Table 7.3. First, consider the conversation at 21 months. This is actually a better than average conversation for this age because Rachel offers information at the beginning – "said bye-bye" and "go in car" – without a specific request for information. In general, the second half of the conversation is more characteristics of conversations at this age, consisting largely of no responses, "yes" responses, and only occasional information responses and offers.

At 24 months, it is apparent that Rachel is producing longer utterances but, more important, offers proportionally more information, especially in response to yes–no questions. At 21 months, most yes–no questions were answered with a "yes" or a "no" or no response. At 24 months, the conversation begins with the question "Did you like the apartment at the beach?" and Rachel answers "Yeah," but adds, "And I have fun, in the, in the, in the water." Later when asked, "Did you play in the ocean," Rachel offers "And my sandals off," and in the rest of the conversation she successfully answers a series of requests for information. At this age, Rachel is providing more information in the conversations, although most information is given in response to specific questions.

By 27 months, the conversation is initiated by Rachel, she offers information, and even probes her mother's memory for the event: "Do you remember the waves, Mommy?" "And do you remember we swimmed?" "Did we play again?" "Do you remember my beach hat?" Clearly, she has mastered the format for initiating and directing conversations about the past.

Effects of repeated recall. One striking aspect of these data is there were almost no significant correlations between the number of repeated conversations and the structure of the conversation. Rachel did not offer more information or provide more information in response to specific questions as a function of how many times an event had been discussed. However, according to both the information-processing and the rote-learning models, repeatedly recalling an event should affect the content of the child's memory, not her conversational skill.

To examine changes in the content of the conversations, each participant's contributions were coded in terms of how many units of different types of information were provided. The units consisted of *setting information,* that is, times and locations, *people, actions, objects, descriptors* (adjectives and adverbs), and *states* such as feeling happy, sad, scared, and so on. Any one statement could include more than one unit. For example, "Grandma gave me a honey bear" included: the person, Grandma; the action, giving; the object, bear; and the descriptor,

Table 7.3. *Examples of mother–child conversations, Study 1*

21 months

M: Did you see Aunt Gail and Uncle Tim last week?
C: Yes, yes, Uncle Tim.
M: What did we do with Aunt Gail and Uncle Tim?
C: Said bye-bye.
M: You said bye-bye to Aunt Gail and Uncle Tim?
C: Yes, go in car, in car.
M: In the car?
C: Yes. Tim went in the car.
M: Tim went in the car?
C: Aunt Gail with Uncle Tim.
M: Aunt Gail was with Uncle Tim in the car? Right. Do you remember what else you did with Aunt Gail and Uncle Tim?
C: (no response)
M: Did we go eat?
C: (no response)
M: What did you have to eat?
C: (unintelligible) chair.
M: Rachel sat in a chair? Did Aunt Gail sit next to you?
C: Yes.
M: What did she read to you?
C: Ernie and Bert book.
M: The Ernie and Bert book?
C: Yeah.
M: She read that to you?
C: Yeah.
M: Yeah, did you eat hamburger?
C: Yeah.
M: And chips?
C: (no response)
M: And did you have ice cream?
C: Yes. Ice cream.
M: What did you do with Uncle Tim?
C: Hug him.
M: What did you do with Uncle Tim?
C: Yeah, Uncle Tim.
M: With Uncle Tim. And did you see some cannons?
C: No.

24 months

M: Did you like the apartment at the beach?
C: Yeah. And I have fun in the, in the, in the water.
M: You had fun in the water?
C: Yeah. I come to the ocean.
M: You went to the ocean?
C: Yeah.
M: Did you play in the ocean?
C: And my sandals off.

Table 7.3. *(cont.)*

M:	You took your sandals off?
C:	And my jamas off.
M:	And your jamas off. And what did you wear to the beach?
C:	I wear hot cocoa shirt.
M:	Oh, your cocoa shirt, yeah. And your bathing suit?
C:	Yeah. And my cocoa shirt.
M:	Yeah. Did we walk to the beach?
C:	Yeah.
M:	Who went to the beach?
C:	Mommy and Daddy.
M:	Did you play in the sand?
C:	Yeah.
M:	What did you do in the sand?
C:	Build sand castles.
M:	Yeah. And did you go in the water?
C:	(no response)
M:	Who went in the water with you?
C:	Daddy and Mommy.
M:	Right. Did the big waves splash you?
C:	Yeah.

27 months

C:	Do you remember the waves, Mommy?
M:	Do I remember the waves? What about the waves?
C:	I go in the waves and I build a sand castle. And do you remember we swimmed? I swimmed in the waves and we did it again. Did we play again?
M:	Yeah, so let's see, you went in the waves and you built sand castles and we did that together?
C:	Yeah.
M:	Yeah. I remember those waves. Did you like the beach?
C:	I cried.
M:	You cried?
C:	Yeah.
M:	Why?
C:	I cried I want to go to the beach.
M:	You cried I want to go to the beach?
C:	Yeah.
M:	Yeah. Did we go to the beach?
C:	Yeah. And I cried I want the beach.
M:	We went together, didn't we?
C:	No.
M:	Who went to the beach?
C:	Grandma Pat.
M:	Grandma Pat was there.
C:	A big wave come and I (unintelligible) my beach chair and my hat. Do you remember my beach hat?
M:	Yeah. The waves came to your beach chair and your hat, right.

honey. Only information not mentioned previously was coded. So if Rachel said, "Grandma gave me a honey bear," after being asked, "What did Grandma give you?" she would only be credited with providing the information – a honey bear – because Grandma had already been mentioned by the mother.

Next, the particular content of each repeated conversation was analyzed. This analysis was based on 15 events discussed two to six times for a total of 42 observations between the ages of 21 and 25 months. Of interest was whether the conversations tended to rehash the same information, as would be predicted by the rote-learning model, or whether Rachel included previously unmentioned information in later conversations, which could be predicted from either the information-processing or the interactive-learning models.

An overall consistency score was computed for each repeated conversation by summing the number of overlapping information units mentioned in both of two consecutive conversations divided by the total number of information units mentioned across both conversations. A score of 1.00 would indicate that the information provided in both conversations was identical, and a score of 0 would indicate that there was no overlap at all in what was discussed in the two conversations. The mean consistency score across both participants was .39, indicating that overall, less than half of what was discussed in a repeated conversation had been discussed in the prior conversation about the event.

This relatively low proportion of overlap could be due to a number of causes. Either the mother or child could have provided new information across conversations, or either or both of the participants might have omitted old information over conversations. Of primary interest for the models of memory development discussed earlier is the degree to which Rachel reported the same information over repeated conversations, and the extent to which she incorporated her mother's contributions into her reports. In fact, only 22% of Rachel's contributions was information previously mentioned by her mother, 34% repeated her own past contributions, and 44% of her contributions to each conversation consisted of new information that had not been provided by either participant in any of the previous conversations.

Conclusions

This study did not find any evidence to support a rote-learning model of early autobiographical memory. Rachel was not simply remembering what had been discussed before – she was continually providing new information in repeated conversations about the same events. The mother also provided different information in repeated conversations.

Although it may be the case that some memories of childhood can be traced to family folklore, rote learning was not a significant determinant of Rachel's memory performance.

What do these data say about the other two models? There was no evidence that repeated recall of particular events affected the overall amount of information Rachel later reported about those events. Thus, these data do not support the information-processing model that predicts that repeated activation of a memory improves recall of the event. However, it is possible that the amount of information reported at any session was more a function of how motivated Rachel was to continue the conversation, not how much she remembered. In other words, information that was activated may not be reported.

These data are consistent with the interactive-learning model. There is more evidence that over the 7 months of talking about the past, Rachel learned a lot about how to remember, that is, about how to participate and, finally, to initiate conversations about the past rather than rehearsing specific content. At first, her mother had the overall structure of the activity in mind, and provided most of the information while directing Rachel's participation. Rachel seemed to have difficulty directing her own memory search and relied heavily on questions to remember events. Eventually, Rachel began to interpret the conversations not as a series of questions to be answered but as an activity of remembering. When she shifted her goal from one of answering questions to one of remembering, she offered more and more information spontaneously and was better able to direct her own memory search. She even attempted to direct her mother's as well.

These developments cannot be explained solely in terms of increased language ability. Surely, Rachel's command of language developed such that she was able to produce longer utterances and communicate more information. Yet, given the structure of the conversation, there was nothing to compel her to offer more information. She could have continued to answer yes–no questions with a yes or a no. Instead, she changed her interpretation of her role in the conversation. Even with only single-word utterances, Rachel could have offered more information than she did in the early conversations. As in the example of the conversation at 21 months, she was certainly capable of offering information and, in fact, did so, but most of the conversation was more directed. Although increasing language ability certainly contributed to the changes in the structure and content of the conversations over time, it cannot explain these changes.

Another important finding is that retention interval influenced Rachel's ability to report information. Longer intervals correlated with fewer offers of information in response to yes–no questions and an overall decrease in amount of information reported. Thus, many of the increases in memory performance were apparent only when retention interval was partialed out, and many effects of retention interval were apparent only when chronological age was partialed out.

Effects of repeated recall, retention interval, and maternal style: An experimental investigation

Although the case study data provided a unique opportunity to examine closely a potentially sensitive period in the development of autobiographical memory, we were concerned with the representativeness of this particuar dyad. The next study (Hudson & Sidoti, 1988) examined memory conversations in a sample of 10 mothers and children from 24 to 30 months of age. We were interested in whether the lack of consistency in content of repeated recall conversations is characteristic of mother–child memory conversations with 2- to 2½-year-olds, and whether the kinds of skills children acquire in memory conversations with their mothers are tied to that particular context, or whether they generalize to a situation when someone who did not participate in the actual events asks a child to remember an event.

Method

Ten 24- to 30-month-olds (mean = 27 months) and their mothers participated in the study (five children were boys and five were girls). We told the mothers we were interested in what young children could remember, and because children this age do not feel comfortable talking to people they don't know we wanted to audiotape them remembering with their children. We visited mothers and children in their homes once a week for 4 weeks and audiotape-recorded conversations about the same four events. Two of the events had occurred in the remote past, or 6 to 10 months ago, and two events had occurred in the recent past, or 1 to 6 months ago. All events were relatively novel events, such as family vacations, going to the fair, Halloween, and Easter. Two weeks after the final session with the mothers an experimenter visited the home and asked the child to remember the same events plus four more – also two remote and two recent events. Conversations were transcribed verbatim and coded in terms of the same structural and content units as the longitudinal study.

We also were interested in effects of the mothers' style of remembering on children's reports both with their mothers and with the experimenter. Fivush and Fromhoff (1988) found evidence for two different elicitation styles in mother–child memory conversations, an elaborative style and a repetitive style. They speculated that a more elaborative elicitation style may provide children with a richer context for learning how to remember. We used a relatively simple measure of elaboration – the number of units of information provided by the mother divided by the number of questions asked in a conversation – and we used these scores to divide our sample into low and high elaborators. The elaboration scores for low elaborators ranged from .57 to .66 with a mean of .62, and the scores for high elaborators ranged from .77 to 1.31 with a mean of .93. Examples of high and low elaboration styles are shown in Table 7.4. It is important to keep in mind that mothers using both styles communicated a good deal of information and asked many questions. The difference between the two styles is that mothers with a high elaboration style provided more information per questions and more propositions per turn than did the low elaboration mothers. Maternal style was not correlated either with age of the children or with children's mean length of utterance.

Mother–child conversations across repeated sessions

The analysis of the four mother–child recall sessions focused on three issues: (1) differences between conversations about recent and remote events; (2) changes in the conversations across session; and (3) effects of maternal style on children's participation.

Mothers' contributions. We first analyzed the number of each of the three question-types asked by the mothers over the four sessions. All mothers asked more information and yes–no questions than general questions, but the number of questions asked did not vary across the four sessions. However, as shown in Table 7.5, all mothers asked more questions about recent events than remote events. They also mentioned more information units when talking about recent events (mean = 15.83) than when talking about remote events (mean = 12.14). Finally, we analyzed the proportion of new information mentioned by the mothers in each conversation that had not been mentioned by either participant in any of the previous conversations. The proportions decreased significantly (from 54% to 32%) over Sessions 2 to 4. Despite the decrease over sessions, one-third of the mothers' contributions in the last session included new information.

Children's contributions. Three structural measures were used to characterize the child's performance. Overall responsiveness was computed as the proportion of questions that were responded to, that is, that were not followed by a no response on the part of the child. Children

Table 7.4. *Examples of maternal styles, Study 2*

High elaboration

M: Do you remember what we did, did we hide something and look for it outside?
C: Grandma's house.
M: (chuckles) Yeah, Grandma's house. What did we look for in the grass and in the bushes?
C: Easter bunny.
M: Yeah, what does the Easter bunny bring, something to eat?
C: Candy eggs.
M: Right, candy. Do you like candy?
C: Yeah.
M: Yeah.
C: Yummy.
M: Did we hide candy eggs outside in the grass?
C: (nods)
M: Remember looking for them? Who found two? Your brother?
C: Yes, brother.
M: Yes, Jimmy kept saying, "Let's hide them again!" (chuckles)
C: Brother.

Low elaboration

M: Who came at Eastertime with Grandma?
C: Daniel!
M: Daniel? What does he call you?
C: Hi, Jelly-Belly!
M: Jelly-Belly?
C: Call funny name!
M: What'd we eat at Eastertime, remember the eggs we had?
C: (nods)
M: What was inside the eggs?
C: (unintelligible)
M: We had chocolate eggs?
C: Yeah.
M: Did you eat one at the table?
C: Yeah.
M: And what did you wear on your head at Eastertime?
C: Hm, a bonnet!
M: A bonnet? Where'd you wear it?
C: In church!
M: Church?
C: Church.
M: Who brought you to church?
C: Nana.
M: And who else?
C: Popa.
M: Was Mommy there, too?
C: Yep.

Table 7.5. *Number of questions asked by mothers about recent and remote events, Study 2*

	Recent event	Remote event
General questions	.89	.55
Information requests	9.70	5.95
Yes–no questions	10.10	7.84

Table 7.6. *Proportion of information requests answered by children in mother–child conversations, Study 2*

	Recent event	Remote event
High elaboration mothers	.65	.69
Low elaboration mothers	.57	.44

did not necessarily produce a memory response – they could repeat the mother's questions, simply say yes or no, or repeat previously mentioned information – but they did produce a relevant response. In general, the responsiveness rate was fairly consistent across sessions. However, the response rate for children of more elaborative mothers increased significantly from 80% to 96% over the four sessions, but only when talking about recent events.

A second measure of memory performance was the proportion of requests for information to which the child responded with appropriate information. As shown in Table 7.6, children of more elaborative mothers responded to proportionally more requests for information, and the difference was more pronounced in talking about the remote events. Children also offered information more often when talking about recent events (mean = 4.09) than in conversations about remote events (mean = 2.68), and they reported more units of information about recent events (mean = 9.68) than remote events (mean = 5.31). Finally, half of children's reports in the second, third, and fourth sessions (mean = 54%) consisted of new information that had not been mentioned by either participant in previous conversations.

Summary. These results address the three main issues as follows: (1) There were striking effects of retention interval on the performance of both mothers and children; both participants reported less about remote events. Because the children's contributions are largely elicited by their mothers, this finding suggests that children's relatively poor memory for remote events is because their mothers report less about these events and ask fewer questions about them. There is however, some evidence that the children themselves have more difficulty remembering the remote events. (2) There was no evidence that the amount of information children reported increased over the four sessions, essentially replicating the longitudinal case study. The specific content of the conversations varied considerably over the four sessions and both participants continually provided new information about the events that had not been discussed before. (3) Maternal style emerged as an important variable. Children of more elaborative mothers became more responsive over sessions when remembering more recent events and were able to respond to proportionally more requests for information about remote events.

Experimenter–child conversations

Here, we were interested in whether differences in memory for recent and remote events generalized to conversations with the experimenter, and whether the events that had been discussed with their mothers (the *old events*) would be remembered better than *new events*.

Experimenter contributions. The experimenter asked fewer questions (means of 1.68 general questions, 4.26 information requests, and 7.34 yes–no questions) than the mothers, but there was no difference in the number of questions asked about recent and remote events. The experimenter also provided considerably less information about the events (mean = 6.56 information units). The kinds of information the experimenter did provide was in the form of probes about predictable aspects of the event. For example, in interviewing a child about Halloween and not meeting with much success, the experimenter sometimes probed predictable aspects of the event: "Did you dress up? Did you wear a costume? What were you for Halloween?"

Children's contributions. There were no effects of retention interval on either structural or content measures. There were also no effects of old versus new events in the general responsiveness, that is, the proportion of questions responded to (mean = .73). However, children responded to proportionally more information requests when asked about old events (mean = .58) than when asked about new events (mean = .43). As shown in Table 7.7, the difference in number of spontaneous offers of information for old and new events was significant only for children of more elaborative mothers. Yet this did not affect the total number of information units reported for old and new events (means of

Table 7.7. *Number of spontaneous offers of information by children in experimenter–child conversations, Study 2*

	Old events	New events
High elaboration mothers	5.3	3.25
Low elaboration mothers	2.5	2.8

6.98 and 6.78, respectively). Finally, 36% of children's contributions to conversations about previously discussed events consisted of information that had not been reported in any of the sessions with their mothers.

Summary. The effects of retention interval found in the conversations with mothers did not generalize to the experimenter–child conversations. Further, children did not recall more about the events they had previously recalled with their mothers. However, they were able to participate more fully in conversations about previously discussed events, as indicated by the proportion of information requests that they were able to respond to and the number of offers of information made by children of more elaborative mothers.

Conclusions

These results indicate that 24- to 30-month olds have a limited ability to remember past events. They were very dependent on their mothers to cue memories and to direct their memory search. There was little change over the four sessions in their ability to contribute to the conversations, and when interviewed by an experimenter they did not remember any more information about events they had repeatedly recalled with their mothers. In addition, children had a great deal of difficulty reporting memories of events more than 6 months in the past. In part, this is because their mothers have difficulty remembering those events and provided less structure and fewer cues for the children. Consequently, when remembering with an experimenter who did not differentiate between recent and remote events, the children's performance did not vary.

What is interesting about children's difficulty in recalling remote events is that over the repeated recall sessions, the mothers provided a lot of information that children could incorporate into their responses, but this did not happen. There was no evidence that any kind of rote learning was going on. The mothers' questions probed the children's memory, but children did not tend to incorporate information mentioned by their mothers into later recall sessions. Moreover, the finding

that children did not benefit much from repeated conversations is surprising in light of many memory studies showing that verbal rehearsal
usually enhances children's recall.

Rather, how mothers talked about the past was more important than
the specific content of what they mentioned. Children whose mothers
used an elaborative style were better able to answer information requests
about more remote events and profited more from prior conversations
when remembering events with an experimenter. All children were better able to answer requests for information from an experimenter when
they were asked about events they had discussed with their mothers.
Thus, there was more evidence of improvement and generalization in
children's performance in terms of the structural aspects of remembering than in the content of children's reports.

This does not mean there was no negotiation of content over the four
mother–child recall sessions. As demonstrated by the first example in
Table 7.8, there were cases in which the same content was discussed in
each session, and over the four sessions the child's version of the event
changed to resemble more closely the mother's version. Here, Tanya
initially recalls a visit to a museum as fairly benign, but her mother makes
the point of reminding her that something scared her there. By the
second session, Tanya admits that she didn't like it, but can't say why and
is once again reminded by her mother. By the last session, Tanya volun-
teers the information that she was scared.

However, there were as many instances when the mother insisted on
her version of the event, which was steadfastly denied by the child in
each of the sessions, as shown in the second example displayed in Table
7.8. Seth repeatedly remembers being scared by clowns at a circus performance when he went to the country fair 10 months ago. His mother
continually corrects him that he was not scared by the clowns at the fair
but was scared a few weeks ago when he saw a clown at a party. Seth is not
swayed: Even in the last recall session with the experimenter he main-
tains his version of the event. Thus, some negotiation of content certainly did occur, and participants did repeat some core content over the
sessions, but the variability in content and the children's ability continually to recall new information was much more striking than the repetition of old information across sessions: Children were not simply repeating what they had been told.

What develops in mother–child conversations about the past?

Together with the findings from the longitudinal study, these results
indicate that 2-year-olds are in the early stages of learning how to recount personal experiences. Through conversations about the past, children adopt the goal of remembering as a jointly constructed activity, and

Table 7.8. *Examples of content negotiation, Study 2*

Tanya (30 months)
Session 1
M: What'd you see there?
C: A fire engine and a tunnel.
M: A fire engine and a tunnel. That's right, and what happened in the tunnel? What happened – did you like the tunnel?
C: (nods)
M: You liked the tunnel? I thought you didn't like the tunnel; it made a lot of noise! Didn't you tell me you got scared? Did you get scared in the tunnel?
C: No.
M: Oh, okay. I thought it made so much noise and it was so dark, you got scared and jumped and held on to Mommy.
C: I jumped up to my Mommy.

Session 2
M: And what else did you see?
C: A tunnel!
M: You didn't like the tunnel; why not?
C: Because I didn't.
M: Because you didn't? What happened in the tunnel?
C: I don't know.
M: What, did it sound like raining in the tunnel; did you get a little scared? It was kind of loud, wasn't it?
C: (nods)
M: Yeah, and you got a little scared in the tunnel. And you jumped up and said, "Mommy hold me!"

Session 4
M: Do you remember the museum?
C: Next time we won't go in the tunnel.
M: What happened in the tunnel?
C: I got scared.
M: You got scared?
C: And I jumped up to you. Next time we go to the museum we won't go in the tunnel!
M: That's right.

Seth (24 months)
Session 2
M: Did you ever see a circus?
C: Parade circus!
M: What? Parade? Parade, I think, parade. Parades are different than circuses. We saw a parade just a few weeks ago, but it wasn't a circus.
C: Clowns in it!
M: Right, we saw clowns in the parade.
C: And circus.
M: Did you see others, see clowns at a circus, though, in a show?
C: We clapped hands.
M: We clapped hands, yeah. Do you know what, what else was in the circus besides the clowns, do you remember being one?
C: Oh.

Table 7.8. *(cont.)*

M: You went to one at the fair.
C: Fair. Outside clapping! Here come clowns!
M: Here comes what?
C: Clowns.
M: Clowns, yeah. (to experimenter) He knows clowns are supposed to be in the circus, but I don't think he remembers that we saw it.
C: I see a clown. Hot outside!
M: Yeah, we went to the fair when it was hot out, and he sat in the stroller. Yeah, I don't know if you remember the circus; did we see some animals in the circus?
C: Yes, I was crying, I was crying circus! Jon cried . . .
M: Were you afraid of the clowns?
C: It was sad.
M: Yeah?
C: Yeah, circus had clowns.
M: (to experimenter) This was a few weeks ago, though, that he was crying at the clowns. Yeah, I don't think he remembers that; he wasn't crying, he wasn't afraid of the clowns last summer.
C: I was crying clowns!
M: Yeah, that wasn't a circus, though, where you saw the clown and you were crying.

Session 3
M: Did we see anything at the fair?
C: Clowns!
M: Clowns at the circus. Do, do you remember being . . .
C: That's sad!
M: Do you remember seeing Jonathan dressed up?
C: Jonathan.

Session 4
M: Do you remember going to a circus?
C: (shakes head)
M: No, huh? Don't ever remember, huh?
C: I don't like clowns.
M: I know you don't like clowns, but was there anything else at the circus?
C: I sit on Mommy!
M: (to experimenter) He doesn't like clowns.
C: I don't like circus clowns!

Session 5 (with experimenter)
E: What'd you see in the circus?
C: Clown circus, clown circus.
E: A clown circus?
C: Yes.
E: Oh, what else?
C: I scared of clowns!
E: You're scared of clowns?
C: Yeah.
E: Yeah? Oh, you were scared of the clowns?
C: That's all right now, okay *now!*
E: It's all right now? (chuckles) Okay.

Table 7.8. *(cont.)*

C:	All right now.
E:	Who, who took you to the fair?
C:	Jonathan.
E:	Jonathan took you, huh? Anybody else?
C:	Daddy.
E:	Daddy came, too? Anybody else?
C:	Daddy carry me.
E:	Daddy carried you; why did he carry you?
C:	'Cause was scared.
E:	'Cause you were scared of the clowns?
C:	Yes, scared.

by participating in the process of remembering, they acquire discourse skills for engaging in memory conversations. They may also develop the cognitive skills for directing their own memory search. However, there is still a very large gap between what 20- to 30-month-olds can remember with their mothers and what they can remember on their own, that is, the zone of proximal development.

In addition, verbal discussions of events may not affect young 2-year-olds' recall of specific events in the same way as for preschool children. That is, young 2-year-olds do not remember more about events they have previously discussed. This finding suggests that talking about events may affect long-term recall differently than reenactment of an event. Although reenactment improves memory in infants as young as 3 months (Rovee-Collier & Hayne, 1987), it is not until at least 33–42 months that talking about events has been shown to improve long-term verbal recall (Hamond, 1988).

Of course, reenactment studies with infants and toddlers have used behavioral measures of memory (Rovee-Collier & Hayne, 1987; Fivush & Hamond, in press), whereas studies of effects of repeated verbal recall in older children have used verbal measures (Hamond, 1988; Hudson, 1990). It should come as no surprise that verbal rehearsal does have an effect before children can talk. But what is particularly interesting about the data presented in this chapter is that for children in the process of learning to recount past experiences, repeated verbal recall does not affect young children's recall of specific events. Rather, effects of talking about the past were more general in the sense that the cumulative effects of talking about many different events over time (Study 1) and the way events were talked about (Study 2) affected children's overall ability to contribute to memory conversations more than what in particular was talked about.

In order for repeated verbal recall to affect children's autobiographical memory, they may have to have acquired the ability to direct their own memory search, that is, be able to recount an event on their own. Thus, memories of events occurring up to about 30 months may depend on physical reenactment in order to prevent forgetting. Once children can retrieve and recount autobiographical memories on their own at about 30–36 months (Fivush, Gray, & Fromhoff, 1987), simply talking about an event can "preserve" it for long-term memory. The fact that 20–30 months coincides with the onset of childhood amnesia suggests that childhood amnesia may, in part, be the result of developmental changes in the types of experiences necessary to prevent long-term forgetting (see also Fivush & Hamond, this volume, and Nelson, this volume, for further discussion of the causes of childhood amnesia).

Thus, two important developments during this time period may lay the foundation for the emergence of autobiographical memory. First, children make the transition from participating in conversations about the past to independently recounting personal memories. This transition reflects the development of children's abilities to search their own memory and organize their own memory narratives. The data presented in this chapter indicate that mother–child conversations about the past provide the interactive context in which young children can make this transition. There is more evidence that children from 20 to 30 months are acquiring the structure of remembering rather than rehearsing specific content. That is, they are learning *how* to remember, not *what* to remember. Second, a shift from physical to verbal reactivation of event memories may occur as a result of the development of children's abilities to retrieve and recount autobiographic memories independently. The ability to narrate events, not just the ability to talk, may herald the emergence of a verbally accessible memory system during the years 2 to 3.

NOTE

This research was supported by a Faculty Research Grant from the State University of New York. Special thanks go to Francesca Sidoti for her assistance in Study 2, to Hollis Wiedenbacher and Judi Moore for their assistance in coding, and to Laura Keup for help in transcribing.

REFERENCES

Eisenberg, A. R. (1985). Learning to describe past experiences in conversation. *Discourse Processes, 8,* 177–204.
Fivush, R., & Fromhoff, F. A. (1988). Style and structure in mother–child conversations about the past. *Discourse Processess, 11,* 337–355.

Fivush, R., Gray, J. T., & Fromhoff, F. A. (1987). Two-year-olds talk about the past. *Cognitive Development, 2,* 393–409.
Fivush, R., & Hamond, N. R. (in press). Time and again: Effects of repetition and retention interval on two year olds' event recall. *Journal of Experimental Child Psychology.*
Gruendel, J. M. (1980). *Scripts and stories: A study of children's event narratives.* Unpublished doctoral dissertation, Yale University.
Hamond, N. R. (1988). *Memories of Mickey Mouse: Young children recount their trip to Disneyland.* Paper presented at the Southeastern Conference on Human Development, Charleston.
Hudson, J. A. (1986). Memories are made of this: Effects of general event knowledge on the development of autobiographic memory. In K. Nelson (Ed.), *Event knowledge: Structure and function in development* (pp. 97–118). Hillsdale, NJ: Erlbaum.
Hudson, J. A. (1988). Children's memory for atypical actions in script-based stories: Evidence for a disruption effect. *Journal of Experimental Child Psychology, 5,* 1–15.
Hudson, J. A. (1990). Constructive processes in children's autobiographic memory. *Developmental Psychology, 26,* 180–187.
Hudson, J., & Hagreen, M. (1987, October). *From script to story: The development of children's narratives.* Paper presented at Boston University Conference on Language Development, Boston.
Hudson, J., & Nelson, K. (1986). Repeated encounters of a similar kind: Effects of familiarity on children's autobiographic memory. *Cognitive Development, 1,* 253–271.
Hudson, J. A., & Shapiro, L. R. (in press). From knowing to telling: The development of children's scripts, stories, and personal narratives. In A. McCabe & C. Peterson (Eds.), *New directions in narrative structure.* Hillsdale, NJ: Erlbaum.
Hudson, J. A., & Sidoti, F. (1988, April). *Two-year-olds' autobiographic memory in mother–child conversation.* Paper presented at the International Conference on Infant Studies, Washington, DC.
Lucariello, J., & Nelson, K. (1987). Remembering and planning talk between mothers and children, *Discourse Processes, 10,* 219–235.
Nelson, K., & Ross, G. (1980). The generalities and specifics of long-term memory in infants and young children. In M. Perlmutter (Ed.), *Children's memory* (New directions for child development, No. 10, pp. 87–101). San Francisco: Jossey-Bass.
O'Connell, B., & Gerard, A. (1985). Scripts and scraps: The development of sequential understanding. *Child Development, 56,* 671–681.
Piaget, J. (1962). *Play, dreams, and imitation in childhood.* New York: Norton.
Pillemer, D., & White, S. (in press). Childhood events recalled by children and adults. In H. W. Reese (Ed.), *Advances in child development and behavior* (Vol. 22). New York: Academic Press.
Ratner, H. H. (1984). Memory demands and the development of young children's memory. *Child Development, 55,* 2173–2191.
Rovee-Collier, C., & Hayne, H. (1987). Reactivation of infant memory: Implications for cognitive development. In H. W. Reese (Ed.), *Advances in child development and behavior* (Vol. 20, pp. 185–238). New York: Academic Press.
Rovee-Collier, C. K., Sullivan, M. W., Enright, M., Lucas, D., & Fagan, J. W. (1980). Reactivation of infant memory. *Science, 208,* 1159–1161.

Sachs, J. (1983). Talking about the there and then: The emergence of displaced reference in parent–child discourse. In K. Nelson (Ed.), *Children's language* (Vol. 4, pp. 1–28). Hillsdale, NJ: Erlbaum.

Stein, N. L. (1988, October). *A model of storytelling skills.* Paper presented at the Boston University Conference on Language Development, Boston.

Vygotsky, L. S. (1978). *Mind in society.* Cambridge, MA: Harvard University Press.

White, S. H., & Pillemer, D. B. (1979). Childhood amnesia and the development of a socially accessible memory system. In J. F. Kihlstrom & F. J. Evans (Eds.), *Functional disorders of memory* (pp. 29–73). Hillsdale, NJ: Erlbaum.

8

The social and functional context of children's remembering

BARBARA ROGOFF AND JAYANTHI MISTRY

Memory development reflects the opportunities individuals have to learn particular skills in the everyday activities practiced in their culture. To understand memory performance, or to compare the performance of different groups, it is essential to examine the subjects' goals in remembering and the social context in which it occurs. Research on memory development has increasingly examined children's skills and strategies in memory tasks that resemble those occurring in children's everyday lives (DeLoache & Brown, 1983; Nelson & Ross, 1980; Paris, Newman, & Jacobs, 1985; Wellman & Somerville, 1980).

In this chapter we argue that understanding the role of context in memory development requires consideration of how individuals' memory performances are embedded in systems of activity integrating what is to be remembered, the purpose of remembering, and the social context of remembering. Specifically, we examine memory performances that involve

1. remembering information embedded in meaningful contexts rather than remembering unrelated bits of information and performing memory tasks with no practical purpose, and
2. variation in the social context of mnemonic activities, especially the "metamnemonic" role of adults in helping children to attend to material to be remembered and to apply appropriate strategies to remember it.

These issues are illustrated with a preliminary study of how preschoolers' free recall is influenced by engaging children in remembering for a practical purpose and by the assistance of their parents in remembering.

Our arguments are consistent with Bartlett's emphasis on remembering as "a matter of social organization, with its accepted scales of value" (1932, p. 248). Bartlett argued that memory is a socially structured process in both "the manner and the matter of recall" (p. 244), challenging the notion that memory is a "pure" process that can avoid the influence of previous knowledge and background experience.

197

Similarly, the Soviet sociohistorical view of the development of higher mental processes stresses the social genesis and structuring of memory (Meacham, 1977; Vygotsky, 1978). Leont'ev stated that "the role of the social medium is not limited . . . simply to its emerging as a central factor of development; man's memory . . . remains associated with it in its very functioning" (1981, p. 363). In the sociohistorical approach, memory and other higher mental processes develop from experience in involving the use of cultural tools and institutions in shared thinking with more skilled companions. Cultural, institutional tools of action and thought include arithmetic and writing systems, mnemonic strategies, and procedures for the use of such tools. This perspective focuses on the social unit of activity and derives individual functioning from social activity, rather than seeking first to explain individual functioning and then adding social influences to presumably "basic" individual functioning.

The notion that individual functioning is derived from social activity suggests that the particular activities in which individuals engage are central to memory development. The Laboratory of Comparative Human Cognition (1983) has drawn distinctions between contrasting assumptions regarding the generality of learning experiences and resulting cognitive skills. They characterize a central-processor approach as fitting the assumptions of traditional developmental theory and research: The events an individual experiences contribute to the strength or power of a central processor consisting of general skills. These general skills are assumed to be broadly applicable to tasks regardless of the nature of specific tasks.

However, evidence indicates that the assumption of generality of processing is questionable (Feldman, 1980; Fischer, 1980; Fowler, 1980), and that memory and other cognitive processes are inherently related to the activities in which they are used (Rogoff, 1982). Memory does not involve context-free competencies to be applied indiscriminately across widely diverse problem domains but, rather, involves skills functionally tied to the context of their use.

The Laboratory of Comparative Human Cognition contrasts the central-processor approach with the distributed-processing approach, which emphasizes that skills are closely tied to the context of practice, as the individual develops skills in particular tasks through experience in related activities. Skills are customized to the task within activities, and thus link particular classes of experience with performance on specific genres of task.

The Laboratory of Comparative Human Cognition (1983) and Scribner and Cole (1981) propose "socially assembled situations" as the appropriate unit of analysis. These are cultural contexts for action and problem solving that are constructed by people in interaction with each other.

Cultural practices employed in socially assembled situations are learned systems of activity in which knowledge consists of standing rules and technologies for thought and action appropriate to a particular situation, embodied in the interaction of individual members of a society.

The central tenet of this chapter is that remembering is organized on the basis of features of the activities in which it occurs, with applicability of developing skills to new situations on the basis of the systems nature of activities – involving not only the form of the problem but also the purpose of solving it and the sociocultural context in which the activity is embedded. People remember in order to achieve practical, interpersonal results in specific socioculturally organized contexts.

People transform novel problems to resemble familiar ones by seeking analogies across problems, according to their interpretation of the task (Duncker, 1945; Gick & Holyoak, 1980). Important aspects of their interpretation of a task derive from the purpose of the task and the social supports of others who assist in the application of cultural tools for problem solution and in the marking of points of similarity across problem situations (Rogoff & Gardner, 1984; Wertsch & Hickmann, 1987).

In this chapter we first examine the functional nature of memory in terms of how everyday remembering involves use of the meaningful organization of information and derives from the meaningful purposes motivating memory. Then we consider the social context of memory performance and development, arguing that memory performances must be considered as social interactional settings and that memory development can be aided by social support. These notions are illustrated with a pilot study we have carried out to examine the role of purpose and social support in young children's memory skills.

The functional nature of memory

Meaningful organization of information according to practice

Developmental differences in memory skills are most notable in the growth with age of use of strategies to organize information (e.g., Flavell & Wellman, 1977; Ornstein, 1978; Naus & Ornstein, 1983; Paris et al., 1985; Wellman, 1988). In many memory tests, subjects are presented with lists of unrelated pieces of information that may be more fully remembered if subjects apply some strategy to coordinate the pieces. This may involve rehearsal – for information to be held in memory for short amounts of time – or organization involving categorizing the items or elaborating meaningful connections between items. Young children have more difficulty using such strategies, even when prompted, than do older children (Flavell, Beach, Chinsky, 1966; Pressley, Heisel, Mc-

Cormick, & Nakamura, 1982). Similarly, older adults are less likely to use such strategies and have trouble with such memory tasks and strategies even when given training in strategy use, compared with younger adults (Mueller, Rankin, & Carlomusto, 1979; Perlmutter, 1979). Consistent with these developmental differences are cross-cultural findings that people in nontechnological cultures have the greatest difficulties with memory tasks in which the structure of the material is not made explicit, and often do not employ organizational strategies spontaneously (Cole & Scribner, 1977).

The use of memory tasks employing unrelated bits of information has a long history in psychology, since Ebbinghaus introduced the nonsense syllable. The presentation of isolated bits of information was seen as simplifying the units of information to be recalled and limiting the role of previous experience brought to the particular associations to be remembered. However, this simplicity is likely to be an illusion, as Bartlett pointed out in his critique of the nonsense syllable:

Uniformity and simplicity of structure of stimuli are no guarantee whatever of uniformity and simplicity of structure in organic response . . . isolation [of response] is not to be secured by simplifying situations or stimuli and leaving as complex an organism as ever to make the response. What we do then is simply to force this organism to mobilise all its resources and make up, or discover, a new complex reaction on the spot. (1932, pp. 3–6)

The processes required to invent connections between isolated bits of information may be quite unrelated to everyday memory where the information can be integrated with a meaningful context rather than requiring imposed organization.

The notion that memory practices are tied to cultural institutions is suggested by the fact that the people who have great difficulty with remembering isolated bits of information, and with inventing organizational strategies to handle them, have less (or less recent) experience in the institution of formal schooling. Young children, older adults, and individuals in nontechnological societies may have less practice and less reason to be concerned with remembering lists than do the comparison groups, which have greater familiarity with school skills.

Western literate young adults have special demands and opportunities to develop the use of memory aids appropriate for remembering lists of isolated pieces of information. Goody (1977) points out that with tests involving lists of "decontextualized" words, facility stems from familiarity with lists and the classification systems that lists promote (e.g., alphabetic, categorical). Goody suggests that making and remembering lists is a product of literacy.

Remembering lists of unrelated items may be an unusual experience outside of school but common in school, where pupils frequently have to use strategies to ensure recall of material they have not understood. And it appears that in the early grades, schoolteachers attempt to provide instruction in the use of such mnemonic strategies (Hart, Leal, Burney, & Santulli, 1985).

While less-schooled individuals may have little practice creating order for isolated bits of information, people from all backgrounds may have similar experience remembering information that is embedded in a structured context and using strategies that incorporate the existing organization of items and context, using meaningful relationships among items as an aid to recall. People use their knowledge of usual relationships among objects and events to organize their memory for items appearing in a meaningful context (Friedman, 1979; Mandler, 1979).

With organized materials, there may be fewer developmental and cultural differences in memory performance, because most memory problems for any individual involve material that is organized in a complex and meaningful fashion rather than lists of items that have been stripped of organization. For example, in remembering the arrangement of the top of a desk, a serial listing of items is generally insufficient, since items are spatially arranged in three dimensions, and they overlap and bear multiple relationships with one another. The contextual and conceptual order of the array helps the user of the desk to locate things.

Consistent with the idea that contextually organized information might show fewer differences between groups is research showing that cultural differences are removed or reduced in two types of memory task – memory for spatial arrangements and memory for organized prose (Cole & Scribner, 1977; Dube, 1982; Kearins, 1981; Mandler, Scribner, Cole, & DeForest, 1980; Neisser, 1982; Ross & Millsom, 1970). To follow up on this idea, Rogoff and colleagues studied memory for organized scenes with populations that ordinarily perform quite differently on memory tasks involving unrelated items.

Similarity across cultures in children's reconstruction of scenes. Rogoff and Waddell (1982) examined the performance of Guatemalan Mayan and U.S. 9-year olds on the reconstruction of contextually organized three-dimensional scenes. Each child watched as a local experimenter placed 20 miniature objects such as cars, animals, furniture, people, and household items into a panorama model of a town, containing a mountain, lake, road, houses, and some trees. All objects were pretested for familiarity to both groups. The 20 objects were removed from the panorama and reintegrated into the pool of 80 objects from which they were drawn, and after a delay of minutes, the child reconstructed the scene.

The Mayan sample had shown strikingly poorer list memory performance than a U.S. comparison group in a previous study (Kagan, Klein, Finley, Rogoff, & Nolan, 1979), but they performed at least as well as (nonsignificantly better than) U.S. children on the test using contextually organized materials. These results challenge the generality of cultural differences usually found with memory for lists of unrelated items; they suggest that meaningful organization of information may be skillfully employed for remembering in cultural communities varying in the skill of their members in using the mnemonic strategies helpful for remembering lists.

The slight advantage of the Mayan children seemed to be due to the counterproductive attempts by some U.S. children to apply a strategy useful for remembering unorganized lists – rehearsal. About a third of the 30 U.S. children (but only 1 of the 30 Mayan children) rehearsed the names of the objects in the panorama as they studied. This is an effective strategy for remembering lists of unrelated items immediately after presentation, but may be inappropriate for remembering contextually organized material. Rehearsal of object names may help only minimally in reconstruction because the objects are present at the time of the delayed test and the problem is remembering their locations. Kearins (1981) suggests that successful reconstruction of spatial arrays is accompanied by remembering the "look" of the arrangement rather than by the use of verbal strategies as in standard list memory tasks.

A child who has learned strategies for remembering lists of words may indiscriminately apply those strategies to inherently organized material, without regard for the relevance of such strategies to the particular task. This occurred in a subsequent study when 7-year-old U.S. children were asked to remember the layout of a large-scale space (a laboratory funhouse). They seemed to remember it as a list of rooms, overlooking the complex nonlinear relations between rooms (Skeen & Rogoff, 1987). Agemates who were not told in advance to remember the space were more effective in recalling the layout of the space. As U.S. children learn to master mnemonic strategies useful for remembering lists, they may overgeneralize the strategies to tasks that might better be approached by attention to meaningful relationships between features of the array.

Everyday life may commonly involve remembering things through attention to the contextual organization of the material. All people have to remember how to get to an acquaintance's house, where to find things at home, and what occurrences have led to an important event. Even children as young as 2 years show impressive memory for the location of interesting objects in meaningful layouts (DeLoache & Brown, 1983).

In order to examine whether contextual organization is the crucial feature differentiating the scene reconstruction task from list memory tasks, the next study varied contextual organization using the same materials, comparing the performance of older and middle-aged U.S. adults. As mentioned previously, older adults show the same pattern of poor performance on list memory tasks as do individuals in nontechnological cultures.

Memory of older and middle-aged adults for contextually organized versus arbitrarily arranged spatial information. There were no differences in the performance of aged and middle-aged adults asked to reconstruct a scene with 30 objects arranged in a panorama resembling a town, whereas the usual age decrement appeared when the same objects were presented in an arbitrary arrangement (Waddell & Rogoff, 1981). To control for the possibility that the difference might involve salience of cues or the spatial modality of the task, performance on the contextually organized array was compared with performance on an arbitrary arrangement of the same props from the panorama (mountains, houses, etc. – see Figure 8.1) in a bank of cubicles. The 30 objects to be replaced in the bank of cubicles were associated with the same props (i.e., mountains, houses, etc.), but the overall arrangement did not constitute a meaningful scene. The items in the scenes were not arranged in already learned locations that would require no effort to remember; they were put in places that they would not necessarily be expected. The subjects had to learn the locations, making use of the meaningful layout of the panorama in which the new information appeared.

The older adults in the United States – like the children from a nontechnological culture – had difficulty remembering unrelated bits of information but were skilled in remembering information that could be integrated into a meaningful arrangement.

The subjects appeared to use a strategy that resembles the method of loci, in which very effective memory performance can be achieved by relating new pieces of information to a meaningful scene that serves as a mnemonic peg system (Higbee, 1979). Subjects reconstructing the panorama often followed paths through the layout, replacing items in one area or along a particular path before going to the next area. They were more likely to follow such a spatial sequencing strategy than to use recognition of objects in the pool to order recall, or to mimic the random order of placement in which items had been presented. Subjects who used the spatial sequencing strategy to a greater extent produced more complete reconstructions of the scene than did subjects who used it less.

The pattern across ages in use of the spatial sequencing strategy supports the idea that contextual organization was useful to both age groups. In the contextually organized scene, aged and middle-aged adults used spatial sequencing to a similar extent. However, in the arbi-

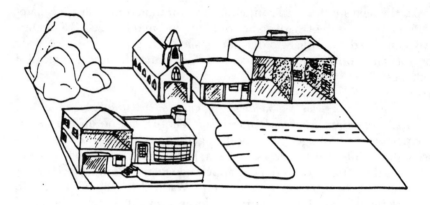

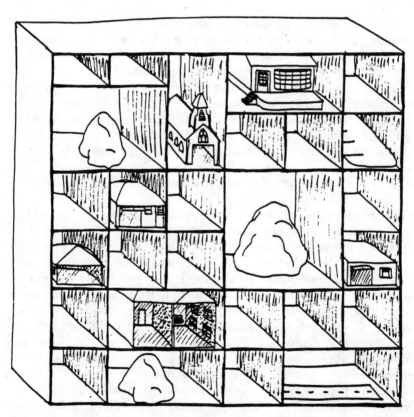

Figure 8.1. The prop arrangements for the panorama and the bank of cubicles in Waddell & Rogoff, 1981. (Reprinted courtesy of the American Psychological Association.)

trary arrangement involving the bank of cubicles, there were great age differences. Middle-aged adults used more sequencing in their replacement of objects in the cubicles than in the panorama, creating paths through the cubicles. The aged adults used spatial sequencing much less frequently in reconstructing the arrangement of the cubicles than did the middle-aged adults, and than did the aged adults reconstructing the panorama. Instead, they appeared overwhelmed, and their efforts in reconstruction were much less orderly and effective. They appeared to attempt to reproduce the order in which the objects were placed in the cubicles by the experimenter, a strategy that correlated with less accurate object placement.

A subsequent study involving incidental as well as intentional memory for the arrangement of objects in the panorama showed that use of contextual organization by both middle-aged and older adults involves active attention to the relationships between objects in the scene (Waddell & Rogoff, 1987). Memory for contextually organized information is not automatic, although it may be impressive even in populations that have difficulty inventing organization for unrelated items. Both the accuracy of placement and the use of the spatial sequencing strategy were much greater when subjects remembered deliberately or else attended incidentally to the spatial relationships among objects.

These studies comparing memory for contextually organized information and memory for unrelated items suggest that exclusively studying memory for items stripped of organization may have led the field to a somewhat skewed picture of memory development. The results stress the importance of considering the role of contextual organization in memory and of examining the relationship of memory tasks to the organized practices of remembering (e.g., in school or other cultural institutions) in which the subjects routinely participate. An emphasis on the contextual relations in the material to be remembered, as well as between the task and cultural practices, is similarly suggested by research on children's memory for organized events, stories, and scripts (Nelson & Gruendel, 1981, as well as many of the other chapters in this volume). The next section expands the consideration of the functional nature of memory to include the role of the purpose of the task.

Meaningful purpose in memory activity

In the cross-cultural literature, outstanding memory performance by non-Western people has been observed in situations in which memory serves a culturally important goal, with remembering the means rather than the goal of the activity. Examples include remembering spatial information to avoid getting lost while navigating on land or sea (Gladwin, 1970; Levy-Bruhl, 1926; Lewis, 1976), and remembering verbal material in narrating stories or oral history (D'Azevedo, 1982; Hunter, 1979; Lord, 1965; Mack, 1976).

Memory research has concentrated on tasks and experimental situations in which memory is a goal in itself rather than a means to a practical goal, such as remembering an important appointment (Brown, 1975; Paris & Cross, 1983; Rogoff, 1982; Smirnov & Zinchenko, 1969). Without a purpose for remembering material, thousands of trials of exposure may still not ensure remembering, as was the case with Professor Sanford's morning prayer, read daily over 25 years but not learned (Sanford, 1917, reprinted 1982). Memory for meaningful events, where the goal of an action is known, is better than memory for less meaningful events (Brewer & Dupree, 1983).

Remembering in everyday life is usually in the service of accomplishing some other goal rather than being itself the end for the activity. Again, the institution of formal schooling appears related to the situation of having to remember something so someone can see if one has remembered it. Outside school, this may be an uncommon experience, especially in some cultural groups in which knowledge is not tested until it is fully consolidated (Cazden & John, 1971), or in which asking a question to which one already knows the answer is not done except to trick the responder (Irvine, 1978). Some cultural differences in memory performance may thus derive from the unfamiliarity or inappropriateness of being asked to remember for no practical purpose. Individuals familiar with schooling may come to regard memory tests as serving a familiar purpose, fitting a recognizable genre of interpersonal endeavor, but those less familiar with schooling (or other contexts involving demonstration of skill for the sake of evaluation) may have difficulty with requests to remember for no other purpose.

For young children, the arbitrariness of being asked to remember in order to demonstrate one's memory skill may contribute (among other reasons for age differences) to poor memory performance. Paris et al. (1985) suggest that conditions of familiar settings and meaningful goals promote young children's understanding of the need to intervene as an agent, to perceive the mnemonic goal, and to act in an instrumental manner, which contribute to children's self-directed use of mnemonic strategies as well as to learning effective techniques for remembering.

A landmark study by Istomina (1977) focused the attention of developmentalists on the role of meaningful purpose in remembering. She reported that preschoolers' performance on a free recall task was much improved when remembering items was essential for carrying out a meaningful activity (a game of shopping in a play store) than when items needed to be recalled simply for the sake of memory performance, as an experimenter asked for recall in a "lesson." In the lesson condition, the experimenter asked the child to listen attentively to the words and try to remember them in order to recount them later to the experimenter.

The game situation combined the themes of playing store and playing school, as six children played together, with three given the roles of store employees and three given kindergarten roles (e.g., teacher, cook, director). In the course of play, the kindergarten leader (the experimenter) invited one of the children to go on an errand to the store to buy some things for the kindergarten, and slowly named the five items. The child was given a permission slip, money, and a basket, and went to the store and told the store manager what was needed. The child completed the purchase and then returned to the kindergarten. The game continued until all the children playing in the "kindergarten" had been to the store. The embeddedness of the memory activity in the play scenario, with remembering essential for the play, is illustrated by the variations in the instructions leading to the memory task: In one example, the target child played the role of the teacher putting the dolls to sleep.

"Lyuba," says the experimenter, "when the children are asleep you can do an errand and go to the store."
Lyuba immediately jumps up and runs up to the experimenter saying: "What should I buy?" (Istomina, 1977, p. 116)

In another example, the experimenter reminds the target child of his role as "cook" and sets up the memory activity as follows:

"Valerik," says the experimenter, "you're our cook. What are you going to prepare for lunch today?"
Valerik answers: "I don't know."
"Well then," say(s) the experimenter, "the children are coming back from a walk and there is nothing to eat. (Valerik smiles and gazes questioningly at the experimenter.) Here is an entry permit to go to the store. Go and buy . . ." (she then names the items). (Istomina, 1977, pp. 114–115)

As the examples suggest, the game situation goes beyond simply motivating the children or providing a familiar situation. It provides a purpose for remembering a list of items without the memory goal being made explicit by the experimenter. Remembering the items was essential for the purpose of carrying out the play activity. The situation was motivating and meaningful, but, more important, the memory aspect of the activity was in the service of the unrolling play, not incidental or arbitrary. "This game involved a specific, defined situation that created a motivation for remembering or recall, i.e., it created conditions that enabled the child to set the goals of remembering and recall for himself explicitly" (Istomina, 1977, p. 104).

We and others have attempted to explore Istomina's suggestion, with attempts varying in their closeness to Istomina's procedure, rationale, and results. Weissberg and Paris (1986) examined how 3- to 7-year-olds remembered six items to be purchased from a pretend grocery store or to be remembered in a standard free recall format. (They also examined children's recall for the first names of six stuffed animals attending a pretend party, but this condition does not seem to satisfy the spirit of having children remember information in the service of a goal besides remembering. The task was a game, but the goal of the game was to remember, not to remember in order to accomplish another goal.)

In contrast with Istomina's results, Weissberg and Paris found poorer performance in the condition involving recall of items to be purchased from the pretend grocery store. Weissberg and Paris's 4- to 5-year-old subjects remembered an average of 3.4 items in the lesson condition and 2.8 items in the shopping condition, while Istomina's 4- to 5-year-olds remembered 1.5 words in the lesson condition and 3 words in the game condition (and 1.8 and 2.6 words, respectively, in a replication reported by Istomina).

Weissberg and Paris conclude that global motivational dispositions do not account for contextual differences in children's remembering. However, in our reading, the issue is not the presence of global motivational dispositions but the extent to which memory is necessary to reach another goal of an activity in which children are engaged. There were subtle but perhaps important differences in the way the shopping task was engineered in the two studies that may have influenced the extent to which it provided purpose for the subjects.

In Istomina's study, the remembering task flowed naturally from an intrinsically motivating activity and served an essential purpose in the flow of the play. The remembering goal was embedded in the task of buying groceries, which in turn was functional in the context of the child's role in the game. Children who did not remember the shopping items needed in the pretense would compromise the further elaboration of the fantasy. An example demonstrating the engagement of the children in the fantasy shopping goal was provided by one child who listed the needed items to the store manager and added, "And hurry, because the children are hungry" (Istomina, 1977, p. 118).

In Weissberg and Paris's shopping situation, the goal of buying groceries presumably made the task more motivating than simply repeating item names back to an experimenter, and the children undoubtedly enjoyed the "game" with the two adults present. But the shopping task did not have a function beyond satisfying an experimenter who asked the child to go to the store and buy groceries. And the context did not sound as though the children could have engaged in developing a fantasy goal in which they needed to remember the items. Although the situation was apparently fun, it appears unlikely that an engaging fantasy would have developed to embed the memory goal as an essential means to another goal. There were no other children present (and although adults often support children's fantasy, they seldom enter into it as participants [Dunn & Dale, 1984; Goncu, personal communication]); the procedure involved two lesson and two "game" free recall lists (each repeated twice) in counterbalanced order, and the experimenter praised the children for their performance. The lack of a real or fantasy purpose for the "shopping trip" that would necessitate efforts to remember could account for the differences between these findings and those of Istomina.

Weissberg and Paris argue that the lesson condition (standard free recall) enhanced children's understanding of the goal of remembering, the need to act deliberately in order to foster recall, and a dawning awareness of rehearsal as a useful mnemonic strategy. But as Weissberg and Paris speculate, it is possible that the lesson (free recall) condition for the U.S. subjects held much greater meaning than it did for Istomina's Soviet children, tested before 1948, who may have been unfamiliar with being tested in a free recall format. Istomina's subjects' preschools may have been less academic than those in the United States in the 1980s; U.S. children receive instruction in free recall on *Sesame Street*, and often possess manufactured memory games in their homes; and the discourse pattern of asking a child to repeat arbitrary pieces of information on demand may be more familiar to current U.S. children than to Soviet children of several decades ago. Istomina's 3-year-old subjects often seemed bewildered in the "lesson" task, whereas Weissberg and Paris's 3-year-old subjects appeared competent. So, as Weissberg and Paris point out, the goals of the lesson task may have been differentially meaningful for the two groups.

Our pilot study, extending Istomina's focus on examining mnemonic activity that serves a meaningful goal, compared children remembering items to ask for from a storekeeper in order to make their own sack lunch, versus remembering the items to be told to an experimenter. (In both conditions, the person to whom the child told the item names was a different person from the person who had told the child the items to remember, to avoid problems that could arise in situations when a person asks for information that they obviously already have.)

The study involved thirteen 4-year-olds recruited from preschools serving middle-class populations in Salt Lake City. Parents (usually mothers) presented the list to their child in a room at the preschool, using a standard list of 10 pictures of items that could go in a sack lunch. (The items were not so standard, however, that even a child who had not received the list would know what items to say. The items were: cheese slice, napkin, apple juice, bread, crackers, paper plate, grapes, cookies, plastic bags, corn chips.)

The parents were constrained in their manner of presenting the list:

They were told to go through the list (the pack of item cards) in the order they were in, twice. The parents presented the list in a standard free recall format – nurturantly but without prompts or suggestions.

In the lunch condition, the parent explained to the child that they were going to make a sack lunch and needed to get all the things for the sack lunch from the experimenter ("grocer") on the other side of the room. After being presented with the list, the child went across the room and asked for the items, which the grocer gave him or her, and the child took them back to the parent in a basket. This constituted the memory test. When it was completed, the child went back to the store to get any forgotten items, and the parent and child put together the lunch for the child to take home as a treat. (At the time of the memory test, the children were working with the information that the items were for making their own sack lunch, but they did not know that they would be allowed to go back for any forgotten items.) Thus the function of the memory task involved remembering a grocery list as a necessary step in making a sack lunch with the parent, and this is how the activity was explained by the parent: needing to remember the items to get them from the "store" for their sack lunch.

In the lab condition, the parent told the child to remember the items in order to go to the experimenter on the other side of the room and tell her the pictures they remembered. When the child was through recalling, the experimenter gave her or him a packed sack lunch to take home – the first mention of the sack lunch for the lab condition.

Results indicated that when a meaningful purpose made it important to try to remember the items (that is, in the lunch condition), 4-year-olds remembered more items than when the purpose was simply to remember the items to report them to someone (free recall condition). Out of 10 items, children in the lunch condition remembered 5.3 and the children in the free recall condition remembered 2.7, a difference significant at the .01 level. These findings support the idea that a meaningful purpose for remembering facilitates preschool children's recall.

Our figures are almost twice as high as those of Istomina, perhaps because in our study the list was presented both orally and with pictures, and was repeated once. Compared with Weissberg and Paris's subjects, our subjects remembered almost twice as many items in the shopping condition (perhaps because of the greater intrinsic connection between remembering and achieving a meaningful goal in our shopping condition), and slightly fewer in the free recall condition.

In our study, we also included a condition in which parents were allowed to assist their children in studying the list. The findings above are limited to the situation in which parents followed standard experimental format (no assistance). After discussing the social context of memory performance, we examine the results of having parents help their children prepare for the test during the presentation of items.

Organization of memory in social practice

In recent years, there has been growing interest in the social context of children's cognitive development, sparked in part by Vygotsky's (1978, 1987) works emphasizing that cognitive development begins as social activity, in which children's intellectual efforts are supported by more experienced partners in shared problem-solving in the zone of proximal development (see Laboratory of Comparative Human Cognition, 1983; Rogoff, 1982; 1990; Wertsch, 1979). Vygotsky emphasized both the role of social institutions and tools such as schooling and literacy, and the mediating context of social interaction.

In the remaining sections, we consider first the social interactional context of memory performance and its relation to cultural rules for communication. Then we examine the possibility that social interaction can assist children in developing their memory skills, reporting the other half of the sack lunch study.

Memory tests as social situations

Experimental situations such as memory tests are social situations, although experimenters seldom explicitly examine the role of their arrangements and interactions with subjects. The participants in a memory study not only are providing a memory performance but are also managing a social relationship with the person who has asked them to remember. We never have pure observations of memory, uninfluenced by the communication context of the elicitation of the performance (except perhaps when the rememberers have set themselves the task of remembering, and then the performance is seldom public).

Some recognition of this issue is available in the literature on the development of children's spatial cognition. This literature considers the role of various methods of eliciting children's understanding of where objects are in space, comparing children's reports, map drawing, way finding, pointing through barriers at target objects, and reconstructing layouts (Newcombe, 1985; Skeen, 1984). Although most of the discussion has been cast in terms of performance-competence concerns, some writers have pointed out that memory performances are embedded in the context of communication, which may channel the performance observed (Gauvain & Rogoff, 1989; Linde & Labov, 1975). Consideration of the communicative context of cognitive performance is particularly important in developmental studies, as older children are more skilled in the use of communicative devices for transmitting spatial information than are younger children (age 8 vs. age 6, Gauvain & Rogoff, 1989). Erickson (1981) argues that it is impossible to separate referential meaning (as in an assessment of understanding) and social meaning.

It is important, from this perspective, to consider the social context of how the memory performance is staged. As mentioned in the section on the purpose of the memory performance, some memory tasks involve asking people to remember material solely for the purpose of remembering, a social situation that may conflict with cultural practices in some societies or that may conflict with familiar situations for some age groups.

The patterns of interpersonal relations involved in a memory test may be familiar to some groups of subjects, and unfamiliar or even inappropriate for other groups. Patterns of interpersonal relations are organized by institutions and cultural tools, and enter into the means by which people communicate, in laboratories as much as anywhere else.

In many cultural groups, the status relations between children and adults do not fit the conversational peer ascription often used in middle class U.S. adult–child interactions. It is not uncommon in traditional societies for the interaction between adults and children to be characterized by directives from adults and compliance by children, rather than incorporating interest in children's opinions (Blount, 1972; Harkness & Super, 1977). The role of schooling in familiarizing children with the kind of communication used in testing is suggested by findings that in a traditional society, a year of school dramatically increases children's ability to finish an experiment – regardless of correctness of answers – and increases the number of words used in responding (Super, 1977).

An example of how conventions for social interaction can influence memory performance is provided by a cross-cultural study of story recall (Rogoff & Waddell, unpublished data, reported in Rogoff & Mistry, 1985). Since non-Western people have shown impressive prose recall (Dube, 1982; Mandler, Scribner, Cole, & DeForest, 1980; Ross & Millsom, 1970), story recall was used as another contextually organized task to parallel the spatial scene reconstruction task in comparing the memory performance of U.S. and Guatemalan Mayan 9-year-old children. However, the Mayan children remembered far less of the stories than did the U.S. children, averaging only 54 information units from the two stories compared with the 79 information units recalled by the U.S. children.

This was despite extensive efforts to make the task culturally appropriate for the Mayan children. The stories were adapted from the Mayan oral literature, told to the children by a familiar teenager speaking the local Mayan dialect, in a local house in which they had become comfortable through prior play sessions, parties, and several tests that they had enjoyed. The children were eager to participate in the sessions. In the effort to make story recall more like telling the story rather than being tested by the same person who had just told it to them, the children told the stories to another local person (an older woman with whom they were familiar and comfortable) who had not been present when the teenager told them the story. With such efforts to make the task culturally appropriate to the Mayan children, why might their performance have been so poor compared with Western children and non-Western groups whose performance on story recall is impressive?

There were unanticipated social features of the test situation that made the Mayan children very uncomfortable. It is culturally inappropriate for Mayan children to speak freely to an adult. When carrying a message to an adult, they must politely add the word *cha* ("so I have been told") in order to avoid conveying a lack of respect by impertinently claiming greater knowledge than the adult. Although they hear stories told by their elders and talk freely among themselves, it was an unfamiliar and stressful situation for Mayan children to attempt to narrate a story to an adult – no matter how comfortable they were with the story content, the testing environment, and the adult.

The Mayan children's recall performances were very bashful and contrasted with their eager performance on other tests. Some barely spoke at all; many spoke in whispers, fidgeting and avoiding eye contact; many punctuated their utterances with the word *cha*. They appeared to be being grilled rather than narrating a story. They usually mentioned a fact from each of the main episodes of the story, but in a disjointed fashion, as if they were listing a few key points. And these points were often provided only in response to the listener asking "What happened next?"

In contrast with the Mayan children's awkward performance, the U.S. children's recalls were fluent, formed connected narratives, and required few prompting questions. (About 75% of the Mayan recalls were rated as disjointed rather than cohesive, whereas only 8% of the U.S. recalls were. The Mayan children were given three to four times as many prompting questions as were the U.S. children.)

Whether Mayan children's story recall would appear more complete and fluent if they were telling the story to a peer rather than an adult is a matter for speculation. The point is that memory performance occurs in a communication context in which social features of the subject's efforts cannot be separated from the cognitive task. Other cultural influences on narrative production have been noted by Cazden (1979), Matsuyama (1983), Nadel (1937), and Tannen (1980). From these illustrations, it is clear that memory functioning is grounded in the social situation of the current performance, the situations in which the subjects are used to remembering things, and the societal values and practices molding the use of memory.

Development of mnemonic skills through social interaction

This final section considers social situations in which children may learn to use mnemonic tools or approach memory problems more skillfully through supportive interaction with more skilled partners. A number of authors, building on Vygotsky's theory, emphasize the formative possibilities of children's joint problem-solving with adults, with the adult supporting the child's efforts in a way that allows the child to participate in a slightly more skilled approach to the problem than is possible for the child working independently, which the child may appropriate for use on subsequent occasions (Rogoff, 1986, 1990; Wertsch, 1979; Wood, Bruner, & Ross, 1976).

There have been a number of suggestions that social interaction can support memory development, and a few studies of the question (Rogoff, 1990). Wertsch (1978) suggests that adults may serve as children's "auxiliary metamemory," handling the executive aspects of remembering as children carry out mnemonic strategies under supervision, and McNamee (1981) suggests that memory for connected text develops between adults and children as they converse. Peters (1986) provides a careful longitudinal analysis of paternal support and child participation in collaborative storytelling between a 2-year-old and his father; DeLoache (1983) notes the supportive role of mothers' memory questions in picturebook reading; Ratner (1984) found correlations between the memory demands placed by mothers on toddlers and the children's performance on later memory tests. Toddlers whose mothers managed conversations about past events by rephrasing and elaborating their questions recounted more information in more coherent narrative form several years later (Fivush, 1988). Guided participation in remembering with adults can facilitate children's memory for a categorization scheme for common objects (Ellis & Rogoff, 1982; Goncu & Rogoff, 1987; Rogoff & Gardner, 1984).

In our sack lunch free recall experiment in which we examined the role of providing children with a meaningful purpose to the activity, we also included parallel conditions in which the parents were asked to assist their children in learning the items. In the comparison of the free recall condition and the sack lunch condition reported earlier, the parents simply presented the list. In the parallel conditions involving both free recall and sack lunch scenarios, another set of parents were encouraged to help their children learn the list during item presentation. In all conditions, the parents were limited to two presentations of the list, with predetermined order of items. Parents who simply presented the list were encouraging and pleasant, but did not elaborate beyond showing and labeling each item. Parents who were encouraged to assist their children were told, "While naming the items and showing the picture you may say whatever you want to ensure your child is remembering."

Results showed a significant interaction between the purpose for the task and the presence of parental assistance ($p < .01$). When the task had a standard free recall purpose, children whose parents assisted them remembered slightly more items than those whose parents simply presented the list ($p < .08$, average recall of 4.2 vs. 2.7 items out of 10). There was no difference due to parental assistance in the conditions involving a meaningful purpose (sack lunch), in which children remembered an average of 4.4 items with assistance and 5.3 without. From these results, it appears that parental assistance can facilitate children's remembering, but when the task already involves a meaningful purpose, parental assistance does not improve children's performance. We are currently expanding our sample size to be able to examine more carefully the effect and nature of parental assistance.

Even with the small sample size, however, it is instructive to explore what the parents did when told they could help their children. Guiding children's attention to the items was possible in all conditions, and all parents in all four conditions used nonverbal gestures (e.g., pointing, deliberately holding the item in the child's line of vision), intent facial expressions, and emphasis in enunciation of the labels as they presented items. The mean frequencies were 19.5 and 18.9 in the no-assistance conditions, and 14.0 and 12.8 in the assistance conditions, indicating that parents who were simply presenting the items without assistance guided their children's attention to the items on almost all of the 20 item presentations, and that those who were encouraged to assist their children guided their children's attention to the items on more than half of their presentations (and these latter parents, of course, engaged in other strategies to assist their children as well).

Most of the parents in all conditions emphasized the mnemonic goal of the task as they explained the task initially, to a similar and great extent across the four conditions. In the free recall conditions, parents emphasized the mnemonic goal, as in the following example: "I'm going to show you the pictures and I'm going to tell you what they are. . . . And you try real hard to remember so you can go and tell J. [Experimenters' assistant] what you saw. Okay?" In the lunch conditions, parents similarly emphasized the mnemonic goal in the context of the activity of making a sack lunch, as in this example: "We need to go to the grocery store and get things for our lunch first. So you need to remember the things we need for lunch."

In the lunch condition encouraging assistance, parents also emphasized the mnemonic goal during item presentation. For example, while showing a child the picture of Baggies, one mother labeled the item, explained that they need it to put the food in, and added, " 'cause you have to remember to get those at the store or we'll be sunk." Half of the parents who were encouraged to assist their children explicitly emphasized the need to remember specific items during item presentation.

Children in all four groups clearly participated in learning the information, through labeling the items (usually when their parents prompted them to provide labels). Beyond this small role, there was little obvious participation possible for the children, given that the list had to be presented twice in a predetermined order. However, many of the children labeled the items while they were being presented, especially in the free recall conditions, in which parents were more likely to prompt children to label rather than providing the labels. In the free recall conditions, 9 of the 15 children labeled five or more items, compared with only 3 of the 13 children in the lunch conditions. Children in the free recall conditions who did not label items recalled fewer items, $r = -.50, p = .03$.

When the parents were encouraged to provide assistance (in both lunch and free recall tasks), there was more child labeling than when the parents were not to provide assistance. In the lunch task (in which parents who were told to assist focused on strategies of embedding items in the lunch theme or elaborating on connections between items – see next paragraph), 3 of the 7 assistance parents prompted child labeling at least five times, whereas no parent in the lunch/no-assistance condition did so ($Ms = 3.6$ vs. .3 prompts to label, respectively). In the free recall task, six of the eight assistance parents prompted child labeling at least five times, whereas only three of the seven parents in the no-assistance condition did so ($Ms = 7.0$ vs. 4.0 prompts to label).

Finally, the parents who were allowed to help their children during item presentation provided their children with strategies for remembering specific items. They marked items by reference to the child's familiar experiences, or related the items to each other (e.g., "Here's cheese to eat with the crackers") or to the overall lunch theme, sometimes categorizing items within the lunch theme (e.g., "We need dessert for our lunch, so let's have grapes"). Provision of organizing strategies linking items to one another or to the lunch theme was frequent, averaging 10 when the purpose was to make a sack lunch, and 9 when the purpose was to remember items to tell the experimenter in a free recall task. It appears that in the standard free recall condition, the provision of parental assistance often led to an adoption of the sack lunch theme similar to that arranged by the experimenters in the condition involving actually making a sack lunch.

The sample size is too small to determine reliably the relation between provision of strategies and children's recall. However, children in the standard free recall purpose condition with parental assistance who remembered five or more items received more parental suggestions of organizational strategies for the items ($Ms = 4.3$ vs. 3.4 references to organizational strategies).

Because of the small sample size, these results must, of course, be considered speculative. However, the findings suggest that parental assistance can facilitate preschool children's learning of a list of items, to about the same extent as providing a meaningful purpose to the task. Parents focus their children's attention on the items and refer to the need to remember whether or not they are encouraged to say things to help children remember as they are presenting the list. And children take part in labeling the items in all conditions, more so when their parents are encouraged to assist them. When parents are encouraged to help their children remember, they add to these forms of assistance the provision of specific suggestions for strategies to organize the items, which may help the children's remembering. The results of this study and others support the idea that children's guided participation (Rogoff, 1990) in shared thinking can contribute to their skills in handling cognitive problems.

In sum, this chapter has argued that the development of memory skill is closely tied to familiar tasks that children and adults practice and to the purpose for remembering the material. Memory development is broadly situated in the social contexts and cultural institutions in which memory skills are practiced. Our perspective is that remembering serves practical and interpersonal goals (in memory tests and naturalistic memory activities alike), which are organized in sociocultural activities and traditions that support and constrain the understanding and skills children develop in their attempts to manage the problem-solving situations of their community in which they participate. Individuals' memory performances are inherently tied to features of tasks, the purpose of the memory activity, and the social and cultural contexts of remembering.

NOTE

We are grateful to Scott Paris for his thoughtful comments on a previous version of this chapter, and are confident that the resulting improvements still leave room for further discussion. Support for research reported here came from National Institute of Child Health and Human Development Grant 5R01HD16973. We appreciate the participation of children and parents and facilitation by administrators of the Jewish Community Center preschool in Salt Lake City. An earlier version of the research was reported at the meeting of the Society for Research in Child Development in Baltimore, April 1987. Revisions were facilitated by the Center for Advanced Study in the Behavioral Sciences, where Barbara Rogoff was a fellow during 1988–1989, with support from the National Science Foundation (#BNS87–00864), the Spencer Foundation, and a Faculty Fellow Award from the University of Utah.

REFERENCES

Bartlett, F. C. (1932). *Remembering*. Cambridge: Cambridge University Press.

Blount, B. G. (1972). Parental speech and language acquisition: Some Luo and Samoan examples. *Anthropological Linguistics, 14*, 119–130.

Brewer, W. F., & Dupree, D. A. (1983). Use of plan schemata in the recalled recognition of goal-directed actions. *Journal of Experimental Psychology: Learning, Memory, and Cognition, 9*, 117–129.

Brown, A. L. (1975). The development of memory: Knowing, knowing about knowing and knowing how to know. In H. W. Reese (Ed.), *Advances in child development and behavior* (Vol. 10). New York: Academic Press.

Cazden, C. (1979). Peek-a-boo as an instructional model: Discourse development at home and at school. In *Papers and reports on child language development* (No. 17). Stanford University, Department of Linguistics.

Cazden, C. B., & John, V. P. (1971). Learning in American Indian children. In M. L. Wax, S. Diamond, & F. O. Gearing (Eds.), *Anthropological perspectives in education* (pp. 252–272). New York: Basic.

Cole, M., & Scribner, S. (1977). Cross-cultural studies of memory and cognition. In R. V. Kail, Jr., & J. W. Hagen (Eds.), *Perspectives on the development of memory and cognition*. Hillsdale, NJ: Erlbaum.

D'Azevedo, W. A. (1982). In U. Neisser (Ed.), *Memory observed: Remembering in natural contexts* (pp. 258–268). San Francisco: W. H. Freeman.

DeLoache, J. S. (1983, April). *Joint picture book reading as memory training for toddlers*. Paper presented at the meeting of the Society for Research in Child Development, Detroit.

DeLoache, J. S., & Brown, A. L. (1983). Very young children's memory for the location of objects in a large-scale environment. *Child Development, 54*, 888–897.

Dube, E. F. (1982). Literacy, cultural familiarity, and "intelligence" as determinants of story recall. In U. Neisser (Ed.), *Memory observed: Remembering in natural contexts* (pp. 274–292). San Francisco: W. H. Freeman.

Duncker, K. (1945). On problem solving. *Psychological Monographs, 58*, 85–93.

Dunn, J., & Dale, N. (1984). I a daddy: 2-year-old's collaboration in joint pretend with sibling and with mother. In I. Bretherton (Ed.), *Symbolic play: The development of social understanding* (pp. 131–158). Orlando, FL: Academic Press.

Ellis, S., & Rogoff, B. (1982). The strategies and efficacy of child versus adult teachers. *Child Development, 53*, 730–735.

Erickson, F. (1981). Timing and context in everday discourse: Implications for the study of referential and social meaning. In W. P. Dickson (Ed.), *Children's oral communication skills* (pp. 241–269). New York: Academic Press.

Feldman, D. H. (1980). *Beyond universals in cognitive development*. Norwood, NJ: Ablex.

Fischer, K. W. (1980). A theory of cognitive development. The control and construction of hierarchies of skills. *Psychological Review, 87*, 477–531.

Fivush, R. (1988). *Form and function in early autobiographical memory.* Unpublished manuscript, Emory University.

Flavell, J. H., Beach, D. R., & Chinsky, J. M. (1966). Spontaneous verbal rehearsal in a memory task as a function of age. *Child Development, 37*, 283–299.

Flavell, J. H., & Wellman, H. M. (1977). Metamemory. In R. V. Kail, Jr., & J. W. Hagen (Eds.), *Perspectives on the development of memory and cognition.* Hillsdale, NJ: Erlbaum.

Fowler, W. (1980). Cognitive differentiation and developmental learning. In H. W. Reese & L. P. Lipsitt (Eds.), *Advances in child development and behavior* (Vol. 15). New York: Academic Press.

Friedman, A. (1979). Framing pictures: The role of knowledge in automated encoding and memory for gist. *Journal of Experimental Psychology, 108*, 316–355.

Gauvain, M., & Rogoff, B. (1989). Ways of speaking about space: The development of children's skill at communicating spatial knowledge. *Cognitive Development, 4*, 295–307.

Gick, M. L., & Holyoak, K. J. (1980). Analogical problem solving. *Cognitive Psychology, 12*, 306–355.

Gladwin, T. (1970). *East is a big bird.* Cambridge, MA: Belknap Press.

Goncu, A. & Rogoff, B. (1987, April). *Adult guidance and children's participation in learning.* Paper presented at the meeting of the Society for Research in Child Development, Baltimore.

Goody, J. (1977). *The domestication of the savage mind.* Cambridge: Cambridge University Press.

Harkness, S., & Super, C. M. (1977). Why African children are so hard to test. In L. L. Adler (Ed.), *Issues in cross-cultural research. Annals of the New York Academy of Sciences, 285*, 326–331.

Hart, S. S., Leal, L., Burney, L., & Santulli, K. A. (1985, April). *Memory in the elementary school classroom: How teachers encourage strategy use.* Paper presented at the meeting of the Society for Research in Child Development, Toronto.

Higbee, K. L. (1979). Recent research in visual mnemonics: Historical roots and educational fruits. *Review of Educational Research, 49*, 611–629.

Hunter, I. M. L. (1979). Memory in everyday life. In M. M. Gruneberg & P. E. Morris (Eds.), *Applied problems in memory.* New York: Academic Press.

Irvine, J. T. (1978). Wolof 'magical thinking': Culture and conservation revisited. *Journal of Cross-Cultural Psychology, 9*, 300–310.

Istomina, Z. M. (1977). The development of voluntary memory in preschool-age children. In M. Cole (Ed.), *Soviet developmental psychology.* White Plains, NY: M. E. Sharpe.

Kagan, J., Klein, R. E., Finley, G. E., Rogoff, B., & Nolan, E. (1979). A cross-cultural study of cognitive development. *Monographs of the Society for Research in Child Development, 44* (5, Serial No. 180).

Kearins, J. M. (1981). Visual spatial memory in Australian aboriginal children of desert regions. *Cognitive Psychology, 13*, 434–460.

Laboratory of Comparative Human Cognition. (1983). Culture and cognitive development. In W. Kessen (Ed.), *History, theory, and methods*, Vol. 1 of P. H. Mussen (Ed.), *Handbook of child psychology* (294–356). New York: Wiley.

Leont'ev, A. N. (1981). The development of higher forms of memory. In A. N.

Leont'ev (Ed.), *Problems of the development of the mind*. Moscow: Progress Publishers.

Levy-Bruhl, L. (1926). *How natives think* (pp. 109–116). London: George Allen & Unwin.

Lewis, D. (1976). Observations on route finding and spatial orientation among the Aboriginal peoples of the Western Desert region of Central Australia. *Oceania, 46*, 249–282.

Linde, C., & Labov, W. (1975). Spatial networks as a site for the study of language and thought. *Language, 51*, 924–939.

Lord, A. B. (1965). *Singer of tales*. New York: Atheneum.

Mack, J. E. (1976). *A prince of our disorder: The life of T. E. Lawrence*. Boston: Little, Brown.

Mandler, J. M. (1979). Categorical and schematic organization in memory. In C. R. Puff (Ed.), *Memory organization and structure*. New York: Academic Press.

Mandler, J. M., Scribner, S., Cole, M., & DeForest, M. (1980). Cross-cultural invariance in story recall. *Child Development, 51*, 19–26.

Matsuyama, U. K. (1983). Can story grammar speak Japanese? *The Reading Teacher, 36*, 666–669.

McNamee, G. D. (1981, April). *Social origins of narrative skills*. Paper presented at the meeting of the Society for Research in Child Development, Boston.

Meacham, J. A. (1977). Soviet investigations of memory development. In R. V. Kail, Jr., & J. W. Hagen (Eds.), *Perspectives on the development of memory and cognition* (pp. 273–295). Hillsdale, NJ: Erlbaum.

Mueller, J. H., Rankin, J. L., & Carlomusto, M. (1979). Adult age differences in free recall as a function of basis of organization and method of presentation. *Journal of Gerontology, 34*, 375–385.

Nadel, S. F. (1937). Experiments on culture psychology. *Africa, 10*, 421–435.

Naus, M., & Ornstein, P. A. (1983). The development of memory strategies: Analysis, questions, and issues. In M. T. H. Chi (Ed.), *Trends in memory development research* (Vol. 9, pp. 1–29). Basel: S. Karger.

Neisser, U. (Ed.). (1982). *Memory observed: Remembering in natural contexts*. San Francisco: W. H. Freeman.

Nelson, K., & Gruendel, J. (1981). Generalized event representations: Basic building blocks of cognitive development. In M. E. Lamb & A. L. Brown (Eds.), *Advances in developmental psychology* (Vol. 1, pp. 131–158). Hillsdale, NJ: Erlbaum.

Nelson, K., & Ross, G. (1980). The generalities and specifics of long-term memory in infants and young children. In M. Perlmutter (Ed.), *Children's memory* (New directions for child development, No. 10). San Francisco: Jossey-Bass.

Newcombe, N. (1985). Methods for the study of spatial cognition. In R. Cohen (Ed.), *The development of spatial cognition*. Hillsdale, NJ: Erlbaum.

Ornstein, P. A. (Ed.). (1978). *Memory development in children*. Hillsdale, NJ: Erlbaum.

Paris, S. G., & Cross, D. R. (1983). Ordinary learning: Pragmatic connections among children's beliefs, motives, and actions. In J. Bisanz, G. L. Bisanz, & R. Kail (Eds.), *Learning in children: Progress in cognitive development research*. New York: Springer-Verlag.

Paris, S. G., Newman, D. R., & Jacobs, J. E. (1985). Social contexts and functions of children's remembering. In C. J. Brainerd & M. Pressley (Eds.), *The cognitive side of memory development* (pp. 81–115). New York: Springer-Verlag.

Perlmutter, M. (1979). Age differences in adults' free recall, cued recall, and recognition. *Journal of Gerontology, 34*, 533–539.

Peters, A. M. (1986). *I wanna tell story: The development of collaborative story telling by a 2-year old blind child and his father.* Unpublished manuscript, University of Hawaii.

Pressley, M., Heisel, B. E., McCormick, C. B., & Nakamura, G. (1982). Memory strategy instruction with children. In C. J. Brainerd & M. Pressley (Eds.), *Progress in cognitive development research: Vol. 2. Verbal processes in children* (pp. 125–159). New York: Springer-Verlag.

Ratner, H. H. (1984). Memory demands and the development of young children's memory. *Child Development, 55,* 2173–2191.

Rogoff, B. (1982). Integrating context and cognitive development. In M. E. Lamb & A. L. Brown (Eds.), *Advances in developmental psychology* (Vol. 2). Hillsdale, NJ: Erlbaum.

Rogoff, B. (1986). Adult assistance of children's learning. In T. E. Raphael (Ed.), *The contexts of school based literacy.* New York: Random House.

Rogoff, B. (1989). The joint socialization of development by young children and adults. In A. Gellatly, D. Rogers, & J. A. Sloboda (Eds.), *Cognition and social worlds.* Oxford: Clarendon Press.

Rogoff, B. (1990). *Apprenticeship in thinking: Cognitive development in social context.* New York: Oxford University Press.

Rogoff, B., & Gardner, W. P. (1984). Adult guidance in cognitive development: An examination of mother–child instruction. In B. Rogoff & J. Lave (Eds.), *Everyday cognition: Its development in social context* (pp. 95–116). Cambridge, MA: Harvard University Press.

Rogoff, B., & Mistry, J. (1985). Memory development in cultural context. In M. Pressley & C. Brainerd (Eds.), *Cognitive learning and memory in children.* New York: Springer-Verlag.

Rogoff, B., & Waddell, K. J. (1982). Memory for information organized in a scene by children from two cultures. *Child Development, 53,* 1224–1228.

Rogoff, B., & Waddell, K. J. *The social context of recalling stories: A cross cultural study.* Unpublished manuscript, University of Utah.

Ross, B. M., & Millsom, C. (1970). Repeated memory of oral prose in Ghana and New York. *International Journal of Psychology, 5,* 173–181.

Sanford, E. C. (1917/1982). Professor Sanford's morning prayer. In U. Neisser (Ed.), *Memory observed: Remembering in natural contexts* (pp. 176–177). San Francisco: W. H. Freeman.

Scribner, S., & Cole, M. (1981). *The psychology of literacy.* Cambridge, MA: Harvard University Press.

Skeen, J. A. (1984). *The effects of planning to remember on children's memory for large-scale space.* Unpublished doctoral dissertation, University of Utah.

Skeen, J., & Rogoff, B. (1987). Children's difficulties in deliberate memory for spatial relationships: Misapplication of verbal mnemonic strategies? *Cognitive Development, 2,* 1–19.

Smirnov, A. A., & Zinchenko, P. I. (1969). Problems in the psychology of memory. In M. Cole & I. Maltzman (Eds.), *A handbook of contemporary Soviet psychology.* New York: Basic.

Super, C. M. (1977). *Who goes to school and what do they learn?* Paper presented at the meeting of the Society for Research in Child Development, New Orleans.

Tannen, D. (1980). A comparative analysis of oral narrative strategies: Athenian Greek and American English. In W. L. Chafe (Ed.), *The pear stories: Cognitive, cultural and linguistic aspects of narrative production* (pp. 51–87). Norwood, NJ: Ablex.

Vygotsky, L. S. (1978). *Mind in society: The development of higher psychological processes.* Cambridge, MA: Harvard University Press.

Vygotsky, L. S. (1987). *Thinking and speech.* In R. W. Rieber, & A. S. Carton (Eds., N. Minick, Trans.), *The collected works of L. S. Vygotsky* (pp. 37–285). New York: Plenum.

Waddell, K. J., & Rogoff, B. (1981). Effect of contextual organization on spatial memory of middle aged and older women. *Developmental Psychology, 17,* 878–885.

Waddell, K. J., & Rogoff, B. (1987). Contextual organization and intentionality in adults' spatial memory. *Developmental Psychology, 23,* 514–520.

Weissberg, J. A., & Paris, S. G. (1986). Young children's remembering in different contexts: A reinterpretation of Istomina's study. *Child Development, 57,* 1123–1129.

Wellman, H. (1988). The early development of memory strategies. In F. E. Weinert & M. Perlmutter (Eds.), *Memory development: University changes and individual differences* (pp. 3–30). Hillsdale, NJ: Erlbaum.

Wellman, H., & Somerville, S. (1980). Quasi-naturalistic tasks in the study of cognition: The memory-related skills of toddlers. In M. Perlmutter (Ed.), *Children's memory* (New directions for child development, No. 10, pp. 33–48). San Francisco: Jossey-Bass.

Wertsch, J. V. (1978). Adult–child interaction and the roots of metacognition. *Quarterly Newsletter of the Institute for Comparative Human Development, 2,* 15–18.

Wertsch, J. V. (1979). From social interaction to higher psychological processes. *Human Development, 22,* 1–22.

Wertsch, J. V., & Hickmann, M. (1987). Problems solving in social interaction: A microgenetic analysis. In M. Hickmann (Ed.), *Social and functional approaches to language and thought* (pp. 251–266). Orlando, FL: Academic Press.

Wood, D., Bruner, J. S., & Ross, G. (1976). The role of tutoring in problem-solving. *Journal of Child Psychology and Psychiatry, 17,* 89–100.

9

Autobiographical memory across the preschool years: Toward reconceptualizing childhood amnesia

ROBYN FIVUSH AND NINA R. HAMOND

Child:	Once on Halloween the kids was over and I had a princess dress on me.
Adult:	You had a princess dress on? Did you get any candy? Did you go door to door? What happened?
Child:	We went treating.
Adult:	You went treating! And who took you?
Child:	Andrea's mother took us. And my mom . . . and we brought a pumpkin too.
Adult:	What did you do with the pumpkin?
Child:	We lighted it.
Adult:	What did it look like? Was it scary?
Child:	Uh-huh. Dad made cuts in it with a razor. He made a face too. That was funny.
	(35-month-old child conversing with an adult)

Even very young children talk about their past experiences with others. Moreover, as the example above illustrates, children are capable of recalling accurate, organized information about events that have occurred in their past. Yet until quite recently, little was known about young children's autobiographical memory. Many researchers had drawn conclusions about the early autobiographical memory system based on adults' difficulty in recalling events that occurred before the age of 3 or 4 years, a phenomenon labeled "childhood amnesia." But when we begin to look at what children themselves are recalling during this early period, we gain a different perspective on memory development in general, and the phenomenon of childhood amnesia in particular.

In this chapter, we present new evidence on developmental changes in autobiographical memory across the preschool years based on a longitudinal study of children between the ages of 2½ and 4 years. Consideration of these data led to a reconceptualization of childhood amnesia. Essentially, we argue, first, that very young children are more attentive to the typical aspects of novel events than to the distinctive and ultimately memorable aspects of these events, and, second, that young children are more dependent on adults to provide retrieval cues for recall than are older children. Both factors lead to impoverished recall of very early memories. Before discussing these arguments in detail, however, we will place the issue of childhood amnesia in a broader theoretical context and give a brief overview of current research on young children's autobiographical memory.

The phenomenon of childhood amnesia

Freud (1953/1924) was the first psychologist to document the paucity of memories from early childhood. He described this amnesia as that "which veils our earliest childhood from us and estranges us from it (p. 335). Probably because he was dealing with a clinical population, Freud believed this amnesia was due to the repression of the emotionally traumatic events of early childhood, most notably the conflict and resolution surrounding children's early sexual identification. Since Freud's time, the phenomenon of childhood amnesia has been amply demonstrated. Although many adults can recall experiences from their preschool years, there does seem to be a general and significant lack of memories before the age of 3 years (Wetzler & Sweeney, 1986). However, the reasons underlying this amnesia are not clear (see White & Pillemer, 1979, for a review). The major alternatives to Freud's psychodynamic explanation include neurological changes in brain structure (Spear, 1979), and schematic reorganizations of the way in which information is encoded and retrieved (Neisser, 1962; Schachtel, 1982).

What these explanations share in common is the idea of a discontinuity in development. If any or all of these explanations are correct (since they are not mutually exclusive), they have serious implications for the way in which we conceptualize the development of human memory. More specifically, it would indicate a reorganization, or structural change in the memory system with age. Thus, an understanding of the phenomenon of childhood amnesia becomes central to our understanding of memory development in general (see Nelson, 1988, for related arguments). However, we cannot rely on what adults recall of their preschool years to examine this issue; we must examine what children themselves are recalling during the critical period between 2 and 4 years of age. In particular, it is essential to examine the content, organization, and duration of young children's memories, and how these might change with age. Only by doing so can we determine possible discontinuities in memory development.

Understanding childhood amnesia is not the only reason for studying early autobiographical memory. Examining what young children recall about personally experienced events is also an ideal domain in which to examine early mnemonic competencies. Asking children to recall their personal experiences differs in fundamental ways from most memory assessment tasks. First, autobiographical memory requires no mnemonic intervention at the time of experience in order to insure subsequent memory. Rather, memory is a natural outcome of interacting in the world. Second, by asking children to recall personally experienced events, we are obviously asking about familiar and probably meaningful events. It is under these conditions that we are most likely to get a clear picture of what children are capable of doing (Brown, Bransford, Ferrara, & Campione, 1983; Donaldson, 1978; Gelman, 1977).

Third, and most important, we as researchers are not deciding in advance what particular material children should remember. Although we do choose what events to ask about, children are free to recall whatever aspects of those events they deem interesting and important. In contrast to virtually all other types of memory tasks, when we ask about past experiences, we are not giving children the material to be remembered and then assessing how much is recalled. Rather, we are allowing children to select the material to be recalled from extended, complex real-world events. This allows us to examine not only the amount and duration of early memories (although these are also important issues), but also more qualitative aspects of what is remembered. In this way, autobiographical memory provides a unique window on children's minds; studying autobiographical memory allows us to examine how young children are naturally and spontaneously selecting and organizing information to be remembered, and how this process might change with development. Thus, a better understanding of early autobiographical memory is an essential part of our growing understanding of how and what young children are doing in the world.

Developmental research on early autobiographical memory

In the last 10 years there has been a surge of research on young children's memory for real-world events.[1] We now know that by age 3, children are able to give well-organized reports about routine events, such as going to McDonald's or a birthday party (see Nelson, 1986, for a review), as well as detailed, accurate reports of novel, one-time events (Fivush, Hudson, & Nelson, 1984; Hudson & Nelson, 1986; Sheingold & Tenney, 1982; Todd & Perlmutter, 1980). But few studies have examined autobiographical memory in children under the age of 3, a critical period for understanding childhood amnesia.

In a study explicitly designed to examine the development of children's ability to recall a novel event, Sheingold and Tenney (1982) asked subjects ranging from 4 years old to adulthood to recall specific aspects of the events surrounding the birth of their sibling. For all subjects, their sibling was born when the subject was 4 years old. Thus, the retention interval varied from a few months to many years. Somewhat surprisingly,

Sheingold and Tenney found virtually no forgetting of this event over this extended period of time. Most interesting, when children in an additional group were asked about the birth of a sibling that occurred when they were 3 years old, they recalled almost nothing. These results suggest that one factor contributing to childhood amnesia may be young children's inability to encode, store, or retrieve as much information about events as older children. However, we must be extremely cautious in drawing such a conclusion. These subjects were only asked about one event, the birth of a sibling. Note that this is an event in which the mother is the central character; the child is only an observer.[2] Moreover, children were asked a highly structured series of questions that the experimenters decided a priori were important about this event, and many of these questions concerned the activities of the mother and the new baby. Thus, the experimenters predetermined the possible content of the memory; children were not free to recall what they thought was interesting about the event. To understand fully possible changes in the early memory system, we must examine what children themselves are choosing to recall.

This is exactly what Nelson (1988) accomplished in a longitudinal study of one young child's bedtime monologues. Nelson tape-recorded Emily's monologues beginning when Emily was 21 months old. Even at this young age, Emily included recountings of past experiences in her monologues, and continued to do so until taping was discontinued 16 months later. Notice that in this situation, Emily was free to recall whatever aspects of events that she found interesting, and under these conditions, what Emily focused on was routines. Novel events such as Christmas and the birth of her baby brother were barely mentioned, but Emily recounted routine events such as going to her baby-sitter's or to preschool again and again. Moreover, she seemed to dwell especially on deviations from these routines, such as the day she had to go to school in a different car when the family car was broken. Finally, Emily rarely recounted an event that occurred more than 3 months in the past. Nelson argues from these data that childhood amnesia can be explained in two ways. First, young children are tuned to routine events because routines are what give the world predictability. Second, if a novel event is not repeated within a certain time frame, possibly 3 months or so, the event will be forgotten. If it is repeated, a "script," or a general representation of the event, will be formed, and the next occurrence of a similar event will be expected to conform to the same general structure as the previous occurrences. Thus, childhood amnesia is due to the forgetting of novel events and the merging of repeated events into scripts.

One problem with this explanation is that it is not the case that novel events are forgotten. We asked children ranging in age from 29 to 35 months to recall specific, novel events that had occurred either in the recent past (up to 3 months ago) or in the distant past (more than 3 months ago) (Fivush, Gray, & Fromhoff, 1987). All children recalled events from the distant past. In fact, all children recalled at least one event that occurred more than 6 months ago. Moreover, children recalled as much accurate, organized information about events in the distant past as they recalled about events in the recent past. Thus Nelson's (1988) arguments cannot be completely right. Children aged 2½ are recalling accurate information about novel events over extended periods of time. Why, then, do adults have such difficulty recalling events from this time period? The critical data for answering this question can only be achieved through an examination of what children are recalling about past events across the age period from 2 to 4 years old. It is to a consideration of these data that we now turn.

A longitudinal study of early autobiographical memory

We have been investigating various aspects of early autobiographical memory over the last 4 years. One methodological tactic has involved extensive interviews with young children about past experiences. In this chapter, we report on one subset of these data, a series of three interviews with the same group of children. During the first interview, mothers conversed with their 2½-year-old children about several past experiences. During the second interview, conducted 6 weeks later, a female experimenter queried the children about the same events that they had discussed with their mothers. A second female experimenter interviewed the children 14 months later, when the children were not quite 4 years old, and asked about some of the same events that had been asked about previously, as well as about some new events. Nine children participated in the first two interviews; seven of these children were available for the third interview. As often happens in exploratory research, the first two interviews were originally conducted to examine one set of issues, but the unexpected results led to a new set of questions, which were addressed by conducting the third interview. Thus, in presenting our findings, we follow, to some extent, the development of our own thinking about the development of autobiographical memory.

Recalling the past with mothers versus strangers

The first two interviews addressed the question of whether or not children are learning what is interesting and important to recount about past events during conversations about these events with adults. This idea is rooted in the developmental theories of Vygotsky (1978). According to Vygotsky, all skills develop on two levels: first on the interpersonal level, and then on the intrapersonal level. For example, Snow & Goldfield (1983) have examined the development of book-reading skills by tracing the way in which mothers and their children read the same books over a period of time. At first, mothers provide the entire structure for this event, pointing to a picture, asking, "What's that?" and providing the answer, "A doggie?" to which children need only agree. With increasing experience, children become more and more competent participants in this interaction, responding to the mothers' questions, and even beginning to ask their own questions.

In the domain of autobiographical memory, where the task can be conceptualized as narrating a past event, the mother may initially provide the entire narrative structure and content, and with time, the child would come to participate more fully in providing the appropriate information. Several recent studies have shown that children are learning about the narrative structure for reporting past events in these early mother–child conversations (Eisenberg, 1985; Fivush, in press; Hudson, 1986a, this volume; Sachs, 1983), but it is not clear whether children are learning what content to include in their reports. That is, are children learning what is interesting and important to report about particular past events by the way in which mothers talk about these events? We investigated this issue by comparing mother–child conversations about the past to the child's subsequent recall of the same events with a stranger. We were particularly interested in whether children would incorporate information provided by the mother on the first interview into their own independent recall of these same events on the second interview.

During the first interview, mothers were asked to engage their 2½ year old child in conversations about a series of novel past events, such as going on an airplane ride, a trip to the beach, last Christmas, the child's second birthday, and so on. All interviews were conducted in the child's home, with a female experimenter present to tape-record and take notes. Mothers were told that we were interested in what young children remember, and were encouraged to try to elicit as much memory as possible while keeping the conversation as natural as possible. Each mother asked her child about approximately 12 different events, and each child recalled information about approximately 10 of those events. Six weeks after the first interview, a second female experimenter returned to the child's home and asked the child to recall the same events that the mother had asked about on the previous interview. The second experimenter had no knowledge of either the mother's questions or the child's recall from the first interview; she had only a list of events asked about on the first interview.

Analyses focused on the amount and source of information recalled by children. All information provided by the mother on the first interview, and recalled by children on both interviews, was broken down into "units," each unit expressing a distinct piece of information about the event. Units were further coded into one of the following five mutually exclusive categories: (1) Activity: reference to any action or activity occurring during the event, such as "I *ran*," or "Billy *jumped* up and down." (2) Object: reference to any object involved in the event, such as "We picked up *shells*." (3) Person: mentioning any person except the child who participated in the event, for example, "*Mommy* came" and "I saw *Santa Claus*." (4) Location: specifying when or where the event occurred, such as, "I was at the *beach*" and "It was *Christmas*." And (5) Attribute: all adjectives, adverbs, and modifiers, for example, "I saw *two* monkeys," ". . . a *big* dog." Only information that was confirmed as accurate by parents was coded. Each unit of information recalled on the second interview was additionally coded for source. That is, each unit of information recalled on the second interview could have been provided by the mother on the first interview, or it could have been recalled by the child on the first interview, or it could be new and different information that was not recounted by either participant on the first interview.

Two somewhat surprising results emerged. First, as can be seen in Figure 9.1, children recalled more information on the second interview with the stranger (a mean of 9.63 units of information) than on the first interview with the mother (a mean of 5.48 units of information). Children also recalled more information about activities and objects than about the other categories of information, and this held for both interviews. However, this probably reflects the kinds of information available to be recalled about events than anything meaningful about young children's memory. There are simply more activities and objects that can be recalled about any given event. Second, 76% of the information that children recalled on the second interview was new and different information than had been recalled on the first interview. Children neither incorporated the information provided by the mother on the first interview into their own recall of the event, nor did they recall what they themselves had recalled on the first interview. Thus children recalled more information and different information with the stranger than with the mother.

There are several reasons why we may have obtained these results: One, the mother had experienced the event with the child, whereas the stranger obviously had not. This changes the social situation in two ways. First, the child is aware that the mother also experienced this event and therefore may view this more as a "test" situation than as "real" questions. The stranger, who was not there, on the other hand, may be perceived as asking "real" questions. Second, and related to the first, because the mother was there, she also has a memory of the event and

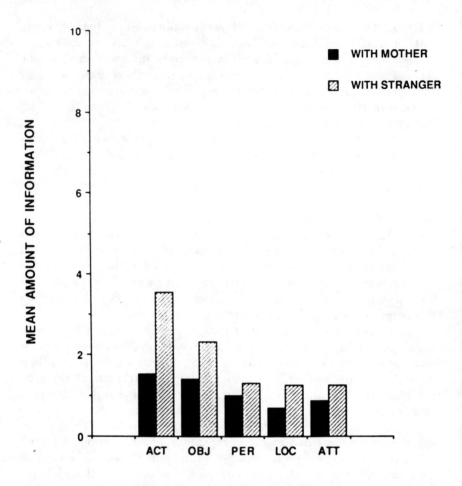

CATEGORY OF INFORMATION

Figure 9.1. Mean amount of each category of information children recalled per event at Interview 1 and 2.

may specifically try to guide the child to recall those aspects of the event that she herself found most interesting. Examination of the protocols suggests that mothers were often trying to elicit a particular piece of information from the child. For example, here is one mother asking her child about a trip they took to Florida (*M* stands for mother and *C* stands for child):

M: And where did we eat breakfast? Where did we go for breakfast?
C: What?

M: Where did we go for breaksfast? Remember we went out, Daddy, you and I? What restaurant did we go to?
C: Gasoline.
M: Gasoline? No, what restaurant did we go have breakfast at?
C: Ummm . . .
M: Do you remember? It was Burger . . . ?
C: King!

Or another mother asking her child about last Halloween:

M: Last year, remember it was Halloween. Remember that? Who did we go trick-or-treating with?
C: (unintelligible)
M: Didn't we go with some friends? Who did we go with? Do you remember who came trick-or-treating with us?
C: With who?
M: With who? You tell me. You had two friends come over. Which ones went trick-or-treating?
C: Stacy.
M: Not Stacy. Who? Come on.
C: Who?
M: Who came dressed as Big Bird?
C: Orly.

In these situations, the mothers are deciding in advance what information children should be remembering, and they work very hard at getting their children to recall just those pieces of information. Notice also that by providing more and more contextual information, mothers are very often successful at getting their children to remember just those pieces of information. But when children are free to recall whatever aspects of these events they choose to remember, as with the stranger asking general, open-ended questions, the children do not recall those pieces of information that the mothers worked so hard to get them to remember. Rather, they recall different information. When we take a closer look at what kind of information children are choosing to talk about, it seems that children recall what could be considered, from an adult's perspective, routine, or typical aspects of events. For example, when asked by the stranger about going camping, one young child recalled sleeping outside in a tent, which is certainly unusual, but then the conversation continues (*E* stands for experimenter and *C* stands for child):

E: You slept outside in a tent? Wow, that sounds like a lot of fun.
C: And then we waked up and eat dinner. First we eat dinner, then go to bed, and then wake up and eat breakfast.
E: What else did you do when you went camping? What did you do when you got up, after you ate breakfast?
C: Umm, in the night, and went to sleep.

Or another child recalling spending the night at a friend's house:

> *E:*   What did you do at Charlotte's house?
> *C:*   Play.
> *E:*   You played. What did you play with?
> *C:*   Toys.
> *E:*   What did you do?
> *C:*   Go to sleep.

Or, finally, a child recalling a visit from his cousin, Jonathan:

> *E:*   What did you do with Jonathan? Anything special?
> *C:*   Yeah.
> *E:*   Where did you go?
> *C:*   Food Giant (a supermarket)

What we are seeing in these examples is children's tendency to report general, or typical, information about novel events, rather than information that distinguishes this one event from all other events. This is not to say that all of children's recall was of this type. The same child who recalled going to the supermarket when his cousin came to visit, also recalled that "Mom gave me the wrong milk and I throwed up" during this event. (This child is allergic to lactose-based milk, and his mother had, in fact, given him the wrong milk during Jonathan's visit, the only time she had ever done so. We will return to this example later in the chapter.) So, although children are recalling a good deal of typical information, they are also reporting distinctive, or unique, information about past events.

In order to explore more fully the content of children's recall, all information recalled was coded as either "distinctive" – that is, any information that uniquely specifies an event, such as recalling the Halloween pumpkin, Easter eggs, or specific people and presents at a birthday party – or as "typical", such as expressing routine activities like "eating lunch," "going to sleep," or "playing with toys." Using these definitions, only 48% of the information that children recalled when conversing with the stranger expressed distinctive information.

At least two problems arise in interpreting this finding. First, we are relying on verbal recall. It is possible that children say, "We played with toys," but they are thinking of specific toys. There is really no way to fully address this issue. However, it is the case that when children provided some information about an event, the experimenter usually tried to elicit additional information of the same type. Thus, children were given every opportunity to provide more specific, distinctive information. Even so, only about half of the information provided by children was distinctive.

Second, the memory status of typical information is not clear. When children recall some distinctive information about an event – for example that the second birthday cake was shaped like Cookie Monster – we can be sure that children are remembering actual details about that event. But when typical information is reported, we don't know whether children are "remembering" the event or "reconstructing" what must have happened based on knowledge about the world. We return to this issue later in this chapter, after the remaining data are presented. Here we address a related question, that of why young children are reporting so much typical information in their recall of novel events.

One reason children report typical information may be that they do not understand the conversational constraints operating in this situation. When adults are asked questions about events such as going to a restaurant, they do not report that they sat down, got a menu, ordered food, and so on, because they assume their conversational partner shares this event knowledge. It is possible that very young children are not aware that other people, especially strangers, share a common set of experiences. To date, no research has addressed this question. An alternative possibility is that children are well aware that others share common experiences but are unaware that there are conversational constraints against reporting this shared knowledge. However, several studies have demonstrated that 2-year-old children are aware of the "given–new" constraint in conversation (Grice, 1975), the idea that one does not repeat information across utterances, but rather is supposed to provide some new information with each conversational turn (Garvey, 1984), and this seems similar to conversational constraints against reporting shared event knowledge.

It is also possible that young children report such a high percentage of typical information because they are trying to understand novel events by assimilating them to events with which they are more familiar. Young children may be relying on their general knowledge about the world in order to understand more novel events. Camping is just like being at home – you eat dinner, go to sleep, wake up, and eat breakfast – except that you do it outdoors. This possibility is obviously related to Nelson's (1988) interpretation of Emily's tendency to recount routine events discussed earlier. Our findings go even further in suggesting that even when explicitly asked to recall novel events, young children tend to place them in the context of more routine occurrences.

When we think about the world of 2-year-old children, this makes perfect sense. Because everything is still so new, young children are in the process of building up expectations so that they can anticipate and predict the world around them. In order to understand a novel experience, young children may need to focus on what is familiar about this event, what makes it similar to events already known about, rather than on what is distinctive or unusual about this event, and thus what makes it different from other events. Focusing on the typical allows children to understand novel events. But focusing on the typical will obviously not provide distinctive memory cues in the future. Thus, these early memories may be particularly vulnerable to forgetting. As children grow older, more and more of their memories may become less accessible because what is remembered is too typical to provide a distinctive memory cue. At the same time, as children begin to gain more experience with the world, they should begin to note and remember more distinctive aspects of novel events leading to more accessible autobiographical memories.

Long-term recall of novel events

In order to explore these developmental implications, we compared children's recall at age 2½ to their recall of some of these same events at age 4, as well as examining their recall for events experienced during the intervening period. We were obviously interested in whether 4-year-old children would be able to recall anything about events that had occurred before the age of 2½, and if so, what kind of information would be recalled. If our interpretation is valid, we would expect 4-year-old children to have difficulty recalling these events at all, and what they do recall should tend to be the more distinctive aspects of those events. In addition, we should see a general shift toward recalling more distinctive information, such that 4-year-old children will recall more distinctive information about events of the previous year than about events occurring even earlier.

The third interview was conducted 14 months after the second interview, when the children were not quite 4 years old, by a different female experimenter, again in the child's home. Events asked about when the child was 2½ years old and again when the child was 4 years old are referred to as *previously recalled events*. Only those events which had not recurred in the intervening period were included; for example, the child's second birthday and last Christmas were eliminated because another birthday and another Christmas had occurred, but an airplane trip was included if the child had not gone on another one. Children were asked about approximately three of the same events that they had been asked about previously, and all children were able to recall information about some of these events. In addition, children were asked about approximately seven events that occurred during the previous year, and they recalled information about approximately five of these events. These events, which were asked about only at age 4, are referred to as *new events*.

All information that children recalled during the third interview was coded, first, for amount and category of information (i.e., activity, object, person, location, or attribute), and, second, for whether it expressed typical or distinctive information, for the previously recalled events and

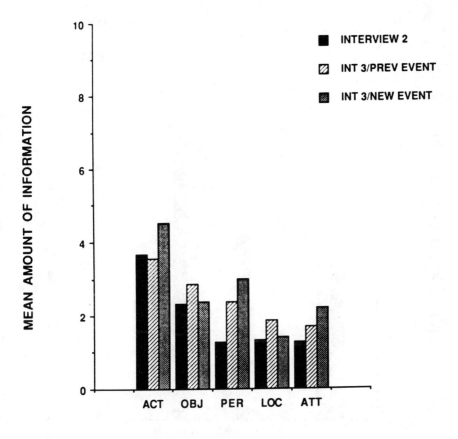

Figure 9.2. Mean amount of each category of information children recalled per event at Interview 2 and 3 for previously recalled and new events.

the new events separately. We were greatly surprised to discover that children recalled as much information about the previously recalled events at age 4 as they had recalled about those events at age 2½ (see Figure 9.2). For the previously recalled events, children recalled a mean amount of 12.25 units of information at age 4, compared to a mean of 9.63 units of information recalled at age 2½, which is not a statistically significant difference. In addition, they recalled just as much information about the previously recalled events (12.25 units) as they did about the new events (a mean of 13.54 units of information). Children also showed the same pattern of recall across the categories of information at all three interviews; they generally recalled more about activities and

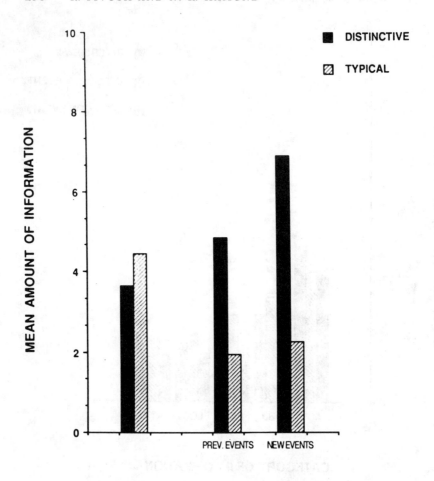

Figure 9.3. Mean amount of distinctive and typical information recounted per event at Interview 2 and 3 for previously recalled and new events.

objects than the other three categories of information. Thus, we are not seeing any differences in the quantity of information recalled either as a function of the child's age or time since experiencing the event.

However, children are reporting more distinctive information at age 4 than they had at age 2½, as shown in Figure 9.3. As already discussed, children recalled about equal amounts of typical and distinctive information when recalling events at age 2½. When recalling these same events at age 4, that is, the previously recalled events, children report slightly, but not significantly, more distinctive information than they had at age 2½, but significantly less typical information. Further, 4-year-old children are reporting significantly more distinctive information about the new events than about the previously recalled events. Hence, some of our expectations were confirmed. When 4-year-old children do recall events that occurred before the age of 2½, they tend to recall distinctive information about those events, and children recall more distinctive information about events that occurred after the age of 2½ than about events that occurred before the age of 2½.

However, it was puzzling that children were recalling so much information about the previously recalled events. We therefore decided to take a closer look at exactly what children were recalling about these events. In particular, we assessed how much of the information recalled about these events at age 4 had also been recalled about these events at age 2½. That is, of all of the distinctive information recalled about a given event at age 4, the percentage of that information that was also recalled at either interview at age 2½ was calculated, and a similar percentage was calculated for the typical information. Information recalled at age 4 that had been recalled in either of the two previous interviews was called "overlapping" information, and information recalled at age 4 that had not been recalled at the previous interviews was called "new" information. As can be seen in Figure 9.4, the results are surprising. First, very little of the information that children recalled at age 4 had been recalled at the previous interviews (only 26%); 74% of all information that children reported about previously recalled events at age 4 had not been reported at either interview at age 2½. Thus, on each of the three recall trials, children reported different information, indicating a great deal of inconsistency in children's recall. Moreover, even when we look just at the distinctive information, children are still recalling a good amount of information at age 4 that had not been recounted at age 2½. Of all the distinctive information recalled at age 4, 44% had not been recalled previously. It is important to stress again that all of this information was accurate, as confirmed by parents.

The fact that children recalled distinctive information at age 4 that they had recalled at age 2½ is not unexpected. It is exactly this kind of information that virtually any theory of memory would predict would be best recalled. For instance, in the earlier example of the child who is allergic to milk and recalled his mother giving him the wrong milk at age 2½, when again asked about his cousin Jonathan's visit 16 months later responded, "Mommy gave me, ummm, Jonathan's milk and I threw up." Another example is from a child whose goldfish had died. When asked about this event at age 4, he responded, "I fed my fish too much food and then it died and my mom dumped him in the toilet." This is essentially the same information recalled at age 2½. In both cases, the infor-

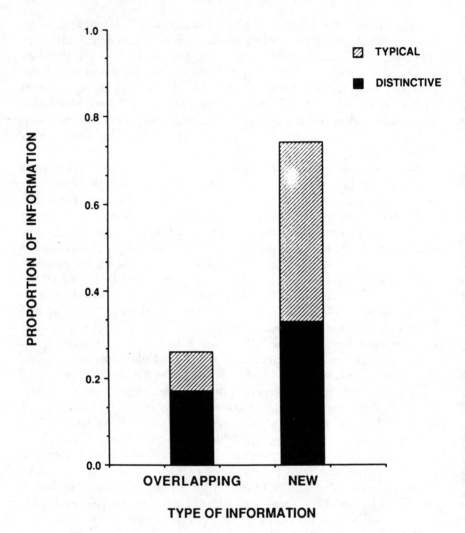

Figure 9.4. Proportion of overlapping and new information recounted about previously recalled events at Interview 3.

mation recalled about the event is distinctive, and is therefore likely to remain accessible over very long periods of time. However, children also recalled accurate and distinctive information about events at age 4 that they had not recalled about these events at age 2½. For example, one child who did not recall anything about seashells when recounting a trip to the beach at age 2½ recalled the following information at age 4:

E: Do you remember going to the beach?
C: A big wave, you know what? Splash! My mom found me a bunch of

shells when she went on her vacation. [This refers to a recent trip the
mother took without the child].

E: Did you find any shells?
C: We didn't bring any home. We found tiny little ones.

Or another child, who in recalling a family trip to Baltimore at age 2½
did not mention going to the beach while there, but when recalling the
event at age 4 reported:

E: Do you remember going to Baltimore?
C: I got to ride in the way back (of the station wagon). We went to the beach
     and my daddy made this big sandcastle.
E: Did you go in the water?
C: We saw waves. We went back and forward. When the wave came, we
     went back.

As these examples illustrate, 4-year old children are reporting accurate detailed information about specific events that occurred before they
were 2½ years old. Moreover, almost half of the distinctive information
reported about these events at age 4 had not been reported about these
events during the previous recall trials.

To summarize, at age 2½, children are just as likely to recount typical
as distinctive information about personally experienced, novel events. At
age 4, children are recounting substantially more distinctive information
about novel events than they had at age 2½, and they are recounting
more distinctive information about events that occurred during the previous year than about events that occurred before the age of 2½. However,
it is also the case that children are not recounting the same distinctive
information over time. Almost half of the distinctive information recalled about the previously recalled events at age 4 had not been recalled
about these events at age 2½. Thus, two major findings emerge from
these data. First, there seems to be a developmental shift with age toward
recounting more distinctive information about novel events. Second,
children tend to be highly inconsistent in the actual information recalled
about a specific event on different recall trials. The implications of each
of these findings are discussed in turn.

The shift toward recounting distinctive information

The fact that children recount more typical information about novel
events when they are 2½ years old than they do when they are 4 years old
supports the suggestion that younger children are attuned to the more
routine aspects of new experiences. However, before any conclusions can
be drawn, we must return to the issue of the status of typical information
in verbal recall that we touched upon earlier. One could argue from the

data presented in this chapter that younger children are, in fact, recalling less information about novel events than are older children. Rather than recalling specific details about past events, younger children are reconstructing what must have happened based on their general knowledge about the world. Obviously, all recall is partly reconstructive (Bartlett, 1932; Neisser, 1988). The crucial question is whether the typical information reported by 2½-year-old children is generated at the time of recall in response to situational memory demands, or whether the typical information is an integrated part of children's memories. Several aspects of children's recall argue against the interpretation that typical information is being generated at the time of recall.

First, virtually all of the typical information that children provide is appropriate information. That is, the child who recalled eating dinner, going to sleep, waking up, and eating breakfast when going camping, did, indeed, engage in these activities, as did the child who reported going to a friend's house, playing with toys and going to sleep. Children did not report possible typical activities that did not actually occur during the event. If children were generating probable activities in response to the experimenter's questions, we would expect at least some intrusion of typical information. In fact, we found just the opposite: Children often commented when expected activities did not occur during the event (e.g., "We didn't eat dinner there" or "Mommy didn't come"). These kinds of comments support the suggestion that young children are placing novel events in the context of more familiar activities.

Second, if children were generating typical information in response to memory demands, we would expect children to provide more typical information as the questioner asked more and more questions. This was not the case. Children provided typical information in response to the experimenter's open-ended questions. On the other hand, mothers, who asked many more questions and many more demanding questions, did not tend to elicit much recall of any type from their children. Children seem to provide the typical information spontaneously, rather than in response to situational demands.

Finally, and related to this last point, children's recall of typical information was interspersed with their recall of distinctive information. Children neither provided all the distinctive information they could recall and then began to generate typical information in response to additional questions, nor did they give only typical information and then provide distinctive information only with more specific questions. Both kinds of information seemed interwoven in children's recall protocols.

Together, these three points argue against an interpretation favoring generation of typical information at the time of recall in response to the interviewer's questions. Rather, they suggest that typical information is an integral part of children's memory for these events. This is also in accord with Nelson's (1988) data on Emily's developing autobiographical memory system. However, our findings require some revision of Nelson's account of childhood amnesia. To recapitulate briefly, Nelson posited that childhood amnesia stemmed from two factors; first, in order to understand and predict the world around them, young children focus on routine events, and, second, that novel events will not be retained for extended periods of time if they are not reexperienced. Clearly, our data support the first factor but not the second.

Young children are, indeed, focusing on routines. So much so, in fact, that they are even placing novel events within the framework of more familiar activities. Young children are still in the process of learning about the everyday world. In order to be able to anticipate and predict what is going to happen, children focus on the repeated, routine aspects of events because it is these aspects that give the world predictability. When a novel event occurs, young children will tend to notice what makes this strange new event familiar, what makes it similar to events already understood. In this way, novel events become more comprehensible.

Understanding novel events in terms of more familiar routines occurs throughout development. For example, Barsalou (1988) found that college students report their summer vacations as a series of routines. Even when recounting something as novel as a vacation in Paris, adults frame their recall in terms of routines and deviations from routines. Thus the tendency to assimilate novel events to more familiar occurrences appears to remain an important way to organize and recount personal experiences. However a critical difference between the 2-year-olds in the present study and the 20-year-olds in Barsalou's study is the amount of experience the individual has had with the world. Clearly, we accrue more experience with increasing age. In order to understand how novel events differ from more routine events, one must have general knowledge about routine events; very young children are still in the process of understanding how the world "usually" works and therefore focus on similarities across diverse events. As children gain more knowledge about the world, they are able to understand novel events in terms of how they differ from familiar events (see Hudson, 1986b, and Nelson & Hudson, in press, for related arguments). Although all events may be understood within the framework of routines, younger children focus on similarities to routines, whereas older children and adults focus on deviations or distinctions from routines. With increasing age, there is an increasing tendency to focus on what makes novel events distinctive, different, and ultimately memorable. Thus, the shift toward recalling more distinctive information with development will lead to more accessible memories from the later preschool years.

The inconsistency of early recall

Framing novel events within the context of more familiar events helps explain part of why events from this early developmental period are forgotten, but it cannot be the whole story. Four-year-old children in our study recalled distinctive information about events that occurred more than 18 months in the past. Thus, it is not the case that novel events are forgotten if not repeated. Young children can and do retain information about novel, one-time events over extended periods of time. However, it is also the case that children recall different information each time they recount the same novel event. Most important, they are recalling different distinctive information when recalling the same event. We would expect some degree of inconsistency between any two recall trials; we all tend to modify what we recount based on situational constraints such as whom we are talking with, why we are recounting this particular event, and so on. However, the degree of instability of children's recall found in this study is remarkably high. Only 24% of the information recounted at the first interview was again recounted at the second interview, and of all information recalled during the first two interviews, only 26% was recounted at the third interview.

These findings are in sharp contrast to the consistency of recall we see in older children and adults when reporting the same event on different recall trials. For example, McCloskey, Wible, and Cohen (1988) assessed the consistency of adults' recall of the *Challenger* disaster over a 9-month retention interval. Although respondents recalled less information over time, they were highly consistent in the content of their recall. Very little of the information reported after 9 months was completely different information than had been reported immediately after the event occurred.

Similar results have been obtained with school-age children. In a recent study, we examined children's long-term recall of a kindergarten class trip to a museum of archaeology (Hudson & Fivush, 1987). Children were asked to recall the event immediately after it occurred, 6 weeks later, 1 year later, and 6 years later. As expected, there was a decrease in amount recalled over this period of time, but the content of what each child recalled was quite consistent. In comparison to the inconsistency in recall we found in the current study with preschoolers, when 6-year-old children recalled the museum trip 1 year after it occurred, 62% of what they recalled had been recalled on the previous recall trials. Thus, although there is some new (accurate) information reported a year later, there is clearly more consistency than we are seeing with younger children.

Impressionistically, one of the major differences in children's memory performance between the current study with preschoolers and kindergarten children's memories of the class trip is the number of questions necessary to elicit recall. Although children recalling their kindergarten class trip to the museum needed more direct questions as the retention interval increased (i.e., they need to be reminded that the Jewish Museum is a museum of archaeology), once they remembered the event at all, they were able to provide a full and coherent account of the event without additional experimenter questions. Preschool children in the current study, however, showed a very different pattern of recall. Although they were able to report a good amount of accurate information, their recall tended to be prompted by the adult's questions. Moreover, this seemed to be especially true when the children were 2½. For these young children, recall tended to be a process whereby the adult asked a question, the child provided a few units of information, the adult asked another question, the child provided a few more units of information, and so on.[3] Young children seem to be relying on the adult's questions to provide retrieval cues, and this may help account for the inconsistency in young children's recall.

To be more specific, it seems quite possible that children in the current study were inconsistent in what they recalled because the interviewers were inconsistent in what they asked. Older children and adults have learned the appropriate kind of information to report about past events; they know to report the "who, what, when, and where" (Neisser, 1982), and can query themselves about these aspects of the event in order to provide a coherent report. Younger children may simply not have learned the appropriate narrative structures yet and so are unable to use the conventional form for reporting an event in order to guide their own retrieval. Rather, they rely on the adult's questions to cue them to the type of information they should report.

This relates to our earlier discussion of what young children are learning in adult–child conversations about the past. Although children do not seem to be learning what specific information to recall about a particular past event, children are learning the appropriate narrative forms during these conversations (Eisenberg, 1985; Fivush, in press; Sachs, 1983). Hudson (1986a; this volume), in particular, has elegantly demonstrated this point. By studying mothers and children recalling both the same and different events over time, she has shown that children are not picking up particular pieces of information about specific events, but they are beginning to learn what categories of information are important to impart.

If this interpretation is correct, it implies that young children will tend to recall information only when it is asked for. Some support for this position comes from a study conducted by Hamond (1987) on children's memories for a family trip to Disney World. Hamond asked children ranging in age from 3 to 6 years old to recall various aspects of their Disney World experience; half of the children had gone to Disney World 6 months in the past, and half had gone 18 months in the past. Surprisingly, there were no effects of age or retention interval on amount of information children recalled about their trip. All children recalled a great deal of information, regardless of how old they were at the time of the interview or how long it had been since the experience. However, there were differences in the way in which the information was recalled. Younger children needed more questions and prompts from the adult in order to recall as much information as the older children did. Similar findings have been found in several studies of young children's recall (see Pillemer & White, in press, for a review). Across many studies, younger children recall as much information as older children do, but they need more memory questions in order to do so. Thus, it seems that younger children are more dependent on adults' questions to guide their recall.

In light of the findings from the current research, this idea needs to be somewhat modified. Notice that mothers, who ask a great many questions, tend to elicit less recall than strangers who ask fewer but more open-ended questions. The crucial difference here is that mothers are asking for very specific pieces of information (e.g., "What kind of cookies did Grandma bake that you liked so much?"), whereas the stranger asked for general categories of information (e.g., "What did you eat?"). Thus, what young children seem to need is for the adult to provide the general category of information that should be recalled rather than for the adult to focus in on a specific detail. With increasing experience in recalling events, children are learning the categories of information that need to be recounted about an event and are becoming better able to cue themselves on these categories.

Developmentally, then, young children may need an adult's questions to provide the framework for event recall, whereas older children have internalized this process and can provide their own retrieval cues. Thus, young children's recall may be inconsistent because they recall only that information that is asked for. We are currently investigating this issue in more detail (Fivush, Hamond, Harsch, Wolf, & Singer, in press). If this possibility proves correct, then it, too, can help account for the phenomenon of childhood amnesia. If young children are recalling only a subset of what is remembered about any given event on any given recall trial, then only this subset will be rehearsed, or reinforced in memory. Each time a particular event is recalled, a different subset of the remembered information will be rehearsed. Thus, there will not be a stable core of remembered material rehearsed across recall trials, resulting in a more fragmented memory that will be more difficult to recall later in time. As children gain experience in recounting events and begin to provide their own internal cues, they will begin to recall similar material across recall trials. Although there will be some different material recounted on each recall, there will also be a subset of remembered information that will form a stable core of the memory, leading to a more integrated, accessible memory.

Conclusion: Toward reconceptualizing childhood amnesia

The research reported in this chapter is a first step in examining autobiographical memory across the preschool years. The work was exploratory, and many of our interpretations were post hoc. A great deal of systematic research is needed to examine the predictions and test the ideas that have emerged from this study. However, we would like to stress that exploratory research is the necessary foundation for generating reasonable hypotheses. Although our theoretical interpretations are speculative, our empirical findings suggest new ways of conceptualizing early autobiographical memory and explaining childhood amnesia.

First and foremost, we have demonstrated that even very young children are able to retain information about novel events over extremely long periods of time. Most impressive, 4-year-old children can recall events that occurred before the age of 2½. Thus, young children are mnemonically competent. Further, these findings call into question explanations of childhood amnesia that rely on basic structural changes in the memory system with development. Rather, our research suggests that childhood amnesia may be better conceptualized within the framework of children's developing understanding of the world around them. In particular, two processes have been identified that might lead to the increasing inaccessibility of early memories.

First, because young children are in the process of trying to understand, anticipate, and predict the world around them, they are attuned to routines. In order to understand novel events, young children try to assimilate them to more familiar routine events. Because the more routine aspects of novel events will not provide distinctive memory cues in the future, these early events will become more and more difficult to recall as time passes. Second, young children have not yet learned the framework for recounting events. They do not spontaneously produce the who, what, where, and when of an event, but rely on adults' questions to guide them through the kinds of information they should recall. Because they are not providing their own retrieval cues, they are not recalling a stable set of remembered information about any given event during any given recall trial. Thus, these early memories will tend to become more fragmented and therefore more difficult to recall later in development.

We are currently investigating these processes in more detail. But regardless of the outcome of future research, it seems clear that childhood amnesia is not a simple phenomenon with a single, simple explanation. Factors that we have not even addressed in this chapter, but that surely play a role in childhood amnesia, include the emotional tone and salience of early memories (Fivush, Gray, & Fromhoff, 1987); verbal and mental rehearsal of early childhood events (Rubin & Kozin, 1984); the construction of a "personal time-line" (Barsalou, 1988); and the interrelations between personal experiences and the developing self-concept (Fivush, 1988). What we have tried to demonstrate in this chapter is that in order to understand the phenomenon of childhood amnesia, we must first understand exactly what it is that young children are recalling about their personal experiences and how this changes with development.

NOTES

This research was supported by an Emory University Faculty Research Grant to the first author. We are indebted to Anne Wolf for her invaluable assistance in all phases of this research.
1 Given the constraints and purposes of this chapter, we will present a very brief and highly selective review of some of the recent research. For more detailed reviews, the reader is directed to Pillemer and White (in press).
2 We thank Eugene Winograd for first pointing this out to us.
3 Young children are not always or completely reliant on adults' questions to guide their recall. About 30% of 2-year-old children's recall of past events is reported in a well-organized narrative structure (see Fivush, Gray, & Fromhoff, 1987, for a more complete discussion of this issue).

REFERENCES

Barsalou, L. (1988). The organization of autobiographical memory. In U. Neisser & E. Winograd (Eds.), *Remembering reconsidered: Ecological and traditional approaches to the study of memory* (pp. 193–243). New York: Cambridge University Press.

Bartlett, F. C. (1932). *Remembering: A study in experimental and social psychology.* New York: Cambridge University Press.

Brown, A. L., Bransford, J. D., Ferrara, R., & Campione, J. (1983). Learning, remembering and understanding. In J. Flavell & E. Markman (Eds.), *Mussen handbook of child psychology* (Vol. 3, pp. 77–166). Somerset, NJ: Wiley.

Donaldson, M. (1978). *Children's minds.* New York: Norton

Eisenberg, A. R. (1985). Learning to describe past experience in conversation. *Discourse Processes, 8,* 177–204.

Fivush, R. (1988). The functions of events memory. In U. Neisser & E. Winograd (Eds.), *Remembering reconsidered: Ecological and traditional approaches to the study of memory* (pp. 277–282). New York: Cambridge University Press.

Fivush, R. (in press). The social construction of personal narratives. *Merrill-Palmer Quarterly.*

Fivush, R., Gray, J. T., & Fromhoff, F. A. (1987). Two year olds talk about the past. *Cognitive Development, 2,* 393–410.

Fivush, R., Hamond, N. R., Harsch, N., Wolf, A., & Singer, N. (in press). Content and consistency of young children's autobiographical memory. *Discourse Processes.*

Fivush, R., Hudson, J., & Nelson, K. (1984). Children's long-term memory for a novel event: An exploratory study. *Merrill-Palmer Quarterly, 30,* 303–316.

Freud, S. (1953/1924). *A general introduction to psychoanalysis.* New York: Pocket Books.

Garvey, C. (1984). *Children's talk.* Cambridge, MA: Harvard University Press.

Gelman, R. (1977). Cognitive development. *Annual Review of Psychology, 29,* 297–332.

Grice, H. P. (1975). Logic and conversation. In P. Cole & J. L. Morgan (Eds.), *Syntax and semantics: Vol 3. Speech acts* (pp. 41–58). New York: Academic Press.

Hamond, N. R. (1987). *Memories of Mickey Mouse: Young children recount their trip to Disney World.* Unpublished masters' thesis, Emory University.

Hudson, J. A. (1986a, April). Effects of repeated recall on autobiographic memory. In J. A. Hudson (Chair), *Learning to talk about the past.* Symposium conducted at the Southeastern Conference on Human Development, Nashville.

Hudson, J. A. (1986b). Memories are made of this: General event knowledge and autobiographical memory. In K. Nelson (Ed.), *Event knowledge: Structure and function in development* (pp. 97–118). Hillsdale, NJ: Erlbaum.

Hudson, J. A., & Fivush, R. (1987). *As time goes by: Sixth grade children recall a kindergarten experience* (Emory Cognition Project Report #13). Emory University, Atlanta.

Hudson, J. A., & Nelson, K. (1986). Repeated encounters of a similar kind: Effects of familiarity on children's autobiographical recall. *Cognitive Development, 1,* 253–271.

McCloskey, M., Wible, C. G., & Cohen, N. J. (1988). Is there a special flashbulb-memory mechanism? *Journal of Experimental Psychology: General, 117,* 171–181.

Neisser, U. (1962). Cultural and cognitive discontinuity. In T. E. Gladwin & W. Sturtevant (Eds.), *Anthropology and human behavior* (pp. 54–71). Washington, DC: Anthropological Society of Washington.

Neisser, U. (1982). Snapshots or benchmarks? In U. Neisser (Ed.), *Memory observed* (pp. 43–48). San Francisco: Freeman.

Neisser, U. (1988). What is ordinary memory the memory of? In U. Neisser & E. Winograd (Eds.), *Remembering reconsidered: Ecological and traditional approaches to the study of memory* (pp. 356–374). New York: Cambridge University Press.

Nelson, K. (1986). *Event knowledge: Structure and function in development.* Hillsdale, NJ: Erlbaum.

Nelson, K. (1988). The ontogeny of memory for real events. In U. Neisser & E. Winograd (Eds.), *Remembering reconsidered: Ecological and traditional approaches to the study of memory* (pp. 244–277). New York: Cambridge University Press.

Nelson, K., & Hudson, J. A. (in press). Scripts and memory: Interrelations in development. In F. Weinhart & M. Perlmutter (Eds.), *Memory development.* Hillsdale, NJ: Erlbaum.

Pillemer, D. B., & White, S. H. (in press). Childhood events recalled by children and adults. In H. W. Reese (Ed.), *Advances in child development and behavior* (Vol. 22). New York: Academic Press.

Rubin, D. C., & Kozin, M. (1984). Vivid memories. *Cognitive Psychology, 16,* 81–95.

Sachs, J. (1983). Talking about the there and then: The emergence of displaced reference in parent–child discourse. In K. E. Nelson (Ed.), *Children's Language* (Vol. 4, pp. 1–27). New York: Gardner Press.

Schachtel, E. G. (1982). On memory and childhood amnesia. In U. Neisser (Ed.), *Memory observed* (pp. 189–200). San Francisco: W. H. Freeman.

Sheingold, K., & Tenney, Y. J. (1982). Memory for a salient childhood event. In U. Neisser (Ed.), *Memory observed* (pp. 201–212). San Francisco: W. H. Freeman.

Snow, C. E., & Goldfield, B. A. (1983). Turn the page please: Situation-specific language acquisition. *Journal of Child Language, 10,* 551–569.

Spear, N. (1979). Experimental analysis of infantile amnesia. In J. F. Kihlstrom & F. J. Evans (Eds.), *Functional disorders of memory* (pp. 75–102). Hillsdale, NJ: Erlbaum.

Todd, C., & Perlmutter, M. (1980). Reality recalled by preschool children. In M. Perlmutter (Ed.), *Children's memory* (New directions for child development, No. 10, pp. 69–86). San Francisco: Jossey-Bass.

Vygotsky, L. S. (1978). *Mind in society: The development of higher psychological processes.* Cambridge, MA: Harvard University Press.

Wetzler, S. E., & Sweeney, J. A. (1986). Childhood amnesia: An empirical demonstration. In D. Rubin (Ed.), *Autobiographical memory* (pp. 191–202). New York: Cambridge University Press.

White, S. H., & Pillemer, D. B. (1979). Childhood amnesia and the development of a socially accessible memory system. In J. F. Kihlstrom & F. J. Evans (Eds.), *Functional disorders of memory* (pp. 29–74). Hillsdale, NJ: Erlbaum.

10

Children's concerns and memory: Issues of ecological validity in the study of children's eyewitness testimony

GAIL S. GOODMAN, LESLIE RUDY,
BETTE L. BOTTOMS, AND CHRISTINE AMAN

Did you ever wet your pants in school? As a child, did you ever hurt yourself so badly that you had to go to a hospital? Were you ever spanked with a belt? These questions can be answered quickly by most people. We seem to know well if such events happened in our childhood or not, at least once the barrier of infantile amnesia has been passed. What unites these questions is that they all concern actions that are personally significant to children, actions that affect a child's sense of well-being, safety, or social acceptance. People often feel that they remember whether such events occurred or not. Yet the study of memory development has been largely silent on how such personally significant events affect children's memory. A main theme of this chapter is that actions affecting a child's sense of well-being, safety, and social acceptance are remembered remarkably well and that, at least by the age of 4 years, children are surprisingly resistant to suggestions about them.

The study of children's testimony, especially as it relates to child abuse, led us to examine children's memory and suggestibility for personally significant actions. Children who testify in courts of law and are involved in legal investigation often do so as victims of child abuse. These child victim/witnesses are interviewed about such personally significant and potentially embarrassing experiences as having their clothes removed, being hit, being kissed, or seeing someone's "private parts." If such experiences are not remembered well, children may be more subject to suggestive influences by adults and hence more easily led to give false reports of abuse.

Currently, there is great public and professional debate concerning children's testimony in child abuse cases. Some fear that the use of leading questioning by legal and mental health professionals is resulting in false allegations of abuse and consequently prosecution and conviction of innocent adults. Others claim that children do not report abuse readily and that leading questioning may be necessary to facilitate children's disclosures. Despite strong claims by both sides, ecologically valid

249

research in which children are asked about bodily injury and sexual acts has been virtually nonexistent.

A second theme of this chapter thus concerns ecological validity. Like studies of children's memory, studies of children's testimony typically suffer from a lack of ecological validity. Trivial stimuli (e.g., cartoons or stories), which children in actual court cases or legal investigations would hardly ever be asked to testify about, are followed by questions concerning peripheral details or descriptions of strangers. In child abuse investigations, central actions and identifications of familiar people are of primary concern. Thus, many of the existing studies are likely to underestimate children's ability to provide accurate testimony in actual child abuse investigations, just as laboratory studies of children's memory have generally underestimated children's cognitive and memory abilities (DeLoache, Cassidy, & Brown, 1985; Donaldson, 1978; Nelson, 1986).

In the present chapter, we describe a series of studies that combine ecological validity with experimental control to examine children's memory for information relevant to personal safety. One of our main motivations for conducting the studies was to determine whether false reports of abuse can be readily elicited from children. Before describing the studies, we will outline the theoretical framework that guides our research.

Conceptual framework

Our guiding assumption is that children's "concerns" play a prominent role in their memories (cf. Frijda, 1986). By concerns we mean children's drives, fears, wishes, and preferences. (We will use the term *personal significance* to refer to events that are relevant to children's concerns.) One primitive concern is physical safety – that is, not being hurt or assaulted. Another concern that emerges fairly early is fear of abandonment. More positive concerns such as interests in food, comfort, and play also exist. These more positive concerns also play an important role in children's memory.

Some concerns, such as ones for personal safety and food, are quite basic, but others rely on cognitive development. For example, a concern not to be embarrassed implies the existence of a symbolic social self (Fischer, Shaver, & Carnochan, 1989). As we grow older, attacks on or bolstering of the symbolic self can be as important as attacks on or nurturance of the real self. Suicide in the name of lost love or social dishonor serves as a somber reminder.

Concerns may also rely on the acquisition of cultural norms. Certain practices (e.g., appearing partially nude in public) may cause little embarrassment in some cultures (e.g., Tahitian) but a great deal of embarrassment in others (e.g., American). Relevant experience and maturity are required for children to learn the values and expectations of the culture in which they are reared.

It has been difficult in laboratory experiments to address children's concerns in relation to their memory, particularly for aversive events. Ethical issues pose the main obstacle. We cannot, for research purposes, actively threaten children's safety or deprive them of food or comfort. Another obstacle is that the more ethically manipulable concerns (e.g., interest in toys) change with time, place, and need. Thus, it is difficult to standardize the importance of stimuli in relation to a child's concerns.

Why should children's concerns have a profound effect on their memory? The answer is evident: Survival of the species requires that we learn – quickly and with lasting impact – to avoid danger and sustain life. Children, who are particularly helpless should be in a sense "prepared" (Seligman, 1970) to have lasting memories for events that threaten or promote their well-being. In that way they can avoid danger and gain nurturance. Garcia's (e.g., Garcia & Koelling, 1966) classic taste-aversion experiments indicate the power of memories for information relevant to self-preservation, and his findings surely have implications for humans as well as for less advanced species.

Physiological, cognitive, and motivational factors may also help explain improved memory for events associated with children's concerns. Recent research suggests that nature wisely provided us with a physiological mechanism to consolidate memory for personally significant events rapidly. Gold (1987) describes an elegant series of studies indicating that certain hormones, such as adrenaline, result in enhanced memory through the release of plasma glucose. Gold proposes that these memory-enhancing hormones, which are released in response to important but not to trivial events, may indicate to brain cells whether information is worthy of more permanent storage or not.

Cognitive research also supports the view that personally significant events are retained in memory better than less significant events, such as those typically used in laboratory studies (Bohannon, 1988; Keenan, MacWhinney, & Mayhew, 1977; Linton, 1982). Keenan and Baillet (1980) argue that better retention of personally significant events results at least in part from the self being the most informationally rich schema in memory. Since semantic structures to which events are encoded influence the amount of elaboration received by a given piece of information, hence influencing its memorability, events encoded in relation to the self will be highly memorable. Such "self-referencing" effects are especially evident when memory tasks require use of self schema and when appropriate retrieval cues are available (Brown, Keenan, & Potts, 1986). Better memory for information relevant to the self has been demonstrated both in adults (Rogers, Kuiper, & Kirker, 1977) and children (Pullyblank,

Bisanz, Scott, & Champion, 1985). Children's concerns, such as the desire for safety and comfort, are by definition highly relevant to the self and should, according to this formulation, be highly memorable. Keenan and Baillet's (1980) view is couched in purely cognitive terms, but, as they acknowledge, motivational factors such as emotion may also ensure a high degree of memorability for personally significant events.

Many have argued that emotions play a primary role in memory (see Rapaport, 1942). Certainly, access to early autobiographical memories is influenced by emotion, since when adults are asked to recount their earliest memories, the vast majority of recollections are associated with either negative or positive affect (see Pillemer & White, 1989, for a review). Motivational and cognitive factors are likely to interact to further strengthen children's memories for personally significant events. For example, the way a child feels about an event is likely to affect how much elaborative processing and how much mental (if not overt) rehearsal that event receives.

In sum, there are a number of reasons to suspect that children's concerns influence their memory. Concerns are linked to survival and as a result to the self, informationally rich memory schemas, and emotion.

Most forms of child abuse have a direct impact on children's concerns. Physical as well as sexual abuse influences a child's sense of physical safety. In addition, to the extent that children are aware of social taboos against sexuality, premature sexual involvement is likely to be embarrassing. We turn now to a discussion of children's concerns for physical safety and avoidance of embarrassment. If we are correct that children's concerns have a powerful effect on memory, it is important for us to identify children's concerns as they pertain to abusive actions. Wherever possible, we relate this discussion to children's memories.

Bodily injury

All victims of child physical abuse and some victims of child sexual abuse suffer bodily injury. Since children, like adults, are interested in maintaining personal safety, abuse violates one of children's most basic concerns. As might be expected, when children are questioned about their fears, bodily injury is mentioned frequently. For example, Lentz (1985) questioned a hundred 5- and 6-year-olds about their fears at home, at school, and at the baby-sitter's. Children's main fears concerned bodily injury, punishment, and abandonment. Although all children expressed considerable concern about these events, females expressed more fear of bodily injury than males did. Similarly, Angelino, Dollins, and Mech (1956) uncovered a number of individual and sex differences in the specific content of children's fears, but generally found that 9- to 18-year-olds expressed the greatest number of fears about safety, a category that included violence, being hurt, and punishments (see also Jersild & Holmes, 1935).

Yamamoto, Soliman, Parsons, and Davies (1987) conducted a cross-cultural study of children's fears. The youngest children were third-graders and the oldest were teenagers. Most of the children's high-fear responses can be grouped into four categories: bodily injury (e.g., going blind, having an operation); abandonment or separation from loved ones (e.g., losing a parent, getting lost); embarrassment (e.g., wetting in class); and punishment (e.g., being sent to the principal). Yamamoto et al. note that adults are not always accurate in assessing children's fears. Parents tend to think that children fear the birth of a sibling, for example, yet children themselves rated this as the least feared event out of 20 possibilities. In contrast, events that caused embarrassment or social rejection figured more prominently in children's fears than adults might expect.

It is thus clear that bodily injury constitutes one of children's primary concerns. But when children sustain physical injury, do they remember it? The link between children's memory and their concerns about bodily injury was recently revealed in a study of very young children's recountings of personal experiences. Miller and Sperry (1988) recorded conversations between children, aged 1 year 7 months to 2 years 8 months, and their mothers. In these conversations, children's memories primarily concerned negative events, especially events of physical harm. When child-initiated conversations were considered, 91% of them concerned negative events and 70% involved events of physical harm. When another person initiated the topic of conversation, recountings of negative events still predominated (53%); mention of physical harm was the largest single category (30%). Overall, the children's recountings were about evenly split as to whether or not the child had been hurt in or witnessed the event, although individual differences on this dimension were strong. Examples of the children's memories of harm included such acts as getting an inoculation, falling, being burned, and being hit, slapped, grabbed, or otherwise physically assaulted.

Embarrassment, punishment, and sexuality

As the surveys just discussed indicate, another childhood concern is embarrassment. Children's reactions to child abuse, especially child sexual abuse, may involve embarrassment. Even questioning children about sexual matters may cause them to blush. Social commentators and researchers alike note that sexuality is characterized in children's minds by embarrassment, mystery, and even fear, particularly fear of punishment

(Goldman & Goldman, 1982, 1988; Jackson, 1982). Young children may not know anything about sex other than having observed that adults treat the topic as something to be avoided or kept secret, or for which one can be punished or ridiculed. Thus, children come to react to situations that carry sexual connotation by becoming embarrassed – a shame that they are taught to feel, without necessarily understanding the reasons why.

Perhaps one of the first things children are taught to be embarrassed about concerning sexuality is the exposure of their own bodies to others. Jackson (1982) comments that

adults' reactions to children's behavior turn previously innocent activities into guilt-ridden ones, but many children will already have an inkling that "sexual" games are taboo, infringing as they do the rules of modesty that have most likely already been learnt. Children are taught early on that certain parts of the body must be kept hidden and that it is "rude" or "dirty" to expose them to others. (pp. 96–97)

Goldman and Goldman (1982, 1988) observed that guilt and inhibition about nudity and sexuality are soon acquired from the child's parents, who reflect not only their own personal restraints but those of the society in which they have been reared.

Goldman and Goldman reached this conclusion after conducting a cross-cultural study in which they asked children, the youngest being 5-year-olds, about many aspects of sexual thinking, including nudity. In the study, children were asked, for example, about their attitudes toward clothing. Responses to such questions as "Do we need to wear clothes in a warm climate?" revealed the taboo, embarrassment, and fear of punishment associated even in the minds of 5-year-olds with exposure of one's genitals. For example, an English 5-year-old boy answered, "Yes, because your father would give you a hiding." And from a 7-year-old Australian girl, "My mom says you shouldn't do that. She says it's not right to go around with nothing on." An 11-year-old American girl focused on the fact that others would laugh.

Other outward signs of embarrassment were revealed in answers given to the question "Would you ask your parents about sex?" A 7-year-old answered, "Sometimes they get very nervous about it." An English teenager replied, "Even if we did ask, . . . we'd be all embarrassed." A 5-year-old Australian girl answered, "I wouldn't tell anyone or ask anyone, 'cos it's supposed to be a secret." Children reported being afraid to ask even their friends for fear of being laughed at. Interestingly, of the four countries studied, American society proved to be the most restrictive in its treatment of sexuality, at least as reflected by the children's statements.

We know of no studies that have traced the very beginnings of embarrassment about nudity in children. Thus, it is difficult to say when this potentially important variable might begin to influence memory. Although research is sparse, anecdotes indicate that embarrassment about nudity starts early, at least for some children. Take the following example from one of the present authors' visits to a relative:

Last year, one of us (GG) was invited to give a talk in Fort Worth, Texas, about her work on children's testimony. She took the occasion to visit a relative whose son, Nick, had just turned 2. Coincidentally, the father arrived home from work at the same time that the child testimony researcher drove up in front of the house. As they entered the house together, Nick raced to the door completely naked to greet his dad. When the little boy saw that his father was not alone, he stopped in his tracks, covered his groin, turned red, let out a loud squeal, and raced back into his room.

Already at the age of 2, Nick knew that nudity in front of strangers was taboo. And he knew exactly what area of his body to conceal.

Research on the development of embarrassment is limited in general (see Edelmann, 1987, and Seidner, Stipek, & Feshbach, 1988, for reviews). Nevertheless, as Seidner et al. point out, it is clear that precursors of embarrassment appear in infancy. In order to feel embarrassment, one must recognize a contingency between one's own behavior and an outcome. The concept of the self as an agent, that actions of the self can produce outcomes, is believed to arise in early infancy (Watson, 1966). The ability to engage in self-evaluation is also believed to be necessary for the feeling of embarrassment. This ability is likely to be present by the second year of life (Lewis & Michaelson, 1983). Thus, there is reason to believe that children might experience embarrassment by the second year. Nevertheless reasons for becoming embarrassed may change developmentally.

Seidner et al. (1988) recently conducted a developmental study of the concept of embarrassment. In it, 5-, 7-, 9-, and 11-year-old children as well as adults were asked to reveal events that made them "very, very embarrassed." Although both children and adults tended primarily to give examples of outcomes for which they were responsible, children tended more than adults to indicate that events outside their control also caused embarrassment. Child sexual abuse, an act that is outside of the child's control, may be one such event.

We have been unable to locate studies of children's memories for embarrassing events generally or sexually related events (such as a nudity) specifically. Our studies address this issue by asking children about acts related to sex. However, our studies concern whether children know that certain potentially sexual acts (e.g., having one's clothes removed) and certain potentially injurious acts (e.g., being hit) did *not* occur.

Young children's conversations about the past consist not only of what did happen but of what did not (Todd & Perlmutter, 1980), indicating that even young children remember both types of information.[1] Todd and Perlmutter give the example of a 3-year-old who, when asked what happened when he climbed the stairs onto an airplane, remarked, "I didn't fall." Thus, this child knew he had not been hurt. Similarly, our studies indicate that children, at least by the age of 4 years on average, generally know that they were not physically or sexually abused when they were not. Moreover, they are able to assert this knowledge even under the force of suggestive questioning.

In summary, nudity and sexuality are associated with embarrassment and secrecy – if not punishment – in children's minds. Previous research provides few insights about when this association first arises or how it affects children's memory. Our own studies, described later in this chapter, provide relevant but indirect information by examining whether children remember that sexually related and potentially embarrassing events did not occur.

Ecological validity

The study of children's concerns and memory highlights the issue of ecological validity, a particularly important consideration in research on children's testimony. Studies of children's testimony, and of adults' testimony, for that matter, have suffered from a lack of ecological validity in numerous ways. Children are typically exposed to nonengaging events presented in stories (e.g., Ceci, Ross, & Toglia, 1987; Saywitz, 1987) or films (Cohen & Harnick; 1980; Dale, Loftus, & Rathbun, 1978). When live events are enacted, they are often of an uninvolving or mundane nature, such as a person watering a plant (King, 1984). The children are typically bystanders to the events, and it is seldom determined whether the events carry much interest to the children. Another serious problem with many studies involves limitations on the legal relevance of the questions asked: Children tend to be queried about peripheral details rather than the main actions that occurred. Children's memory for main actions is typically superior to their memory for other forms of information (Fivush, Gray, & Fromhoff, 1987; Goodman, Hirschman, and Rudy, 1987; Pear & Wyatt, 1914), and in child abuse cases, the main actions and who performed them are of primary interest. It is important for psychologists to determine if the findings of their studies generalize to the types of events children in fact testify about. Otherwise, we may mislead ourselves and the legal system.

In a clever experiment, Ochsner and Zaragoza (1988) directly tested the issue of ecological validity for bystander child witnesses to a "crime."

They examined whether viewing what appeared to be a real purse-snatching led first-graders to provide more accurate testimony than viewing a neutral event. In their study, three children at a time were brought to an empty schoolroom to complete a puzzle. While the children worked on the task a man entered the room, introduced himself by saying that he was looking for the principal, and fumbled about by, for example, dropping a pencil. At that point, one of two things happened. In the theft condition, the confederate stole a purse that was in the room. In the no-theft condition, the confederate simply walked out in search of the principal. The researcher soon reentered the room and interviewed the children.

Several interesting findings emerged, the main one being that in almost every way children in the theft condition were more accurate than children in the no-theft condition. Compared to the no-theft group, the theft group produced more correct statements in free recall while at the same time producing fewer incorrect statements; were less willing to select a suggested (misleading) alternative on a forced-choice test; were more likely to correct the interviewer when an incorrect alternative was presented; and were less suggestible overall.

This study demonstrates that much of the former research on children's testimony is likely to have underestimated children's ability to provide accurate eyewitness reports. As Ochsner and Zaragoza point out, the control condition in their experiment was probably more involving than the stories and films used in many investigations of children's testimony. Thus, studies that rely on uninvolving stimuli would be expected to widen the performance gap even further than the study by Ochsner and Zaragoza.

The present studies

The studies described in this chapter examine a number of issues related to children's testimony. The studies are united by our interest in children's memory and suggestibility about actions associated with child abuse, actions pertinent to children's concerns. Our primary focus is on whether false reports of abuse can be created through suggestive questioning. A number of other issues, such as the effects of participation and stress on children's reports, are addressed in individual experiments. In the first set of studies, children were involved to varying degrees in social interactions. In Study 1 we compared the testimony of bystander and participant witnesses. One child was actively engaged in games with an unfamiliar man while the other child merely watched. After a delay, the children were interviewed as if they were in a child abuse investigation. The second study examined children's use of anatomically detailed dolls to recount an event. Children were again involved in a social interaction with an adult. But in contrast to the first study, some of the children were later interviewed with anatomically detailed dolls. We can therefore examine whether these controversial forms of "stimulus support" increase children's suggestibility about acts related to sexual and physical abuse.

The second set of studies concerns children's testimony about a stressful event, one that simulates victimization. The effects of stress and of long delays on children's reports are examined. Finally, we describe a study that explores the effects of intimidation on children's reports of a stressful event.

The questions used in our interviews were often strongly leading. They were at times repeated, so that the children's initial reports were challenged. If a child disclosed abuse in an actual legal or social service interview that included questions such as ours, the interviewer would likely face severe criticism from the accused that the child was led into making a false accusation. Child abuse charges have often been dismissed by judges on this ground. These criticisms are based on the assumption that children are highly suggestible (see, for example, Loftus, 1979). If children are indeed as suggestible as some have claimed, then we should be able in our studies to create false reports of abuse.

Children's testimony about social interactions

Study 1: Child participant versus bystander witnesses

The goal of this study was to examine the influence of participation on children's memory. There is reason to believe that participation leads to better memory in children (see Slackman, Hudson, & Fivush, 1986). We were interested in the participation–bystander distinction for two reasons. One is that child victims will be forced to participate in abusive events, whereas other children may not be victimized themselves but may be in a position to watch. The second is that most former research on children's testimony has focused almost exclusively on child-bystander witnesses. To the extent that participation leads to better memory, former studies may have underestimated children's abilities.

In our experiment, children experienced a neutral event. A neutral event was chosen because it is often argued in child abuse cases that nothing abusive happened to the child but that a false report of abuse was created through interviewer questioning. The use of a neutral event permitted us to examine this claim. Three specific questions thus motivated the study: (1) What are the effects on memory of children's participation in, versus observation of, social interactions? (2) How suggestible are children about actions associated with child abuse? And (3) Are there age differences in children's susceptibility to such suggestions?

The setting of the study was a fairly dilapidated research trailer equipped with a one-way mirror and a few chairs. We selected the trailer as the site of the first session for two reasons. One was that it provided a unique retrieval cue; the children could later be asked what happened when they went into the trailer, which was presumably a more memorable cue than asking them what happened when they went into an ordinary room. The second reason concerned ecological validity; several actual cases of child abuse of which we were aware took place in trailers.

In the study, thirty-six 4- and 7-year-old children, in same-age and same-sex pairs, were escorted to the trailer. The children, randomly selected from subject files maintained by the Department of Psychology at the University of Denver, were strangers to each other. On entering the trailer, the children were introduced to a male confederate who had been waiting for them inside. The trio sat and talked, using puppets to make the children feel at ease. At one point the confederate put on a funny mask for the children's entertainment. After that, the participant–bystander manipulation began. One of the children (the "participant") was randomly selected to engage in further games with the confederate, while the other (the "bystander") was randomly selected to observe. To ensure that the children would believe that the decision was made by chance and not because the confederate favored one child, the children were presented with a box containing two marbles, and each child was asked to select one. The children in the participation condition were told that they had selected the marble that permitted them to play further games, whereas the bystanders were told that they would do an equally important task, that of watching. The participants were engaged in the following activities: playing Simon Says, during which time the confederate and child, in the midst of performing other actions, touched each others' knees; the confederate dressing the child in a clown costume that was placed over the child's clothes; the child being lifted onto a table and having her or his photograph taken in several poses; thumb wrestling; and playing a game invented for the experiment called "Funny Things That Clowns Do," which involved such actions as the child tickling the confederate. The bystander was frequently told to watch carefully and was complimented for paying attention. At the end of the session, each child received a small toy. The session lasted approximately 12 minutes.

The activities used in the study were selected based on actual cases of child abuse. In actual cases, children at times report that: their clothes were removed; their picture was taken while posing naked, presumably for pornographic purposes; the sexual acts were described as tickling; the perpetrator used a mask to scare them; and they were touched in the context of games. The events in the trailer permitted us to ask about such events because related (but nonabusive) actions occurred. They also permitted us to investigate whether innocent actions would be confused with abusive actions under conditions of suggestive questioning.

From 10 to 12 days after the trip to the trailer, the children were interviewed. Each was first asked three recall questions. Specifically, they were asked to tell the interviewer everything about what happened in the trailer, what the man in the trailer looked like, and what kinds of games were played. They were then asked a series of misleading and specific questions about the appearance of the confederate, the activities played in the trailer, the appearance of the inside of the trailer, and the timing of the event. For example, the children were asked: "He had a beard and a mustache, right?" (In fact, the confederate was clean-shaven.) "Did he take a picture of you?" "What color were the curtains on the windows of the trailer?" (In fact, there were no curtains.) "How long were you in the trailer with the man?"

The questions about the activities in the trailer were of two types: Some concerned actions that might lead to an accusation of child abuse, such as "He took your clothes off, didn't he?" whereas others did not, such as "He took you to another room and took your shoes off, right?" All of the action questions were asked in relation to the child being questioned and also in relation to the other child. Therefore, each child was asked, "Did he kiss you?" and "Did he kiss the other child?" In addition, each child was asked to pick the confederate's picture from a "blank" lineup, in which the confederate was not pictured.

The purpose of the specific questions was to obtain more detailed information from the children compared to that obtained during free recall, since it is well known that children's free recall is sketchy and does not reflect all that they know (Goodman & Reed, 1986; Johnson & Foley, 1984; Nelson, 1986). In addition, we wanted to mimic the kind of questioning often included in legal and social service investigations. Some would consider our specific questions, such as "Did he hit you?" as leading because they included specific information that the children did not spontaneously mention (White & Quinn, 1988). Nevertheless, the misleading questions were clearly more suggestive than the specific questions and placed greater pressure on the children to conform to the implied answer.

The findings support a view of children as having specific strengths and weaknesses in their reports, with one of the strengths being an ability to answer abuse-related questions accurately. The older children recalled more correct information in response to both the initial question ("I need you to tell me exactly what happened"), $M = 10.78$, and the second question ("What did the man look like?"), $M = 1.72$, than the younger children did, $M = 4.61$, and $M = 0.78$, $F(1, 34) = 10.30$, $p < .01$, and $F(1, 34) = 4.20$, $p < .05$, respectively. The difference between the two groups in the amount of correct information recalled in response to the third question ("What kinds of games did you play?") was nonsignificant; 7-year-olds, $M = 3.11$; 4-year-olds, $M = 2.22$. The children recalled little incorrect or ambiguous information. On average, they provided less than one incorrect or ambiguous item of information, and there were no significant age differences on these two measures. Thus, although older children recalled more information than younger children, they were not more accurate in absolute terms. The younger children recalled very little, but what they did recall was typically correct.

Overall, the older children were more accurate in response to the specific questions, $M = .69$, than the younger children were, $M = .59$, $F(4, 29) = 10.00$, $p < .001$. Univariate tests revealed, however, that although the older children were more accurate in response to questions about the person – $M = .89$, and actions, $M = .90$ – than the 4-year-olds – $M = .71$ and $M = .80$, respectively – there was very little difference between the age groups in response to questions about the room, $M = .61$, and $M = .66$, or time, $M = .24$ and $M = .30$, for the 4- and 7-year-olds, respectively. Apparently, both age groups were still unfamiliar with the concept of time as communicated in adult units of measure such as minutes. The room represented the most peripheral information queried; it is likely that both age groups paid little attention to the barren appearance of the inside of the trailer.

The children were also asked misleading questions about the person, actions, room, and time. Responses were scored as correct if the child actively resisted the suggestion by disagreeing with it. It is also possible to consider "don't know" responses as resistance to suggestion, and so analyses were conducted in two ways, once including "don't know" responses and once excluding them. In either case, higher scores indicate greater resistance to suggestion. When "don't know" responses were included, 4-year-olds, $M = .68$, were significantly more suggestible than 7-year-olds, $M = .82$, $F(1, 32) = 5.63$, $p < .05$, although this difference is only marginally significant when "don't know" responses were excluded. Univariate analyses revealed that the older children, $M = .94$ and $M = .95$, compared to younger children, $M = .74$ and $M = .84$, were better able to resist suggestions about the person, $F(1, 34) = 11.31$, $p < .01$, and the actions, $F(1, 34) = 10.07$, $p < .01$. The two age groups did not reliably differ in their ability to resist suggestions about the room, 7-year-olds, $M = .74$, and 4-year-olds, $M = .63$, and about time, 7-year-olds, $M = .67$, and 4-year-olds, $M = .50$. This pattern matches that for the children's answers to the specific questions, indicating that age differences in suggestibility result at least in part from younger children having weaker memories than older children for certain types of information.

Surprisingly, there were few overall differences in the amount of information recalled or the proportion of specific or misleading questions answered correctly as a function of participation, although as we shall see shortly, other effects of participation did emerge.

Of particular interest in this study were children's responses to the abuse questions. If questioning about actions associated with abuse leads to false allegations, as is often claimed, we would expect children to use such questions as a basis for generating fictitious reports of abusive events. On the other hand, the children could be especially accurate in response to these questions because of their direct relevance to the child's body and physical well-being. Table 10.1 presents the accuracy of the children's responses to the abuse questions. In general, the children were very accurate in answering these questions. The 7-year-olds answered 93% of them correctly, and the 4-year-olds answered 83% correctly.

Despite the high accuracy rates, it was of interest to examine the types of errors made. Not all errors would be considered legally dangerous. Perhaps the most dangerous error from a legal perspective is to say that something occurred when it actually did not, a "commission" error. Another legally relevant but often less serious error is to leave out something that did occur, an error of "omission." The relevant findings are also included in Table 10.1. Out of 252 opportunities, the 7-year-olds made only one commission error. This error was made by a 7-year-old bystander child who responded affirmatively but without elaboration to the correctly leading question "The person in the trailer didn't touch you, did he?" Thus, commission errors were rare for the 7-year-olds. The more common error was to omit actions that did occur. Even then, virtually all the omission errors made by the 7-year-olds were in response to a specific subset of questions – those concerning touching.

The 4-year-olds made 13 out of a possible 252 commission errors. Thirty-eight percent of the commission errors made by 4-year-olds were to the questions about touching, again reflecting the children's difficulty with these questions. None of the children produced any sexualized answers to these questions, however. The only elaboration was offered by a 4-year-old, who said, in response to the question about whether he had touched the man, "Yes, but only to get the puppet."

Two of the three commission errors to the question about kissing were made by a single child. She answered "yes" to both questions about kissing and then spontaneously added, "I am a boy. I pretend to be a boy every time." The significance of her response remains a mystery to us. The third commission error about kissing was produced by a boy who

Table 10.1. *Number of children who provided a correct response, a commission error (CO), an omission error (OM), or a "don't know" (DK) in response to abuse questions*

	4-year-olds				7-year-olds			
	Correct	CO	OM	DK	Correct	CO	OM	DK
He took your clothes off, didn't he?	18	0	0	0	18	0	0	0
He took the other girl's (boy's) clothes off, didn't he?	18	0	0	0	18	0	0	0
How many times did he spank you?	17	1	0	0	18	0	0	0
How many times did he spank the other girl (boy)?	17	1	0	0	18	0	0	0
The person in the trailer didn't touch you, did he?	10	1	6	1	13	1	2	2
The person in the trailer didn't touch the other girl (boy), did he?	10	2	4	2	13	0	2	3
Did he kiss you?	17	1	0	0	18	0	0	0
Did he kiss the other girl (boy)?	16	2	0	0	18	0	0	0
Did he put anything in your mouth?	18	0	0	0	18	0	0	0
Did he put anything in the other girl's (boy's) mouth?	17	1	0	0	18	0	0	0
Did he take a picture of you?	13	2	2	1	18	0	0	0
Did he take a picture of the other girl (boy)?	18	0	0	0	17	0	1	0
Did you touch him?	10	2	5	1	5	0	4	0
Did the other girl (boy) touch him?	11	0	5	2	9	0	7	2

also made the only two commission errors about spankings. He made no spontaneous comments in relation to these errors.

Three other commisssion errors were made by a single child. This boy was the most inaccurate child in the whole study and one of the most inaccurate children we have ever seen after testing more than 400 children in studies of this sort. He confused the visit to the trailer with a visit his class had just taken to an anatomy museum, and thus described blood and bones as having been in the trailer. He claimed that the man in the trailer had used a magic wand to make the other little boy disappear. He also gave some accurate testimony, but in a way that made it seem incredible: He said there had been a turtle in the trailer that flew through the air. In fact, there had been a turtle that flew through the air – it was one of the puppets that the confederate pretended could fly. The boy never qualified his response by indicating that the turtle was a puppet, which made his statement sound bizarre. The extent of this boy's inaccuracies is exceptional in our experience. It is important to note, however, that his commission errors were generally not the kind that would lead to a false accusation of abuse, especially in the context of his other bizarre statements. His worst error on the abuse questions was to say that the man had put a hot dog in the other boy's mouth. Interviewers in child abuse cases are instructed to determine the children's own words for genitals (e.g., Jones & McQuistin, 1986). Without knowing this little boy's terms for sexual anatomy, it is unclear how his response would be interpreted had he produced it in an actual investigation. It might well have caused concern, however.

Even for the 4-year-olds, omission errors on the abuse questions were more prevalent than commission errors. Twenty-two omission errors were made. As was true for the 7-year-olds, the 4-year-olds made the majority of these errors in response to the questions about touching. Given that so many of the errors were made to these questions, some discussion of them is warranted. These questions were intentionally vague in that they did not indicate what parts of the body might have been touched. Within the context of our questioning, it seemed to be unclear to children what constituted a touch: Was it a touch when the man helped the participant put on the costume? Is a tickle a touch? Is it a touch to tweak someone's nose, as they did in the Funny Things That Clowns Do game? Both the 7- and the 4-year-olds tended to add qualifiers to their answers to the touch questions, such as "I don't think so" or "Only to get the clown costume on," indicating that they felt our questions about touching were unclear. Or perhaps they realized our questions concerned inappropriate touching. One child recounted to us that there is good touch and bad touch, but that there had been no bad touch in the trailer.

Because most studies of children's testimony have not included questions that relate to abusive, embarrassing, or personally significant actions, we felt it would be enlightening to compare the children's responses to the abuse questions with their responses to the other action questions. These latter, nonabuse questions would be more comparable to those asked in previous research. If the children were more accurate in answering our abuse questions, it might suggest that former studies underestimated children's ability to provide accurate testimony about abuse-related actions. We conducted separate analyses for the specific and misleading abuse questions. For this purpose, we compared the children's answers to the abuse questions with their answers to the nonabuse questions. When the questions were divided into abuse and

Table 10.2. *Mean proportion of correct answers to misleading questions as a function of participation condition and type of question*

	Participation condition	
Type of question	Participants	Bystanders
Abuse	.91	.92
Nonabuse	.94	.79

nonabuse specific questions, the younger children provided fewer commission errors in response to the abuse, $M = .05$, as opposed to the nonabuse questions, $M = .09$; the same pattern held true for the 7-year-olds (who made very few errors), $M = .00$ and $M = .03$, respectively. Given that 95% of the 4-year-olds' answers to the abuse-specific questions were either correct, "don't know" responses, or omission errors, these findings suggest that children as young as 4 years of age can provide largely accurate testimony in response to specific questions that are particularly relevant in child abuse investigations.

The mean proportion of commission errors to the misleading questions were similarly analyzed. The participants, regardless of age, did not make a single commission error to the abuse or the nonabuse questions. Of the bystanders, only one 7-year-old made a commission error and it was to a nonabuse question. Only one 4-year-old bystander made any commission errors to the abuse questions, resulting in a group mean of .05 for this condition. On the other hand, the 4-year-old bystanders made an average of .13 commission errors to the nonabuse questions.

Interestingly, and in accord with our predictions, participants, $M = .93$, were more resistant than bystanders, $M = .86$, to suggestions about the actions, $F(1, 32) = 4.05$, $p = .05$. Given that the children's roles differed for the activities in the trailer, the action questions should be particularly sensitive to possible differences between the bystanders' and the participants' memories. This effect must be considered, however, in light of an interaction of participation condition with type of question, $F(1, 32) = 8.33$, $p < .01$ (see Table 10.2). The interaction reflects the fact that the participants' and bystanders' resistance to suggestion did not vary for the abuse questions: Both groups were highly resistant to these suggestions. The participants' and bystanders' resistance to suggestion did differ, however, for the nonabuse questions. The participants maintained a high resistance to suggestion, but the bystanders did not. This finding is important because most studies have examined the suggestibility of bystander witnesses when asked nonabuse questions, the kind of questions that led to the poorest performance in our study.

Children thus evidenced considerable accuracy in answering specific abuse questions and even in resisting strongly worded suggestions about actions associated with abuse. We also noticed that children's demeanor changed once we began to ask the abuse questions. Many showed signs of embarrassment by giggling or smiling. Others looked surprised. Some covered their eyes with their hands, puckered up their faces in disgust, asked in disbelief if we would repeat the question, or, if their parent was in the room during the questioning, glanced over at her or him in an act of "social referencing" (Klinnert, Campos, Sorce, Emde, & Svejda, 1983), with a look of "good grief!" on their faces. We scored the children's nonverbal responses to three of the most blatant abuse questions: "Did he kiss you?" "He took your clothes off, didn't he?" and "Did he hit you?" in comparison to the questions preceding that line of questioning, which mostly concerned the confederate's appearance. The children showed significant increases in smiling and surprise as soon as the abuse questions began.

The children were also asked to identify the "trailer man" in a blank lineup consisting of photographs of five men similar in appearance to the confederate, but not the confederate himself. The 7-year-olds made a greater number of correct nonidentifications, $M = .62$, than did the 4-year-olds, $M = .39$, although the difference was not reliable. It is disturbing that 38% of the 7-year-olds and 61% of the 4-year-olds made a false identification. In the majority of child abuse cases, however, the perpetrator is known to the child and identification of a stranger is not an issue (Goodman et al., 1988). Research indicates that children's identification of familiar persons is substantially better than their identification of strangers (Diamond & Carey, 1977), as is also true for adults (Bahrick, Bahrick, & Wittlinger, 1975).

In conclusion, the data indicate that even very young children can give accurate, unsuggested testimony about actions that are significant to them. If it were true that children within the age range we tested are highly suggestible in relation to questions about abuse, we might have seen many children make claims of abuse in response to our questioning. We did not.

In contrast, the children evidenced a number of weaknesses in their testimony. They made many false identifications on the blank photo-identification task. Their performance in answering questions about the timing of the event was poor. Thus, children show specific strengths and weaknesses in their testimony. At least by the age of 4 years, one of their strengths was in correctly answering questions that relate to physical safety and sexuality.

Nevertheless, a few 4-year-olds provided answers that might lead to the suspicion of child abuse (e.g., an affirmative response to a question about being hit or kissed). Such responses were given by so few children that it was difficult to identify factors predicting their performance.

Study 2: Children's use of anatomically detailed dolls

Although significant age differences were not evident in the children's ability to answer abuse questions, there was a hint that such differences might exist if even younger children were tested. Perhaps the few 4-year-olds who produced commission errors to the abuse questions were developmentally delayed compared to the other 4-year-olds. We therefore conducted a study in which 3-year-olds were included. Previous research indicates that 3-year-olds' performance on eyewitness testimony tasks is inferior to that of older children and adults in almost every way (e.g., Ceci et al., 1987; Goodman & Reed, 1986). These studies have not included questions directly related to children's physical safety or to sexually abusive acts, however. Therefore, it was still possible that even 3-year-olds would be resistant to the abuse suggestions. Nevertheless, we suspected that in addition to 3-year-olds' having general cognitive and memorial deficits, they might not fully understand the implications of many of our abuse questions. If, for example, they did not fully understand that some of the questions concerned acts that had sexual or embarrassing connotations (e.g., kissing, the removal of one's clothes), they might be more suggestible in regard to these questions than older children. After all, adults innocently kiss children and young children's clothes are taken off by some people, such as relatives and baby-sitters, without embarrassment or distress necessarily occurring.

Another interest was to examine the effects of stimulus support on children's testimony. Stimulus support has been shown to enhance young children's ability to report events (Price & Goodman, 1985), although it is not always successful in doing so (see Perlmutter, 1984, for a review). In the present case, we were interested in a very special type of stimulus support, namely, anatomically detailed dolls. These dolls are often used in investigations of child sexual abuse, on the assumption that children can demonstrate sexual acts that might be difficult or embarrassing for them to express verbally. The dolls have sexual characteristics such as breasts and penises and openings for orifices such as the mouth and vagina. Although the dolls were designed to provide stimulus support for accurate reporting, concern has been raised that the dolls may lead to false reports of abuse. Critics have argued that the dolls' sexual characteristics might falsely suggest abuse to children, elicit sexual fantasies, or lead interviewers to misinterpret children's play with and curiosity about the dolls' "privates" as signs of abuse. These effects, it is argued, would be especially likely to occur under conditions of suggestive questioning (e.g., Gabriel, 1985).

In our study, we investigated 3- and 5-year-olds' use of anatomically detailed dolls to report an event. Because our focus was again on whether false reports of abuse could be easily elicited from children, participants were engaged in a neutral, real-life experience rather than a stressful one. Specifically, 80 children (forty 3-year-olds and forty 5-year-olds) individually engaged in games, such as playing with a Hula-Hoop and pretending to have a tea party, with a male confederate. One week later the children were interviewed. The interview consisted of first having the children name body parts of dolls. They then recalled their interactions with our confederate. In the two doll conditions, the children were encouraged to show as well as tell what happened. Several other toy props such as two chairs and a distractor bed were available to the children. After they recalled/reenacted what happened, children in all groups answered a set of specific and misleading questions about the confederate's appearance and actions. A subset of the questions related to abuse; for example, we asked, "Did he touch your private parts?" "Did he keep his clothes on?" "Did he ask you to keep a secret about your private parts?" and "How many times did he spank you?" Within each age group, one-fourth of the children were interviewed with anatomically detailed dolls, one-fourth with regular dolls, one-fourth with dolls out of touch but in view, and one-fourth with no dolls in the room. The regular dolls were identical to the anatomically detailed ones except that they did not possess the sexual characteristics associated with anatomically detailed dolls. The four conditions permitted us to determine whether or not the use of anatomically detailed dolls leads to false reports of abuse and whether dolls, anatomically detailed or not, help or hinder children in recounting an event.

When the children's free recall/reenactment was analyzed so that both correct verbal responses and gestures were scored, the 5-year-olds communicated more correct information in both doll conditions than in the no-doll condition (see Table 10.3). The 3-year-olds' reports were not significantly affected by the presence or absence of dolls, although their mean performance was highest in the regular doll condition. When the children's responses were scored in terms of a checklist of the games played, the 5-year-olds recalled or reenacted more correct information than the 3-year-olds. On both measures, the age and doll groups did not differ in the amount of incorrect information communicated, although 3-year-olds, $M = .13$, verbally recalled a significantly greater proportion of incorrect information than 5-year-olds, $M = .04$.

On the specific questions overall, doll condition did not significantly

Table 10.3. *Mean number of correct items of information communicated by 3- and 5-year-olds as a function of doll condition (Study 2)*

	Age	
Doll condition	3-year-olds	5-year-olds
No dolls	7.40	9.70
Dolls in view	5.90	10.80
Regular dolls	10.50	20.50
Anatomically detailed dolls	5.30	16.80

Table 10.4. *Mean proportion of correct answers to specific questions as a function of age group and doll condition (Study 2)*

	Age	
Doll condition	3-year-olds	5-year-olds
No dolls	.67	.74
Dolls in view	.62	.73
Regular dolls	.58	.77
Anatomically detailed dolls	.52	.77

affect the children's accuracy, but age did (see Table 10.4). On the misleading questions overall, the 5-year-olds were again more accurate than the 3-year-olds, but the doll condition did not influence either age group's performance.

Again, we were particularly interested in the children's responses to abuse questions (see Table 10.5). The 3- and 5-year-olds differed reliably in the proportion of commission errors made to specific as well as misleading questions related to abuse, with 3-year-olds committing significantly more commission errors. Moreover, the younger 3-year-olds, $M = .36$, made significantly more commission errors than the older 3-year-olds, $M = .14$, $F(1, 57) = 12.50$, $p < .001$, on the misleading questions. Whether or not the children were interviewed with anatomically detailed dolls, regular dolls, dolls in view, or no dolls did not influence their responses to the specific or misleading abuse questions, however.[2]

Most of the commission errors made by the children would not be likely to lead to a prosecution of child abuse, with one prominent exception. Several 3-year-olds and a few 5-year-olds answered affirmatively to the questions about their private parts ("Did he touch your private

Table 10.5. *Proportion correct answers and commission errors to the abuse questions as a function of age and doll condition (Study 2)*

	Age	
	3-year-olds	5-year-olds
No dolls		
Specific questions		
Correct	.75	.79
Commission	.10	.02
Misleading questions		
Correct	.80	1.00
Commission	.20	.00
Dolls in view		
Specific questions		
Correct	.74	.74
Commission	.08	.06
Misleading questions		
Correct	.77	.93
Commission	.23	.07
Regular dolls		
Specific Questions		
Correct	.62	.78
Commission	.18	.02
Misleading questions		
Correct	.68	1.00
Commission	.32	.00
Anatomically detailed dolls		
Specific questions		
Correct	.62	.73
Commission	.19	.09
Misleading questions		
Correct	.73	.97
Commission	.27	.03

parts?" and "Did he ask you to keep a secret about your private parts?"). We therefore began asking the children where their private parts were. The children pointed to their ears, to their arms, and to other not so private places. Thus, we were using a term that the children did not understand. It should also be noted that when the children made commission errors to the abuse questions, these errors consisted almost entirely of nods of the head without any elaboration or detail.

In summary, age differences in answering the abuse questions did occur when children as young as 3 years were interviewed. Their greater suggestibility may result from deficits in the ability to encode or retain the original event (Brainerd & Reyna, 1988), from a lack of understanding of the implications of some of our questions, or from social factors, such as a desire to please the interviewer or the inability to resist intimidation. We examine this third possibility in connection with a study reported in a later section. In any case, the use of anatomically detailed dolls in and of itself did not increase the chances of obtaining a false report of abuse. Moreover, anatomically detailed and regular dolls helped the 5-year-olds recount what happened.

Children's testimony concerning stressful events

Study 3: The effects of stress and long delays

As mentioned earlier, it is important for the sake of ecological validity to understand children's memory and suggestibility about actions associated with abuse even in the context of neutral events. This is so because such research is responsive to claims that children can be easily led to make false reports even when nothing "bad" happened. It is also important to study children's testimony about more stressful events, ones that simulate acts of violence against a child. Such studies can provide valuable information on the effects of stress on children's reports.

It is commonly accepted in the eyewitness testimony literature that stress inhibits accuracy. This conclusion is based on the Yerkes–Dodson law and on research with adults in which various stress manipulations have been attempted, such as the viewing of violent films (e.g., Loftus & Burns, 1978). These studies have concentrated on bystander witnesses' memory for peripheral details or confederates' faces. The few studies to investigate victimization focused on the loss of possessions such as a watch or calculator (e.g., Hosch & Cooper, 1982; Leippe, Wells, & Ostrom, 1978). They did not investigate memory as a function of the stress produced by attacks on a person's body. Such studies are difficult to conduct because of the obvious ethical considerations.

Recently, researchers have avoided this problem by studying memory for naturally occurring stressful situations. Peters (1987), for example, examined children's memory of a visit to the dentist's office, with a focus on children's subsequent ability to recognize the dentist's face from target-present and target-absent photo lineups. On most of his measures, there was no significant relation between stress and anxiety. The vast majority of the children (95%) went to the dentist for checkups and teeth cleaning, however. Thus, the children's anxiety may not have reached high levels.

These findings not withstanding, there is reason to believe that high levels of stress will have a beneficial effect on memory. As discussed earlier, physiological studies show that high levels of stress are associated with better memory (Gold, 1987). Psychological studies reveal that events of high emotionality and personal significance are retained better than events of low emotionality and little personal significance (Keenan & Baillet, 1980; Linton, 1982).

Over the last few years, we investigated children's memory for naturally occurring stressful events. Specifically, we conducted a series of studies on children's reactions to stressful medical procedures (Goodman, Aman, & Hirschman, 1987; Goodman, Hepps, & Reed, 1986; Goodman, Hirschman, & Rudy, 1987), such as venipuncture and inoculations, which children receive as part of their standard health care. Several of these studies have been reported in detail elsewhere (see Goodman et al., 1987, for a review). Here, we present new data concerning the effects of stress and long delays on children's reports. In regard to the effects of stress on memory, we predicted that more highly stressed children would evidence better memory than less stressed children. In regard to the effect of delay on children's reports, we predicted that although the completeness and accuracy of children's memory would decrease over time, they would remain resistant to suggestion about actions associated with abuse.

We selected medical procedures, and inoculations in particular, because they are known to be stressful for many children. Children associate syringes with their least favorite part of going to the doctor's office (Steward & Steward, 1981), as many adults undoubtedly do. As Steward and Steward report, "medical procedures [are] embedded in an emotional context that is heavily weighted with negative feelings (fear, pain, abandonment, punishment, loss of control) . . . there is often extreme agitation and lack of compliance during a procedure" (p. 79). Thus, for our purposes, studying children's memory for inoculation experiences seemed close to ideal.

In one of our studies, forty-eight 3- to 6-year-old healthy children received inoculations at a medical clinic. Most of the children also received an oral polio vaccine. We did not impose the inoculations on the children or alter the clinic's practices in any way. The ages included reflected practical considerations. Children within this age range are still receiving the standardly prescribed sequence of inoculations and are required to receive certain vaccinations for entry into school. At it happens, children within this age range are particularly frightened by medical procedures. Melamud (1976) found that children under the age of 7 years are more emotional in response to all medical procedures than are older children.

Table 10.6. *Children's eyewitness testimony performance as a function of stress level (Study 3)*

Measure	Stress level			
	3	4	5	6
Number correct recall	3.46	3.24	3.25	5.20
Number incorrect recall	0.00	0.09	0.13	0.00
Proportion specific questions answered correctly	0.70	0.69	0.66	0.70
Proportion misleading questions answered correctly	0.56	0.63	0.44	0.82
Proportion correct identifications	0.62	0.33	0.25	0.40

Note: None of the children received a stress rating of 1 or 2.

We unobtrusively videotaped the children as they received their shots, and coded the children's reactions in terms of the stress the children evidenced. The children's reactions varied widely. Most looked frightened, but some were quite stoic, relatively unfazed, and said, "It didn't hurt." Others, however, became nearly hysterical. These children had to be physically restrained, often by two or three people. They cried, screamed, yelled for help, tried to run out of the room, and sobbed afterward while complaining that it hurt. In sum, they reacted as if they were being attacked. We know of no other scientific studies in which the stress levels were as high as they were for our most stressed children, perhaps the only exception being two studies involving adults reported by Baddeley (1972). Depending upon one's own experiences, readers can probably best envision the stress these children experienced by thinking back to their own childhood inoculations, to the times their own children received vaccines, or possibly to the experience of sitting in pediatric clinic waiting rooms and hearing other children scream as they receive their shots.

The stress ratings were coded on a scale ranging from 1 (*very happy* or *very relaxed*) to 6 (*very unhappy* or *very frightened*). After either 3 to 4 or 7 to 9 days, the children were interviewed about what happened. The children's performance as a function of their stress level is reported in Table 10.6.

Our general finding was that stress had a facilitative effect on the children's reports. Specifically, planned comparisons revealed that children at the highest stress levels recalled more information than the other children and were less suggestible. Interestingly, the children had to reach a level of great distress before beneficial effects on memory were evidenced. These effects were maintained even when the amount of time the child spent in the inoculation room was statistically controlled.

Because we could not randomly assign children to different stress groups, there was a possibility that the more stressed children differed in ways correlated with stress that could affect their memories. It might be argued, for instance, that the more intelligent children could better anticipate that the shot might hurt or that they could better remember the last time they received a shot. In an attempt to examine this possibility, a digit-span test was given to the children at the beginning of their interviews. Digit span correlates with IQ and serves as a common test of children's memory. The children's digit-span scores did not reliably differ as a function of stress level.

The highly stressed children's recall was more detailed than the less stressed children's. Here are some examples of their statements:

"I got a shot. I got a band aid on it. I got some stuff in my mouth. Gerald [his brother] was first. He spit it out on the floor. I didn't spit it out. It was gross. Then I went home and played and ride [sic] on my bike and went to my friends" (5-year-old).[3]

"They gave me my shots. My dad had to talk. They gave me two shots on the arms. Then I gave my dad's friend a stomp on the foot and gave my dad a kick in the shin. I don't want anyone holding and touching me because I get mean and that's all that happened. And then we left" (5-year-old).

These children's reports were completely accurate. Not a single error in free recall was made by the highly stressed children. It would not have been surprising if increased quantity of report had been accompanied by an increase in error, with highly stressed children saying more but providing no more accurate statements proportionally. Nevertheless, this did not happen; there was no effect of stress in terms of a greater number of inaccurate statements recalled.

The less-stressed children provided some very skeletal but still very accurate reports. For example:

"They gave me a shot" (6 ½-year-old).

"I got a shot on this leg" (points to his leg). "It hurt bad" (5-year-old).

It is noteworthy that the effects of stress on the children's ability to identify accurately the nurse who gave them the shot appeared to be in the direction opposite to the effects of stress on recall and suggestibility. Although this effect did not reach statistical significance, it nevertheless points to the possibility that our findings may be consistent with those of other studies showing adverse effects of stress on photo identification (see Deffenbacher, 1983, for a review).

When children suffer abuse, the experience may remain a secret for months or even years. When children become involved in child abuse

Table 10.7. *Children's eyewitness testimony performance one year after receiving their inoculations (Study 3)*

Measure	Time of test		
	Time 1 (3 to 9 days)	Time 2 (One year)	
Number correct recall	3.50	2.32	$p < .05$
Number incorrect recall	.04	.27	n.s.
Proportion specific questions answered correctly overall	.71	.67	n.s.
Action questions	.87	.73	$p < .05$
Person questions	.57	.66	n.s.
Room questions	.70	.61	n.s.
Central questions	.82	.70	$p < .05$
Peripheral questions	.52	.58	n.s.
Proportion misleading questions answered correctly overall	.64	.51	$p < .05$
Action questions	.75	.59	$p < .05$
Person questions	.62	.51	n.s.
Room questions	.54	.44	n.s.
Central questions	.68	.58	n.s.
Peripheral questions	.57	.47	n.s.
Identifications			
Correct	.50	.14	$p < .01$
False	.41	.32	n.s.

investigations, they are interviewed by authorities soon after disclosure, but again months if not years may elapse before a trial commences. Because such long delays are often involved in actual cases, we waited a year and reinterviewed as many children as we could find who had participated in the study just described. The delay we chose corresponds well to the delays experienced by child victim/witnesses who testify in court (Goodman et al., 1988). After the 1-year delay, we were able to find and reinterview 22 of the original 48 children. The interview was the same as before. We compared the accuracy of the 22 children's earlier reports with their reports after the long delay.

The findings are shown in Table 10.7. The children evidenced significant decreases on several memory measures: the amount of correct information recalled; the number of specific questions answered correctly about actions and about central information (which mostly consisted of action questions); and the ability to identify accurately the nurse in the photo identification task. The children also showed significant increases in their suggestibility generally and in their suggestibility about the ac-

Table 10.8. *Children's responses to the abuse questions initially and after a one year delay (Study 3) (in percentages)*

| | Time of test | | | | | |
| | Time 1 (3 to 9 days) $n = 48$ | | | Time 2 (one year) $n = 22$ | | |
Question	Correct	Omission	Commission	Correct	Omission	Commission
Did she hit you?	100	0	0	100	0	0
Did she kiss you?	96	0	4	95	0	0
Did she put any- thing in your mouth?	81	19	0	68	22	0
Did she touch you any place other than your arm?	50	50	0	50	22	14

Note: All percentages add to 100 when "don't know" responses are included.

tions that took place. The children did not, however, evidence a significant increase in the amount of incorrect information recalled, which still averaged less than one item of incorrect information per child. And they did not show significant declines in memory on several of the other measures. Nor did they make a significantly larger number of false identifications. (There was an increase in the number of "don't know" responses.) Unfortunately, too few of the high-stress children were reinterviewed to track the course of their initially more vivid memories.

We were particularly interested in how the children's responses to our "abuse" questions would fare. Only four such questions were included in the study, but it is instructive to examine the children's answers to them as a function of time (see Table 10.8). We included in this comparison the responses of all 48 children at the initial testing and of the 22 children at the 1-year testing. The pattern of the children's responses to the questions "Did she hit you?" and "Did she kiss you?" remained virtually unchanged. Even after a year, all of the children knew they had not been hit and all of them knew they had not been kissed. In response to the question "Did she put anything in your mouth?" there was a slight increase in omission errors and in "don't know" responses. When the children were asked, "Did she touch you anywhere other than your arm?" there was an increase in both "don't know" responses and in commission errors. When we examined the commission errors, none of them involved sexual touching. Rather, the children who made this error claimed, for example, that they had been touched on the wrist, the other arm, or the leg, when the videotape showed they had not been. Thus, despite the long delay, repeated questioning, and the leading nature of our interview, the children did not make false reports of abuse. It could be argued that the lack of false reports resulted in part because children do not expect nurses to abuse them. We agree that such expectations might have made the children less likely to say yes to the questions "Did she hit you?" and "Did she kiss you?" It should be noted, however, that children also do not expect teachers, church officials, Boy Scout leaders, and baby-sitters to abuse them, yet such people have been accused fairly often in child abuse cases. Thus, our findings are still relevant to such cases.

Study 4: Improving young children's reports

So far we have seen that children by the age of 4 years are, on average, quite resistant to suggestions about abuse; that anatomically detailed dolls do not in and of themselves lead to false reports; that high levels of stress actually strengthen rather than detract from memory; and that even after a year's time, children still know whether they have been abused or not. But we have also seen that 3-year-olds and some 4-year-olds make more commission errors on abuse questions than other children do.

We were intrigued by the young children's suggestibility and by what might cause it. Two factors indicated by former research are the interviewer's status and degree of intimidation. In eyewitness testimony studies, it has been found that 3-year-olds, compared to older children and adults, tend to look less at the confederate (Goodman & Reed, 1986), indicating that the younger children are more shy and easily intimidated. The status of an interviewer, whether the interviewer is an adult or another child, for example, can also influence children's suggestibility (Ceci et al., 1987; but see Brigham, Van Verst, & Bothwell, 1986). We therefore sought a way to lessen the intimidation produced by an adult interviewer. "Being nice" came to mind.

Clinicians and developmental psychologists typically begin their interviews with children by building rapport. Substantial encouragement of children and reinforcement of their performance are often required to keep them interested and involved in interviews and experiments. Nevertheless, in actual investigations of child abuse, interviewers have been severely criticized for these behaviors. Critics claim, for example, that the responsiveness and encouragement children receive during interviews might lead to false reports because the interviewer would reinforce inaccuracies. We were therefore interested in the effects of such "reinforcements" on children's reports.

In our study, 72 children, ranging in age from 3 to 7 years, were interviewed about their inoculations after either 2 or 4 weeks. The children were divided into two age groups, 3- to 4-year-olds and 5- to 7-year-olds. Half of the children in each age group were interviewed in a "reinforcement" condition. These children were given considerable support and encouragement during the interview. At several points, the children were complimented for their performance, regardless of their accuracy. The interviewer smiled frequently, and the children received cookies and juice. In the no-reinforcement condition, the interviewer was more distant. For example, the interviewer was permitted to say "Okay" and "All right," but not to comment positively on the children's performance. The interviewer smiled less and the children did not receive cookies or juice. Regardless of reinforcement condition, the children were asked a set of specific and misleading questions, including a subset of abuse questions. We restrict our discussion here to the abuse questions, most of which were misleading; for example, "She touched your bottom, didn't she?" "How many times did she kiss you?"

The results of the study were quite informative. The reinforcement condition did not affect the older children's error rate to the abuse questions. They made an equal proportion of commission errors with reinforcement, $M = .09$, or without it, $M = .08$. In contrast, reinforcement had a significant effect on the younger children's answers. The 3- to 4-year-olds made twice as many commission errors to the abuse questions in the no-reinforcement, $M = .23$, as in the reinforcement, $M = .10$, condition. In fact, in the reinforcement condition, the younger and older children's performances were nearly identical; the use of reinforcement brought the younger children's performance up. The interaction of age group and reinforcement was significant, $F(1, 62) = 4.20, p < .05$. When encouraged and supported, the younger children typically knew that they had not been hit or kissed and that their clothes had not been removed or their bottoms touched. Thus these children were best able to resist adult suggestions about such actions when they were made comfortable enough to do so.

Conclusion

Freud believed that children are easily led to fantasize sexually and even physically abusive events (Freud, 1905/1963; Freud, 1919/1963). Many contemporary psychologists and psychiatrists have also claimed that children are so suggestible that they can easily be led into false reports of abuse. It may be possible to obtain false reports if one relies on nods of the head by 3-year-olds, but we have so far never seen a 3-year-old provide any sexualized detail. By the age of 4 years, most children we have tested are surprisingly resistant to abuse suggestions. Thus, producing false reports of abuse in children has not been easy. Why?

The answer may lie in the fact that child abuse involves actions directed against a child's body, actions that violate their concerns. These acts also violate children's expectations, which may additionally bolster their memory. But there is undoubtedly more to it than that. The violation of trivial expectations would probably not be very memorable. The violation of one's body is.

According to Piagetian theory, children's earliest organizations involve their bodies. Development seems to flow from self-organization outward. For example, infants' primary circular reactions tend to involve their bodies and children's egocentrism consists of relating information to the self. A focus on the self may be one of nature's ways of promoting self-protection.

Much previous research, starting at the turn of the century and continuing into the 1980s, indicates that children are highly suggestible (e.g., Berenda, 1950; Ceci et al., 1987; Dale et al., 1978; Marple, 1933; Varendonck, 1911; Whipple, 1912; see also Loftus, 1979). They clearly are more suggestible than adults about some kinds of information, particularly information that is not remembered as well (Goodman, Aman, & Hirschman, 1987; Goodman & Reed, 1986). But the study of children's concerns demonstrates that resisting suggestion, like most cognitive abilities, shows considerable unevenness or decalage (Fischer, 1980). It is influenced by age but also by how memorable certain information is (Goodman & Reed, 1986) and, moreover, by the social context under which children are tested. Young children are easily intimidated and cannot necessarily evidence their skills in all contexts.

Unevenness in children's abilities across tasks and contexts has important implications for ecological validity. We may well under- or overestimate children's ability to provide accurate testimony when we test children's memory and suggestibility in artificial situations and for trivial stimuli. The evidence presented in this chapter, supported by work in other laboratories (e.g., Ochsner & Zaragoza, 1988), indicates that the tendency has been toward underestimation. The field of memory development evolved from a study of children's memory for artificial stimuli in decontextualized laboratory tasks to one of greater ecological validity. The study of children's testimony requires a similar transition.

This is not to say that any one study can simulate everything that children experience in legal settings. Because every case is different this would be an impossible task. Rather, it is to say that our studies need to match as closely as possible important aspects of children's experiences, and that in our conclusions we need to guard against overgeneralization.

In an attempt to follow our own advice, we would like to mention several caveats regarding our own findings. Our studies mainly address children's testimony about one-time events experienced with unfamiliar people. We did not test children's memory about repeated events or the actions of familiar people. Moreover, we did not conduct as many repeated interviews as children often experience in actual cases. None of the children had been taken out of their homes or had reason to fear that they might be. We did not imply to the children that our confederates were criminals, and we did not pose as legal authorities. Moreover, our children did not undergo direct or cross-examination as might take place in a courtroom. And the children had no reason to lie to us as they might if they were trying to protect a loved one. Thus, even though we have attempted to conduct more ecologically valid studies in relation to child abuse cases than have heretofore been attempted, the generality of our findings is still open to question.

The ecological validity of studies of children's testimony affects not only our understanding of children's development but also the lives of those who partake, as victims or defendants, in actual cases. Currently, there is such great concern with children's testimony that findings in this area are almost immediately applied to actual cases, even if researchers do not mean them to be, or even if researchers propose to be investigating only theoretical issues. These studies are nevertheless used to gauge the accuracy of actual child witnesses. Because they influence whether a victimized child receives protection, on the one hand, or an innocent person is falsely convicted, on the other, it is not enough to worry solely about the internal validity of our studies. External validity is also of paramount importance.

Our research indicates that children's concerns, such as a desire for personal safety, influence the quality of their testimony. Children are more resistant to suggestion about personally significant actions than one would predict based on previous research. We believe that children's concerns also effect memory generally. In fact, it is unlikely that a complete theory of memory development can ignore this importance influence. The study of children's testimony about abusive actions provides one window into the corner of children's minds that deals with their concerns. Through this window we may gain important insights both for psychology and for justice.

NOTES

The research reported in this article was supported by grants to Gail S. Goodman from the Department of Health and Human Services and from the W. T. Grant Foundation (the latter awarded through the Developmental Psychobiology Research Group, Department of Psychiatry, University of Colorado Health Sciences

Center). We are grateful to: Migima Company for donating several anatomically detailed dolls for use in Study 2; Marilyn Shahan (Head Nurse), Dr. Franklin Judson (Director Disease Control Center), and the entire staff of the Colorado State Department of Health and Hospital's Immunization Clinic in Denver for permitting us to conduct Studies 3 and 4 on their premises; Phillip Shaver for editing suggestions; and Stewart Beyerle, Patricia England, Jodi Hirschman, Daniel MacIntosh, Annette Rice, and Christine Wilson for research assistance.

1 In considering whether children remember what did not as well as what did happen, we were reminded of Piaget's often cited example of how he "remembered" being kidnapped as an infant only to find out years later that the kidnapping never occurred. It is possible that children will be more susceptible to suggestion when the suggestions relate to the period of life associated with infantile amnesia. In any case, it should also be kept in mind that Piaget's example is an anecdote and is not scientifically based.

2 For the present report of this study, children's responses to the abuse questions were scored as commission errors if they indicated actions consistent with abuse. For example, in response to the question "Show me where he touched you?" the child had to indicate genital touching or the like for a commission error to be scored.

3 The children's recall was scored based on the videotape made at the clinic. We did not score the children's statements about what they did after they left the clinic.

REFERENCES

Angelino, H., Dollins, D., & Mech, E. V. (1956). Trends in the "fears and worries" of school children as related to socio-economic status and age. *Journal of Genetic Psychology, 89*, 263–276.

Baddeley, A. D. (1972). Selective attention and performance in dangerous environments. *British Journal of Psychology, 63*, 537–546.

Bahrick, H. P., Bahrick, P. O., & Wittlinger, R. P. (1975). Fifty years of memory for names and faces: A cross-sectional approach. *Journal of Experimental Psychology: General, 104*, 54–75.

Berenda, R. W. (1950). *The influence of the group on the judgments of children.* New York: King's Crown Press.

Bohannon, J. N. (1988). Flashbulb memories for the space shuttle disaster. *Cognition, 29*, 179–196.

Brainerd, C. J., & Reyna, V. F. (1988). Memory loci of suggestibility development: Comment on Ceci, Ross, and Toglia (1987). *Journal of Experimental Psychology: General, 117*, 197–200.

Brigham, J., Van Verst, M., & Bothwell, R. K. (1986). Accuracy of children's eyewitness identifications in a field setting. *Basic and Applied Social Psychology, 7*, 295–306.

Brown, P., Keenan, J. M., & Potts, G. R. (1986). The self-referencing effect with imagery encoding. *Journal of Personality and Social Psychology, 51*, 897–906.

Ceci, S. J., Ross D. F., & Toglia, M. P. (1987). Suggestibility of children's memory: Psycholegal implications. *Journal of Experimental Psychology: General, 116*, 38–49.

Cohen, R. L., & Harnick, M. A. (1980). The susceptibility of child witnesses to suggestion. *Law and Human Behavior, 4*, 201–210.

Dale, P. S., Loftus, E. F., & Rathbun, L. (1978). The influence of the form of the question on the eyewitness testimony of preschool children. *Journal of Psycholinguistic Research, 7,* 269–277.

Deffenbacher, K. (1983). The influence of arousal on reliability of testimony. In B. R. Clifford & S. Lloyd-Bostock (Eds.), *Evaluating eyewitness evidence* (pp. 235–251). Chichester: Wiley.

DeLoache, J., Cassidy, D. J., & Brown, A. L. (1985). Precursors of mnemonic strategies in very young children's memory. *Child Development, 56,* 125–137.

Diamond, R., & Carey, S. (1977). Developmental changes in the representation of faces. *Journal of Experimental Child Psychology, 23,* 1–22.

Donaldson, M. (1978). *Children's minds.* New York: Norton.

Edelmann, R. J. (1987). *The psychology of embarrassment.* New York: Wiley.

Fischer, K. W. (1980). A theory of cognitive development: The control and construction of hierarchies of skills. *Psychological Review, 87,* 477–531.

Fischer, K. W., Shaver, P., & Carnochan, P. (1989). From basic- to subordinate-category emotions. In W. Damon (Ed.), *Child development today and tomorrow* (pp. 107–136). San Francisco: Jossey-Bass.

Fivush, R., Gray, J., & Fromhoff, F. A. (1987). Two-year-olds talk about the past. *Cognitive Development, 2,* 393–409.

Freud, S. (1963). My views on the part played by sexuality in the aetiology of the neuroses. In P. Rieff (Ed.), *Sexuality and the psychology of love.* New York: Macmillan. Originally published in 1905.

Freud, S. (1963). A child is being beaten. In P. Rieff (Ed.), *Sexuality and the psychology of love.* New York: Macmillan. Originally published in 1919.

Frijda, N. (1986). *The emotions.* New York: Cambridge University Press.

Gabriel, R. M. (1985). Anatomically correct dolls in the diagnosis of sexual abuse of children. *Journal of the Melanie Klein Society, 3,* 40–51.

Garcia, J., & Koelling, R. (1966). Relation of cue to consequence in avoidance learning. *Psychonomic Science, 4,* 123–24.

Gold, P. E. (1987). Sweet memories. *American Scientist, 75,* 151–155.

Goldman, R., & Goldman, J. (1982). *Children's sexual thinking.* London: Routledge & Kegan Paul.

Goldman, R., & Goldman, J. (1988). *Show me yours: Understanding children's sexuality.* Ringwood, Australia: Penguin Books.

Goodman, G. S., Aman, C., & Hirschman, J. (1987). Child sexual and physical abuse: Children's testimony. In S. J. Ceci, M. P. Toglia, & D. F. Ross (Eds.), *Children's eyewitness memory* (pp. 1–23). New York: Springer-Verlag.

Goodman, G. S., Hepps, D., & Reed, R. S. (1986). The child victim's testimony. In A. Haralambie (Ed.), *New issues for child advocates* (pp. 167–177). Phoenix: Arizona Association of Council for Children.

Goodman, G. S., Hirschman, J., & Rudy, L. (1987, April). Children's testimony: Research and policy implications. In S. Ceci, (Chair), *Children as witnesses: Research and social policy implications.* Symposium conducted at the meeting of the Society for Research in Child Development, Baltimore, MD.

Goodman, G. S., Jones, D. P. H., Pyle, E., Prado, L., Port, L. P., England, T., Mason, R., & Rudy, L. (1988). The emotional effects of criminal court testimony on child sexual assault victims: A preliminary report. In G. Davies & J. Drinkwater (Eds.), *The child witness: Do the courts abuse children?* Oxford: British Psychological Association.

Goodman, G. S., & Reed, R. S. (1986). Age differences in eyewitness testimony. *Law and Human Behavior, 10,* 317–332.

Hosch, H. M., & Cooper, D. S. (1982). Victimization as a determinant of eyewitness accuracy. *Journal of Applied Psychology, 67*, 649–652.

Jackson, S. J. (1982). *Children and sexuality.* Oxford: Basil Blackwell.

Jersild, A. T., & Holmes, F. B. (1935). Children's fears. *Child Development Monographs, 20*, 358.

Johnson, M. K., & Foley, M. A. (1984). Differentiating fact from fantasy: The reliability of children's memory. *Journal of Social Issues, 40*, 33–50.

Jones, D. P. H., & McQuistin, M. (1986). *Interviewing the sexually abused child.* Denver: C. Henry Kempe National Center.

Keenan, J. M., & Baillet, S. D. (1980). Memory for personally and socially relevant events. In R. S. Nickerson (Ed.), *Attention and performance* (Vol. 8, pp. 651–669). Hillsdale, N.J.: Erlbaum.

Keenan, J. M., MacWhinney, B., & Mayhew, D. (1977). Pragmatics in memory: A study of natural conversation. *Journal of Verbal Learning and Verbal Behavior, 16*, 549–560.

King, M. A. (1984). *An investigation of the eyewitness abilities of children.* Unpublished doctoral dissertation, University of British Columbia.

Klinnert, M., Campos, J., Sorce, J., Emde, R., & Svejda, M. (1983). Emotions as behavior regulators: Social referencing in infancy. In R. Plutchik & H. Kellerman (Eds.), *Emotions in early development: Vol. 2. The emotions* (pp. 57–86). New York: Academic Press.

Leippe, M. R., Wells, G. L., & Ostrum, T. M. (1978). Crime seriousness as a determinant of accuracy in eyewitness identification. *Journal of Applied Psychology, 63*, 345–351.

Lentz, K. (1985). Fears and worries of young children as expressed in a contextual play setting. *Journal of Child Psychology and Psychiatry, 26*, 981–987.

Lewis, M., & Michaelson, L. (1983). *Children's emotions and moods: Developmental theory and measurement.* New York: Plenum.

Linton, M. (1982). Transformations of memory in everyday life. In U. Neisser (Ed.), *Memory observed: Remembering in natural contexts* (pp. 71–91). New York: W. H. Freeman.

Loftus, E. F. (1979). *Eyewitness testimony.* Cambridge, MA: Harvard University Press.

Loftus, E. F., & Burns, T. E. (1978). Mental shock can produce retrograde amnesia. *Memory and Cognition, 10*, 318–323.

Marple, C. H. (1933). The comparative suggestibility of three age levels to the suggestion of group versus expert opinion. *Journal of Social Psychology, 4*, 176–184.

Melamud, B. G. (1976). Psychological preparations for hospitalizations. In S. Rachman (Ed.), *Contributions to medical psychology* (pp. 43–74). Oxford: Pergamon.

Miller, P. J., & Sperry, L. L. (1988). Early talk about the past: The origins of conversational stories of personal experience. *Journal of Child Language, 15*, 293–315.

Nelson, K. (1986). *Event knowledge: Structure and function in development.* Hillsdale, NJ: Erlbaum.

Ochsner, J. E., & Zaragoza, M. S. (1988, March). *The accuracy and suggestibility of children's memory for neutral and criminal eyewitness events.* Paper presented at the American Psychology and Law Association Meetings, Miami, FL.

Pear, T. H., & Wyatt, S. (1914). The testimony of normal and mentally defective children. *British Journal of Psychology, 3*, 388–419.

Perlmutter, M. (1984). Continuities and discontinuities in early human memory paradigms, processes, and performance. R. Kail & N. Spear (Eds.), *Comparative perspectives on the development of memory* (pp. 253–286). Hillsdale, NJ: Erlbaum.

Peters, D. P. (1987). The impact of naturally occurring stress on children's memory. In S. J. Ceci, M. P. Toglia, & D. F. Ross (Eds.), *Children's eyewitness memory* (pp. 122–141). New York: Springer-Verlag.

Pillemer, D. B., & White, S. H. (1989). Childhood events recalled by children and adults. In H. W. Reese (Ed.), *Advances in child development and behavior* (Vol. 21, pp. 297–340). New York: Academic Press.

Pullyblank, J., Bisanz, J., Scott, C., & Champion, M. A. (1985). Developmental invariance in the effects of functional self-knowledge on memory. *Child Development, 56,* 1447–1454.

Price, D., & Goodman, G. S. (1985, April). *Preschool children's comprehension of a recurring episode.* Paper presented at the meeting of the Society for Research in Child Development, Toronto.

Rapaport, D. (1942). *Emotions and memory.* Baltimore: Williams & Wilkins.

Rogers, T. B., Kuiper, N. A., & Kirker, W. S. (1977). Self-reference and the encoding of personal information. *Journal of Personality and Social Psychology, 35,* 677–688.

Saywitz, K. J. (1987). Children's testimony: Age-related patterns of memory errors. In S. J. Ceci, M. P. Toglia, & D. F. Ross (Eds.), *Children's eyewitness memory* (pp. 36–52). New York: Springer-Verlag.

Seidner, L. B., Stipek, D. J., & Feshbach, N. D. (1988). A developmental analysis of elementary school-aged children's concepts of pride and embarrassment. *Child Development, 59,* 367–377.

Seligman, M. E. P. (1970). On the generality of the laws of learning. *Psychological Review, 77,* 406–418.

Slackman, E. A., Hudson, J. A., & Fivush, R. (1986). Actions, actors, links, and goals: The structure of children's event representations. In K. Nelson (Ed.), *Event knowledge* (pp. 47–70). Hillsdale, NJ: Erlbaum.

Steward, M. S., & Steward, D. S. (1981). Children's conceptions of medical procedures. In R. Bibace and M. E. Walsh (Eds.), *Children's conceptions of health, illness, and bodily functions* (New directions for child development, No. 14, pp. 67–84). San Francisco: Jossey-Bass.

Todd, C. M., & Perlmutter, M. (1980). Reality recalled by preschool children. In M. Perlmutter (Ed.), *Children's memory* (New directions in child development, No. 10, pp. 69–86). San Francisco: Jossey-Bass.

Yamamoto, K., Soliman, A., Parsons, J., & Davies, O. L., Jr. (1987). Voices in unison: Stressful events in the lives of children in six countries. *Journal of Child Psychology and Psychiatry, 28,* 855–864.

Varendonck, J. (1911). Les tesmoignages d'enfants dans un proces retentissant. *Archives de Psychologie, 11,* 129–171.

Watson, J. (1966). The development and generalization of "contingency" awareness in early infancy: Some hypotheses. *Merrill-Palmer Quarterly, 12,* 123–135.

Whipple, G. M. (1912). Psychology of testimony and report. *Psychological Bulletin, 9,* 264–269.

White, S., & Quinn, K. (1988). Investigatory independence in child sexual abuse evaluations: Conceptual considerations. *Bulletin of the American Academy of Psychiatry and Law, 16,* 269–278.

11

The suggestibility of preschoolers' recollections: Historical perspectives on current problems

STEPHEN J. CECI, MICHAEL P. TOGLIA, AND
DAVID F. ROSS

In the year 1692 a strange series of events took place in and around Salem Village and Salem Farms, Massachusetts. During the period between June 10 and September 19 at least 20 residents of Salem were accused, tried, and convicted of being witches and wizards by the Salem magistrates. Sentencing was swift; all 20 were hung, burned, or pressed to death. An additional 10 persons were convicted but not executed. In the villages surrounding Salem, from Andover to Wells, the historical record shows that more than 100 others were accused of witchcraft. Although no record is available to discern how many of these were convicted and executed, surely some, and perhaps many, were.

The important aspect of this epoch in American history for us today is the crucial role played by children in the Salem witch trials. The charges of practicing witchcraft were made primarily by children, the so-called circle girls. Not only were children the accusers, they were often the "evidence," purporting to have been physically afflicted by the defendants. For example, the vomiting of bent nails and pins during the trials were alleged to have been the work of the defendants, as was going into apoplectic fits and total paralysis at the sight of them. Finally, children often were the principal witnesses for the state: Little Ann Putnam alone testified in 19 cases and her friends Elizabeth Hubbard testified in 20, Mary Walcott in 16, and Mary Warren in 12. Between them, they provided the key eyewitness testimony that led to the conviction of all but one of those accused in Salem.

In this chapter we delve into the sociocultural context of the Salem trials for clues that could help us to better understand contemporary cases in which children have given eyewitness testimony that, upon cross-examination, has turned out to be as fabulous and contrived as that provided by the children of Salem. Following this expedition backward in time, we shall review some recent experimental findings of ours and others that indicate some of the factors that influence children's susceptibility to erroneous postevent suggestions. Finally, we conclude by mentioning the important caveats regarding ecological validity needed be-

285

fore advocates, policy makers, and jurists can make generalizations based on current psychological research in this area.

The children of Salem

Despite the attempts of writers from succeeding generations to make sense of these events (e.g., Gemmill, 1924; Nevins, 1892), it is fair to say we remain largely puzzled about some aspects of the Salem witch trials. It is unknown, for example, whether the child accusers had deliberately misled the Salem elders about their observations or whether they truly were convinced of the accuracy of their testimony. Similarly, it is unclear how such otherwise reasonable and astute magistrates and jurors could accept the inconsistencies and the often fabulous nature of the children's recollections.

As an aside, it is unfortunate that these individuals have so often been maligned in both popular and "historical" accounts of the Salem trials. Their behavior at the time of the trials was, more often than not, quite reasonable, save for one or two individuals who were clearly guilty of excesses. For instance, the adults of Salem frequently devised clever tests and experiments to determine the veracity of the children's accounts. When one child went into a paralytic fit upon the sight of the accused, which according to tradition could only be removed by the touch of a real witch, the magistrates had her blindfolded and touched by someone other than the accused to determine whether she was feigning bewitchment. When two sisters had vomited more than 30 pins during a pretrial hearing, adults removed all pins from their clothing and stitched them instead, so that they would not be able to find pins to consume, if that was what they had done. In short, the adults at that time were not particularly irrational or hysterical, and therefore attempts to describe them in that way are not likely to help us understand those times or the possibility of modern parallels.

Within little more than a decade following the Salem witch trials, most of the adults – including the ministers, magistrates, and jurors – acknowledged their errors and offered repentance for the role they played in the trials. Several of the child accusers also recanted and begged the forgiveness of the survivors of defendants who had been executed. Yet it is not exactly clear what to make of these recantations, as all of these persons (child and adult alike) continued to believe in witchery and in the validity of such practices as vestral apparitions. No one, to our knowledge, ever stopped believing that witches walked among them, inhabiting the bodies of innocents and afflicting others. All continued to believe that witches should be pursued and prosecuted, including even some of the most notable dissenters at the Salem trials. Consider the confession made by Ann Putnam – the most notorious of the child accusers – to the pastor of the Village Church in 1706.

> I desire to be humbled before God for that sad and humbling providence that befell my father's family in the year 1692: that I, then being in my childhood, should by such a providence of God, be made an instrument for the accusing of several persons of a grievous crime, whereby their lives were taken away from them, whom now I have just grounds and good reason to believe they were innocent persons; and that it was a great delusion of Satan that deceived me in that sad time, whereby I justly fear that I have been instrumental, with others, though ignorantly and unwitting, to bring upon myself and this land the guilt of innocent blood; though what was said or done by me against any person I can truly say and uprightly say before God and man, I did it not out of anger, mallice or ill-will to any person, for I had no such thing against . . . them, but what I did was ignorantly, being deluded of satan . . . I desire to lie in the dust, and to be humbled for it, in that I was the cause, with others of so sad a calamity to them and their families. (From the Witchcraft Papers, State House, Boston, cited in Nevins, 1892, p. 250)

How can we make sense of such recantations? It is evident that Ann Putnam, and others who joined with her in providing eyewitness testimony against those accused of practicing witchcraft, bore no malice toward any of them. So what induced her and the others to become a "deluded instrument of Satan"? To answer this question we need to understand the social and cultural context in which the circle girls were recruited to provide their testimony. By unearthing that context we may be in a better position to understand some of the modern parallels in which children have testified of having seen adults participate in criminal acts that later turned out to be fictitious.

To begin with, at the time leading up to the witch trials, Salem was an emotionally charged place, with accounts of witchcraft commonplace. *Everyone* believed in the power of witches; over the course of the 100 years preceding the trials there evolved a set of expectations in both the American colonies and in Europe about the customs of witches. These expectations included special "devil markings" that were supposed to appear on the bodies of witches; these might be discolorations, birthmarks, transient blushes, and so forth. Often they were thought to take on the resemblance of animals, especially rams. (In retrospect, the zeal with which those accused of being witches were examined for devil's marks would be quite humorous, were the practice not so deadly serious. The accused were often stripped to the waist in public, and if this did not result in blush spots anywhere on the body, their interior eyelids, lips, and so on were scutinized for marks that might resemble animals.) In addition to devil's marks, witches were also expected to possess "witches' marks" – protuberances, such as warts and moles, from which Satan's milk supposedly flowed.

The acceptance by the public of other expectations about the practices and characteristics of witches can be charted over the century as well. It came to be expected, for example, that witches attended sabbats, or local meetings, at which the devil appeared. These seem to have been sexual and emotional orgies, according to the written accounts of persons who attended. Around the middle of the 17th century, the symbols of dark animals, especially black cats, and flying broomsticks became part of the accepted lore about witches, with abundant stories about those accused of witchery assuming the bodies of animals. One of the signs that some-one was a witch, which appeared around this time, was if death or mis-chief followed their cursing. Of the many forms of mischief, a common one was the vomiting of crooked nails. Numerous accounts appear in which children who provided testimony against the witches would vomit nails and bent pins, sometimes 30 or more at once, in the presence of magistrates, jurors, and onlookers. Witches were thought to implant the nails in the stomachs of the children through several means, for instance, by having a bumblebee fly into their mouths to leave the pins. That children did vomit nails and pins can hardly be doubted: Numerous public records attest to such behavior.

Thus, the close of the 17th century found the villagers in Salem living amid a widespread – indeed, universal – belief in the reality of witches and a set of expectations about their behavior and appearance. It was a time when one was particularly careful to avoid any display of behaviors that resembled those of witches, unless, of course, one was deranged and wished to be thought of as a witch. (This was undoubtedly true of some of the defendants.)

Aside from the social conditions existing in Salem in 1692, what were the characteristics of the children who gave eyewitness accounts of defen-dants turning themselves into cats, flying over their pastures on broom-sticks, and instructing insects to implant crooked nails in their stomachs? These children fell into two categories: those whose own behaviors were suspicious and therefore whose testimony can be viewed as a means of diverting attention from themselves; and those whose parents actively encouraged and shaped their "recollections." Some of the older children had been tutored in the ways of witches by an individual who had come from the West Indies and was the maid of a local minister. She told the girls about the practices of witches, and it appears that the girls in turn told their friends. At these tutorials, the children engaged in unusual practices that began to draw attention to themselves (e.g., they crawled on their hands and knees and made strange sounds). From all accounts, some of these girls were prone to neurotic bouts of anxiety and depres-sion. When their behavior began to draw attention, they were among the first to accuse others. To bolster their accusations, they reported having observed the defendants exhibit many of the commonly expected characteristics just mentioned. More will not be said about these cases, as the motive of the accusers was apparent.

Several of the earliest cases in Salem involved individuals who were not on good terms with some of the village elders. One man had incurred the wrath of an elder for neglecting to pay his rum bill; another, because she had insulted a fishmonger's wife over a sale; and still another, because he testified on behalf of his son in a claim brought against him by a member of the Putnam family for driving two horses into a river, where they drowned. These cases and others like them illustrate that there often were adults who were motivated to seize on the children's accusations and encourage them to elaborate, always providing leading questions and positive attention for answers congruent with the charge of witchcraft. Thus, parents, ministers, and judges frequently tried to persuade children that they had in fact observed some occurrence of witchery, believing that if the children really had no such observation, it would become evident. This setting was perfect to bias children's recollections. The Salem records vividly illustrate the use of suggestive questions, biased prompts, and so on. But one final ingredient needs to be mentioned in order to understand fully what transpired in 1692. It concerns the cultural zeitgeist regarding the innocence of children.

At the time of Salem, it was commonly thought that "breaking the will or spirit of a child" was an important means of discipline. It was a time when our forefathers took literally the biblical aphorism Out of the mouths of babes cometh forth truth. Adults believed that a child's innocence enabled him or her to recognize evils that they as adults could not – by virtue of their having dwelt in a tainted world. Anyone so evil as to make a pact with the devil (an act supposedly engaged in by witches) could be recognized by an innocent child for their vileness. Adults not only *could* accept a child's testimony in this regard, they *had* to accept it because their lost innocence compromised their own ability to recognize evil. This appears to have been an important aspect of colonial culture; it encouraged adult interrogators to pursue vigorously children's consciences for evidence of witchcraft against the defendants because the same innocence that enabled children to recognize evil would protect them from confabulations in the face of intense suggestions. Thus, we now have the cultural basis for the seemingly strange recollections of the child witnesses in Salem. The child witnesses were relentlessly questioned, and from the few accounts of the actual interviews it is clear that the interviews were made up of leading questions and repeated insinuations. It is unsurprising that some children eventually turned evidence against even their parents, reporting to have seen them flying on broomsticks and turning their bodies into black cats. In fact, the "social" context of children's remembering cannot be understood in the absence of this cultural context. Breaking children's spirit, coupled with the belief in their innocence, fueled the events at that sad time.

We have gone over these early accounts of the Salem witch trials because we think it informs our present appreciation of some contemporary parallels. Throughout most of the Middle Ages, children younger than 14 were not permitted to give testimony. This rule was suspended to make it possible for children to testify in the Salem witch trials. For the next 200 years the courts noted the excesses of the Salem children and used this example repeatedly during the 19th and 20th centuries as grounds for not allowing their uncorroborated testimony. Today the pendulum has swung back toward permitting children's participation in courts. Children have increasingly regained the opportunity to offer eyewitness testimony, as states have abandoned the corroboration rule in cases of sexual abuse, and Federal Rules of Evidence are tilted in favor of accepting all witnesses as competent, regardless of age or mental status. As a positive consequence of the abandonment of corroboration rules, more and more perpetrators of crimes against children have been convicted on the weight of the child victim's testimony, or pleaded guilty during pretrial bargaining on the assumption that the child's testimony would result in such conviction. The negative side of this trend has been that more and more instances of incredible assertions and recantations are appearing in newspapers. The nationally reported cases in Jordan, Minnesota, and in both El Escondido and Bakersfield, California, are just several recent examples in which children alleged that they saw adults abusing and even killing children, only to recant later when their "recollections" were shown to be physically impossible.

If we look at some of the testimony offered by children in these cases, we find some interesting parallels to the children in Salem. In the summer of 1985 in Bakersfield, California, a group of children alleged that adults, including some of their parents, had engaged in satanic practices that included animal sacrifice and drinking of blood, which culminated in sexual abuse of the children. After a lengthy investigation, the judge ruled their testimony inadmissible on the grounds that their stories showed signs of "cross-fertilization" and implausibility.

Around the same time, in El Escondido, California, a group of children riding a school bus testified that the driver had assaulted some of the children on the way home from school. Three months after his incarceration pending trial, the children recanted and admitted their story had been contrived. Apparently some of the older children on the bus were angered by the driver's insistence that they remain seated on the bus, and they devised the story to punish him. Younger children were swept along with them when investigators queried them about the abuse.

Finally, in the well-known case that took place in Jordan, Minnesota, two children testified that they had witnessed a murder and had seen the defendant dispose of the victim's body in the nearby Minnesota River. Later, when confronted with several serious implausibilities in the children's allegations, the investigators reversed the nature of their interrogation from trying to gain evidence against the accused to trying to verify the children's story. As a consequence, the two children recanted. Although these cases captured national attention, hundreds, if not thousands, of others have cropped up across the country.

Another parallel with the Salem trials suggests itself: In both cases, there was an atmosphere of excitement surrounding the investigation and a proclivity on the part of the investigators to question children relentlessly about cases in which the children already had learned a great deal from others in the community. Although there is no modern cultural counterpart to Salem (save in some fundamentalist countries where religious beliefs govern all aspects of life), there is still a willingness among adults to believe children and to ask them leading questions. Is this unwarranted? To answer this question, we turn to some recent experimental data on the suggestibility of child witnesses. Although the context for much of this research in no way resembles some important features of real-world crimes about which children are called to testify, it does enable us to see some of the mechanisms that might foster distortion in the recollections of young children.

Recent experimental studies of suggestibility

What do we know in a scientifically adequate way about children's vulnerability to suggestions from adults? Surprisingly much has been written about this topic, starting around the turn of the 20th century, and we will not review it here because of detailed treatments elsewhere (Ceci, Ross, & Toglia, 1987, Goodman, 1984). In general, the procedures in these experimental studies share the following similarities: Children first witness an event; then someone suggests to them that the event was somehow different from what they originally observed; and finally, children are asked to recollect the original event. Beneath this similarity is a wide divergence of procedures, settings, and stimuli. Some studies, like our own, which we will briefly report, present stories to children during the regularly scheduled "story time" activities in their nursery schools. Several days later someone interviews the children and provides misleading information about some of the details of the story. Then, 2 days later, the children are given a memory test for the original details. Other studies, such as those of Goodman and her colleagues (Goodman et al., 1987) and Peters (1987, in press) have taken advantage of naturally occurring situations (such as a child's first visit to the dentist) that come closer to mimicking the stressful circumstances associated with some of the cases in which children might be called upon to testify.

Age differences in suggestibility

Perhaps the first question that needs to be addressed is not whether young children are suggestible but, rather, *how* suggestible are they compared to older children and adults. The average adult forms the standard for our views about competency to testify. If children are suggestible, but no more so than the average adult, then it would not be seen as particularly problematic for them to testify. In the first study to be reported, the procedure was simple: Children between 3 and 12 years of age were presented a story about a girl's first day at school. Her name is Lauren. In the course of rushing to bathe, dress, and eat quickly to catch the bus, Lauren becomes sick. The story was accompanied by pictures that illustrated the key points. The children were told after they saw and heard the story that they would be interviewed later about its interest for them and about its comprehensibility. Two days later the children were interviewed and asked, for example, whether they thought other children would enjoy the story.

In the course of this interview, half of the children in each age group were asked questions that contained erroneous information about the story. For example, the children in the *biased* condition were asked: "Do you remember the story we listened to the other day, the one about the little girl named Lauren who ate *cereal* too fast and became sick?" (The original story showed Lauren eating *eggs*, not *cereal*.) As can be seen, the suggestion was subtle in the sense that the interviewer did not dwell on the misinformation and did not pause for the child to think about it or offer corrections. The control children were interviewed in a similar manner, but no misleading information was provided to them. The interviews were conducted by adults and lasted approximately 2 minutes. Two days following these interviews, children were tested for their memory of the original story. They were asked to select the original pictures that accompanied the story. They were confronted with a choice between a picture that was actually in the story (Lauren eating *eggs*) and one that was not in the story but was suggested via misleading questions (Lauren eating *cereal*).

As can be seen in Figure 11.1, the youngest children were more vulnerable to this type of biased interviewing than were older children. Analyses of these data indicated that age differences in susceptibility to misleading suggestions during the interview ceased by around the age of 6 or 7, as there were no reliable differences between first-graders and 12-year-olds

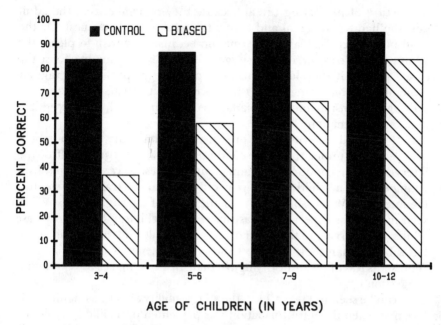

Figure 11.1. Mean percentage correct recognition as a function of age and condition in Experiment 1.

in susceptibility, but large differences between preschoolers and all of the other age groups. Interestingly, there were no reliable age differences in recognition memory in the control condition. The near ceiling effect here may be responsible for this finding because from the literature we expected to find younger children doing less well than older children when the interviewer did not provide erroneous information.

The next question we asked concerned the basis for the preschoolers' susceptibility to erroneous information. Did the erroneous information about Lauren's breakfast alter children's memory of what she ate, or did they continue to remember what she actually ate but choose the wrong picture for other reasons? The first possibility has been referred to as the "erasure" hypothesis (Loftus & Loftus, 1980; McCloskey & Zaragoza, 1985). According to this hypothesis, the original memory of Lauren eating *eggs* is overwritten by the suggested information that she ate *cereal*. Thus, the original trace for eggs is permanently lost. Another explanation has been called the "coexistence" hypothesis. According to it, children may remember what they saw Lauren eating but may refrain from selecting it for a variety of reasons, many of them social (i.e., not having to do with memory processes per se in nature). For example, they may think that although they remember Lauren eating eggs, they will choose the picture of her eating cereal because they remember that the adult said she had eaten cereal and surely the adult must know best. Or the child may select the biased information because they wish to please the adult who made the erroneous suggestion. Finally, they might choose the cereal picture if they lost all memory of the eggs picture but vaguely remembered something having been said about cereal. So, there is no shortage of non-mnemonic explanations for young children's susceptibility to misinformation.

In the second experiment we presented the same story to a group of 3- to 5-year-olds under the same conditions but with a twist: Half of the interviews were conducted by adults and the rest were conducted by a young child. The child was a 7-year-old boy who was trained to conduct the interview. We reasoned that if some or all of the suggestibility effect seen in the first experiment was the result of children trying to please adults, or deferring to the "memories" of an adult who they assume must know better than they, the effect should be lessened when a child, who represents less of an authority figure than an adult, makes the erroneous suggestion.

As can be seen in Figure 11.2, the suggestibility effect was significantly lessened when the misinformation was presented by a child interviewer. One might suppose this could be due to attentional factors, such as children paying greater attention to the adult interviewer than they did to the child interviewer. We have conducted additional studies that indicated those who heard the child interviewer attended to what he said as well as did those who heard the adult interviewer. However, the influence of the interviewer's age (and, more generally, his social status) was not the only important factor in producing the suggestibility effect. As seen in Figure 11.2, there was still a greater degree of faulty recognition over and above that associated with the age of the interviewer. Even children who were misled by the 7-year-old performed worse than the children who were not misled at all. Thus, these social factors do not appear to be the entire explanation for children's susceptibility to misinformation.

In our third experiment, in addition to a group of children who were given biased information and a control group, we included a third group who were given incorrect information that was not one of the later memory test options. For example, in addition to suggesting that Lauren had eaten cereal (when she had been shown eating eggs), we included a condition suggesting she had eaten pancakes. At the time of testing, the options were always between choosing an original picture and the biased one. There was never a choice to make between her eating cereal versus her eating pancakes. This condition, called the *modified* test, was first described by McCloskey and Zaragoza (1985) as a means of disentangling the "erasure" and "coexistence" hypotheses. According to their

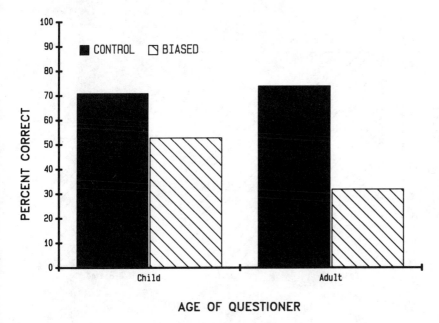

Figure 11.2. Mean percentage correct recognition as a function of age of questioner and condition in Experiment 2.

logic, if the original memory is intact and the biased interview questions have no effect on the level of memory, then children who had seen Lauren eating eggs but were told she had eaten pancakes should be as likely to choose eggs over cereal as the control group children. This would suggest that the insertion of postevent erroneous suggestions (e.g., pancakes) had no mnemonic effect on the original (eggs) trace, only a social effect. If the children in the modified condition choose eggs as often as the control children, then the difference between the control group and the biased group would be the result of children giving up their memories either to please the adult interviewer or to defer to their belief that his memory is superior to their own. The data from this manipulation are shown in Figure 11.3.

As can be seen in Figure 11.3, children in the modified condition chose the correct original picture more often than those in the biased condition. However, they still recognized the original picture less often than the control group did. The differences between all three groups are statistically significant.

A final experiment can best be viewed as an extension of the second study reported above. As alluded to, a prestige effect is one explanation for why the biasing manipulation was so powerful among preschoolers in

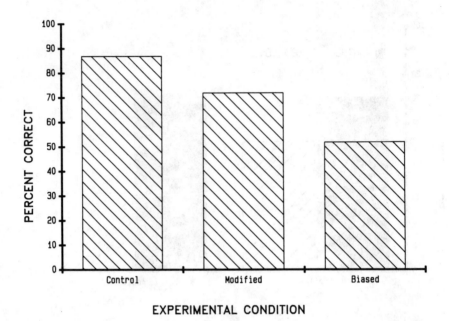

EXPERIMENTAL CONDITION

Figure 11.3. Mean percentage correct recognition by condition in Experiment 3.

our first experiment. That is, children may have, in part, responded to the demands of an adult authority figure whom they may have perceived as highly credible. Recall that the results of our second experiment revealed that when the interviewer (age 7) was of similar social status to the witness, the suggestibility effect, though still significant, was substantially reduced (control, 71% correct; biased, 53% correct).

The fact that the biasing manipulation was less powerful with a child interviewer suggests the importance of "demand characteristics" in young children's vulnerability to misinformation. An alternative explanation, however, is raised by the work of Lindsay and Johnson (1987). They discussed an external-source monitoring interpretation of suggestibility effects, arguing that misleading information may lead some subjects to believe mistakenly that the source of the misinformation was the original event. As applied to our findings, it could be argued that test discriminations are more difficult when both the presenter and interviewer are adults (Experiment 1) than when widely different sources, an adult and a child, serve as presenter and interviewer, respectively (Experiment 2).

Accordingly, the fourth experiment was designed to compare empirically the source-monitoring and prestige explanations. The presenter (adult, child) of the original event was varied, and so was the interviewer (adult, child) on Day 2. The third factor was condition for which there

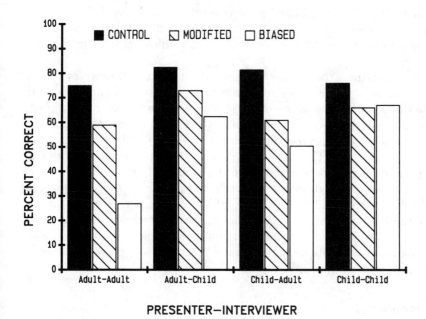

Figure 11.4. Mean percentage correct recognition as a function of presenter–interviewer combination and condition in Experiment 4.

were three levels (control, biased, and modified). As in the previous experiments, recognition testing occurred 2 days after the second session. These recognition results are shown in Figure 11.4.

The analysis of the data revealed no main effect of presenter, a main effect of interviewer such that performance was better with a child interviewer (.70) than an adult interviewer (.60), and a main effect of condition as control performance (.78) was the best followed by the modified (.64) and then biased (.52) groups. Simple effects testing revealed that recognition memory was significantly better in the control group than both the modified and biased groups. Also, subjects in the modified condition were reliably superior to those in the biased condition. These condition comparisons are consistent with those observed in the third experiment. The overall pattern of findings in Experiment 4 appears to be accommodated best by the prestige–authority interpretation.

Recently, Zaragoza (in press) has reported the results of four experiments. Although she found that preschoolers were impaired by the presentation of erroneous postevent information (i.e., the control group outperformed the bias group), she was unable to find evidence for actual memory destruction (i.e., the control group was not reliably different from the modified group). Thus, the poorer performance of these preschoolers in the face of biased postevent information may have resulted entirely from social pressures. Such a view accords with the recantations discussed earlier, as these individuals clearly still retained the original memories.

Taken together, these experiments indicate that a number of forces are operating on children's recognition performance, some social and some that appear to be mnemonic in the sense of the erasure hypothesis. It can always be argued that perhaps nothing as fundamental as erasure occurs but that our procedures are too blunt to detect the crucial nonerasure factors. This may be, but until then, the available evidence suggests that preschoolers' memories for details of emotionally neutral, pictorial events are disproportionately susceptible to the influence of misleading questions. At least some of their poor performance can be accounted for on the basis of social factors, but clearly not all of it. Finally, it is important to remember that preschoolers still were able to provide many accurate memories in these studies, suggesting that under appropriate conditions they can be valuable eyewitnesses.

Conclusion

In conclusion, our findings present a perplexing picture for those interested in making decisions about when and under what circumstances to admit testimony by young children. On the one hand, preschoolers often provide accurate recollections of the events they observe, and when they do not there is often a social or "prestige" factor operative that can, under appropriate interviewing, be counteracted. On the other hand, there is some evidence that preschoolers are more suggestible than older persons.

Of course, this volume is about the memory capabilities of contemporary children in everyday settings and the types of distortion exhibited both by the children in our experiments (and to some extent even by the children who testified at the Salem trials) may not be appropriate backdrop for this topic. Important differences exist that should be confronted, namely, all of our experiments use emotionally neutral events as stimuli, and the events occur only once in a child's life and have no special meaning attached to them. Often the memory being probed in these studies is peripheral to the story, unlike many actual cases in which children are asked to recall events associated with their own victimization. Finally, children in our experiments were passive observers, not participants or victims. All of these features could have important memorial consequences (e.g., Goodman et al., 1987), although Peters's (in press) recent work, as well as our own (Ceci, in press, footnote 1), suggest that altering such features leads to similar results.

But the current prevalence of child victims of abuse and child witnesses to criminal acts makes these experimental studies an enticing point of departure because the same mechanisms that produced distortion of children's memory in research settings *could* be operative in trials in which children are the key eyewitnesses. In a recent case in El Paso, Texas, a defendant was sentenced to death for a murder felony based on the eyewitness account offered by a young girl who reported that she had observed the defendant washing "red stuff" off his hands 6 months previously. At the time, she attached no special meaning to the red stuff, believing it to be seasoning, because most of the adults in her life worked in a nearby chili seasoning plant and would routinely come home from work with red liquid splattered on their hands and clothes. Interestingly, her recollection in this case was fairly similar to that in our own experimental procedures, as the event was emotionally neutral (the little girl was unaware that a murder had been committed) and an important, powerful adult appears to have strongly suggested details of the event that were erroneous. Three years following her damaging testimony, she recanted, stating that she had become so confused by what adults had suggested to her during the interviews that she said things that she should not have said, in an effort to be "helpful" to police.

As far as the study of children's memory in contexts similar to that associated with their own victimization is concerned, reports are appearing with greater frequency in the literature, producing interesting and sometimes conflicting findings. For instance, Goodman et al. (this volume) report several studies that converge on the view that naturally induced high levels of stress are associated with superior memory and better resistance to erroneous suggestion than are low levels of stress. This finding is at odds with Peters's series of studies of children's recollections for stressful events (e.g., visits to the dentist, inoculations, and witnessing staged thefts). The hope is that a resolution of such conflicting findings and a better understanding of the conditions that foster (as well as derail) children's memory will come about only through a combination of laboratory examinations that are able to disentangle variables that may be causing the conflicts and field studies that provide experiments of nature in which a mixture of well-understood variables can be reentangled.

REFERENCES

Ceci, S. J. (in press). Some overarching issues in the child suggestibility debate. In J. L. Doris (Ed.), *The Cornell Conference on the Suggestibility of Children's Recollections, with a View Toward the Child Witness*. Washington, D.C.: American Psychological Association.
Ceci, S. J., Ross, D. F., & Toglia, M. P (1987). Age differences in suggestibility:

Psycho-legal implications. *Journal of Experimental Psychology: General, 116,* 38–49.

Gemmill, W. N. (1924). *The Salem witch trials.* Chicago: A. C. McClurg.

Goodman, G. S. (1984). The child witness: Conclusions and future directions for research and legal practice. *Journal of Social Issues, 40,* 157–173.

Goodman, G. S., Aman, C., & Hirschman, J. (1987). Child sexual and physical abuse: Children's testimony. In S. J. Ceci, M. P. Toglia, & D. F. Ross (Eds.), *Children's eyewitness memory* (pp. 79–91). New York: Springer-Verlag.

Lindsay, D. S., & Johnson, M. K. (1987). Reality monitoring and suggestibility: Children's ability to discriminate among memories from different sources. In S. J. Ceci, M. P Toglia, & D. F. Ross (Eds.), *Children's eyewitness memory* (pp. 92–121). New York: Springer-Verlag.

Loftus, E., & Loftus, G. (1980). On the permanence of stored information in the human brain. *American Psychologist, 35,* 409–420.

McCloskey, M., & Zaragoza, M. (1985). Misleading postevent information and memory for events: Arguments and evidence against memory-impairment hypotheses. *Journal of Experimental Psychology: General, 114,* 3–18.

Nevins, W. S. (1892). *Witchcraft in Salem Village.* Salem, MA: Salem Observer Press.

Peters, D. (1987). The impact of naturally occurring stress on children's memory. In S. J. Ceci, M. P Toglia, & D. F. Ross (Eds.), *Children's eyewitness memory* (pp. 122–141). New York: Springer-Verlag.

Peters, D. F. (in press). The influence of stress and arousal on the child witness. In J. L. Doris (Ed.), *The Cornell Conference on the Suggestibility of Children's Recollections, with a View Toward the Child Witness.* Washington, D.C.: American Psychological Association.

Zaragoza, M. (in press). Preschool children's susceptibility to memory impairment. In J. L. Doris (Ed.), *The Cornell Conference on the Suggestibility of Children's Recollections, with a View Toward the Child Witness.* Washington, D.C.: American Psychological Association.

12

Remembering, forgetting, and childhood amnesia

KATHERINE NELSON

A little more than a decade ago a search of the literature revealed essentially no reports on episodic memory in children between about 10 months and 4 years of age. In 1979 an APA symposium provided the first look at some early exploratory studies of this topic, which were subsequently published in a small but apparently influential volume (Perlmutter, 1980). By the fall of 1987 those few exploratory studies had been succeeded by numerous systematic research programs, enough to fill a full-scale conference and then some. This development is both gratifying and exciting. The data that have emerged provide a picture that is becoming more and more complete but that also raises new and intriguing questions.

Before addressing some of the themes raised by the contributors to this volume, let me briefly review where we've come from. As late as 1975 there was widespread acceptance of the notion (articulated by Piaget among others) that young children's memories were all jumbled up. Young children were held to be "memory deficient," as they were similarly held to be deficient in other areas of cognitive development, and studies of memory during the preschool years were undertaken primarily as a comparison with the more advanced skills of older children. Further, the fact that older children and adults could remember little or nothing of their life experiences before the age of 3 or 4 years (the childhood amnesia phenomenon) seemed to indicate that such memories either did not exist or were too fragmentary to persist. Presumably this belief prevented researchers from investigating the question directly.

Strangely, any parent might have reported the opposite belief – that young children have very good memories for experienced events – and a large number of psychologists are also parents. This is not the first (or last) time that a belief based on formal learning overrode empirical evidence.[1] Young scholars would do well to view this conflict between theoretical belief and experiential evidence as a cautionary lesson, however.

During the 1970s, first at Yale and then at CUNY, my students and I began to investigate the problem of early memory as part of a larger program concerned with cognitive development in the transition years

301

from infancy to childhood (Nelson, 1978; Nelson & Gruendel, 1981). Initially I collaborated with Gail Ross on a study in which mothers of toddlers kept diary records of their young children's memories, resulting in one of the first reports of episodic memory during this age range (Nelson & Ross, 1980). Other studies were directed toward an understanding of children's general event knowledge. Through these we showed that preschoolers, contrary to the then generally accepted wisdom, had very good *general* representations of familiar events, which were well structured in terms of focus on central goal-related acts and accurate temporal sequencing, contrary to the assumption that children's memories were all jumbled up. But that still left open the question of to what extent very young children remembered *specific* extended episodes. It was tempting to suggest – and, indeed, we did suggest it – that children needed to establish a general representation of a class of events before they could recognize that a specific happening was unusual and therefore memorable on its own. This hypothesis, it seemed, could go far toward explaining the childhood amnesia phenomenon. Yet it would not explain many other facts about early memory. As our research accumulated, particularly as Robyn Fivush and Judy Hudson produced their innovative studies of the relation between general and specific event memory (Fivush, 1984; Fivush, Hudson, & Nelson, 1984; Hudson & Nelson, 1986), and as the research from other laboratories emerged, it became clear that there was more to early event memory than our first forays into it had suggested.

The essays collected here provide a good overview of the present state of knowledge in this area, and in this commentary on them I want to explore further a few of the issues they address. In particular, I want to focus on three themes: (1) memory competence in early childhhood; (2) social influences, particularly the role of maternal assistance in remembering; (3) explanations for childhood amnesia. In the course of this discussion I emphasize the importance of taking a functional view of memory and its development as a key to understanding these and other issues.

Memory competence in early childhood

Much of the recent literature in this area is in striking contrast to earlier claims about deficiencies in the early memory system. Subsequent to the early studies demonstrating that, indeed, 2- and 3-year-old children have knowledge of both general and specific events have come a flood of confirmatory findings suggesting that the memory system in early childhood is in basic ways equivalent to the memory system in older children and adults.

The research reported by Pat Bauer and Jean Mandler (this volume) has extended the age at which sensitivity to temporal and causal relations in an event is evidenced down to 16 months, suggesting that this is a basic, perhaps automatic, processing component of human cognition. In these studies children younger than 2 years are shown to be remembering events as temporally organized wholes and not as unorganized sets of disparate components. Equally important is the finding that these young children remembered events experienced only one time over a period of 2 to 6 weeks. Difficult as it is to carry out good research with children between 1 and 2 years, and given the relatively uninteresting and brief events in question, these findings seem far from having reached the limit of competence in terms of young age, length of time span, or complexity of event. For culturally and personally significant events, or for repeated experiences, the child's memory could be expected to be even better. For example, my analysis of the child Emily's memory recounts indicated that at 23 months she could recall in correct temporal order a sequence of at least six component actions from a specific episode of a more or less familiar event (being awakened at her baby-sitter's and taken home). Her recounting was carried out in the course of a crib monologue, lacking any external cues or social support (Nelson, 1989b). Such evidence lends credence to the suggestion that the findings presented by Bauer and Mandler may be but the tip of the iceberg as far as children's early memory competencies are concerned.

But if children remember events over a period of weeks, does that mean there is no limit on the length of time over which a memory may last? Fivush and Hamond's research (this volume) suggests that at least by the age of 2½ years children can retain memory of an event for a period of a year and a half. And the follow-up study by Hudson and Fivush (1987) of the memory of a kindergarten trip to a museum indicated that by 5 years children might store a memory that could be retained for as long as 6 years. The latter finding is impressive, but it does not bear on the childhood amnesia mystery in that the children in their initial study were 5, not 3, years old; thus, they were presumably over the amnesia barrier. Moreover, no child in their study produced a spontaneous account of the museum event 6 years later; all were dependent on external cuing in order to dredge up fragments of the memory. I will return to these issues later, when I consider the childhood amnesia question in more detail.

In general, then, the studies presented here provide support for the claim that after the age of 18 months or 2 years, young children's episodic memory is not different in kind from that of older children. Preschool children are not memory deficient, as once thought. But there are limitations on this claim. All studies find quantitative differences between older and younger children: Older children remember more, younger children seem to be more "schema-bound," and younger children are more dependent on specific cues than older children are.

In this collection perhaps Judy DeLoache's studies of children's use of models present the most intriguing and dramatic evidence of real development, but, as she documents, this does not seem to be development of memory per se. DeLoache was one of the first investigators of toddlers' memory, demonstrating that they could remember the location of hidden objects even after a 24-hour delay (DeLoache, 1980, 1986). Now she has discovered a peculiar limitation on the 2½-year-old's memory for object locations: the inability to transfer from a model to a large environment or vice versa. But as her research clearly shows, this is not a limitation on memory for the actual location of the object; rather, it is a limitation on the ability to use a three-dimensional model as a representational structure. This is fascinating and important research, but it does not limit the conclusions to be drawn about memory from the earlier research.

Bearing in mind that there are some quantitative and perhaps qualitative changes in children's memory over the preschool years, let us turn to the emerging evidence for the important role of social assistance in remembering.

Social influences on early memory

In the research reviewed in this volume, as in most other related research, memory is generally considered as an internal component of cognitive functioning. The usual assumption is that you don't have to learn memory – it just grows, like any physical organ (to adapt Chomsky's formulation regarding the so-called language module). But, however basic some features of memory are, there are clear suggestions in the literature that for some functions of human memory children may have to learn *how* to remember, and that this is the significance of social (often maternal) support (e.g., Eisenberg, 1985; Engel, 1986; Ratner, 1980, 1984; Tessler, 1986).

Consider, then some of the findings from the present series of studies, a few of which seem on the face of it to be contradictory. First, Fivush and Hamond's work seems to indicate that children do not remember what mothers try to get them to remember, and that they remember different things – and more things – with an experimenter than they remember with their mothers. But Hudson (this volume) emphasizes that 2-year-olds have to learn how to remember by learning how to participate in memory talk, and that mothers induct them into this kind of talk. Is there a conflict here? I think not. Hudson suggests that children are extracting a general format: how to narrate an account of an event. This learning is then extended to talk about experienced events in general. The younger children Hudson describes are *learning how* to engage in memory talk, while the somewhat older children that Fivush and Hamond observed were applying already acquired skills. By 3 or 4 years, moreover, as Fivush and Hamond suggest, children may make a distinction between people who have participated in an event with them and therefore do not need to be told about it, and people who were not there and therefore do need or want to be filled in on more details. This could explain the difference at this age in children's accounts to mothers and experimenters.

Some interesting characteristics of maternal support have emerged from these studies. Several researchers have noted that there are different types of memory talk, and that different mothers have a tendency to engage more in one of these types than the other. Mothers who engage in memory narratives, elaborating on an experience and asking questions that encourage the child to contribute information to the narrative, tend to have children who are better able to recount an episode than the children of mothers who use memory talk only in a pragmatic, reminding mode. This difference in maternal style may be important at input, that is, at the time of the original experience, as well as at output, when the experience is being recounted. Tessler (1986) found that children whose mothers talked with them in a narrative style during the experience of going to a museum remembered more of the experience a week later than children whose mothers simply pointed out objects or responded to the child's comments. But another finding from that study was that the children remembered what both mother and child talked about together and failed to remember what the mother talked about alone or what the child commented on alone. This finding emphasizes the importance of the social context both in sharing an experience and in sharing the memory of the experience to what is remembered from it. It suggests that memory cannot be viewed solely as an internal cognitive mechanism but, rather, must be viewed as a function that is at least partially dependent on a nurturing social context.

These considerations may also shed light on the findings of Fivush and Hamond. In their study, the mother chose the topics she wanted the child to remember and talk about. But what the mother remembered from the experience might not match what the child had experienced at the time. In particular, Tessler's results suggest that unless the mother and child had talked about something *together,* the child might have failed to notice and therefore to remember it.

Rogoff and Mistry's study of maternal support (this volume) is also important to this story. They suggest that maternal coaching is important under some conditions but seems unimportant in others. In particular, when children were internally motivated to remember items that they needed to prepare a bag lunch, maternal assistance on the task was not needed; but when the task was motivated only as a memory task, without a functional goal, parental assistance improved children's performance.

Taken together then, the studies presented here indicate that young children can and do remember aspects of specific experiences that seem important or salient to them. What is remembered under these circumstances is often somewhat impoverished, however, consisting of a skeletal framework plus a few details. These findings also suggest that what is salient to children is often not what seems important or interesting to adults, and thus efforts to extract specific bits of information about an event from the child may fail. But adults do support the development of more elaborated memory in a variety of ways. I consider the significance of these findings further in the following section.

The roots of autobiographical memory (or, What happens to childhood amnesia?)

If children do remember episodes for long periods – years – why are early memories blocked after age 3 (or age 4, 5, or even later; there is considerable individual variability as to the exact cut-off)? For many years developmentalists have neglected the study of childhood amnesia, and it has been a peripheral topic in the general study of the psychology of memory. Whatever the eventual correct explanation of the phenomenon, it seems apparent now that it must have an important bearing on our understanding of early cognitive, social, and personality development. It well deserves our attention; and thanks to Neisser's (1982) prodding to study memory in its ecological context, it, among other topics, has begun to yield results from empirical research efforts, as the studies presented in this volume have demonstrated.

This is not the place to review the various theories that have been put forth to explain childhood amnesia (see Fivush, 1988b; Nelson, 1988, 1989b; Pillemer & White, in press; White & Pillemer, 1979). I want to note, however, that the problem of childhood amnesia has often been misrepresented. In Freud's (1905/1963) repression theory, as well as in Schachtel's (1947) reconstruction account, Neisser's (1962) and White and Pillemer's (1979) theories of cognitive reorganization, the implication has been that something happens to block early memories. But this seems a misleading way to look at the matter, tempting the theorist (and the practitioner) to try to unblock the hidden memories, almost invariably unsuccessfully. The fact that virtually *no* early memories slip through the barrier (although we now know that they are formed) suggests not that something happens to close down memory but that something opens up: Some positive development takes place that makes it possible for the individual to retain a memory over a long period of time, when this was not possible in the previous developmental state. This development, I believe, is a specifically human characteristic of memory (Nelson, 1989b).

In this section I will briefly outline the facts of the case and suggest a social-functional explanation, drawing on some of the findings reported here.[2] My outline will be skeletal. Much of the supporting data has been summarized in the preceding section and is considered in detail in the chapters cited there; Pillemer and White (in press) also provide a comprehensive survey.

Data-based propositions

1. Remembrances by older children and adults of specific life events do not normally begin to appear until 3 years at the youngest.
   1a. The cutoff point can be as late as 8 years.[3]
   1b. A few individuals have occasional memories from the age of 2 years or younger.
   1c. The age of earliest memory has been negatively correlated with IQ, language ability, and social class. Females tend to have earlier memories than males.[4]
2. Young preschool children are more reliable – give more complete and better organized accounts – in reporting generic memory (of repeated events) than specific memory for a particular episode.
3. Specific memories may be retained for as long as 6–18 months in early childhood.
   3a. Recall of specific memories by young children is often dependent on extensive external cuing.
   3b. Children's specific memories of familiar events are subject to fusion, confusion, and loss of detail.
   3c. Children's memory of the details of a specific episode may vary in unpredictable ways from the adult account. Children often remember different details than adults do of the same event.
   3d. Some early memories may confuse real experience with repetitions of what others have reported, or may distort what actually happened. Early memories seem to be more vulnerable to these effects than later memories.
   3e. Specific details that seem to be lost or inaccessible at one point may reappear in recall at a later point. There is a lack of consistency in what is accessible to verbalization. This seems to indicate instability in what is remembered and how it is organized.
   3f. Internally cued memory (e.g., crib monologues) seems to involve reworking and resolving ambiguities and to lead to additions to the general knowledge system.
   3g. Specific memories tend to be lost unless they are reinstated at least once within a specific limited time period.
4. Adults teach children to remember in different ways. How they engage in memory talk affects what and how children remember.

Together these propositions can be used to explain childhood amnesia and its release. This explanation relies on the interpretation of memory as a particular kind of functional system.

Memory as a functional system

Human memory like all human capacities is a product of evolutionary forces, resulting in a system that is functionally adapted to enable the organism to interact flexibly with the social and physical environment. The basic learning-memory function is shared with other mammalian species (Oakley, 1983), and there is evidence that the more recently evolved "late memory" system (characterized in terms similar to Tulving's episodic memory) matures in the human infant during the first year of life (Mandler, 1984; Schacter & Moscovitz, 1984).

The most basic general function of memory for any organism is to provide guidance for action. The mammalian memory system not only supports action in the present but also prepares for future action. What has happened is used as the basis for predicting what will happen. For this purpose the most useful type of evidence comes from events that are frequently repeated, and thus the most useful (and banal) type of memory is that for familiar routine events, the type of generalized event memory realized as scripts. This type of memory is the one that young children seem to be especially good at (Proposition 2, above).

Obviously, an event that is experienced once and never again is of little use in guiding action and predicting the future. Memory for single episodes therefore is less functional in this basic sense than memory for repeated events. But how can one know whether a novel event is singular or only the first of its kind? Often the child cannot tell. It would be optimal, then, to remember the salient features of an event for a period of time in case it should be repeated, so that the memory could then guide action, and could be retained for its future utility. The memory system itself might even have a trigger of the kind that says: "If repeated within x amount of time (days, weeks), file for future use; if not, drop." Such a trigger would explain findings such as Rovee-Collier and Hayne's (1987) with infants, and Fivush and Hamond's (in press) with 3- and 4-year-olds. Both these investigators found that a one-time reminder of an experience led to memory of the experience, while an unreminded experience was forgotten over the same period of time. Rovee-Collier calls this "reinstatement." It is not clear, however, how long an event reinstated only once would be held in memory.

These considerations suggest that whereas specific memories will be held for a period of time (and the length of that period might be variable, depending on factors such as emotional significance, excitement, or salience of some other kind), they will be subject to automatic erasure if not repeated. This is not to suggest that such episodes might not include important information that is entered into the general knowledge system. For example, Emily at 2½ formulated a rule that when you go to the airport you have to bring some luggage. But the episode that was the basis for the formation of this rule (a trip to her grandmother's) was soon lost to the episodic memory system.

Still, as we know, at some point specific memories of both one-time and repeated events do become entered into an autobiographical memory system that is capable of preserving them for years, even decades. How does this happen? Does the memory system change in some way at some point so that it is functional to retain some specific memories indefinitely?

To account for this change it seems reasonable to assume that specific memories become recognized as significant for reasons other than that of guiding action and predicting the future. On the basis of the considerations advanced thus far, it would seem that such significance might be established through social means, specifically, through the use of language to recount and to share an experience with others. In other words, childhood amnesia is overcome when children learn that their memories can be shared with others.

There is another aspect of function that is relevant to what children remember. As Gail Goodman (this volume) emphasizes, children remember what concerns them, and their concerns include safety, comfort, and security. This dimension is not independent of the recurrent event dimension, for the most basic conditions of children's lives are composed in the events of caretaking (feeding, sleeping, bathing, and so on) and in sharing the attention and affection of caregivers. The stability of these events is of great concern to children. Of course, there are other concerns, other aspects of experience that have functional significance for children because they are fun, scary, exciting, or puzzling even though they may never be repeated. Rogoff and Mistry's research identifies still another functional component: the importance of memory within the context of the activity – its relevance to a goal, to a meaningful purpose. In each of these ways – the way the event impinges on basic concerns, its affective or motivational salience, and the child's goals – the functional component of memory for the child may vary systematically from that of the adult's for the same event. When this is the case, opportunities for sharing memories of the event will be lessened; adults may not be able to cue the child's memory effectively. On the other hand, the child might be equally capable of conveying the essence of his or her experience to a nonparticipant regardless of whether the content of the memory varied from that of a participating adult's.

The hypothesis that childhood amnesia is overcome through sharing memories with others is supported from a number of directions. As discussed earlier, considerable research has established that young children learn to engage in memory talk, and that mothers guide them in what to remember, both during an experience and later, when the experience is recalled. This research has also indicated that mothers vary in the way they engage their children in memory talk, and that children's memory tends to co-vary with mothers' styles. The usual age of onset of autobiographical memory is consistent with the age of learning to talk about what is remembered as reported in this research, typically between 2 and 4 years. Fivush and Hamond's finding that 2½-year-olds seem uninterested in talk about the past, whereas 4 year olds find such talk interesting, underscores this point: By 4½, children have learned how to engage in such talk, even, in some cases, how to make an interesting story of their experience.

Additional indirect support for this hypothesis comes from the literature on adult memory, which has revealed the relations itemized above under Proposition 1. Variability in the age of earliest memory from 2 to 8 years cannot be explained by any simple maturation function but, rather, must draw on an explanation based on the variability of experience, such as engaging in the "right kind" and the "right degree" of memory talk. That girls generally have earlier memories than boys could be attributable to the possibly greater propensity of mothers to engage in such talk with their daughters. Correlations with language facility would clearly be explicable from this account, and correlations with IQ and social class, although not so obviously related, might be expected. Most of the data on learning to engage in memory talk comes from middle-class educated parents, and most of the data on childhood amnesia comes from college students or educated adults. Thus, the coincidence of age of earliest memory and age of learning to engage in memory talk might be valid, but the particular age found in these studies might be culturally specific. Comparisons with practices in other cultures and social classes, together with investigations of early memories, should shed light on this relation.

This general proposal is consistent with the Vygotskian account of memory development, as Hudson (this volume) has emphasized. In this account, children are inducted into cultural practices through the social mediation of adults. As Hudson notes, the 2- to 3-year-old child has to learn how to narrate an event, through guidance by the adult. After experience with learning the format of "memory talk" the child may generalize this mode of discourse to other events not already discussed with another. That is, the activity first experienced on the external plane becomes internalized and available as an independent function for the child. This statement, however, oversimplifies the process involved. We have seen that memory has certain functions for the child, but the culture (instantiated in parental guidance) values other functions as well, for example, telling a coherent story, telling the truth, getting the facts right, remembering particular details, emphasizing some parts of an event and not others. The problem that faces the child in learning to engage in "memory talk" is, then, the problem of coordinating two functional systems, the child's and the culture's. Accomplishing this coordination takes time.

There is another possibility to consider. Rather than establishing the cultural significance of memories and promoting an appropriate narrative format for conveying them, sharing memories with others through verbal means may become a form of reinstatement that enables a specific memory to persist beyond the hypothesized "drop" trigger. Reinstatement by verbal means is not possible until a certain degree of facility with language is attained, a degree sufficient to enable the child to establish a mental representation of an event from a verbal account given by someone else. It is not the simple ability to talk about events, but the capacity to use a linguistic representation presented by another person as the basis for establishing one's own cognitive representation, that is essential. This ability develops gradually, and from other evidence (Nelson, 1986) seems to come into play some time after 3 years of age.

Fivush and Hamond (this volume) emphasize the lack of consistency in what is verbalized by the younger child, implying that a stable core of information is not retained. This implies that the crucial factor is entertaining a verbal representation of the event, that it is not enough to "bring the episode to mind." In addition, Hudson (this volume) emphasizes that verbal discussions with 2-year-olds do not affect the specifics of what is remembered in their later recall. The implication here is that for the child under 3, sharing memories is not effective in leading to a reinstatement of the memory. Hudson suggests that the ability to produce an event narrative independently is a prerequisite for reactivation through verbal recall.

These suggestions shed light on the findings from the study of Emily's early memory (Nelson, 1989a). Recall that I reported that Emily recounted events to herself from at least 21 months when she talked to herself at night. By 2 years she was very verbal and capable of recounting quite long and complex events. Later, when she was 6 years old, we attempted to access her memory for some of the events that she had talked about at length at 2 to 2½ years, but failed to elicit any memories from that period of her life. The explanation for this failure seems to be that, as I suggested earlier, her recounting appeared to be serving the function of comprehension, of integrating information into her general knowledge system. The implication here is that before a certain point, the child's own recount will not be effective as a reactivating mechanism, because the recount is serving not as a specific memory-enhancer but as a comprehension mechanism. Early recounting to self, then, should be viewed not as rehearsal but as knowledge construction. The child needs to learn that recounting can serve another, more social, function as well.

We may then speculate that memory talk with adults first facilitates the ability to narrate events, then supports independent narrations, and, finally, enables the child to interpret the narrations of others and coordinate or integrate them with his or her own accounts. These developments seem to take place for many children between the ages of 2 and 4 years. Thus, again, the age of establishment of autobiographical memory is consistent.

Note that this account requires that children accord significance to the verbal accounts of others as well as to their own remembering. At first, internalizing others' accounts might result in a lack of differentiation between what is heard and what is remembered from experience, as well as in the distortions in memory from biased questioning that Ceci et al. (this volume) have found to be more characteristic of preschool than of older children. This lack of differentiation would be expected to be a temporary phenomenon, overcome as the child became experienced in distinguishing between first- and secondhand memories. Again, the timing seems generally right, in that 5-year-olds' memory is less subject to distortion or confusion than 3-year-olds' in the research reported by Ceci et al. and by Goodman et al. (this volume).

Even if the child becomes able to use the verbal account of another effectively to reinstate a memory, however, this would not be sufficient to sustain it indefinitely, as the previous research indicates. Although re-experience of part of an event prolongs the memory of the event for the very young child, there is apparently a limit on how long the reinstated memory will last. Thus, the question is not whether verbal recounting of memories simply reinstates them and thus enables them to persist, or whether it establishes the social significance of memories and thus preserves them because of their socially valued function. Rather, it seems that both factors must be involved.

In any case, the evidence supports the verbal recounting explanation of the onset of enduring memory for specific experiences. But not all of our enduring memories from early childhood are shared with others, as psychoanalytic studies have clearly brought out. Although children may be inducted into the process of remembering experiences, it seems that they must go on from there to select which experiences to remember. What is remembered no doubt depends upon its personal significance, its importance to one's self-image (good or bad) and sense of self-history, as Fivush (1988a) has argued elsewhere. Covert recounting of memories to oneself no doubt takes the place of recounting them with others.

Memories that are neither overtly or covertly recounted for many years may fade from sight but, as a number of researchers have suggested, may be retrievable given the right cues (e.g., Hudson & Fivush, 1987).

This view of the matter suggests a number of lines of research. For example, what difference does it make if a child is shifted from one linguistic community to another during childhood? Are the earlier memories lost? One might expect that children with close siblings would remember more from childhood than only children because they would be likely to share with siblings as well as with adults. What about deaf children? Under this hypothesis, deaf children without sign language should be late in establishing an autobiographical memory system because they lack the means for recounting with others.[5] The hypothesis also suggests interesting cross-cultural and cross-linguistic studies. Cultures in which storytelling is valued, and in which children are encouraged to participate in such sessions, should enhance early memories, whereas cultures that discourage children's participation (for example, the Mayan culture that Rogoff reported on) should retard the establishment of the autobiographical memory system.

In summary, I have tried to pull together the various empirical studies reported in this volume and elsewhere in the recent literature, to determine how they may bear on the longstanding mystery of childhood amnesia. This account does not contradict that put forth by Fivush and Hamond; rather, it both extends and limits their conclusions. To recapitulate briefly: Reinstatement is essential for a single memory to persist beyond a brief period of time. Talk to oneself about an event at first is effective not in reinstating but only in integrating the event into the general knowledge system. Talk with others about the experience is effective in reinstating the memory only after the child has reached a certain level of linguistic and cognitive ability sufficient to enable the verbal presentation of another to be internalized in the child's memory system as a mental representation of an event. Finally, talk with others is necessary to learn the culturally valued aspects of memories and format of narrating events. Shared memory talk provides the conditions for establishing an autobiographical memory system, which, once established, serves both social and personal functions. These functions are specifically human; they go beyond – and draw on different kinds of information than – those served by the more basic memory systems (early and late) that are shared with all other mammalian species.

It is gratifying at this point to have so much original and important research relating to this problem. But clearly these proposals imply the need for much more work to be carried out to verify, test, and challenge the implications drawn on the basis of present knowledge. We can all look forward to a conference on this topic 5 or 10 years hence; the picture will no doubt look quite different then – clearer, we can hope, and no doubt more complex.

NOTES

1 Psychologists should not feel unduly embarrassed by this situation: It has a long and respectable history. For example, physicians until the late Renaissance relied on the (often mistaken) writings of Galen (c. 130–200) on human anatomy and physiology, rather than on evidence from firsthand investigation (Boorstin, 1983).
2 Pillemer and White (in press) outline a social account of the overcoming of childhood amnesia that is similar in many ways to the present one. See also Fivush (1988b).
3 This finding from the older literature (Dudycha & Dudycha, 1941; Waldfogel, 1948) is frequently ignored in contemporary accounts, but my own informal surveys of students indicate that the evidence for great variability in age of cutoff is probably reliable.
4 See Dudycha & Dudycha (1941) and Waldfogel (1948). This kind of variability has also been overlooked in recent accounts.
5 A study by Williams and Bonvillian (n.d.) indicates that the age of earliest memories of deaf college students is no different from that of hearing students, and falls within the same age range shown by other studies. There are some problems with the interpretation of this study, however, and I believe the issue remains open to further investigation.

REFERENCES

Boorstin, D. J. (1983). *The discoverers: A history of man's search to know his world and himself.* New York: Random House, Vintage.

DeLoache, J. S. (1980). Naturalistic studies of memory for object location in very young children. In M. Perlmutter (Ed.), *Children's memory* (New directions for child development, No. 10). San Francisco: Jossey-Bass.

DeLoache, J. S. (1986). Memory in very young children: Exploitation of cues to the location of a hidden object. *Cognitive Development, 1,* 123–137.

Dudycha, G. J., & Dudycha, M. M. (1941). Childhood memories: A review of the literature. *Psychological Bulletin, 38,* 668–682.

Eisenberg, A. R. (1985). Learning to describe past experiences in conversation. *Discourse Processes, 8,* 177–204.

Engel, S. (1986). *Learning to reminisce: A developmental study of how young children talk about the past.* Unpublished doctoral dissertation, City University of New York.

Fivush, R. (1984). Learning about school: The development of kindergarteners' school scripts. *Child Development, 55,* 1697–1709.

Fivush, R. (1988a). The functions of event memory: Some comments on Nelson and Barsalou. In U. Neisser and E. Winograd (Eds.), *Remembering reconsidered: Ecological and traditional approaches to the study of memory* (pp. 277–282). New York: Cambridge University Press.

Fivush, R. (1988b). *Form and function of early autobiographical memory.* Unpublished manuscript, Emory University.

Fivush, R., & Hamond, N. R. (in press). Time and again: Effects of repetition and retention interval on two-year olds' event recall. *Journal of Experimental Child Psychology*.

Fivush, R., Hudson, J., & Nelson, K. (1984). Children's long-term memory for a novel event: An exploratory study. *Merrill-Palmer Quarterly, 30,* 303–316.

Freud, S. (1963). Three essays on the theory of sexuality. In J. Strachey (Ed.), *The standard edition of the complete works of Freud* (Vol. 7). London: Hogarth Press. Originally published in 1905.

Hudson, J. A., & Fivush, R. (1987). *As time goes by: Sixth grade children recall a kindergarten experience* (Emory Cognition Project Report #13). Emory University, Atlanta.

Hudson, J., & Nelson, K. (1986). Repeated encounters of a similar kind: Effects of familiarity on children's autobiographical memory. *Cognitive Development, 1,* 253–271.

Mandler, J. M. (1984). Representation and recall in infancy. In M. Moscovitch (Ed.), *Infant memory: Its relation to normal and pathological memory in humans and other animals* (pp. 75–101). New York: Plenum.

Neisser, U. (1962). Cultural and cognitive discontinuity. In T. E. Gladwin & W. Sturtevant (Eds.), *Anthropology and human behavior.* Washington, DC: Anthropological Society of Washington, DC.

Neisser, U. (1982). *Memory observed: Remembering in natural contexts.* San Francisco: W. H. Freeman.

Nelson, K. (1978). How young children represent knowledge of their world in and out of language. In R. S. Siegler (Ed.), *Children's thinking: What develops?* (pp. 225–273). Hillsdale, NJ: Erlbaum.

Nelson, K. (1986). *Event knowledge: Structure and function in development.* Hillsdale, NJ: Erlbaum.

Nelson, K. (1988). The ontogeny of memory for real events. In U. Neisser & E. Winograd (Eds.), *Remembering reconsidered: Ecological and traditional approaches to the study of memory* (pp. 244–276). New York: Cambridge University Press.

Nelson, K. (1989a). Monologue as re-presentation of events. In K. Nelson (Ed.), *Narratives from the crib.* Cambridge, MA: Harvard University Press.

Nelson, K. (1989b). Remembering: A functional developmental perspective. In P. R. Solomon, G. R. Goethals, C. M. Kelley, B. R. Stephens (Eds.), *Memory: An interdisciplinary approach.* New York: Springer-Verlag.

Nelson, K., & Gruendel, J. (1981). Generalized event representations: Basic building blocks of cognitive development. In A. Brown & M. Lamb (Eds.), *Advances in developmental psychology* (Vol. 1). Hillsdale, NJ: Erlbaum.

Nelson, K., & Ross, G. (1980). The generalities and specifics of long-term memory in infants and young children. In M. Perlmutter (Ed.), *Children's memory* (New directions for child development, No. 10, pp. 87–101). San Francisco: Jossey-Bass.

Oakley, D. A. (1983). The varieties of memory: A phylogenetic approach. In A. Mayes (Ed.), *Memory in animals and humans* (pp. 20–82). Workingham, England: Van Nostrand–Reinhold.

Perlmutter, M. (Ed.). (1980). *Children's memory* (New directions for child development, No. 10). San Francisco: Jossey-Bass.

Pillemer, D., & White, S. (in press). Childhood events recalled by children and adults. In H. W. Reese (Ed.), *Advances in child development and behavior* (Vol. 22). New York: Academic Press.

Ratner, H. H. (1980). The role of social context in memory development. In M.

Perlmutter (Ed.), *Children's Memory* (New directions for child development, No. 10). San Francisco: Jossey-Bass.

Ratner, H. H. (1984). Memory demands and the development of young children's memory. *Child Development, 55,* 2173–2191.

Rovee-Collier, C., & Hayne, H. (1987). Reactivation of infant memory: Implications for cognitive development. In H. W. Reese (Ed.), *Advances in child development and behavior* (Vol. 20, pp. 185–283). New York: Academic Press.

Schachtel, E. G. (1947). On memory and childhood amnesia. *Psychiatry, 10,* 1–26.

Schacter, D. L., & Moscovitz, M. (1984). Infants, amnesics, and dissociable memory systems. In M. Moscovitz (Ed.), *Infant memory: Its relation to normal and pathological memory in humans and other animals* (pp. 173–216). New York: Plenum.

Tessler, M. (1986). *Mother–child talk in a museum: The socialization of a memory.* Unpublished manuscript, City University of New York.

Waldfogel, S. (1948). The frequency and affective character of childhood memories. *Psychological Monographs, 62* (Whole No. 291).

White, S. H., & Pillemer, D. B. (1979). Childhood amnesia and the development of a socially accessible memory system. In J. F. Kihlstrom & F. J. Evans (Eds.), *Functional disorders of memory* (pp. 29–47). Hillsdale, NJ: Erlbaum.

Williams, R. L., & Bonvillian, J. D. (n.d.). *Early childhood memories in deaf and hearing college students.* Unpublished manuscript, Gallaudet University.

13

Recall and its verbal expression

JEAN M. MANDLER

"Where did you go?" "Out." "What did you do?" "Nothing." This is a familiar characterization of parental frustration in trying to elicit accounts from their children about the events of the day. But do children really remember as little detail as this wry commentary suggests? Children's recall – in particular, autobiographical recall of personally experienced events – is the main focus of this volume. The questions center on such issues as how recall develops, how accurate it is, what accounts for improvement in recall, and why it is that we can no longer remember so many events from early childhood that are still recallable for many months after they occur. The authors are largely in agreement about many of these issues, giving a coherence to the account of memory development that is often lacking in a collection of research reports from different laboratories. I do not wish to breach the consensus that is being built, because it provides a much more complete account than we have had until now. Nevertheless, I would suggest some additional considerations about the phenomena under study. To do this, I need to make a few general comments about memory before addressing the issue of what young children remember and why. Following a brief discussion about the what and the why, I concentrate on how much children remember and for how long, focusing on memory in very young children and emphasizing the difficulties in assessment that their verbal protocols pose.

What kind of memory is recall?

Memory is one of the most basic functions of the human organism, involved in everything it does. Even newborns learn to recognize things, as shown by their habituation to previously presented stimuli and dishabituation to new ones. Infants a few months old learn to recognize a patterned sequence of events sufficiently well that they can anticipate the next event to occur (Haith, Hazan, & Goodman, 1988; Smith, 1984). Infants of the same age who have learned a conditioned response, such as kicking their feet to make a mobile turn, "forget" this habit over a few weeks' time, but if the mobile is presented again, it helps reactivate or reinstate the conditioned response (Rovee-Collier & Hayne, 1987).

It is tempting to call these phenomena "remembering," but they are not, at least not in the sense that the term is usually used and as it is used in this volume. What children remember and why refers to what children *recall*. Recall is a specialized and advanced form of memory that brings something not perceptually present to conscious awareness. It is a function that seems likely to be restricted to the higher mammals. Many organisms display the memory phenomena discussed in the previous paragraph, but we credit few of them with the ability to bring their past lives to mind or to think about absent objects and events. It is an interesting commentary on our field that it is so rarely mentioned that recall involves conscious processing. Yet, if pressed, psychologists who study memory to define a term they use all the time typically agree that recall involves bringing some aspect of the past or some bit of previously acquired knowledge to conscious awareness. Thus, recall is a form of conscious thought, in which we re-present (or, more accurately, reconstruct) information to ourselves.

It is possible to have an organism maintaining a fully functional recognition-memory system that enables it to learn and to differentiate new stimuli from old, while at the same time lacking the ability to recall information that is not perceptually present. This discussion suggests a dual memory system, one that is automatic in operation and not accessible to conscious report, and another whose contents can be brought to mind and thought about. Dual memory systems have been given various names in the literature, such as early and late memory systems (Schacter & Moscovitch, 1984); implicit and explicit memory (see Schacter, 1987, for a review); procedural and declarative memory (Cohen, 1984; J. Mandler, 1984); integrative and elaborative memory (G. Mandler, 1989); and sensorimotor and conceptual memory (J. Mandler, 1988). Not everyone agrees that these systems are always separate or completely dissociable, but the distinction between the two kinds of memory functioning is ubiquitous in current theory and research. Memory theorists vary somewhat in their descriptions of these different systems, but one thread appears in all accounts: early, implicit, procedural, integrative, sensorimotor memory operates automatically and beyond the reach of awareness, whereas late, explicit, declarative, elaborative, conceptual memory involves information that has been encoded in such a way as to be accessible to consciousness.

If we are to study what young children remember (recall) and why, and if only some kinds of information are recallable, we need to determine in principle what they are. I have suggested (J. Mandler, 1988) that the only kinds of information available for recall are those that are encoded conceptually. Much of the information we encode is probably not conceptual in nature. We go about our daily business guided by continual perceptual input, most of which we ignore, insofar as our conscious attention is concerned. Our perceptual schemas encode huge amounts of information and continually update our implicit memory system, but unless we attend to something and encode it conceptually, that information will not be accessible later. The efficiency of our perceptual and motor-processing systems enable us to get around the world without paying much attention to their inputs, thus freeing our conscious attention for thinking, planning, and troubleshooting, and for noticing new or unusual events. It is for this reason that we are so poor at recalling the myriad details of an experience; much of that information was never noticed in the first place, so it will not be available later to be brought to mind or to tell someone else about.

There seem to be two major reasons why people's memory of a situation vary. First, what they *notice* will vary as a function of their interests, prior knowledge, and what they are doing in the situation (see Nelson, 1986). Second, raw experience is never recallable; it must be interpreted in some way by the conceptual system, and how people *conceptualize* a situation will vary as a function of what they know. Let me illustrate these points with a homely example. Many of us are poor at recalling what people look like. Not only can we not describe faces adequately, we usually cannot image them very well either. Others – artists, for example – have a rich set of concepts about the human face that not only encourage them to encode things most of us miss, but that enable them to recall a much more detailed description. I was in my mid-forties (attending a rather dull seminar that encouraged my attention to wander off the topic) before I noticed for the first time that people's ears tended to be at the same level as their eyes. After noticing this bit of information I found that I began to encode information about faces I had not in the past; I could even say sometimes *why* a particular face looked odd, having noticed that the ears were set at a slightly different level than normal. Presumably, my perceptual apparatus had been responsive to such information for the first forty years, since it is the kind of information we use to recognize faces, but it would have been impossible for me to recall this information before I had attended to and conceptualized it (however crudely in comparison with an artist's description). It is important to note that my conceptual information about ears may or may not have been encoded in an imaginal format; whether imaginal or linguistic, however, it was a redescription of information into a kind of conceptual form that had not been there before. My concept of a face had changed, and therefore, what I could recall about a face had changed as well.

What do young children remember?

So there are only some kinds of information that either children or adults can recall. They must have *noticed* the information and been able to *conceptualize* it in some way. Already we can see some important reasons why a young child's recall might differ from that of the adult even if the type of processing they do is in principle the same. That the nature of the processing children and adults do *is* the same is one aspect of the consensus we see building in this volume. However, many of the chapters comment on the fact that young children pay attention to different aspects of events than do adults. And the younger the child, the higher the probability that their conceptualizations of an event differ as well. For example, Ratner, Smith, & Padgett (this volume) provide several indications that young children understand making clay less well and organize this event differently than do adults. Not surprisingly, then, some of the details of their recall differ even though the same kind of processes appear to be at work for both groups.

Farrar and Goodman's chapter offers a processing explanation for why children notice different things than do adults, using an intriguing theory of schema confirmation and schema deployment. Schema confirmation refers to the attempt to find or build an appropriate schema for new events. In the earliest stage of this process attention is thought to be allotted in an unbiased fashion. Once a schema has been selected or formed, however, there follows a period in which one tries to verify its appropriateness by looking for confirming evidence. After a schema has been confirmed, one enters a period of schema deployment, in which attention is no longer needed for purposes of overall comprehension of the situation, and so is redirected to new and unusual information instead. Each of these phases is associated with remembering different kinds of things. If one experiences an event during the first stage, one's memory should be relatively unbiased. During the next phase of schema confirmation, one remembers what appear to someone who already understands the situation to be its mundane or expected aspects. If one has reached the phase of schema deployment (the state adults are typically in), because attention has been directed toward the unusual or new aspects of the situation, these distinctive aspects are more frequently recalled, at least for a time. (Eventually the reconstructive aspect of memory leads to reproduction of the familiar once again.) The recall of distinctive information is well documented in the adult literature, in which the materials are almost always highly familiar (lists of words, stories, etc.). Farrar and Goodman suggest quite reasonably that young children might be in the stage of schema confirmation much more often than is the case for older children and adults. One might expect, therefore, that young children will recall the mundane and expected more often, and have greater difficulty with unusual events. Evidence for this hypothesis is provided by Farrar and Goodman's finding (this volume) that 4-year-olds have more difficulty than 7-year-olds in keeping new, unusual events separate from repeated scriptlike ones.

Fivush and Hamond in their chapter also provide data that are directly relevant to this hypothesis. They report that 2½-year-olds tended to recall the mundane, scriptlike aspects even of new and unusual events rather than emphasize the distinctive happenings. Such data are consistent with the notion that very young children experiencing novel events are apt to be in a schema-confirmation stage. As Farrar and Goodman would predict, to the extent that children are trying to make sense out of new experiences, they may emphasize their relationship to the already known.

However, Fivush and Hamond also report data that do not fit quite so well with a schema-confirmation hypothesis. The same 2½ year old children were asked to recall the same events once more when they were 4. Now the children tended to recall the distinctive aspects of the events rather than the expected ones – a fascinating finding that raises a host of issues. For one thing, it suggests a closer look at the schema-confirmation hypothesis. What else might be happening when a child is experiencing a new event beyond attempting to match it to an appropriate schema? We assume that new schemas are usually formed on the basis of extension and generalization from existing ones. Even very young children already know about eating before going to McDonald's for the first time and about going to bed at home before their first camping trip. It would be surprising if the child's attention were not captured by at least some of the new variations on the old activities. Indeed, this is one of the functions that we believe conscious attention is designed to perform. Why, then, do young children not recount these distinctive aspects? Is it only because they are emphasizing to themselves the familiar in the effort to organize and conceptualize the new situation? Even if this were so, one would expect children to dwell on the variations they are working to understand and incorporate, to mull them over and ponder them. One might have predicted, then, that the new, distinctive aspects of an event would loom even larger in their recall than in that of adults, since most "new" variations that adults experience are only minor wrinkles on highly familiar sequences.

Fivush and Hamond suggest several reasons, other than the tendency of the children at 2½ to focus on the familiar, to account for this shift in recall. Mothers cued the children's recall at 2½, and a stranger cued their recall at age 4. These two types of adults varied considerably in their cuing techniques. They also point out that the 4-year-olds had learned more about the conversational requirements of telling people about an event. I would like to offer still another explanation, one that Fivush and Hamond mention but do not emphasize. Perhaps the reason the 2½ year olds recounted the familiar aspects of events was due not so much to lack of attention to the distinctive new information, but to difficulty in formulating ways to express it. If we are to understand what young children recall, it seems we must determine the relationship between what they remember and what they say. It may help to approach this topic from the vantage point of preverbal children's recall, in which the relationship between remembering and verbal report is not at issue.

When do children first remember?

The age at which recall first manifests itself in infancy is still uncertain. I have suggested that the ability is present at least from 6 months (J. Mandler, 1988), but the evidence at this age is still slim. We have very few techniques for demonstrating awareness of the past in such young subjects. For example, Smith (1984) calls the anticipation of the next event in a sequence recall, but we have no independent evidence that her 5-month-old infants were consciously thinking about the event sequences. To learn to track a rapidly occurring series of events appears to be part of the automatic workings of our perceptual mechanisms, akin to the learning mechanisms found in conditioning phenomena. Similarly, in Rovee-Collier's work when a conditioned response is reinstated by re-presenting part of the stimulus context, we have no evidence that the infants *recall* the previous events; they may, but this kind of conditioning phenomenon can occur without conscious memory of what has been experienced in the past.

There does begin to be solid evidence for recall of past events by about 9 months, when it has been shown both in the laboratory (Meltzoff, 1988) and in diary accounts (Ashmead & Perlmutter, 1980) that infants can reproduce events observed the day before – either where an object was hidden or novel actions that they watched. Presumably there are no verbal elements in such recall, but the infants demonstrate that they are bringing a past event to mind by looking for the object in the correct place or by imitating what they had observed. Neither simple learning nor perceptual mechanisms can account for such behavior. By 16 months, as discussed in Bauer's and my chapter, both familiar and uniquely new events can be reproduced even after several weeks have passed. Again, no verbalization is required, nor is it likely that the past experience being re-created is represented in verbal form. Thus, the roots of recall are early enough that they are necessarily grounded in nonverbal experience.

Even as adults, much of what we recall spontaneously from our past is couched in imaginal rather than verbal form. Yet most studies of recall in the laboratory involve verbal material – lists of words, stories, and so forth. As a result, the relationship of recall of personal events to verbal report has not often been discussed. In addition, because for adults the translation from experience to verbal expression comes so easily it may not seem problematical. We know it is often difficult to express the details of a new experience, but we are so accustomed to expressing the gist of things in language that we forget how childlike our descriptions become when we are forced to describe some event that is truly new to us. The chapters by Fivush and Hamond and by Hudson make the important point that part of the apparent improvement in recall during the preschool years is due to the development of linguistic facility and of the narrative form we use to communicate our experiences to others.

One of the major tasks of studying the development of the recall function, then, is to disentangle recall, in the sense of remembering the events in question, from verbal report of those memories. Young children do not produce the same kind of verbal recall as do adults – especially for individual events – but the relationship of what they say to what they remember is something about which we have relatively little evidence. It is true that by the age of 3, as Nelson and her colleagues have demonstrated, children show the same overall form in their accounts of scripted events as do adults, recounting sequences in correct order, emphasizing the central actions, and even using the correct verb forms of the timeless present (Nelson & Gruendel, 1986). But these reports are of general knowledge, not the autobiographical recall of individual events that is the focus of this volume. As far as recall of one's personal past is concerned, young children are largely silent. But should we conclude from their silence that they don't remember anything, or that they are having trouble expressing in words what they do remember?

How much do young children remember?

The ambiguity of verbal report is one of the major stumbling blocks in our attempts to formulate a precise theory of both what and how much young children recall. The hypothesis put forth by Fivush and Hamond, and by Hudson as well, that young children rely on adults' cuing to provide retrieval cues is a very reasonable one. Its implication is that children cannot provide retrieval cues on their own and so cannot actually remember much without adults to guide them. However, it is probably not the whole story. First, there is evidence that even very young children often remember a lot on their own, as Nelson's (1984) study of crib memories indicates. Second, adults often give the wrong retrieval cues, as Fivush and

Hamond amply illustrate, which may interfere with adequate verbal production and even with the remembering process itself. In one of their protocols a mother is trying to get a child to remember a trip. She probes for the name of a restaurant they went to; the child says "Gasoline," apparently trying to express something entirely different about the trip. The mother persists until the child conforms to her agenda, and so we never find out what the child was originally trying to say. Third, adults typically don't wait very long for children to speak their minds: They tend to remind and fill in at any point a child seems to be struggling for words. This tendency does not disappear even when children become verbally more fluent than preschoolers usually are. An interesting study by Rowe (1974) found that the average time teachers waited for a reply when questioning children in elementary school science classes was only one second. Training teachers to wait even two seconds longer resulted in a significant increase in the amount of information the children recalled.

How are we to determine, then, whether the child has not recalled something or simply does not express it out loud? Or, more difficult still, how do we determine whether the effort of formulating a statement about a recalled event interferes with the expression of other aspects of the event or distorts the meaning the child is trying to express? Take the case of a child recalling her first camping trip. As mentioned earlier, Fivush and Hamond found that 2-year-olds tended to recall the routine aspects of such novel experiences, saying things like "We ate dinner and went to sleep." But could it be that the child remembers the novel elements of the experience but finds 'it too difficult to express the concept of, say, a sleeping bag? The child might be experiencing a vivid memory image, but one that defeats his or her descriptive capabilities. The verbal result might well be "We went to bed." In itself, then, the verbal statement is not proof that the child has recalled only the mundane aspects of the event.

So it may not be safe to assume that verbal protocols are straightforwardly associated with what is remembered about an event. The younger the child, the more problematical the relationship becomes. Certainly verbal reports underestimate the amount of information that is represented. A dramatic example of such underestimation is provided in the chapter by Goodman, Rudy, Bottoms, and Aman describing children's recall of an event when they could use dolls to reenact what had happened. Although the 3-year-olds' recall was low in either verbal or enactment conditions, the 5-year-olds' recall was twice as great when they acted out the event than when they recounted it verbally.

An equally dramatic instance of the underestimation of memory that verbal protocols provide is shown by the recall data that Fivush and Hamond collected from their 2½-year-olds. Only a quarter of what they said at this time was recounted when they were 4; that is, most of the information recalled at 4 had not been mentioned at 2½. I think we must assume from these data that the 2½-year-olds remembered much more than they reported. Such data do not imply that the memory itself is unstable. Indeed, Fivush and Hamond (in press) have reported other data, involving enactment rather than verbal recall, that indicate much greater consistency across repeated recalls than they found in the study reported in this volume.

One of the important points that Fivush and Hamond make is that 2½-year-olds tend to verbalize material mainly in response to adult questions. They also note, as just mentioned, that 4-year-olds have learned more about the narrative forms of recall. Both of these factors seem to be playing a role in the more abundant verbalizations of 4-year-olds, but they are just as consistent with the view that 2-year-olds talk less, not that they necessarily remember less. Such a view is also consistent with many studies in the literature reporting that younger children recall as much as older children do, but it takes a lot more work to extract the information from them.

Similar comments can be made about the dependency of young children's remembering on the retrieval cues provided by adults. The chapters by Fivush and Hamond and by Hudson provide clear demonstrations that parents initiate, lead, and guide very young recallers' verbal descriptions. They also show that how well children do on such reports is a function of the parents' interactive style. Although these results are consistent with the proposition that the children do not actually bring the relevant information to mind without the adults' retrieval cues, we cannot be sure that this is the case. The nagging worry remains that the children may be thinking about the event with a great deal more richness than they express. Several of the chapters in this volume allude to this problem. For example, Hudson offers three models of the way in which repeated verbal recall might affect memory development, pointing out that some aspects of each may be correct. In the information-processing model, repeated memory conversations are said to reactivate memories and strengthen retrieval paths. In the rote-learning model, repeated conversations provide children with a narrative about an event that eventually replaces the original memory. In the interactive learning model, memory conversations enable children to acquire both narrative skills for talking about the past and retrieval strategies for searching their own memory. Hudson mentions a fourth possibility but does not consider it further – namely, that repeated conversations improve language ability but do not affect memory per se, only the ability to talk about what one remembers. It is the last possibility that I stress here, if only to say it must be tested before we can be confident of the other explanations.

I think it is fair to say that at this point in our research we do not know the limits on how much young children remember. It may be the case that young children remember less or that their memory is skeletal and impoverished, but it may also be the case that they just talk less and less well. Two-year-olds' language is primitive, their fluency is poor, and the effort of production may even interfere with the remembering task at hand. The difficulties with language are apparent, but at the same time we must be careful not to confound them with the capacity to remember itself. It will tax our ingenuity to separate the ability to recall from the ability to report what one recalls, but this must be one of the major goals of future research in the field of memory development.

How long do children remember?

Recent research has produced some surprising information as to just how long young children can remember things. As reported in Bauer's and my chapter, 16- to 21-month-olds recall novel events experienced 2 to 6 weeks earlier. Nelson (1984) found that a 2-year-old spontaneously recalled events that occurred several months earlier. And quite remarkably, Fivush and Hamond's data indicate that 4-year-olds remember events that occurred at least 1½ years in the past. Most such data reflect experimenter-imposed time intervals, and because this type of research is quite recent there has not yet been enough time to study systematically the limits on such remembering.

One can at least suspect that there are in principle no limits (beyond one's age itself) in how long something can be remembered. Indeed, Sheingold and Tenney (1982), in one of the rare studies of long-term memory for childhood events, found no loss of information about the birth of a sibling at age 4 over a period of 16 years. Furthermore, I do not believe we can reject this hypothesis out of hand on the basis of the phenomenon of childhood amnesia. For one thing, childhood amnesia usually involves preverbal memories, and these must be the most difficult of all to cue after one has reached the age at which one's thought processes become saturated with language. For another, childhood amnesia is an ill-charted phenomenon. Some of us seem to have escaped its clutches at least partially, only to be barren of memories during other portions of our lives. I have great sympathy for researchers investigating this phenomenon, because it is such a difficult topic to study, yet the fact remains that we do not yet know how many memories escape the amnesia trap of early childhood. My own first memory was entirely visual and undated in my recollections until late adolescence, when by accident I learned from an adult who had been there what exactly had happened and how old I was at the time (18 months). It must be relatively rare that we are provided with confirmation about our earliest memories, and it is hardly surprising that we often have no idea when they took place. Calendar time is not something that looms large in young children's interests, and even vivid images do not necessarily include information about the surrounding context in which they were formed. Such lack of dating must make it difficult to be sure which are one's earliest memories.

The new work on early memories reported in this volume must also make us suspect the ubiquity of childhood amnesia. Of course, we are unlikely to have any conscious memories of the period in infancy before the late, explicit memory system is fully operational and recall makes its first appearance, whether that be at 6 months or slightly later. But do we have any reason to believe that Fivush and Hamond's 4-year-olds would be unable to recall anything about the events that took place at 2½ if asked again at 5? With the continual cuing that repeated recalls provide, it seems likely that these memories would remain accessible indefinitely. Of course, it is possible that they would become frozen into the verbal forms used in the telling, but this seems to be a common fate of frequently discussed memories at any age, not something peculiar to recall of very early experiences.

To the extent that with age we rely increasingly on verbal rehearsal of early memories (or on the verbal accounts of others about them), we might well end in the situation described by Fivush and Hamond. The images that escape report (as in the case of the 2-year-old who recounted about her camping trip only that she went to sleep) may become increasingly inaccessible or even eventually blocked by verbal accounts that were produced in the interim. Fivush and Hamond's data indicate that such blockage does not happen for many months, but as far as we know no verbal rehearsal took place during that period. In trying to report memories from childhood many years later, a great deal of talk about the events we do remember is more likely to have occurred. If this is the information that is most accessible, they may be all that we as experimenters hear about early memories. If no verbal rehearsal has been carried out, we may not hear anything at all.

All recall is cued, whether we are merely reminded of something or respond on the basis of a query. When others ask us about the past, typically we have only verbal cues to rely on. What a pity we cannot reinstate the rich contextual cues – the sights and sounds and smells – that surrounded the events as they occurred. We might be astounded – and gratified – to discover how much we remembered. There are many anecdotal accounts of children spontaneously recalling very old events when they visit a vacation home or a house where the family used to live. Until we can find a way to systematically cue such memories, we probably will not know just how much of our past survives.

Addendum

I want to end with a few comments on DeLoache's chapter, because even though her topic is not recall, her finding that 2½-year-olds have such great difficulty in understanding the correspondence between a room and its scale model is fascinating and surprising to most of us. We are surprised not only because of the insightlike abruptness with which the understanding seems to be gained, but also because we have ample evidence that children of this age can easily carry out event sequences using toy models of participants and props as substitutes for the real things. Even a 1½-year-old seems to have no difficulty in understanding that one can act out the event of bathing with a teddy bear and a dishpan, that a tiny tea set is satisfactory for a tea party, or even that in a pinch a banana can be used to make a pretend phone call (Bates, Bretherton, Shore, & McNew, 1983). All of these examples are called symbolic play, in which the child uses tiny models, or appropriately shaped substitutes in place of the real-world items. Why, then, can they not use a small model to stand for a real-world room, to imitate in one room what they see happening in the other?

DeLoache suggests that part of the difficulty is a problem of scale, since her children had less difficulty in understanding the correspondence between a small model of a room and a slightly larger model. But as DeLoache herself points out, there do not seem to be such problems of scale in symbolic play. Indeed, in playing with toys young children seem to be singularly uninfluenced by scale differences. Many of us have observed 2-year-olds seriously try to sit in a tiny toy chair, or try to squeeze a tiny shoe onto their own foot.

These observations may be a clue to the difficulty: Perhaps young children engaging in symbolic play are not being symbolic in quite the way we have usually assumed. They may be treating the tiny models as adequate *substitutes* for the real thing, not as symbolic representations of the real thing. They clearly use perceptual similarity to recognize both the similarities and the differences between the toy and the object; for example, they see that a doll looks like a real person, and they also see it is small and doesn't move or talk by itself (Massey & Gelman, 1988; Sera, Troyer, & Smith, 1988). But apparently there is a difference between understanding an object as a pretend or not-quite-real person and understanding that it is can be treated as a symbol for a person. I believe that DeLoache correctly places the source of difficulty in the lack of *awareness* that the model is supposed to be treated and used as a symbolic representation of the larger room (or vice versa). Apparently this is not a lack of awareness of similarity between model and room per se, but a lack of awareness that the correspondence can be used symbolically.

DeLoache also suggests that part of the difficulty 2½-year-old children experience in their understanding of models is because of the difficulty in treating a real thing in the world in two ways at once, both as itself and as standing for something else. The difficulty seems to lie not so much in understanding that a thing can have two different functions, because even younger children seem capable of doing that in other situations, but in understanding that a real thing can have a *symbolic* function in addition to being itself. Children *use* symbols long before this time; they speak, point, gesture, and engage in symbolic play. But apparently none of these activities requires being consciously aware of the symbolic function that is being carried out. It is interesting that this insight appears first with photographs, perhaps because photographs have no obvious functions of their own. No dual understanding is required, which, as DeLoache suggests, may make it easier to conceptualize the single symbolic function that they do have. What is still missing at this point seems to be the realization that objects as well as pictures can be treated as symbolic representations.

Both speech and symbolic play may involve simpler representational capacities than is required by the symbolic use of a model to locate a hidden object in the world. I find it interesting that chimpanzees experience exactly the same difficulty with the use of models as DeLoache describes for 2½-year-olds, even though language-trained chimps can manipulate symbols, solve fairly abstract analogical reasoning problems, and seem to understand the intentions of others (Premack & Premack, 1983). Language-trained chimps seem to show awareness of correspondence, but it is not clear that even they show awareness that correspondence can be used symbolically.

These speculations may well be wrong. Perhaps the difficulty 2½-year-old children have with DeLoache's task is due to something more mundane, such as the greatly different viewpoint one has when standing inside a real room that surrounds one compared to looking at a small space from the outside. Some such possibility is suggested by the children's success when the two spaces were both small enough to view from the outside. On the other hand, the fact that 2½-year-olds who failed the model task were successful when a picture was used returns us to DeLoache's hypothesis that the difficulty comes from lack of awareness of the symbolic possibilities of objects. Exactly what is involved in *awareness* of symbol use as opposed to symbol use itself is something that we do not yet understand very well and is a problem of outstanding importance for further research.

REFERENCES

Ashmead, D. H., & Perlmutter, M. (1980). Infant memory in everyday life. In M. Perlmutter (Ed.), *Children's memory* (New directions for child development, No. 10). San Francisco: Jossey-Bass.

Bates, E., Bretherton, I., Shore, C., & McNew, S. (1983). Names, gestures and objects: Symbolization in infancy and aphasia. In K. Nelson (Ed.), *Children's Language* (Vol. 4). Hillsdale, NJ: Erlbaum.

Cohen, N. J. (1984). Preserved learning capacity in amnesia: Evidence for multiple memory system. In L. R. Squire & N. Butters (Eds.), *Neuropsychology of memory*. New York: Guilford Press.

Fivush, R., & Hamond, N. R. (in press). Time and again: Effects of repetition and retention interval on two year olds' event recall. *Journal of Experimental Child Psychology*.

Haith, M. M., Hazan, C., & Goodman, G. S. (1988). Expectation and anticipation of dynamic visual events by 3.5-month-old babies. *Child Development, 59,* 467–479.

Mandler, G. (1989). Memory: Conscious and unconscious. In P. R. Solomon, G. P. Goethals, C. M. Kelley, & B. R. Stephens (Eds.). *Memory: Interdisciplinary approaches*. New York: Springer-Verlag.

Mandler, J. M. (1984). Representation and recall in infancy. In M. Moscovitch (Ed.), *Infant memory*. New York: Plenum.

Mandler, J. M. (1988). How to build a baby: On the development of an accessible representational system. *Cognitive Development, 3,* 113–136.

Massey, C. M., & Gelman, R. (1988). Preschoolers' ability to decide whether a photographed unfamiliar object can move itself. *Developmental Psychology, 24,* 307–317.

Meltzoff, A. N. (1988). Infant imitation and memory: Nine-month-olds in immediate and deferred tests. *Child Development, 59,* 217–225.

Nelson, K. (1984). The transition from infant to child memory. In M. Moscovitch (Ed.), *Infant memory*. New York: Plenum.

Nelson, K. (1986). Event knowledge and cognitive development. In K. Nelson (Ed.), *Event knowledge: Structure and function in development*. Hillsdale, NJ: Erlbaum.

Nelson, K., & Gruendel, J. (1986). Children's scripts. In K. Nelson (Ed.), *Event knowledge: Structure and function in development*. Hillsdale, NJ: Erlbaum.

Premack, D., & Premack, A. J. (1983). *The mind of an ape*. New York: Norton.

Rovee-Collier, C., & Hayne, H. (1987). Reactivation of infant memory: Implications for cognitive development. In H. W. Reese (Ed.), *Advances in child behavior and development*. New York: Academic Press.

Rowe, M. B. (1974). Wait-time and rewards as instructional variables, their influence on language, logic, and fate-control: Part One: Wait-time. *Journal of Research on Science Teaching, 2,* 81–94.

Schacter, D. L. (1987). Implicit memory: History and current status. *Journal of Experimental Psychology: Learning, Memory, and Cognition, 13,* 501–518.

Schacter, D. L., & Moscovitch, M. (1984). Infants, amnesics, and dissociable memory systems. In M. Moscovitch (Ed.), *Infant memory*. New York: Plenum.

Sera, M. D., Troyer, D., & Smith, L. B. (1988). What do two-year-olds know about the size of things? *Child Development, 59,* 1489–1496.

Sheingold, K., & Tenney, Y. J. (1982). Memory for a salient childhood event. In U. Neisser (Ed.), *Memory observed: Remembering in natural contexts*. San Francisco: W. H. Freeman.

Smith, P. H. (1984). Five-month-old infant recall and utilization of temporal organization. *Journal of Experimental Child Psychology, 38,* 400–414.

14

Learning from the children

ULRIC NEISSER

The detour problem, illustrated in Figure 14.1, is a well-known test of problem-solving skill. The eager protagonist (*EP*), hoping to reach the unusually attractive morsel (*UAM*), would be wise to take a detour to one side (*DS*); the direct route may look inviting, but it does not lead to success. The research reported in this volume suggests, surprisingly often, that the same principle may apply to the study of memory. Experimental psychologists (*EP*) have sought an understanding of adult memory (*UAM*) for many years, but the results have not been entirely satisfactory. Traditional memory experiments, despite the significant findings they have produced, still fail to answer certain fundamental questions – most notably the one that Alan Baddeley (1988) has recently rephrased as "But what the hell's it for?" In the mid-1970s, some of us reacted to this situation by turning away from traditional memory tasks and materials in favor of more naturalistic studies (Neisser, 1978). But this "ecological movement," which has in fact managed to widen the scope of acceptable memory research to some extent (Neisser, 1988a), has so far enjoyed only modest success in grappling with functional questions like Baddeley's. Fortunately, help is at hand. The study of knowing and remembering in young children, reviewed in this volume, is beginning to produce a significant body of findings – work that is critically revelant to functional questions about memory. Like the attractive morsel in the diagram, understanding of adult memory (*UAM*) may be more easily accessible if we take a detour via developmental studies (*DS*).

But is it really reasonable to take this route? Is the course of human development continuous enough to warrant generalization from children to adults? Until recently, the dominant view in developmental psychology was just the opposite. Following Piaget, it was widely assumed that the mental life of young children is radically different from that of adults. Children in the "sensorimotor stage" were incapable of reasoning; they did not understand narrative or causal sequences, lived only in the present moment, and were radically egocentric. If this were really an

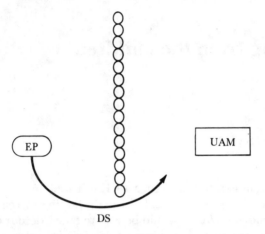

DS

Figure 14.1. The detour problem.

accurate picture of childhood, developmental studies would hold few attractions for psychologists interested in adult memory.

Fortunately, recent work suggests that matters are otherwise. Many lines of evidence now point to the existence of substantial continuities across development – continuities that were obscured by particular features of traditional experimental paradigms (cf. Gelman, 1977; Keil, 1986). Indeed, at least two chapters of the present volume provide further evidence of that continuity: one by Patricia Bauer and Jean Mandler, the other by Judy DeLoache. Bauer and Mandler tackle the issue explicitly: Can very young children (16 to 20 months old) understand and reproduce causal sequences? Contrary to what would once have been expected, their results give a clear affirmative answer to this question. In one experiment, even 16-month olds successfully reproduced a novel causally linked three-event sequence after a single presentation. At the age of 20 months, there was evidence of correct reproduction even after a 2-week delay. To be sure, this behavior does not necessarily demonstrate "recall of order" in any literal sense; the subjects may have remembered the outcome of the sequence and figured out how to make it happen again. But whatever the correct interpretation, it is clear that children understand the domain of causes and consequences well before their second birthday.

DeLoache's study of scale models bears on the continuity issue in a very different way. At first glance, she seems to have discovered a striking new *discontinuity* effect. Two-and-a-half-year-old children who watch a toy being hidden in the model have no notion where to find it in the corresponding room, whereas 3-year-olds go directly to the matching location. Doesn't this mean that an important new mode of logical reasoning (perhaps something like "symbolic representation") emerges at the age of 3? Well, no: DeLoache's ingenious follow-up experiments reveal quite a different story. It turns out that the 2½-year-olds have no difficulty in using a *picture* of the room to guide their search. Moreover, once they have done so (and thus been alerted to the relevance of symbolic representation in this particular task) they often succeed with the scale model as well. And the 3-year-olds, who seemed to have such a good grasp of representation, begin to fail the task as soon as the correspondence between model and room is made less obvious by decreasing the visual similarity of their contents. Development has not produced a fundamental shift from one kind of thinking to another, only a change in the probability of noticing a particular relationship under particular circumstances.

This does not mean, of course, that there are no cognitive differences between 30- and 36-month-old children, or between children and adults. But they are less differences of *kind* than of *situation and experience;* much the same mechanisms are at work, but they are being deployed in different circumstances and with access to different resources. Consider, for example, Robyn Fivush and Nina Hamond's discussion of childhood amnesia in this volume. Their data show that 2½-year-olds can recall things that happened to them 6 months earlier. What's more, the same children can still describe aspects of those events when they are interviewed 18 months later, at the age of 4; at that point, the events themselves lie 2 full years in the past. Why, then, do adults remember so little from this period of their lives? Fivush and Hamond suggest two reasons that have not previously been considered in this context. First, what the youngest children actually recall consists mostly of routine aspects of the events ("What did you do there?" "Went to sleep!"). Such routine matters are not very memorable at any age, so it is easy to understand that they do not persist into adulthood. Second, the children's memories of particular events are not very stable: Being more dependent than adults on the cues offered by their conversational partners, they tend to recall different aspects of an event on different occasions. This, in turn, is because they cannot yet provide their own internal retrieval cues; such cues arise from narrative schemata that they have not had the time to acquire. These interpretations illustrate how large differences between the achievements of adults and children can easily appear despite basic continuity of the underlying mechanisms.

Given that continuity, what can we learn from the developmental studies reported here? It seems to me that they shed light on three interrelated problems: (1) the role of social factors in memory; (2) the functions of schemata; and (3) the role of arousal and involvement in determining the accuracy of recall. The first of these may be the most important, if only because it has been so widely neglected by students of adult memory. An examination of the studies typically reported in journals like *Memory and Cognition* would never lead one to think of recall as a social process, but it usually is. Indeed – as Barbara Rogoff and Jayanthi Mistry point out in their chapter – even a standard memory experiment creates a social situation. But it is a situation with rather unusual rules: One party (the subject) does all the remembering, while the other (the experimenter) has very little to say. In more natural settings people often remember the past together, establishing a valuable and continuing community of experience as they do so.

In principle, there is no reason why joint remembering could not be studied at any age. Nevertheless the topic has held little interest for students of adult memory: Bartlett (1932) was concerned with it half a century ago, but few modern investigators have followed his lead. Most of those few have been engaged either in cross-cultural research or in studies of aging, and have appealed to social factors to explain group differences in achievement (see Rogoff & Mistry's chapter for a partial review of this work). One research group that has studied the social determinants of recall from a somewhat different perspective is worth mentioning here: that of Derek Edwards and David Middleton (1986a, 1986b, 1987, 1988) at Loughborough University in England. These authors have shown, for example (1986a), that a group of young adults recalling a film they have all seen use their memories very differently than do subjects in typical laboratory recall paradigms. Indeed, each of us has a whole range of social memory skills that those recall paradigms never tap. We know how to participate in many kinds of discussion about the past: what to say, and to whom, and about what; when to say it and when to remain silent; whom to listen to and whom to interrupt and whom to believe; what to expect as a consequence of such a discussion.

Whatever its status in adult studies, the social function of memory is front and center in the developmental work reported here. Three chapters address it explicitly. Judith Hudson shows how joint remembering first emerges in mother–child dialogue; Fivush and Hamond explore the role of the adult partner in that dialogue, whether mother or experimenter (a topic that Hudson also addresses); Rogoff and Mistry describe how the social practices of different societies support (or do not support) memory performances of different kinds. But these three chapters do not exhaust the topic; even when the social function of memory is not the main focus of a developmental study, it is never far out of sight. Young children cannot simply be asked to "remember" in the same casual way that we address our adult subjects. What and how much they will recall depends crucially on how comfortable they are in the test situation. Because children generally prefer friendly games to meaningless tasks (although there may be exceptions to this principle – cf. Weissberg &

Paris, 1986), most developmentalists try to establish a gamelike atmosphere in their laboratories. That is why DeLoache used a Snoopy doll as her hidden target object, why Jeff Farrar and Gail Goodman hired an actor to dress up in different animal costumes to mark the different phases of their experiment, why Hilary Ratner and her collaborators found themselves making many more batches of clay than they probably wanted. For developmental psychologists, the role of social factors in memory is not so much a hypothesis as a fact of life.

To understand why the social setting of recall is so important for children, we must begin with the first appearance of memory in family conversations about past events. Remembering seems to follow a quintessentially Vygotskian course of development, appearing first as a social activity and only later as a private one: "Every function in the child's cultural development appears twice, first on the social level and later on the individual level; first *between* people (*interpsychological*) and then *inside* the child (*intrapsychological*)" (Vygotsky, 1978, p. 57; italics in original). Just this development is traced out in Hudson's longitudinal study of her daughter Rachel's memory conversations. When the study began at 21 months, Rachel could already give some evidence of memory. She answered some yes–no questions ("Did you see Aunt Gail and Uncle Tim last week?" "Yes, yes, Uncle Tim."), and would occasionally offer single items of information in response to specific inquiries ("What did we do with Aunt Gail and Uncle Tim?" "Said bye-bye."). But she did not initiate or actively sustain such conversations; each mnemonic tidbit was produced in response to a specific cue provided by her mother. When the study ended at 27 months, matters were very different. Rachel now remembered things spontaneously and was beginning to ask her mother about them. ("Do you remember the waves, Mommy?" [. . . What about the waves?] "I go in the waves and I build a sand castle. And do you remember we swimmed? I swimmed in the waves and we did it again. Did we play again?") Although even this recall is still very much a social event, Rachel's easy initiation of it suggests that she would be quite capable of remembering things privately as well.

Hudson's analysis of these data permit her to rule out certain counterhypotheses that would otherwise present themselves. Rachel did not simply repeat the same words, for example, or remember the same things over and over again. On the contrary, repeated recalls of the same event typically produced new material every time. This is, apparently, a very general tendency in young children's memory. Hudson also observed it in her follow-up study of 10 other children in the same age range, each of whom was tape-recorded in four different conversations with his or her mother. More than half of the children's reports in the three later sessions consisted of material that had not been mentioned before. In a fifth session with an experimenter, more than a third of the children's reports consisted of information that had not been reported in any of four earlier conversations with the mother about the same event. An even stronger effect of this kind is reported by Fivush and Hamond. In their study, children first recalled a past event with their mothers and then, 6 weeks later, with an unfamiliar experimenter. Under these conditions, *three-quarters* of what the children told the experimenter had gone unmentioned in the earlier recalls with their mothers. This must be partly because the subjects were aware that the experimenter (unlike the mother) had not shared the experience that was being recalled, but it also suggests again that young children are very dependent on cues from their partners in memory conversations.

What young children acquire by engaging in such conversations, then, is not just specific familiarity with particular bygone events; it is a more general ability to talk about the past with other people. This achievement can be described from two different perspectives, one cultural and one psychological. At the cultural level, the children are being introduced to what Rogoff and Mistry call a *cultural practice*. The term *practice* is widely used across several disciplines; it can refer to any coherent shared activity that has its own rules and values. A particularly interesting definition has been offered by the philosopher Alisdair MacIntyre:

By a "practice" I am going to mean any coherent and complex form of socially established cooperative human activity through which goods internal to that activity are realized. (1984, p. 187)

Conversation is surely just such an activity, and the "goods internal to it" are the experiences of community and mutual understanding achieved by both partners in the dialogue. To be sure, MacIntyre himself is thinking primarily of more formalized practices – sports, music, or science, for example – in which standards of excellence are explicitly applied. For that reason he continues his definition as follows:

... in the course of trying to achieve those standards of excellence which are appropriate to, and partially definitive of, that form of activity, with the result that human powers to achieve excellence, and human conceptions of the ends and goods involved, are systematically extended. (1984, p. 187)

All this emphasis on *excellence* sounds a bit heavy for mother–child conversation, but perhaps it is not entirely wide of the mark. I do tend to think of Rachel's later conversations as not only more complex but genuinely "better" than her earlier ones. Similar judgments can be made about adults: It is often remarked that some people are better conversationalists than others. So far we know rather little about this dimension, but the distinction between more and less "elaborative" maternal speaking styles – first proposed by Engel (1986) and Fivush & Fromhoff (in

press), and replicated here by Hudson – may help us to understand it
eventually. MacIntyre himself gives "the making and sustaining of family
life" (1984, p. 188), an activity that surely includes the conduct of
parent–child conversations, as an example of a practice.

I wish to treat conversation about the past as a practice because, as
MacIntyre points out, practices define *virtues*. Good conversation requires not just memory but also sensitivity and honesty and intelligence,
and occasionally courage as well. And, of course, it is not something that
one person does but that two or more people do together. If we take
Baddeley's question seriously, we may now be closing in on some idea of
what memory is *for*. It is to allow people to exercise those virtues that
exhibit themselves most clearly in social intercourse – to be thoughtful
and forthcoming and honest and mutually attentive, for example. (To be
sure, it is also the prerequisite for many vices, including manipulation
and hypocrisy. That's life!) On such an account, Rachel's conversations
with her mother represented her first initiations into a highly significant
social practice.

From the psychological point of view, what Rachel has learned can be
described somewhat differently. As adults, we are familiar with a standard format for recalling past events. Unless they know it already, for
example, our listeners will want to know what happened, whom it happened to, where and how the events took place. They will be particularly
interested in the *unique* aspects of the experience, taking routine matters
for granted; they often ask how we felt about it, and what the consequences were. All this constitutes the so-called narrative schema, which
adults have but young children have not yet acquired. Lacking this
schema, children cannot provide themselves with the right retrieval cues
at the right times; hence (as Fivush and Hamond point out), they are
dependent on whatever their conversational partner may provide. Hudson's longitudinal study is, then, an account of one child's acquisition of
this narrative schema, or at least the beginnings of it. On either interpretation it is important for students of adult memory, documenting the
origins of some of the schemata (or some of the practices) on which our
own research implicitly depends.

Rogoff and Mistry are less concerned with autobiographical recall
than with the kinds of memory tasks that experimenters typically set for
their subjects. Because such tasks draw heavily on the skills developed by
formal schooling, they pose special difficulties for three groups of subjects: (1) preschool children; (2) unschooled children and adults from
traditional societies; and (3) elderly individuals who have been away
from school for many years. Here is another example of the influence of
social factors on memory: This time the critical practice is not conversational remembering but the recall of isolated and meaningless pieces of

information on demand. The special contribution of Rogoff and Mistry's chapter is to show that relatively subtle aspects of the recall situation can affect the perceived meaningfulness of such a task.

Some years ago the Soviet psychologist Z. M. Istomina (1975) reported a demonstration of the importance of recall context that has become rather well known. Preschool children were given a number of items to remember, either as a laboratory task or as part of a game that involved "shopping" at a play store. Recall was markedly higher in the latter case. Recently, however, Weissberg and Paris (1986) have reported a failure to replicate Istomina's result; *their* subjects remembered more in the laboratory setting. I have elsewhere (Neisser, 1988b) interpreted this finding as evidence that American 4- and 5-year-olds of the 1980s can deploy more sophisticated schemata than did their Soviet counterparts of a generation ago: for better or worse, our children are already quite accustomed to arbitrary memory tasks. But Rogoff and Mistry, while also admitting this possibility, suggest another and more testable interpretation: the "shopping game" that was used by Weissberg and Paris may just not have been very involving for the subjects. When they conducted their own replication using a more convincing activity – one in which the child's parents also participated – the Istomina result reappeared in full force.

Perhaps the most interesting contribution of Rogoff and Mistry's chapter stems from their cross-cultural perspective on interactions between parents and children. Most modern American middle-class parents enjoy talking with their children, and often engage them in conversation. The studies reported here by Hudson and by Fivush and Hamond took full advantage of this propensity: Parents and children were explicitly asked to talk to each other about the past, and they did so without hesitation. Nevertheless, this custom is by no means universal. In the Mayan culture described by Rogoff and Mistry, children do not readily offer information to any adult, not even their parents. To do so would be perceived as an impertinence by both parties to the conversation. Not surprisingly, such children perform poorly in experiments that require them to repeat stories to adult listeners; they are reluctant to put themselves forward. Although *adult* conversation about the past is surely as common a practice (in MacIntyre's sense) among the Maya as it is anywhere else, the course of its development is evidently somewhat different than in the United States.

The discussion so far suggests that the first two points of contact between developmental and adult studies of memory – social factors and schemata – actually overlap quite a bit. The social forms of memory we have considered constitute *practices,* supported by cultural institutions and conducted in relevant social settings, but they are also dependent on particular knowledge structures. Without a narrative schema, one can-

not engage in effective, self-cued recall; without some schema for organizing and remembering indifferent material, one cannot do well in
laboratory recall tasks. Two other chapters in this volume – those by
Ratner, Smith, and Padgett and by Farrar and Goodman – also examine
the functioning of memory schemata in young children. The chapter by
Ratner and her collaborators is a straightforward examination of how
children organize a complex clay-making task, and needs no elaboration
here. The work reported by Jeff Farrar and Gail Goodman, however, is
especially relevant to my argument.

Farrar and Goodman take for granted what I have been at such pains
to point out: that a detour via developmental studies can shed important light on issues in the study of adult memory. Their experiments
were explicitly designed to test a theory that Goodman herself had
already advanced in an adult context: the *schema confirmation–deployment
hypothesis* (Goodman & Golding, 1983). That hypothesis addresses one
of the oldest and most vexing problems in memory research: When an
event does not conform to one's schemata, does its novelty make it *more
difficult* or *easier* to remember? Both possibilities make intuitive sense,
and both have some empirical support. On the one hand, Bartlett
(1932) originally proposed the schema concept to explain why unfamiliar material was difficult to recall, and it often is. On the other hand,
unique and surprising events are typically remembered better than the
schema-conforming background with which they contrast. Goodman's
hypothesis resolves this paradox by postulating two successive phases in
the establishment of schemata. She suggests that a new schema must be
"confirmed" – that is, put on a solid footing – before contrast effects
can appear. During this initial phase, schema-congruent material is well
remembered, whereas incongruent material is typically absorbed or ignored. Once solidly established, however, the schema can be "deployed"; at that point, contrasting events will be noticed and remembered better than schema-typical ones.

In the experiments reported here, Farrar and Goodman use the development of young children's memory as a vehicle to test this theory. Both
4- and 7-year-old children underwent a complex series of novel and
repeated experiences – "episodic visits" and "script visits," respectively, in
the authors' terminology. How should recall of the (relatively deviant)
episodic visits compare with recall of visits that conformed to the (increasingly familiar) script? The theory predicts that the *episodic* visits should be
better recalled by the 7-year-olds, because older children are more likely
to have reached the stage of schema deployment during the course of the
experiment. The younger children should take longer to catch on, and
may remain engaged in schema confirmation throughout the whole series of experiences. If so, they will do better with the *scripted* visits instead.

The results of the study are complex, but in general they bear out the authors' predictions. The 4-year-olds tended to ignore deviations from the script, and assimilated the deviant events to the overall schema that they were still in the process of mastering. The 7-year-olds, in contrast, often noticed and recalled the special characteristics of the episodic visits. Farrar and Goodman are careful to remind us that this outcome does not reflect general characteristics of the age groups involved. Four-year-olds can certainly notice and remember novel events on occasion, and 7-year-olds often fail to do so. According to the schema confirmation–deployment hypothesis, the outcome does not depend primarily on the age of the subject but only on whether the novelty in question is with respect to a well-confirmed schema. Here, then, is a paradigmatic instance of a productive detour through developmental studies: A problem that has long vexed the study of adult memory has been clarified by a study comparing two groups of children.

Three other chapters remain to be considered. Two of them – those by Ceci, Toglia, and Ross and by Goodman, Rudy, Bottoms, and Aman – deal with the critically important issue of suggestibility in child witnesses; the third, by Ann Renninger, emphasizes the importance of children's interests in determining what they will remember. At first glance the controversy over children's testimony appears to be a self-contained problem, with little bearing on classical issues in the study of adult memory. We shall see, however, that this impression is mistaken: The findings reported in these chapters may have profound implications for theories about the accuracy of memory at any age.

Ceci et al. argue that children are appreciably more suggestible than adults, and hence that courts should be especially wary in evaluating their testimony (e.g., in cases of alleged child abuse). They support their argument with both historical and experimental evidence: the Salem witch trials on the one hand and their own "misinformation" experiments on the other. It seems to me, however, that the witch trials are largely irrelevant to the issues under consideration here. We cannot now be sure of the reason for the Salem witnesses' bizarre testimony and behavior: The possibilities include ergot poisoning (Caporael, 1976; but cf. Spanos & Gottlieb, 1976); mass hysteria (whatever that is); and just plain malicious lying. Whatever was going on, one thing is clear – the witnesses were adolescent girls in the age range from 10 to 16 years, not "young children" in the sense that that term is used in the present volume. More important, they were not in the age range identified by Ceci et al. themselves as especially vulnerable to suggestion. The lesson of Salem is that we must beware of waves of excited witnesses who testify to outrageous things, whatever their age. It is *not*, I think, that very young children are especially likely to engage in this behavior.

The suggestibility experiments of Ceci et al. are extensions of the misinformation paradigm introduced by Elizabeth Loftus some years ago (e.g., Loftus & Palmer, 1974). The subjects first hear a story; in this case, one about a girl eating breakfast. Later on they are asked questions that include misleading information about the story; still later, they are given a test of recognition memory. The results show that preschool children are more vulnerable to such suggestions than older children (and, presumably, than adults), and that misinformation presented by an adult carries more weight with them than similar misinformation presented by another child. These findings dovetail nicely with those reported by Farrar and Goodman, whose 4-year-olds tended to confuse characteristics of the "episodic visits" with those of the "script visits." In both studies, children of preschool age experienced greater difficulty than older children in distinguishing between sources of information: two kinds of visits in Farrar and Goodman, a story and a set of leading questions in Ceci et al.

The misinformation effects reported by Ceci, Toglia, and Ross, like those originally described by Loftus and her associates, have important implications for the study of testimony. Nevertheless, we must be careful how we generalize from these effects. So far, they have only been demonstrated in a rather narrow range of situations. This point, also noted by Ceci et al., is stressed by Gail Goodman and her collaborators in their chapter entitled "Children's Concerns and Memory." The subjects of such experiments do not *participate* in the to-be-remembered events; they only observe them, or hear about them, or see slides depicting them. It is more than a little dubious to extend their conclusions to situations where children are deeply and personally involved, as in accusations of sexual abuse.

Goodman, Rudy, Bottoms, and Aman are not content with pointing out this potential confound; they report the results of several ingenious studies in which it is overcome. It is characteristic of their research that children must recall situations in which they *were* personally involved; in the course of the recall interview children are systematically exposed to leading questions about possible sexual abuse. The first of the Goodman et al. experiments was designed to permit a direct comparison between participants' and bystanders' memories of the same event. Two young children (either two 4-year-olds or two 7-year-olds) spend 12 minutes with a friendly young man; one child gets to play games with him – to tickle him, to put on a clown costume, to have his or her own photograph taken, and so on – while the other child simply observes. Each child recalls the event 10 or 12 days later, in an interview that includes a number of leading questions. Some of these are relatively neutral: "He had a beard and mustache, right?" (In fact, the man was clean-shaven.)

Others are clearly suggestive or sexual abuse: "He took your clothes off, didn't he?" "Did he kiss the other boy?" If young children are really very suggestible, questions like these would be expected to induce serious errors of memory.

In fact, they rarely did. The bystanders were somewhat more suggestible than the participants, but even they proved strongly resistant to leading questions about sexual abuse. In agreement with the findings of Ceci et al., 4-year-olds were more suggestible than 7-year-olds; again, however, this tendency did not reach statistical significance when the questions concerned possible abuse. The older children were completely suggestion-proof in such matters; except for one obscure response about "touching," none of the 7-year-olds answered even a single question in a way that might indicate the occurrence of abusive behavior. Very few of the 4-year-olds did either, but one (out of 18) did assent to "Did he kiss you?" and "Did he kiss the other child?"; another answered positively to both "Did he kiss you" and two questions about spanking. It is also noteworthy that one of the 4-year-olds gave a number of unpredicted bizarre responses: He said there had been blood and bones in the trailer, and that the man had used a magic wand to make the other little boy disappear.

Viewing the data as a whole, one has the impression that most of the children knew very well what had happened and were not about to accept what they considered to be absurd suggestions. If this experience had become the focus of allegations about sexual abuse, the overwhelming majority of the subjects – even of the 4-year-olds – would have given trustworthy reports. But it is also worth noting that one child spontaneously produced a series of odd and potentially frightening statements at the interview; it is easy to imagine situations in which such an account would be taken as evidence that something untoward had occurred. These data remind us that while it is foolish to rule all testimony by young children out of court, it would also be rash to take everything that a child says at face value. Children differ from one another at least as much as adults do, and the credibility of a potential witness can never be taken for granted.

Goodman et al. report several further experiments on children's susceptibility to leading questions, all tending to the same general conclusion. When an event closely concerns a child, he or she will remember it much more accurately (and much less "suggestibly") than might be expected on the basis of studies that have used less personally involving material. In my view, this conclusion has much in common with the argument of Ann Renninger's chapter on children's interests. Renninger examined videotapes of her subjects' free play to establish what they were most interested in, and used toys representing those interests in subsequent experiments. It turns out that children not only attend more to objects that interest them but also remember such objects better and play with them in more sophisticated ways. The effects are substantial, and would probably generalize to other experimental situations. It seems to me, for example, that the paradigms of Ceci, Goodman, and Renninger could profitably be combined: Children should resist suggestions most strongly when they concern personally interesting material.

Perhaps these results are not surprising. Don't we already know that people remember best what interests them most? If we do, it is not on the basis of any systematic research. Most students of adult memory have shied away from motivational variables. Indeed, there are good reasons for doing so: Variables like "interest" are hard to control and even harder to conceptualize. As a consequence, however, the psychology of memory has been largely the study of how people remember things they don't much care about. That might be all very well if the same principles apply at every level of interest and concern, but what if they don't? Here is another area where a detour via developmental studies may be very productive. Young children wear their hearts on their sleeves; neither their interests nor their dislikes long escape the notice of anyone around them. If we want to know the effect of strong personal feelings on what will subsequently be remembered, they may be exactly the experimental subjects we need.

This point is vividly illustrated in another study reported by Goodman et al. Young children were videotaped as they received inoculations at a clinic, and were interviewed later – some as much as a year later – about what had happened. Again the interviews included potentially suggestive questions about abuse: "Did she hit you? Did she kiss you?" The results for leading questions were very clear: Few children responded "yes" to any such question at any point. Even more interesting (to me) was the effect of high stress levels on the overall accuracy of the recalls. Some children take their shots rather calmly, but others do not; sometimes it takes two or three adults to hold a screaming child down long enough for the inoculation to proceed. Surprisingly, the more agitated children recalled the event *more completely* (when interviewed a few days later by Goodman et al.) than those who had seemed to take it in their stride.

These findings are extremely important. They offer a new perspective on yet another traditional problem in the study of memory: Does high arousal improve or worsen recall? As in the (possibly related) case of novelty, both alternatives are intuitively plausible. We all have vivid memories of at least a few very arousing personal experiences, and are reluctant to believe that we could be wrong about them. On the other hand, it is widely agreed that cognition becomes less efficient under conditions of high arousal; this is one aspect of the so-called Yerkes–Dodson law. In fact, however, there is surprisingly little research in this area. Loftus and Burns (1982) have shown that recall of details in a film is sharply reduced by the presentation of an unexpected violent episode, but their subjects were spectators rather than participants. It is usually assumed that so-called flashbulb memories, like one's recollection of hearing the news of President Kennedy's assassination, are essentially correct (Brown & Kulik, 1982), but real assessment of their accuracy is rarely possible. They may well be mistaken: Harsch and Neisser (1989) have found that subjects' very confident memories of the explosion of the space shuttle *Challenger* three years earlier are often wildly inaccurate. Even here, however, the emotions and activities connected with the to-be-recalled event were those of a spectator rather than a participant.

At this point, any discussion of recall accuracy for highly emotional experiences must remain inconclusive. Even the Goodman et al. inoculation study, which makes such an important contribution to that discussion, is subject to various interpretations. The more highly aroused children in that study were also those who underwent a more complex and differentiated experience; perhaps, then, they just had more to remember. (A bystander experiment would be very useful here: How much would a young *witness* to the drama of another child's stressful inoculation remember about it?) Most children receive a number of inoculations over a period of several years: Do they thus establish "scripts" for the process, which can later mediate recall? Do some children have screaming and fussing as part of their inoculation scripts? Would children remember what happened just as well if it were their first experience of this kind? These comments are not intended as criticisms of the Goodman et al. study. They only show that the question is still open, and illustrate some of the fruitful possibilities that the inoculation-memory paradigm may afford.

The psychology of memory has already benefited substantially from these developmental studies, and can expect to gain a great deal more in the future. The social aspects of recall, long ignored by those of us who study only adults, are moving into the foreground where they belong; the study of memory schemata may be especially productive in children, whose understanding of the situations in which they find themselves is often still incomplete; the role of emotion in memory may soon be clarified by research with subjects whose emotions are so easily aroused and so publicly apparent. We have every reason to appreciate the contribution made by the investigators whose work is represented here. If their young subjects still have a lot to learn, so do the rest of us.

REFERENCES

Baddeley, A. (1988). But what the hell's it for? In M. M. Gruneberg, P. E. Morris, & R. N. Sykes (Eds.), *Practical aspects of memory: Current issues and research* (Vol. 1). Chichester: Wiley.

Bartlett, F. C. (1932). *Remembering.* Cambridge: Cambridge University Press.

Brown, E. F., & Kulik, J. (1982). Flashbulb memories. In U. Neisser (Ed.), *Memory observed* (pp. 23–40). San Francisco: W. H. Freeman.

Caporael, L. R. (1976). Ergotism: The Satan loosed in Salem? *Science, 192,* 21–36.

Edwards, D., & Middleton, D. (1986a). Joint remembering: Constructing an account of shared experience through conversational discourse. *Discourse Processes, 9,* 423–459.

Edwards, D., & Middleton, D. (1986b). Text for memory: Joint recall with a scribe. *Human Learning, 5,* 125–138.

Edwards, D., & Middleton, D. (1987). Conversation and remembering: Bartlett revisited. *Applied Cognitive Psychology, 1,* 77–92.

Edwards, D., & Middleton, D. (1988). Conversational remembering and family relationships: How children learn to remember. *Journal of Social and Personal Relationships, 5,* 3–25.

Engel, S. (1986). The role of mother–child interaction in autobiographical recall. In J. A. Hudson (Chair), *Learning to talk about the past.* Symposium at the Southeast Conference on Human Development, Nashville.

Fivush, R., & Fromhoff, F. A. (in press). Style and structure in mother–child conversations about the past. *Discourse Processes.*

Gelman, R. (1977) Cognitive development. *Annual Review of Psychology, 29,* 297–332.

Goodman, G. S., & Golding, J. (1983). Effects of real-world knowledge on memory. In K. Nelson (Chair), *Memory and representation of the real world.* Symposium at the Society for Research in Child Development, Detroit.

Harsch, N., & Neisser, U. (1989). Substantial and irreversible errors in flashbulb memories of the *Challenger* explosion. Poster presented at meeting of the Psychonomic Society, Atlanta.

Istomina, Z. M. (1975). The development of voluntary memory in children of preschool age. *Soviet Psychology, 13,* 7–64.

Keil, F. C. (1986). On the structure-dependent nature of stages of cognitive development. In I. Levin (Ed.), *Stage and structure.* Norwood NJ: Ablex.

Loftus, E. F., & Burns, T. E. (1982). Mental shock can produce retrograde amnesia. *Memory and Cognition, 10,* 318–323.

Loftus, E. F., & Palmer, J. C. (1974). Reconstruction of automobile destruction. *Journal of Verbal Learning and Verbal Behavior, 13,* 585–589.

MacIntyre, A. (1984). *After virtue* (2nd ed.). Notre Dame, IN: University of Notre Dame Press.

Neisser, U. (1978). Memory: What are the important questions? In M. M. Gruneberg, P. E. Morris, & R. N. Sykes (Eds.), *Practical aspects of memory.* London: Academic Press.

Neisser, U. (1988a). Domains of memory. In P. R. Solomon, G. R. Goethals, C. M. Kelley, & B. R. Stephens (Eds.), *Memory: Interdisciplinary approaches.* New York: Springer-Verlag.

Neisser, U. (1988b). Time present and time past. In M. M. Gruneberg, P. E.

Morris, & R. N. Sykes (Eds.), *Practical aspects of memory: Current research and issues* (Vol. 2). Chichester: Wiley.

Spanos, N. P., & Gottlieb, J. (1976). Ergotism and the Salem Village witch trials. *Science, 194,* 1390–1394.

Vygotsky, L. S. (1978). *Mind in society: The development of higher mental processes.* Cambridge, MA: Harvard University Press.

Weissberg, J. A., & Paris, S. G. (1986). Young children's remembering in different contexts: A reinterpretation of Istomina's study. *Child Development, 57,* 1123–1129.

Name index

Abbott, V., 32
Ableson, R. P., 9, 31, 32, 33 66
Acredolo, L. P., 111
Alba, J., 11
Aman, C., 6, 272, 279, 291, 298, 299, 312, 324, 340, 341–342, 343, 344
Ames, E. W., 39
Anderson, R. C., 31, 134
Angelino, H., 252
Arnold, F., 141
Ashmead, D. H., 21, 322
Austin, G. A., 129

Baddeley, A. D., 272
Bahrick, H. P., 266
Bahrick, P. O., 266
Baillargeon, R., 96
Baillet, S. D., 251, 252, 272
Baird, W., 131, 134
Baldwin, J. M., 132
Barrett, M., 65
Barsalou, L., 4, 32, 44, 66, 241, 246
Bartlett, F. C., 31, 33, 129, 141–142, 197, 200, 240, 334, 339
Bates, E., 10, 124n1, 328
Bauer, P. J., 3, 14, 16, 22, 25, 27n2, 27n4, 168, 303, 322, 326, 332
Beach, D. R., 199
Beeghly, M., 10
Beiderman, I., 38
Benigni, L., 124n1
Berenda, R. W., 279
Berko, J., 78
Berlyne, D. E., 129
Bessel, F. W., 128
Billman, D. O., 94, 104
Bisanz, J., 252
Bjorklund, D. F., 2
Black, J. B., 32
Blount, B. G. 212
Bluhm, C., 66
Bohannon, J. N., 251
Bonvillian, J. D., 314n5
Boorstin, D. J., 314n1

Borke, H., 1
Bothwell, R. K., 277
Bottoms, B. L., 6, 299, 312, 324, 340, 341–342, 343, 344
Bower, G. H., 32
Boyes-Braem, P., 75
Brainerd, C. J., 271
Bransford, J. D., 31, 130, 131, 225
Bretherton, I., 10, 14, 124n1, 328
Brewer, W. F., 31, 206
Bridger, W. H., 39
Brigham, J., 277
Broadbent, D. E., 129
Brown, A. L., 2, 94, 96, 98, 104, 105, 118, 130, 131, 145, 197, 202, 206, 225, 250
Brown, E. F., 344
Brown, P., 251
Brown, R., 1, 78
Bruner, J. S., 31, 75, 122, 129, 214
Bukatko, D., 114
Burney, L., 201
Burns, T. E., 271, 344

Camaioni, L., 124n1
Campione, J. C., 94, 145, 225
Campos, J., 266
Cantor, J. H., 103
Caporael, L. R., 340
Carey, S., 135, 266
Carlomusto, M., 200
Carlson, D. F., 38
Carnochan, P., 250
Case, R., 10
Cassidy, D. J., 2, 96, 98, 250
Cazden, C. B., 206, 213
Ceci, S. J., 6, 79, 256, 267, 277, 279, 291, 298, 312, 340–341, 342, 343
Champion, M. A., 252
Charney, R., 86
Chi, M. T. H., 2, 79, 80, 131, 135
Chiesi, H. L., 135
Chinsky, J. M., 199
Chomsky, N., 304
Cohen, N. J., 242, 318

Subject index